perspectives

Social Psychology

perspectives

Social Psychology

Academic Editor
Michele Acker
Otterbein College

coursewise
publishing
inc.

Boulder • Bellevue • Dubuque • Madison

Our mission at **coursewise** is to help students make connections—linking theory to practice and the classroom to the outside world. Learners are motivated to synthesize ideas when course materials are placed in a context they recognize. By providing gateways to contemporary and enduring issues, **coursewise** publications will expand students' awareness of and context for the course subject.

For more information on **coursewise** visit us at our web site: http://www.coursewise.com

coursewise publishing editorial staff

Thomas Doran, ceo/publisher: Journalism/Marketing/Speech
Edgar Laube, publisher: Geography/Political Science/Psychology/Sociology
Linda Meehan Avenarius, publisher: **courselinks**
Sue Pulvermacher-Alt, publisher: Education/Health/Gender Studies
Victoria Putman, publisher: Anthropology/Philosophy/Religion
Tom Romaniak, publisher: Business/Criminal Justice/Economics

coursewise production staff

Victoria Putman, production manager
Lori A. Blosch, permissions coordinator
Mary M. Monner, production coordinator, print/online

Cover photo: Copyright © 1997 T. Teshigawara/Panoramic Images, Chicago, IL. All Rights Reserved.

Interior design and cover design by Jeff Storm

Printed in the United States of America by **coursewise publishing,** Inc.
1379 Lodge Lane, Boulder, CO 80303

10 9 8 7 6 5 4 3 2

from the
Publisher

coursewise publishing

Edgar Laube

Any bets on how long we'll all be watching "Seinfeld" reruns?? And are they our real "bridge to the twenty-first century"? However long it is, I'll be watching. This stuff is great. Part of it is the interpersonal chemistry, but part is also the bird's-eye view of the interior life of these characters. Their little games and foibles are constantly on display. Trivial concerns dominate their to-worry lists. They deceive themselves more often than they deceive others. In the end, they might even remind us of ourselves occasionally.

The study of social psychology is an important (and mostly serious) undertaking. That's why you're spending your time and money to take the class. But as I read through some of the articles here, I was struck again and again by how useful, how practical, the study of social psychology can be. In this reader, you'll find plenty of good science, but you'll also see how relevant it is to life beyond the classroom. The science helps you make a bit more sense out of reality—of which games and foibles ala "Seinfeld" are a significant part.

Wanting to publish a reader that offered this kind of blend of science and our daily reality, I called an acquaintance who is a social psychologist. I described the type of person I was looking for and asked him to mull the question over a bit. The mulling lasted about two seconds, after which he mentioned Michele Acker. She would be great, he said. He gave me three other names, but the endorsements sounded a bit lukewarm.

That bit of ancient history led to the reader that you're now looking at, as well as to Michele Acker's work on the **courselinks**™ site for social psychology. From our first conversation, Michele "got it." She understood the value you place on relevance. It was her idea to ask students to participate on the Editorial Board. She was in full sympathy with the **coursewise** mission to keep prices within a reasonable range. And, as one of the webmasters for International Society for the Study of Personal Relationships, she's 'netwise'. The only minor problem I had was containing her enthusiasm—she kept finding "an even better" article than the one we had agreed to. This is the type of problem that publishers should have more of. And so, Michele, thanks for your initiative and concern and sense of humor. Your fingerprints are all over this volume, and a lot of students of social psychology will benefit as a result.

This reader (unlike most "Seinfeld" episodes) passed through the **coursewise** R.E.A.L. filter. I think that these selections are **R**elevant, **E**xciting, **A**pproved, and **L**inked. But what do publishers know? Please let me know, via our website, whether or not you agree. Thank you!

from the
Academic Editor

Michele Acker

Welcome to the first edition of *Perspectives: Social Psychology*. I think you will find this an interesting and useful complement to your standard textbook. When **coursewise publishing** approached me about compiling a reader that would showcase social psychology in our everyday lives, I was eager to begin looking for articles. Textbook social psychology is pretty interesting already, but social psychology in the real world can be even more exciting.

Another reason I wanted to work with **coursewise** was their emphasis on the World Wide Web as a learning tool. The web opens up so many possibilities that students just 5 years ago simply did not enjoy. With the click of a mouse button, you can read newspapers from around the world, find extensive information about nearly any topic, and in effect, create your own education. When I teach, my students look for a new web site each week and share it with me and their classmates; the only criteria are that the web site is relevant to that week's topic and that the student finds it interesting. People in my classes have discovered some wonderful web sites, some of which you can find at the **courselinks**™ site (http://www.courselinks.com) for this book. Even if you don't have a similar assignment, I advocate that you experiment with the web as a tool for learning social psychology. Pick the study or concept that interests you the most during your reading, and search for it on the web. I must caution you to have patience and to be discriminating. You'll find a good deal of information on the web that is not at all useful, and some that is just plain wrong. When in doubt about a source, check with a professor or a librarian. I believe that you will find that this exercise will improve your grades. You could even try it for your other courses.

When I teach social psychology, I tell my students that I see the course as Social Psychology for Life. I am always delighted when students can apply some of what they learn to their lives beyond the classroom. To me, the field of social psychology is like a handbook for human existence—where else can you find information that is so central to our everyday lives? Many people, from talk-show hosts to magazine columnists to your next-door neighbor, freely offer their opinions on how you should live your life, as both an individual and as a member of different communities. But how many of these opinions are backed up by objective scientific research? Aside from offering provocative insights into human experience, social psychological research yields personal benefits by helping you to resist propaganda campaigns, make sensible judgments about yourself and others, avoid common pitfalls in your family and romantic relationships, and lessen biases and prejudices, to name but a few.

I have tried to select articles for this volume that are relevant to both social psychology and your current life. Of course, I had to eliminate many other fine articles simply because of practical space limitations. I expect that after reading some of these articles you will begin to recognize the relevance and applicability of social psychology when you read the newspaper or watch the news. I encourage you to let me know of your opinions about the selections in this volume. Some of what seems interesting and relevant to me may not strike you the same way, and that type of feedback will help me to improve future volumes of this reader. You can provide feedback at the **coursewise** web site (http://www.coursewise.com).

This book is divided into eight broad sections. There are many ways of dividing up social psychology, and all of them are artificial to some extent, as categories or chapters or units overlap a good deal. This book may not perfectly correspond with your textbook, but the Topic Key will help you to match up the articles and web sites with your text.

I wish you luck in your class and hope that, with the help of your textbook, this volume, and the web, you come to find social psychology as interesting and useful as I have.

Editorial Board

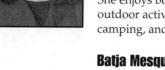

Thomas E. Nelson

Dr. Thomas E. Nelson is an Associate Professor of Political Science and Psychology at The Ohio State University, where he teaches courses in political psychology, public opinion, and experimental research methods. He is co-director of Ohio State's Summer Institute in Political Psychology. He conducts research on the effects of the mass media on public opinion; intergroup relations in the political domain; and social judgment and stereotyping. He enjoys music, reading, movies, and the great outdoors.

Nicole Nugent

Nicole Nugent is an undergraduate psychology major at Wittenberg University. She plans to pursue a Ph.D. in clinical psychology, with research interests in pediatric psychology, control, and body image. In her spare time, she enjoys hiking, drawing and sports.

John W. Reich

Dr. John W. Reich teaches undergraduate courses in social psychology and methodology in applied social psychology and graduate seminars. His research interests include studying emotional and social processes in the mental health of at-risk populations, such as those experiencing chronic physical illness. His nonprofessional interests include biking, hiking the wilds of Arizona, watching foreign films, and reading early American and nineteenth-century British history.

Ann Weber

Dr. Ann Weber, of the University of North Carolina–Asheville, is a social psychologist with a special interest in close relationships, loss, and grief. She teaches courses on those topics, as well as general psychology, social psychology, and history and systems of psychology. She is personally as well as professionally interested in people-animal relationships. She and her husband and their five cats and one dog all enjoy reading, hiking, and napping.

Sabrina Zirkel

Dr. Sabrina Zirkel teaches at the Saybrook Graduate School and Research Center in San Francisco. She teaches courses in personality and social psychology, research methods, gender, and multiculturalism. Her research interests include adolescent identity development and academic underachievement among minority students and women in traditionally male-dominated fields. In her spare time, she enjoys spending time with her own teenager, traveling, skiing, reading, and her cat.

WiseGuide Introduction

Question Authority

Critical Thinking and Bumper Stickers

The bumper sticker said: Question Authority. This is a simple directive that goes straight to the heart of critical thinking. The issue is not whether the authority is right or wrong; it's the questioning process that's important. Questioning helps you develop awareness and a clearer sense of what you think. That's critical thinking.

Critical thinking is a new label for an old approach to learning—that of challenging all ideas, hypotheses, and assumptions. In the physical and life sciences, systematic questioning and testing methods (known as the scientific method) help verify information, and objectivity is the benchmark on which all knowledge is pursued. In the social sciences, however, where the goal is to study people and their behavior, things get fuzzy. It's one thing for the chemistry experiment to work out as predicted, or for the petri dish to yield a certain result. It's quite another matter, however, in the social sciences, where the subject is ourselves. Objectivity is harder to achieve.

Although you'll hear critical thinking defined in many different ways, it really boils down to analyzing the ideas and messages that you receive. What are you being asked to think or believe? Does it make sense, objectively? Using the same facts and considerations, could you reasonably come up with a different conclusion? And, why does this matter in the first place? As the bumper sticker urged, question authority. Authority can be a textbook, a politician, a boss, a big sister, or an ad on television. Whatever the message, learning to question it appropriately is a habit that will serve you well for a lifetime. And in the meantime, thinking critically will certainly help you be course wise.

Getting Connected

This reader is a tool for connected learning. This means that the readings and other learning aids explained here will help you to link classroom theory to real-world issues. They will help you to think critically and to make long-lasting learning connections. Feedback from both instructors and students has helped us to develop some suggestions on how you can wisely use this connected learning tool.

WiseGuide Pedagogy

A wise reader is better able to be a critical reader. Therefore, we want to help you get wise about the articles in this reader. Each section of *Perspectives* has three tools to help you: the WiseGuide Intro, the WiseGuide Wrap-Up, and the Putting It in *Perspectives* review form.

WiseGuide Intro

In the WiseGuide Intro, the Academic Editor introduces the section, gives you an overview of the topics covered, and explains why particular articles were selected and what's important about them.

Also in the WiseGuide Intro, you'll find several key points or learning objectives that highlight the most important things to remember from this section. These will help you to focus your study of section topics.

At the end of the Wiseguide Intro, you'll find questions designed to stimulate critical thinking. Wise students will keep these questions in mind as they read an article (we repeat the questions at the start of the articles as a reminder). When you finish each article, check your understanding. Can you answer the questions? If not, go back and reread the article. The Academic Editor has written sample responses for many of the questions, and you'll find these online at the **courselinks**™ site for this course. More about **courselinks**™ in a minute. . . .

WiseGuide Wrap-Up

Be course wise and develop a thorough understanding of the topics covered in this course. The WiseGuide Wrap-Up at the end of each section will help you do just that with concluding comments or summary points that repeat what's most important to understand from the section you just read.

In addition, we try to get you wired up by providing a list of select Internet resources—what we call R.E.A.L. web sites because they're Relevant, Exciting, Approved, and Linked. The information at these web sites will enhance your understanding of a topic. (Remember to use your Passport and start at http://www.courselinks.com so that if any of these sites have changed, you'll have the latest link.)

Putting It in *Perspectives* Review Form

At the end of the book is the Putting It in *Perspectives* review form. Your instructor may ask you to complete this form as an assignment or for extra credit. If nothing else, consider doing it on your own to help you critically think about the reading.

Prompts at the end of each article encourage you to complete this review form. Feel free to copy the form and use it as needed.

The courselinks™ Site

The **courselinks**™ Passport is your ticket to a wonderful world of integrated web resources designed to help you with your course work. These resources are found at the **courselinks**™ site for your course area. This is where the readings in this book and the key topics of your course are linked to an exciting array of online learning tools. Here you will find carefully selected readings, web links, quizzes, worksheets, and more, tailored to your course and approved as connected learning tools. The ever-changing, always interesting **courselinks**™ site features a number of carefully integrated resources designed to help you be course wise. These include:

- **R.E.A.L. Sites** At the core of a **courselinks**™ site is the list of R.E.A.L. sites. This is a select group of web sites for studying, not surfing. Like the readings in this book, these sites have been selected, reviewed, and approved by the Academic Editor and the Editorial Board. The R.E.A.L. sites are arranged by topic and are annotated with short descriptions and key words to make them easier for you to use for reference or research. With R.E.A.L. sites, you're studying approved resources within seconds—and not wasting precious time surfing unproven sites.

- **Editor's Choice** Here you'll find updates on news related to your course, with links to the actual online sources. This is also where we'll tell you about changes to the site and about online events.

- **Course Overview** This is a general description of the typical course in this area of study. While your instructor will provide specific course objectives, this overview helps you place the course in a generic context and offers you an additional reference point.

- **www.orksheet** Focus your trip to a R.E.A.L. site with the www.orksheet. Each of the 10 to 15 questions will prompt you to take in the best that site has to offer. Use this tool for self-study, or if required, email it to your instructor.

- **Course Quiz** The questions on this self-scoring quiz are related to articles in the reader, information at R.E.A.L. sites, and other course topics, and will help you pinpoint areas you need to study. Only you will know your score—it's an easy, risk-free way to keep pace!

- **Topic Key** The Topic Key is a listing of the main topics in your course, and it correlates with the Topic Key that appears in this reader. This handy reference tool also links directly to those R.E.A.L. sites that are especially appropriate to each topic, bringing you integrated online resources within seconds!

- **Web Savvy Student Site** If you're new to the Internet or want to brush up, stop by the Web Savvy Student site. This unique supplement is a complete **courselinks**™ site unto itself. Here, you'll find basic information on using the Internet, creating a web page, communicating on the web, and more. Quizzes and Web Savvy Worksheets test your web knowledge, and the R.E.A.L. sites listed here will further enhance your understanding of the web.

- **Student Lounge** Drop by the Student Lounge to chat with other students taking the same course or to learn more about careers in your major. You'll find links to resources for scholarships, financial aid, internships, professional associations, and jobs. Take a look around the Student Lounge and give us your feedback. We're open to remodeling the Lounge per your suggestions.

Building Better Perspectives!

Please tell us what you think of this *Perspectives* volume so we can improve the next one. Here's how you can help:

1. Visit our **coursewise** site at: http://www.coursewise.com

2. Click on *Perspectives*. Then select the Building Better *Perspectives* Form for your book.

3. Forms and instructions for submission are available online.

Tell us what you think—did the readings and online materials help you make some learning connections? Were some materials more helpful than others? Thanks in advance for helping us build better *Perspectives*.

Student Internships

If you enjoy evaluating these articles or would like to help us evaluate the **courselinks**™ site for this course, check out the **coursewise** Student Internship Program. For more information, visit:

http://www.coursewise.com/intern.html

Brief Contents

Contents

section

3

**Attitudes and
Persuasion**

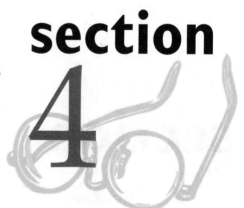

section

4

**Conformity,
Compliance, and
Obedience**

section 5

Group Dynamics

section 6

Stereotypes and Prejudice

section 7

Prosocial Behavior and Aggression

section 8

Interpersonal Relationships

Topic Key

This Topic Key is an important tool for learning. It will help you integrate this reader into your course studies. Listed below, in alphabetical order, are important topics covered in this volume. Below each topic you'll find the article or articles and R.E.A.L. web site addresses relating to that topic. Note that the Topic Key might not include every topic your instructor chooses to emphasize. If you don't find the topic you're looking for in the Topic Key, check the index or the online topic key at the **courselinks**™ site.

Advertising
12   Sex, Lies, and Advertising
13   Hooked on Tobacco: The Teen Epidemic
R.E.A.L. Site
Social Influence: The Science of Persuasion and Compliance
http://www.public.asu.edu/~kelton/

Aggression
21   Contested Community
28   It's Not Easy, But Inner-City Youth Can Unlearn Aggressive Behavior
29   Road Rage: Tailgating, Giving the Finger, Outright Violence
30   Violence, Reel to Real
R.E.A.L. Sites
Human Development and Family Studies at Pennsylvania State University
http://www.personal.psu.edu/faculty/n/x/nxd10/family3.htm
Center for the Study and Prevention of Violence
http://www.colorado.edu/cspv/

Attachment
32   Trust Me, Please

Attitudes
11   America Today: Malaise and Resiliency
14   A University of California Psychologist Investigates New Approaches to Changing Human Behavior
R.E.A.L. Sites
Steve's Primer of Practical Persuasion and Influence
http://www.as.wvu.edu/~sbb/comm221/primer.htm
Social Influence: The Science of Persuasion and Compliance
http://www.public.asu.edu/~kelton/

Attribution
6   It's Not as Bad as You Think It Is: Misguided Handwringing About Our Society's Decline Distracts Us from the Real Crises

R.E.A.L. Sites
Cyberia Shrink's Tests, Tests, Tests
http://www.queendom.com/tests.html
Social Psychology Class Paper
http://www.student.richmond.edu/~nberkebi/social1.html
Atlantic Unbound
http://www.theatlantic.com/atlantic/atlweb/flashbks/blacked/steele.htm

Biology
34   The Love Lab
R.E.A.L. Sites
Human Development and Family Studies at Pennsylvania State University
http://www.personal.psu.edu/faculty/n/x/nxd10/family3.htm

Cognitive Biases
1   Some Systematic Biases of Everyday Judgment
5   Why Bogus Therapies Seem to Work
6   It's Not as Bad as You Think It is: Misguided Handwringing About Our Society's Decline Distracts Us from the Real Crises
R.E.A.L. Sites
Counterfactual Research News
http://www.psych.nwu.edu/psych/people/faculty/roese/research/cf/cfnews.htm
Committee for the Scientific Investigation of Claims of the Paranormal
http://www.csicop.org/
The Public Service Commission of Canada: Stereotyping
http://www.psc-cfp.gc.ca/audit/prcb/mono3-e.htm

Cognitive Dissonance
14   A University of California Psychologist Investigates New Approaches to Changing Human Behavior

Conformity
16   What Messages Are Behind Today's Cults? Cults Are Coming. Are They Crazy or Bearing Critical Messages?
17   Secrets of the Cult

R.E.A.L. Sites
Social Influence: The Science of Persuasion and Compliance
http://www.public.asu.edu/~kelton/
American Family Foundation Cult Group Information
http://www.csj.org/
Social Psychology Class Paper
http://www.student.richmond.edu/~nberkebi/social1.html

Culture
7   To Thine Own Selves Be True: A New Breed of Psychologists Says There's No One Answer to the Question "Who Am I?"
R.E.A.L. Sites
Human Development and Family Studies at Pennsylvania State University
http://www.personal.psu.edu/faculty/n/x/nxd10/family3.htm
Access to Justice Network Publications
http://acjnet.org/docs/bystajhs.html

Deception
2   The Truth about Lying
4   Jurors Look to Mannerisms for Clues to Truth
R.E.A.L. Site
Exploring Nonverbal Communication
http://zzyx.ucsc.edu/~archer/

Decision Making
20   Letterman or Leno: A Groupthink Analysis of Successive Decisions Made by the National Broadcasting Company (NBC)
22   Organization of Information and the Detection of Gender Discrimination
35   Current Perspectives on Dual-Career Families
R.E.A.L. Sites
Counterfactual Research News
http://www.psych.nwu.edu/psych/people/faculty/roese/research/cf/cfnews.htm
Steve's Primer of Practical Persuasion and Influence
http://www.as.wvu.edu/~sbb/comm221/primer.htm

section

1

Learning Objectives

- Explain how normal social judgment processes can be biased and how that impacts our everyday life.

- Discuss the motivation behind deception.

- Understand how memories are formed and the ways in which they may be altered.

- Discuss some techniques for detecting lies and evaluate their effectiveness.

Social Cognition

WiseGuide Intro It is quite likely that one of the things that attracted you to a psychology course was a desire to know what makes people do the things they do. Of course, it's not just psychology students who try to assess and evaluate the people who surround them, or to understand what makes others think and behave the way they do. Perceiving, judging, and making inferences about others is a common and inevitable part of social life. These activities are examples of *social cognition:* the reception, processing, and storage of information that we use to form judgments and make inferences about ourselves and our social universe.

The "cognitive revolution" in social psychology is a relatively recent development, but we can detect its influence in every area of social psychological research. Some of the themes discussed in this section having to do with the capabilities and shortcomings of the social thinker will be repeated in subsequent sections. For example, some of the articles in this section concern how we form impressions of others. Later, in Section 6 on stereotypes and prejudice, we will examine how we form impressions of others when they belong to different social groups.

A recurring theme in this area is the comparison of social and nonsocial cognition. Do we think of a person in the same way we consider inanimate objects, such as an apple or a table, or is there something special about people that leads us to think differently about them? One of the discoveries that seems especially important for social cognition is the influence of goals and motives on social thinking—that is, our tendency to see the social world the way we want or expect it to be, rather than as it really is. This phenomenon is especially apparent in the way we think about ourselves. We may not even be able to trust our own memories of what we think *really* happened. Of course, while we may all benefit from telling ourselves a little white lie now and then, nobody likes to be deceived, whether by a friend or a mountebank peddling a bogus "miracle diet." Distinguishing truth from lies is another challenge for the social thinker.

The first article in this section examines the processes by which we form judgments about ourselves and others, and our frequently inflated sense of our own social judgment skills. Most of us see ourselves as people who perceive the world accurately—as "good judges of character"—in fact, as better than average at detecting others' feelings, thoughts, and even their lies. The previous statement is an example of one of the ways in which we can easily be misled or mislead others. In fact, it is impossible for everyone to be "better than average," but we often have a self-serving bias that informs the ways in which we view ourselves. We all share a number of other common biases in judgment as normal human beings. Dr. Gilovich discusses these biases, and suggests how to recognize and avoid them.

In our next article, "The Truth About Lying," Allison Kornet uncovers all of those little white lies and half-truths we have told in our

Questions

R1. Why is it important to know where a statistic comes from and what it is being compared to? What are the major errors of everyday hypothesis testing? According to Gilovich, what are some additional ways that our memory may be distorted?

R2. Who is likely to deceive others? What are some of the motivations for lying? Why is it potentially problematic to believe that you are good at detecting lies?

R3. How does memory construction occur? How is the process of altering memories demonstrated in scientific studies? What are some potential problems caused by the way our memory works?

R4. What are some nonverbal cues that someone is lying? Who is actually skilled at detecting deception in our society, and what makes them that way?

R5. Why are individual testimonials not sufficient proof for the effectiveness of a therapy? How does the self-serving bias influence our judgments about the effectiveness of a course of treatment? How would you counsel people who were interested in evaluating an alternative medical treatment for themselves?

R6. How can faulty reasoning give us an overly pessimistic view of the state of the world?

lives. As much as people pride themselves on honesty, it turns out that we lie one-fifth of the time! Knowing that, we all must wonder how we can tell when someone is telling the truth. The article discusses a number of research studies that have examined this question. Not only do we lie to others, we frequently lie to ourselves.

If we can't be sure about our impressions of others, can we at least trust our own memories? In "Creating False Memories," you will read about a series of research studies that the author, Dr. Elizabeth Loftus, has conducted over the last ten years. Her studies demonstrate some of the ways in which our memories of others and of ourselves can be altered—both purposefully and accidentally. Her research indicates some of the critical issues to consider as we hear and read more about Recovered Memory Syndrome.

The article by Elaine Woo was written during the unforgettable O. J. Simpson trial. She interviews a number of social psychologists who specialize in research on lying and the detection of lying. There are obvious practical implications of this research, such as sharpening the ability of jurors to detect whether witnesses and defendants are telling the truth. Woo also discusses some of the nonverbal body language that accompanies lying and that might be obvious in a courtroom.

The article by Barry Beyerstein illustrates the practical application of some of the ideas discussed in earlier articles. This timely article discusses why many rational people who, as he says "wouldn't buy a toaster without consulting *Consumer Reports*," are flocking to unproved, potentially dangerous alternative health therapies. He believes that the blame rests partly with those who are selling such alternative therapies, and partly with consumers' inability (or unwillingness) to critically evaluate these therapies. Our judgment of bogus therapies can be compromised by a lack of scientific (or critical) thinking skills and by cognitive biases that distort perceptions and judgments. Beyerstein provides specific examples of these biases and ways to combat them.

Although he is not a social psychologist, Nicholas Lehman offers some interesting social-cognitive explanations for a curious phenomenon in contemporary American society: the increasing sentiment that "things are falling apart," even though, by many objective standards, America has never been better off. Lehman argues that such pessimism is not only based on faulty reasoning, but can have dangerous social and political consequences.

Why is it important to know where a statistic comes from and what it is being compared to? What are the major errors of everyday hypothesis testing? According to Gilovich, what are some additional ways that our memory may be distorted?

Some Systematic Biases of Everyday Judgment

Thomas Gilovich

Thomas Gilovich, professor of psychology at Cornell University and a fellow of CSICOP, is the author of How We Know What Isn't So: The Fallibility of Human Reason in Everyday Life. *This article is based on his presentation at the twentieth-anniversary conference of CSICOP, June 20–23, 1996, Amherst, N.Y.*

Skeptics have long thought that everyday judgment and reasoning are biased in predictable ways. Psychological research on the subject conducted during the past quarter century largely confirms these suspicions. Two types of explanations are typically offered for the dubious beliefs that are dissected in *Skeptical Inquirer*. On one hand, there are motivational causes: Some beliefs are comforting, and so people embrace that comfort and convince themselves that a questionable proposition is true. Many types of religious beliefs, for example, are often ex-

plained this way. On the other hand, there are cognitive causes: faulty processes of reasoning and judgment that lead people to misevaluate the evidence of their everyday experience. The skeptical community is convinced that everyday judgment and reasoning leave much to be desired.

Why are skeptics so unimpressed with the reasoning abilities and habits of the average person? Until recently, this pessimism was based on simple observation, often by those with a particularly keen eye for the foibles of human nature. Thus, skeptics often cite such thinkers as Francis Bacon, who stated:

. . . all superstition is much the same whether it be that of astrology, dreams, omens, retributive judgment, or the like . . . [in that] the deluded believers observe events which are fulfilled, but neglect or pass over their failure, though it be much more common. (Bacon 1899/1620)

John Stuart Mill and Bertrand Russell are two other classic scholars who, along with Bacon, are often quoted for their trenchant observations on the shortcomings of human judgment. It is also common to see similar quotes of more recent vintage—in *Skeptical Inquirer* and elsewhere—from the likes of Richard Feynman, Stephen Jay Gould, and Carl Sagan. During the past twenty-five years, a great deal of psychological research has dealt specifically with the quality of everyday reasoning, and so it is now possible to go beyond simple observation and arrive at a truly rigorous assessment of the shortcomings of everyday judgment. In so doing, we can determine whether or not these scholars we all admire are correct. Do people misevaluate evidence in the very ways and for the very reasons that Bacon, Russell, and others have claimed? Let us look at the research record and see.

Thomas Gilovich, Some systematic biases of everyday judgment, SKEPTICAL INQUIRER, March 13, 1997, No. 2, Vol. 21, p. 31. Used by permission of the SKEPTICAL INQUIRER, Amherst, NY.

The "Compared to What?" Problem

Some of the common claims about the fallibility of human reasoning stand up well to empirical scrutiny. For example, it is commonly argued that people have difficulty with what might be called the "compared to what" problem. That is, people are often overly impressed with an absolute statistic without recognizing that its true import can only be assessed by comparison to some relevant baseline.

For instance, a 1986 article in *Discover* magazine (cited in Dawes 1988) urges readers who fly in airplanes to "know where the exits are and rehearse in your mind exactly how to get to them." Why? The article approvingly notes that someone who interviewed almost two hundred survivors of fatal airline accidents found that ". . . more than 90% had their escape routes mentally mapped out beforehand." Good for them, but note that whoever did the study cannot interview anyone who perished in an airplane crash. Air travel being as scary as it is to so many people, perhaps 90 percent or more of those who died in airline crashes rehearsed their escape routes as well. Ninety percent sounds impressive because it is so close to 100 percent. But without a more pertinent comparison, it really does not mean much.

Similarly, people are often impressed that, say, 30 percent of all infertile couples who adopt a child subsequently conceive. That is great news for that 30 percent to be sure, but what percentage of those who do not adopt likewise conceive? People likewise draw broad conclusions from a cancer patient who goes into remission after steadfastly practicing mental imagery. Again, excellent news for that individual, but might the cancer have gone into remission even if the person had not practiced mental imagery?

This problem of failing to invoke a relevant baseline of comparison is particularly common when the class of data that requires inspection is inherently difficult to collect. Consider, for example, the commonly expressed opinion, "I can always tell that someone is wearing a hairpiece." Are such claims to be believed, or is it just that one can tell that someone is wearing a hairpiece . . . when it is obvious that he is wearing a hairpiece? After all, how can one tell whether some have gone undetected? The goal of a good hairpiece is to fool the public, and so the example is one of those cases in which the confirmations speak loudly while the disconfirmations remain silent.

A similar asymmetry should give pause to those who have extreme confidence in their "gaydar," or their ability to detect whether someone is gay. Here, too, the confirmations announce themselves. When a person for whatever reason "seems gay" and it is later determined that he is, it is a salient triumph for one's skill at detection. But people who elude one's gaydar rarely go out of their way to announce, "By the way, I fooled you: I'm gay."

At any rate, the notion that people have difficulty invoking relevant comparisons has received support from psychological research. Studies of everyday reasoning have shown that the logic and necessity of control groups, for example, is often lost on a large segment of even the educated population (Boring 1954; Einhorn and Hogarth 1978; Nisbett and Ross 1980).

The "Seek and Ye Shall Find" Problem

Another common claim that stands up well to empirical research is the idea that people do not assess hypotheses even-handedly. Rather, they tend to seek out confirmatory evidence for what they suspect to be true, a tendency that has the effect of "seek and ye shall find." A biased search for confirmatory information frequently turns up more apparent support for a hypothesis than is justified.

This phenomenon has been demonstrated in numerous experiments explicitly designed to assess people's hypothesis-testing strategies (Skov and Sherman 1986; Snyder and Swann 1978). But it is so pervasive that it can also be seen in studies designed with an entirely different agenda in mind. One of my personal favorites is a study in which participants were given the following information (Shafir 1993):

Imagine that you serve on the jury of an only-child sole-custody case following a relatively messy divorce. The facts of the case are complicated by ambiguous economic, social, and emotional considerations, and you decide to base your decision entirely on the following few observations. To which parent would you award sole custody of the child?

Parent A:
average income
average health
average working hours
reasonable rapport with the
 child
relatively stable social life

Parent B:
above-average income
minor health problems
lots of work-related travel
very close relationship with the
  child
extremely active social life

Faced with this version of the problem, the majority of respondents chose to award custody to Parent B, the "mixed bag" parent who offers several advantages (above-average income), but also some disadvantages (health problems), in comparison to Parent A. In another version of the problem, however, a different group is asked to which parent they would deny custody of the child. Here, too, a majority selects Parent B. Parent B, then, is paradoxically deemed both more and less worthy of caring for the child.

The result is paradoxical, that is, unless one takes into account people's tendencies to seek out confirming information. Asked which parent should be awarded the child, people look primarily for positive qualities that warrant being awarded the child—looking less vigilantly for negative characteristics that would lead one to favor the other parent. When asked which parent should be denied custody, on the other hand, people look primarily for negative qualities that would disqualify a parent. A decision to award or deny, of course, should be based on a comparison of the positive and negative characteristics of the two parents, but the way the question is framed channels respondents down a narrower path in which they focus on information that would confirm the type of verdict they are asked to render.

The same logic often rears its head when people test certain suppositions or hypotheses. Rumors

of some dark conspiracy, for example, can lead people to search disproportionately for evidence that supports the plot and neglect evidence that contradicts it.

The Selective Memory Problem

A third commonly sounded complaint about everyday human thought is that people are more inclined to remember information that fits their expectations than information at variance with their expectations. Charles Darwin, for example, said that he took great care to record any observation that was inconsistent with his theories because "I had found by experience that such facts and thoughts were far more apt to escape from the memory than favourable ones" (cited in Clark 1984).

This particular criticism of the average person's cognitive faculties is in need of revision. Memory research has shown that often people have the easiest time recalling information that is inconsistent with their expectations or preferences (Bargh and Thein 1985; Srull and Wyer 1989). A little reflection indicates that this is particularly true of those "near misses" in life that become indelibly etched in the brain. The novelist Nicholson Baker (1991) provides a perfect illustration:

[I] told her my terrible story of coming in second in the spelling bee in second grade by spelling keep "c-e-e-p" after successfully tossing off microphone, and how for two or three years afterward I was pained every time a yellow garbage truck drove by on Highland Avenue and I saw the capitals printed on it, "Help Keep Our City Clean," with that impossible irrational K that had made me lose so humiliatingly. . . .

Baker's account, of course, is only an anecdote, possibly an apocryphal one at that. But it is one that, as mentioned above, receives support from more systematic studies. In one study, for example, individuals who had bet on professional football games were later asked to recall as much as they could about the various bets they had made (Gilovich 1983). They recalled significantly more information about their losses—outcomes they most likely did not expect to have happen and certainly did not prefer to have happen.*

Thus, the simple idea that people remember best that which they expect or prefer needs modification. Still, there is something appealing and seemingly true about the idea, and it should not be discarded prematurely. When considering people's belief in the accuracy of psychic forecasts, for example, it certainly seems to be fed by selective memory for successful predictions. How then can we reconcile this idea with the finding that often inconsistent information is better recalled? Perhaps the solution lies in considering when an event is eventful. With respect to their capacity to grab attention, some events are one-sided and others two-sided. Two-sided events are those that stand out and psychologically register as events regardless of how they turn out. If you bet on a sporting event or an election result, for example, either outcome—a win or a loss—has emotional significance and is therefore likely to emerge from the stream of everyday experience and register as an event. For these events, it is doubtful that confirmatory information is typically

*Illustration for figure 1 not included in this publication.

better remembered than disconfirmatory information.

In contrast, suppose you believe that "the telephone always rings when I'm in the shower." The potentially relevant events here are one-sided. If the phone happens to ring while showering, it will certainly register as an event, as you experience great stress in deciding whether to answer it, and you run dripping wet to the phone only to discover that it is someone from AT&T asking if you are satisfied with your long-distance carrier. When the phone does not ring when you are in the shower, on the other hand, it is a non-event. Nothing happened. Thus, with respect to the belief that the phone always rings while you are in the shower, the events are inherently one-sided: Only the confirmations stand out.

Perhaps it is these one-sided events to which Bacon's and Darwin's comments best apply. For one-sided events, as I discuss below, it is often the outcomes consistent with expectations that stand out and are more likely to be remembered. For two-sided events, on the other hand, the two types of outcomes are likely to be equally memorable; or, on occasion, events inconsistent with expectations may be more memorable.

But what determines whether an event is one- or two-sided? There are doubtless several factors. Let's consider two of them in the context of psychic predictions. First, events relevant to psychic predictions are inherently one-sided in the sense that such predictions are disconfirmed not by any specific event, but by their accumulated failure to be confirmed. Thus, the relevant comparison here is between confirmations and non-confirmations, or between events and non-events. It is no surprise, surely, that events are typically more memorable than non-events.

In one test of this idea, a group of college students read a diary purportedly written by another student, who described herself as having an interest in the prophetic nature of dreams (Madey 1993). To test whether there was any validity to dream prophecy, she decided to record each night's dreams and keep a record of significant events in her life, and later determine if there was any connection between the two. Half of the dreams (e.g., "I saw lots of people being happy") were later followed by events that could be seen as fulfilling ("My professor cancelled our final, which produced cheers throughout the class"). The other half went unfulfilled.

After reading the entire diary and completing a brief "filler" task, the participants were asked to recall as many of the dreams as they could. As figure 2 shows, they recalled many more of the prophecies that were fulfilled than those that were not.* This result is hardly a surprise, of course, because the fulfillment of a prophecy reminds one of the original prediction, whereas a failure to fulfill it is often a non-event. The relevant outcomes are therefore inherently one-sided, and the confirmations are more easily recalled. The end result is that the broader belief in question—in this case, dream prophecy—receives spurious support.

The events relevant to psychic predictions are one-sided in another way as well. Psychic predictions are notoriously vague

*Illustration for figure 2 not included in this publication.

about when the prophesied events are supposed to occur. "A serious misfortune will befall a powerful leader" is a more common prophecy than "The President will be assassinated on March 15th." Such predictions are temporally unfocused, in that there is no specific moment to which interested parties are to direct their attention. For such predictions, confirmatory events are once again more likely to stand out because confirmations are more likely to prompt a recollection of the original prophecy. The events relevant to temporally unfocused expectations, then, tend to be one-sided, with the confirmations typically more salient and memorable than disconfirmations.

Temporally focused expectations, on the other hand, are those for which the timing of the decisive outcome is known in advance. If one expects a particular team to win the Super Bowl, for example, one knows precisely when that expectation will be confirmed or refuted—at the end of the game. As a result, the events relevant to temporally focused expectations tend to be two-sided because one's attention is focused on the decisive moment, and both outcomes are likely to be noticed and remembered.

In one study that examined the memory implications of temporally focused and unfocused expectations, participants were asked to read the diary of a student who, as part of an ESP experiment, was required to try to prophesy an otherwise unpredictable event every week for several weeks (Madey and Gilovich 1993). The diary included the student's weekly prophecy as well as various passages describing events from that week. There were two groups of participants in the experiment. In the temporally unfocused condition, the prophecies made no mention of when the prophesied event was likely to occur ("I have a feeling that I will get into an argument with my Psychology research group"). In the temporally focused condition, the prediction identified a precise day on which the event was to occur ("I have a feeling that I will get into an argument with my Psychology research group on Friday"). For each group, half of the prophecies were confirmed (e.g., "Our professor assigned us to research groups, and we immediately disagreed over our topic") and half were disconfirmed (e.g., "Our professor assigned us to research groups, and we immediately came to a unanimous decision on our topic"). Whether confirmed or disconfirmed, the relevant event was described in the diary entry for the day prophesied in the temporally focused condition. After reading the diary and completing a short distracter task, the participants were asked to recall as many prophecies and relevant events as they could.

Knowing when the prophesied events were likely to occur helped the respondents' memories, but only for those prophecies that were disconfirmed.* Confirmatory events were readily recalled whether temporally focused or not. Disconfirmations, on the other hand, were rarely recalled unless they disconfirmed a temporally focused prediction. When one considers that most psychic predictions are temporally unfocused, the result, once again, is that the evidence for psychic predictions can appear more substantial than it is.

Conclusion

There is, of course, much more psychological research on the quality of everyday judgment than that reviewed here (see, for example, Baron 1988; Dawes 1988; Gilovich 1991; Nisbett and Ross 1980; Kahneman, Slovic, and Tversky 1982). But even this brief review is sufficient to make it clear that some of the reputed biases of everyday judgment turn out to be real, verifiable shortcomings. Systematic research by and large supports the suspicions of much of the skeptical community that everyday judgment is not to be trusted completely. At one level, this should not come as a surprise: It is precisely because everyday judgment cannot be trusted that the inferential safeguards known as the scientific method were developed. It is unfortunate that those safeguards are not more widely taught or more generally appreciated.

References

Bacon, F. 1899. *Advancement of Learning and the Novum Organum* (rev. ed.). New York: Colonial Press. (Original work published 1620).

Baker, N. 1991. *Room Temperature*. New York: Vintage.

Bargh, J. A., and R. D. Thein. 1985. Individual construct accessibility, person memory, and the recall-judgment link: The case of information overload. *Journal of Personality and Social Psychology* 49: 1129–1146.

Baron, J. 1988. *Thinking and Deciding*. New York: Cambridge University Press.

Boring, E. G. 1954. The nature and history of experimental control. *American Journal of Psychology* 67: 573–589.

Clark, R. W. 1984. *The Survival of Charles Darwin: A Biography of a Man and an Idea*. New York: Random House.

Dawes, R. M. 1988. *Rational Choice in an Uncertain World*. San Diego, Calif.: Harcourt Brace Jovanovich.

Einhorn, H. J., and R. M. Hogarth. 1978. Confidence in judgment: Persistence in the illusion of validity. *Psychological Review* 85: 395–416.

Gilovich, T. 1983. Biased evaluation and persistence in gambling. *Journal of Personality and Social Psychology* 44: 1110–1126.

———. 1991. *How We Know What Isn't So: The Fallibility of Human Reason in Everyday Life*. New York: Free Press.

Kahneman, D., P. Slovic, and A. Tversky. 1982. *Judgment under Uncertainty: Heuristics and Biases*. Cambridge: Cambridge University Press.

Madey, S. F. 1993. Memory for expectancy-consistent and expectancy-inconsistent information: An investigation of one-sided and two-sided events. Unpublished doctoral dissertation, Cornell University.

Madey, S. F., and T. Gilovich. 1993. Effect of temporal focus on the recall of expectancy-consistent and expectancy-inconsistent information. *Journal of Personality and Social Psychology* 65: 458–468.

Nisbett, R. E., and L. Ross. 1980. *Human Inference: Strategies and Shortcomings of Social Judgment*. Englewood Cliffs, N.J.: Prentice-Hall.

Shafir, E. 1993. Choosing versus rejecting: Why some options are both better and worse than others. *Memory and Cognition* 21: 546–556.

Skov, R. B., and S. J. Sherman. 1986. Information-gathering processes: Diagnosticity, hypothesis-confirmatory strategies, and perceived hypothesis confirmation. *Journal of Experimental Social Psychology* 22: 93–121.

Synder, M., and W. B. Swann. 1978. Hypothesis-testing processes in social interaction. *Journal of Personality and Social Psychology* 36: 1202–1212.

Srull, T. K., and R. S. Wyer. 1989. Person memory and judgment. *Psychological Review* 96: 58–83.

 Article Review Form at end of book.

*Illustration for figure 3 not included in this publication.

Who is likely to deceive others? What are some of the motivations for lying? Why is it potentially problematic to believe that you are good at detecting lies?

The Truth About Lying

Has lying gotten a bad rap?

We do it as often as we brush our teeth, yet until recently lying received little attention from psychologists. Could we really get through life without it?

Allison Kornet

If, as the cliche has it, the 1980s was the decade of greed, then the quintessential sin of the 1990s might just be lying. After all, think of the accusations of deceit leveled at politicians like Bob Packwood, Marion Barry, Dan Rostenkowski, Newt Gingrich, and Bill Clinton. And consider the top-level Texaco executives who initially denied making racist comments at board meetings; the young monk who falsely accused Cardinal Bernardin of molestation; Susan Smith, the white woman who killed her young boys and blamed a black man for it; and Joe Klein, the *Newsweek* columnist who adamantly swore for months that he had nothing to do with his anonymously-published novel *Primary Colors.* Even Hollywood has noticed our ap-

parent deception obsession: witness recent films like *Quiz Show, True Lies, The Crucible, Secrets & Lies,* and comedian Jim Carrey's latest release, *Liar, Liar.*

What's going on here? Nothing out of the ordinary, insists Leonard Saxe, Ph.D., a polygraph at Brandeis University. "Lying has long been a part of everyday life," he says. "We couldn't get through the day without being deceptive." Yet until recently lying was almost entirely ignored by psychologists, leaving serious discussion of the topic in the hands of ethicists and theologians. Freud wrote next to nothing about deception; even the 1500-page *Encyclopedia of Psychology,* published in 1984, mentions lies only in a brief entry on detecting them. But as psychologists delve deeper into the details of deception, they're finding

that lying is a surprisingly common and complex phenomenon.

For starters, recent work by Bella DePaulo, Ph.D., a psychologist at the University of Virginia, confirms Nietzche's assertion that the lie is a condition of life. In a 1996 study, DePaulo and her colleagues had 147 people between the ages of 18 and 71 keep a diary of all the falsehoods they told over the course of a week. Most people, she found, lie once or twice a day—almost as often as they snack from the refrigerator or brush their teeth. Both men and women lie in approximately a fifth of their social exchanges lasting 10 or more minutes; over the course of a week they deceive about 30 percent of those with whom they interact one-on-one. Furthermore, some types of relationships, such as those between parents and teens, are virtual magnets for deception: "College students lie to their mothers in one out of two conversations," reports DePaulo. (Incidentally, when researchers refer to lying, they don't include the mindless pleasantries or polite equivocations we offer each other in passing, such as "I'm fine, thanks" or "No trouble at all." An "official" lie actually misleads, deliberately conveying a false impression. So complimenting a friend's awful haircut or telling a creditor that the check is in the mail both qualify.)

Saxe points out that most of us receive conflicting messages about lying. Although we're socialized from the time we can speak to believe that it's always better to tell the truth, in reality society often encourages and even rewards deception. Show up late for an early morning meeting at work and it's best not to admit that you overslept. "You're punished far more than you would be if you lie and say you were stuck in traffic," Saxe notes. Moreover, lying is integral to many occupations. Think how often we see lawyers constructing far-fetched theories on behalf of their clients or reporters misrepresenting themselves in order to gain access to good stories.

Of Course I Love You

Dishonesty also pervades our romantic relationships, as you might expect from the titles of books like *101 Lies Men Tell Women* (Harper Collins), by Missouri psychologist Dory Hollander, Ph.D. (Hollander's nomination for the #1 spot: "I'll call you.") Eighty-five percent of the couples interviewed in a 1990 study of college students reported that one or both partners had lied about past relationships or recent indiscretions. And DePaulo finds that dating

couples lie to each other in about a third of their interactions—perhaps even more often than they deceive other people.

Fortunately, marriage seems to offer some protection against deception: Spouses lie to each other in "only" about 10 percent of their major conversations. The bad news? That 10 percent just refers to the typically minor lies of everyday life. DePaulo recently began looking at the less frequent "big" lies that involve deep betrayals of trust, and she's finding that the vast majority of them occur between people in intimate relationships. "You save your really big lies," she says, "for the person that you're closest to."

Sweet Little Lies

Though some lies produce interpersonal friction, others may actually serve as a kind of harmless social lubricant. "They make it easier for people to get along," says DePaulo, noting that in the the diary study one in every four of the participants' lies were told solely for the benefit of another person. In fact, "fake positive" lies—those in which people pretend to like someone or something more than they actually do ("Your muffins are the best ever")—are about 10 to 20 times more common than "false negative" lies in which people pretend to like someone or something *less* ("That two-faced rat will never get my vote").

Certain cultures may place special importance on these "kind" lies. A survey of residents at 31 senior citizen centers in Los Angeles recently revealed that only about half of elderly Korean Americans believe that patients diagnosed with life-threatening metastatic cancer should be told the truth about their condition. In contrast,

nearly 90 percent of Americans of European or African descent felt that the terminally ill should be confronted with the truth.

Not surprisingly, research also confirms that the closer we are to someone, the more likely it is that the lies we tell them will be altruistic ones. This is particularly true of women: Although the sexes lie with equal frequency, women are especially likely to stretch the truth in order to protect someone else's feelings, DePaulo reports. Men, on the other hand, are more prone to lying about themselves—the typical conversation between two guys contains about eight times as many self-oriented lies as it does falsehoods about other people.

Men and women may also differ in their ability to deceive their friends. In a University of Virginia study, psychologists asked pairs of same-sex friends to try to detect lies told by the other person. Six months later the researchers repeated the experiment with the same participants. While women had become slightly better at detecting their friends' lies over time, men didn't show any improvement—evidence, perhaps, that women are particularly good at learning to read their friends more accurately as a relationship deepens.

Who Lies?

Saxe believes that anyone under enough pressure, or given enough incentive, will lie. But in a study published in the *Journal of Personality and Social Psychology*, DePaulo and Deborah A. Kashy, Ph.D., of Texas A&M University, report that frequent liars tend to be manipulative and Machiavellian, not to mention overly concerned with the impression they make on others. Still, DePaulo warns that liars "don't always fit the stereotype of caring only about themselves." Further research reveals that extroverted, sociable people are slightly more likely to lie, and that some personality and physical traits—notably self-confidence and physical attractiveness—have been linked to an individual's skill at lying when under pressure.

On the other hand, the people *least* likely to lie are those who score high on psychological scales of responsibility and those with meaningful same-sex friendships. In his book *Lies! Lies!! Lies!!! The Psychology of Deceit* (American Psychiatric Press, Inc.), psychiatrist Charles Ford, M.D., adds depressed people to that list. He suggests that individuals in the throes of depression seldom deceive others—or are deceived themselves—because they seem to perceive and describe reality with greater accuracy than others. Several studies show that depressed people delude themselves far less than their nondepressed peers about the amount of control they have over situations, and also about the effect they have on other people. Researchers such as UCLA psychologist Shelley Taylor, Ph.D., have even cited such findings as evidence that a certain amount of self-delusion—basically, lying to yourself—is essential to good mental health. (Many playwrights, including Arthur Miller and Eugene O'Neill, seem to share the same view about truth-telling. In *Death of a Salesman* and *The Iceman Cometh*, for example, lies are life sustaining: The heroes become tragic figures when their lies are stripped away.)

Detecting Lies

Anyone who has played cards with a poker-faced opponent can appreciate how difficult it is to detect a liar. Surprisingly, technology doesn't help very much. Few experts display much confidence in the deception-detecting abilities of the polygraph, or lie detector. Geoffrey C. Bunn, Ph.D., a psychologist and polygraph historian at Canada's York University, goes so far as to describe the lie detector as "an entertainment device" rather than a scientific instrument. Created around 1921 during one of the first collaborations between scientists and police, the device was quickly popularized by enthusiastic newspaper headlines and by the element of drama it bestowed in movies and novels.

But mass appeal doesn't confer legitimacy. The problem with the polygraph, say experts like Bunn, is that it detects fear, not lying; the physiological responses that it measures—most often heart rate, skin conductivity, and rate of respiration—don't necessarily accompany dishonesty.

"The premise of a lie detector is that a smoke alarm goes off in the brain when we lie because we're doing something wrong," explains Saxe. "But sometimes we're completely comfortable with our lies." Thus a criminal's lie can easily go undetected if he has no fear of telling it. Similarly, a true statement by an innocent individual could be misinterpreted if the person is sufficiently afraid of the examination circumstances. According to Saxe, the best-controlled research suggests that lie detectors err at a rate anywhere from 25 to 75 percent. Perhaps this is why most state and federal courts won't allow polygraph "evidence."

Some studies suggest that lies can be detected by means other than a polygraph—by tracking speech hesitations or changes in vocal pitch, for example, or by identifying various nervous adaptive habits like scratching, blinking, or fidgeting. But most psychologists agree that lie detection is destined to be imperfect. Still, researchers continue to investigate new ways of picking up lies. While studying how language patterns are associated with improvements in physical health, James W. Pennebaker, Ph.D., a professor of psychology at Southern Methodist University, also began to explore whether a person's choice of words was a sign of deception. Examining data gathered from a text analysis program, Pennebaker and SMU colleague Diane Berry, Ph.D., determined that there are certain language patterns that predict when someone is being less than honest. For example, liars tend to use fewer first-person words like *I* or *my* in both speech and writing. They are also less apt to use emotional words, such as *hurt* or *angry*, cognitive words, like *understand* or *realize*, and so-called exclusive words, such as *but* or *without*, that distinguish between what is and isn't in a category.

Not Guilty

While the picture of lying that has emerged in recent years is far more favorable than that suggested by its biblical "thou shalt not" status, most liars remain at least somewhat conflicted about their behavior. In DePaulo's studies, participants described conversations in which they lied as less intimate and pleasant than truthful encounters, suggesting that people are not entirely at ease with their deceptions. That may explain why falsehoods are more likely to be told over the telephone, which provides more anonymity than a face-to-face conversation. In most cases, however, any mental distress that results from telling an everyday lie quickly dissipates. Those who took part in the diary study said they would tell about 75 percent of their lies again if given a second chance—a position no doubt bolstered by their generally high success rate. Only about a fifth of their falsehoods were discovered during the one-week study period.

Certainly anyone who insists on condemning all lies should ponder what would happen if we could reliably tell when our family, friends, colleagues, and government leaders were deceiving us. It's tempting to think that the world would become a better place when purged of the deceptions that seem to interfere with our attempts at genuine communication or intimacy. On the other hand, perhaps our social lives would collapse under the weight of relentless honesty, with unveiled truths destroying our ability to connect with others. The ubiquity of lying is clearly a problem, but would we want to will away all of our lies? Let's be honest.

 Article Review Form at end of book.

How does memory construction occur? How is the process of altering memories demonstrated in scientific studies? What are some potential problems caused by the way our memory works?

Creating False Memories

Researchers are showing how suggestion and imagination can create "memories" of events that did not actually occur.

Elizabeth F. Loftus

In 1986 Nadean Cool, a nurse's aide in Wisconsin, sought therapy from a psychiatrist to help her cope with her reaction to a traumatic event experienced by her daughter. During therapy, the psychiatrist used hypnosis and other suggestive techniques to dig out buried memories of abuse that Cool herself had allegedly experienced. In the process, Cool became convinced that she had repressed memories of having been in a satanic cult, of eating babies, of being raped, of having sex with animals and of being forced to watch the murder of her eight-year-old friend. She came to believe that she had more than 120 personalities—children, adults, angels and even a duck—all because, Cool was told, she had experienced severe childhood sexual and physical abuse. The psychiatrist also performed exorcisms on her, one of which lasted for five hours and included the sprinkling of holy water and screams for Satan to leave Cool's body.

When Cool finally realized that false memories had been planted, she sued the psychiatrist for malpractice. In March 1997, after five weeks of trial, her case was settled out of court for $2.4 million.

Nadean Cool is not the only patient to develop false memories as a result of questionable therapy. In Missouri in 1992 a church counselor helped Beth Rutherford to remember during therapy that her father, a clergyman, had regularly raped her between the ages of seven and 14 and that her mother sometimes helped him by holding her down. Under her therapist's guidance, Rutherford developed memories of her father twice impregnating her and forcing her to abort the fetus herself with a coat hanger. The father had to resign from his post as a clergyman when the allegations were made public. Later medical examination of the daughter revealed, however, that she was still a virgin at age 22 and had never been pregnant. The daughter sued the therapist and received a $1-million settlement in 1996.

About a year earlier two juries returned verdicts against a Minnesota psychiatrist accused of planting false memories by former patients Vynnette Hamanne and Elizabeth Carlson, who under hypnosis and sodium amytal, and after being fed misinformation about the workings of memory, had come to remember horrific abuse by family members. The juries awarded Hamanne $2.67 million and Carlson $2.5 million for their ordeals.

In all four cases, the women developed memories about childhood abuse in therapy and then later denied their authenticity. How can we determine if memories of childhood abuse are true or false? Without corroboration, it is very difficult to differentiate between false memories and true ones. Also, in these cases, some memories were contrary to physical evidence, such as explicit and detailed recollections of rape and abortion when medical examination confirmed virginity. How is it possible for people to acquire elaborate and confident false memories? A growing number of investigations demonstrate that under the right circumstances false memories can be instilled rather easily in some people.

My own research into memory distortion goes back to the early 1970s, when I began studies of the "misinformation effect." These studies show that when people who witness an event are later exposed to new and misleading information about it, their recollections often become distorted. In one example, participants viewed a simulated automobile accident at an intersection with a stop sign. After the viewing, half the participants received a suggestion that the traffic sign was a yield sign. When asked later what traffic sign they remembered seeing at the intersection, those who had been given the suggestion tended to claim that they had seen a yield sign. Those who had not received the phony information were much more accurate in their recollection of the traffic sign.

My students and I have now conducted more than 200 experiments involving over 20,000 individuals that document how exposure to misinformation induces memory distortion. In these studies, people "recalled" a conspicuous barn in a bucolic scene that contained no buildings at all, broken glass and tape recorders that were not in the scenes they viewed, a white instead of a blue vehicle in a crime scene, and Minnie Mouse when they actually saw Mickey Mouse. Taken together, these studies show that misinformation can change an in-dividual's recollection in predictable and sometimes very powerful ways.

Misinformation has the potential for invading our memories when we talk to other people, when we are suggestively interrogated or when we read or view media coverage about some event that we may have experienced ourselves. After more than two decades of exploring the power of misinformation, researchers have learned a great deal about the conditions that make people susceptible to memory modification. Memories are more easily modified, for instance, when the passage of time allows the original memory to fade.

False Childhood Memories

It is one thing to change a detail or two in an otherwise intact memory but quite another to plant a false memory of an event that never happened. To study false memory, my students and I first had to find a way to plant a pseudomemory that would not cause our subjects undue emotional stress, either in the process of creating the false memory or when we revealed that they had been intentionally deceived. Yet we wanted to try to plant a memory that would be at least mildly traumatic, had the experience actually happened.

My research associate, Jacqueline E. Pickrell, and I settled on trying to plant a specific memory of being lost in a shopping mall or large department store at about the age of five. Here's how we did it. We asked our subjects,

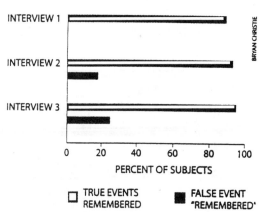

Recall of planted childhood events in this study appears to increase slightly after the details become familiar to the subject and the source of the information is forgotten. Ira Hyman and his colleagues at Western Washington University presented subjects with true events provided by relatives along with a false event—such as spilling a punch bowl on the parents of the bride at a wedding. None of the participants remembered the false event when first told about it, but in two follow-up interviews, initially 18 percent and later 25 percent of the subjects said they remembered something about the incident.

24 individuals ranging in age from 18 to 53, to try to remember childhood events that had been recounted to us by a parent, an older sibling or another close relative. We prepared a booklet for each participant containing one-paragraph stories about three events that had actually happened to him or her and one that had not. We constructed the false event using information about a plausible shopping trip provided by a relative, who also verified that the participant had not in fact been lost at about the age of five. The lost-in-the-mall scenario included the following elements: lost for an extended period, crying, aid and comfort by an elderly woman and, finally, reunion with the family.

After reading each story in the booklet, the participants wrote what they remembered about the event. If they did not remember it, they were instructed to write, "I

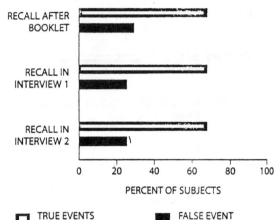

RECALL AFTER BOOKLET

RECALL IN INTERVIEW 1

RECALL IN INTERVIEW 2

0   20   40   60   80   100

PERCENT OF SUBJECTS

☐ TRUE EVENTS REMEMBERED   ■ FALSE EVENT "REMEMBERED"

False memory took root in roughly 25 percent of the subjects in this study by the author and her co-workers. The study was designed to create a false recollection of being lost at age five on a shopping trip. A booklet prepared for each participant included the false event and three events that he or she had actually experienced. After reading the scenarios, 29 percent of the subjects "recalled" something about being lost in the mall. Follow-up interviews showed there was little variation over time in recalling both the false and true events.

do not remember this." In two follow-up interviews, we told the participants that we were interested in examining how much detail they could remember and how their memories compared with those of their relative. The event paragraphs were not read to them verbatim, but rather parts were provided as retrieval cues. The participants recalled something about 49 of the 72 true events (68 percent) immediately after the initial reading of the booklet and also in each of the two follow-up interviews. After reading the booklet, seven of the 24 participants (29 percent) remembered either partially or fully the false event constructed for them, and in the two follow-up interviews six participants (25 percent) continued to claim that they remembered the fictitious event. Statistically, there were some differences between the true memories and the false ones: participants used more words to de-

scribe the true memories, and they rated the true memories as being somewhat more clear. But if an onlooker were to observe many of our participants describe an event, it would be difficult indeed to tell whether the account was of a true or a false memory.

Of course, being lost, however frightening, is not the same as being abused. But the lost-in-the-mall study is not about real experiences of being lost; it is about planting false memories of being lost. The paradigm shows a way of instilling false memories and takes a step toward allowing us to understand how this might happen in real-world settings. Moreover, the study provides evidence that people can be led to remember their past in different ways, and they can even be coaxed into "remembering" entire events that never happened.

Studies in other laboratories using a similar experimental procedure have produced similar results. For instance, Ira Hyman, Troy H. Husband and F. James Billing of Western Washington University asked college students to recall childhood experiences that had been recounted by their parents. The researchers told the students that the study was about how people remember shared experiences differently. In addition to actual events reported by parents, each participant was given one false event—either an overnight hospitalization for a high fever and a possible ear infection, or a birthday party with pizza and a clown—that supposedly happened at about the age of five. The parents confirmed that

neither of these events actually took place.

Hyman found that students fully or partially recalled 84 percent of the true events in the first interview and 88 percent in the second interview. None of the participants recalled the false event during the first interview, but 20 percent said they remembered something about the false event in the second interview. One participant who had been exposed to the emergency hospitalization story later remembered a male doctor, a female nurse and a friend from church who came to visit at the hospital.

In another study, along with true events Hyman presented different false events, such as accidentally spilling a bowl of punch on the parents of the bride at a wedding reception or having to evacuate a grocery store when the overhead sprinkler systems erroneously activated. Again, none of the participants recalled the false event during the first interview, but 18 percent remembered something about it in the second interview and 25 percent in the third interview. For example, during the first interview, one participant, when asked about the fictitious wedding event, stated, "I have no clue. I have never heard that one before." In the second interview, the participant said, "It was an outdoor wedding, and I think we were running around and knocked something over like the punch bowl or something and made a big mess and of course got yelled at for it."

Imagination Inflation

The finding that an external suggestion can lead to the construction of false childhood memories helps us understand the process by which false memories arise. It is natural to wonder whether this research is applicable in real situations such as being interrogated by law officers or in psychotherapy. Although strong suggestion may not routinely occur in police questioning or therapy, suggestion in the form of an imagination exercise sometimes does. For instance, when trying to obtain a confession, law officers may ask a suspect to imagine having participated in a criminal act. Some mental health professionals encourage patients to imagine childhood events as a way of recovering supposedly hidden memories.

Surveys of clinical psychologists reveal that 11 percent instruct their clients to "let the imagination run wild," and 22 percent tell their clients to "give free rein to the imagination." Therapist Wendy Maltz, author of a popular book on childhood sexual abuse, advocates telling the patient: "Spend time imagining that you were sexually abused, without worrying about accuracy, proving anything, or having your ideas make sense. . . . Ask yourself . . . these questions: What time of day is it? Where are you? Indoors or outdoors? What kind of things are happening? Is there one or more person with you?" Maltz further recommends that therapists continue to ask questions such as "Who would have been likely perpetrators? When were you most vulnerable to sexual abuse in your life?"

The increasing use of such imagination exercises led me and several colleagues to wonder about their consequences. What happens when people imagine childhood experiences that did not happen to them? Does imagining a childhood event increase confidence that it occurred? To ex-plore this, we designed a three-stage procedure. We first asked individuals to indicate the likelihood that certain events happened to them during their childhood. The list contains 40 events, each rated on a scale ranging from "definitely did not happen" to "definitely did happen." Two weeks later we asked the participants to imagine that they had experienced some of these events. Different subjects were asked to imagine different events. Sometime later the participants again were asked to respond to the original list of 40 childhood events, indicating how likely it was that these events actually happened to them.

Consider one of the imagination exercises. Participants are told to imagine playing inside at home after school, hearing a strange noise outside, running toward the window, tripping, falling, reaching out and breaking the window with their hand. In addition, we asked participants questions such as "What did you trip on? How did you feel?"

In one study 24 percent of the participants who imagined the broken-window scenario later reported an increase in confidence that the event had occurred, whereas only 12 percent of those who were not asked to imagine the incident reported an increase in the likelihood that it

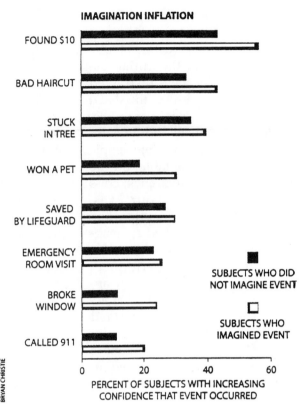

IMAGINATION INFLATION

BRYAN CHRISTIE

PERCENT OF SUBJECTS WITH INCREASING CONFIDENCE THAT EVENT OCCURRED

■ SUBJECTS WHO DID NOT IMAGINE EVENT

□ SUBJECTS WHO IMAGINED EVENT

Imagining an event can increase a person's belief that the fictitious event actually happened. To study the "imagination inflation" effect, the author and her colleagues asked participants to indicate on a scale the likelihood that each of 40 events occurred during their childhood. Two weeks later they were given guidance in imagining some of the events they said had not taken place and then were asked to rate the original 40 events again. Whereas all participants showed increased confidence that the events had occurred, those who took part in actively imagining the events reported an even greater increase.

had taken place. We found this "imagination inflation" effect in each of the eight events that participants were asked to imagine. A number of possible explanations come to mind. An obvious one is that an act of imagination simply makes the event seem more familiar and that familiarity is mistakenly related to childhood memories rather than to the act of imagination. Such source confusion—when a person does not remember the source of information—can be especially acute for the distant experiences of childhood.

Studies by Lyn Goff and Henry L. Roediger III of Washington University of recent rather than childhood experiences more directly connect imagined actions to the construction of false memory. During the initial session, the researchers instructed participants to perform the stated action, imagine doing it or just listen to the statement and do nothing else. The actions were simple ones: knock on the table, lift the stapler, break the toothpick, cross your fingers, roll your eyes. During the second session, the participants were asked to imagine some of the actions that they had not previously performed. During the final session, they answered questions about what actions they actually performed during the initial session. The investigators found that the more times participants imagined an unperformed action, the more likely they were to remember having performed it.

Impossible Memories

It is highly unlikely that an adult can recall genuine episodic memories from the first year of life, in part because the hippocampus, which plays a key role in the creation of memories, has not matured enough to form and store long-lasting memories that can be retrieved in adulthood. A procedure for planting "impossible" memories about experiences that occur shortly after birth has been developed by the late Nicholas Spanos and his collaborators at Carleton University. Individuals are led to believe that they have well-coordinated eye movements and visual exploration skills probably because they were born in hospitals that hung swinging, colored mobiles over infant cribs. To confirm whether they had such an experience, half the participants are hypnotized, age-regressed to the day after birth and asked what they remembered. The other half of the group participates in a "guided mnemonic restructuring" procedure that uses age regression as well as active encouragement to re-create the infant experiences by imagining them.

Spanos and his co-workers found that the vast majority of their subjects were susceptible to these memory-planting procedures. Both the hypnotic and guided participants reported infant memories. Surprisingly, the guided group did so somewhat more (95 versus 70 percent). Both groups remembered the colored mobile at a relatively high rate (56 percent of the guided group and 46 percent of the hypnotic subjects). Many participants who did not remember the mobile did recall other things, such as doctors, nurses, bright lights, cribs and masks. Also, in both groups, of those who reported memories of infancy, 49 percent felt that they were real memories, as opposed to 16 percent who claimed that they were merely fantasies. These findings confirm earlier studies that many individuals can be led to construct complex, vivid and detailed false memories via a rather simple procedure. Hypnosis clearly is not necessary.

Memories of infancy—such as a mobile hanging over a crib—can be induced even though it is highly unlikely that events from the first year of life can be recalled. In a study by the late Nicholas Spanos and his colleagues at Carleton University, "impossible" memories of the first day of life were planted using either hypnosis or a guided mnemonic restructuring procedure. The mobile was "remembered" by 46 percent of the hypnotized group and by 56 percent of the guided group.

How False Memories Form

In the lost-in-the-mall study, implantation of false memory occurred when another person, usually a family member, claimed that the incident happened. Corroboration of an event by another person can be a powerful technique for instilling a false memory. In fact, merely claiming to have seen a person do something can lead that person to make a false confession of wrongdoing.

This effect was demonstrated in a study of Saul M. Kassin and his colleagues at Williams College, who investigated the reactions of individuals falsely accused of damaging a computer by pressing the wrong key. The innocent participants initially denied the charge, but when a confederate said that she had seen them perform the action, many participants signed a confession, internalized guilt for the act and went on to confabulate details that were consistent with that belief. These findings show that false incriminating evidence can induce people to accept guilt for a crime they did not commit and even to develop memories to support their guilty feelings.

Research is beginning to give us an understanding of how false memories of complete, emotional and self-participatory experiences are created in adults. First, there are social demands on individuals to remember; for instance, researchers exert some pressure on participants in a study to come up with memories. Second, memory construction by imagining events can be explicitly encouraged when people are having trouble remembering. And, finally, individuals can be encouraged not to think about whether their constructions are real or not. Creation of false memories is most likely to occur when these external factors are present, whether in an experimental setting, in a therapeutic setting or during everyday activities.

False memories are constructed by combining actual memories with the content of suggestions received from others. During the process, individuals may forget the source of the information. This is a classic example of source confusion, in which the content and the source become dissociated.

Of course, because we can implant false childhood memories in some individuals in no way implies that all memories that arise after suggestion are necessarily false. Put another way, although experimental work on the creation of false memories may raise doubt about the validity of long-buried memories, such as repeated trauma, it in no way disproves them. Without corroboration, there is little that can be done to help even the most experienced evaluator to differentiate true memories from ones that were suggestively planted.

The precise mechanisms by which such false memories are constructed await further research. We still have much to learn about the degree of confidence and the characteristics of false memories created in these ways, and we need to discover what types of individuals are particularly susceptible to these forms of suggestion and who is resistant.

As we continue this work, it is important to heed the cautionary tale in the data we have already obtained: mental health professionals and others must be aware of how greatly they can influence the recollection of events and of the urgent need for maintaining restraint in situations in which imagination is used as an aid in recovering presumably lost memories.

Further Reading

The Myth of Repressed Memory. Elizabeth F. Loftus and Katherine Ketcham. St. Martin's Press, 1994.

The Social Psychology of False Confessions: Compliance, Internalization, and Confabulation. Saul M. Kassin and Katherine L. Kiechel in *Psychological Science,* Vol. 7, No. 3, pages 125–128; May 1996.

Imagination Inflation: Imagining a Childhood Event Inflates Confidence That It Occurred. Maryanne Garry, Charles G. Manning, Elizabeth F. Loftus and Steven J. Sherman in *Psychonomic Bulletin and Review,* Vol. 3, No. 2, pages 208–214; June 1996.

Remembering Our Past: Studies in Autobiographical Memory. Edited by David C. Rubin. Cambridge University Press, 1996.

Searching for Memory: The Brain, the Mind, and the Past. Daniel L. Schacter. BasicBooks, 1996.

 Article Review Form at end of book.

What are some nonverbal cues that someone is lying? Who is actually skilled at detecting deception in our society, and what makes them that way?

Jurors Look to Mannerisms for Clues to Truth

Elaine Woo

Times *staff writer*

When Ron Shipp urged his friend O. J. Simpson to "tell the truth," when Denise Brown heaved sighs and sobbed on the stand, and when Detective Mark Fuhrman snapped his head back while viewing the letter of a woman who has accused him of racism, what was the jury doing?

Were they watching to see if Brown, detailing Simpson's alleged abuse of her sister, ever looked at Simpson from the witness box? Taking mental note of how Shipp, during a break in the proceedings, stared pointedly at the accused double-murderer and mouthed a message to him? Wondering what Fuhrman's sudden movement meant?

Wouldn't we all like to know? As armchair jurors glued to the broadcasts of Simpson's televised trial, we size up the witnesses not only by weighing their statements but by observing their demeanor, believing that mannerisms sometimes speak louder than words.

Behavioral experts say the real jurors are no different, seeking out clues of truthfulness or deception in the shrug of a shoul-

der, the twitch of a brow, the steadiness of a gaze.

"When we're placed in a new situation or confronted with people we don't know, we generally place more importance on the nonverbals," said Donald Vinson, chairman of DecisionQuest, the Torrance trial consulting firm advising the prosecution in the Simpson case. Jurors, he added, "have got nothing to do all day but sit and watch. So (nonverbal communication) matters a great deal."

Jude Nelson will attest to that. The former rock band manager from Sylmar sat in a Van Nuys courtroom for six months in 1993 as a member of the Lyle Menendez jury. He remembers one defense witness who leaned toward Lyle and "kept eyeballing him" from the stand, as if trying to communicate with him. The juror concluded that the witness was "lying through her teeth."

"Body language," insists Nelson, who voted for first-degree murder on a jury that ultimately deadlocked, "is incredibly important."

The idea—that a person's behavior while testifying can be a powerful gauge of honesty—is embedded in the American judicial system.

"The courts assume that you are better at judging someone's truthfulness if you can see them," said Phoebe Ellsworth, a professor of law and psychology at the University of Michigan law school who has studied how juries make decisions.

That is why most witnesses are questioned in open court before a judge and jury, and why jurors are commonly instructed by judges to use demeanor on the stand as one of several important tests of believability.

The irony is, a growing body of research shows that most people are mediocre at best when they try to judge truthfulness from facial expressions, tone of voice, body movements and other facets of demeanor. This weakness has been found even in professionals for whom lie-catching is crucial, such as customs inspectors and psychiatrists.

In the courtroom, a leading authority on lie detection says, the odds are stacked almost hopelessly against intuiting deception from behavior.

"The courtroom is the most difficult situation of all," said Paul Ekman, a psychology professor and researcher at UC San Francisco's Human Interaction Laboratory.

In Superior Court Judge Lance A. Ito's courtroom, the 20 jurors and alternates have kept poker faces for the most part, giving away few clues to their thoughts about the witness parade under way for the past several weeks. But jury specialists who have conducted extensive post-trial interviews with jurors in other cases say it's likely that little is escaping their gaze.

Sequestered jurors may be especially attuned to nonverbal messages from courtroom players, said Jo-Ellan Dimitrius, the Pasadena trial consultant advising the Simpson defense team.

"What happens is the courtroom becomes their home. They know everybody who walks in and out of that door. They notice not only what you have on but how all the people in the courtroom interact with one another, not just the defendant and the attorneys, but the reporters, the judge, the bailiff and the people in the audience," she said. "Trials get to be monotonous, so (the jurors) look around the courtroom for reactions."

Jurors also use courtroom behavior as a sounding board. "We all look for validation. How do you do that when you're sitting in the jury box and you're told you cannot talk about the case or anything having to do with the case?" Dimitrius said.

"The validation you get is through the body language of everybody in that courtroom. That's a very important part of the process."

Courts can try to regulate behavior, as Ito did when he issued an order against emotional displays among courtroom spectators while the jury is present. "This includes the rolling of eyes, facial grimaces, hand gestures and all other obvious expressions," Ito wrote. The prohibition came after members of the Brown family were noticed visibly sighing or rolling their eyes during defense presentations before the jury was brought in. Simpson has reacted similarly during testimony by prosecution witnesses.

University of Washington forensic psychologist Elizabeth Loftus says jurors, like most of us, are also sensitive to "para-linguistic cues," especially those that express confidence or uncertainty.

Studies by many researchers have shown that confident speech is very persuasive, particularly from an eyewitness to a crime. Verbal tics or hedges, such as preceding a statement with "I think" or "I kind of feel," are a turnoff.

Given that, jurors might have difficulty believing Rosa Lopez.

The maid to Simpson's next-door neighbor was a vital alibi witness who was expected to testify that she saw Simpson's white Bronco parked in front of his Brentwood estate around the time that the prosecution alleges the murders of Nicole Brown Simpson and Ronald Lyle Goldman were committed.

Instead, she seemed tentative and confused when she was questioned about the time. And, during her videotaped testimony—which the jury might be shown when the defense presents its case—she often used phrases such as "if you say so, sir" when responding to prosecution questions.

During the Menendez trial, juror Ruth Slike recalls being impressed—negatively—by Lyle's manner of speech. "It was kind of chopped. It seemed to imply a kind of arrogance about him," she said.

"I looked at the transcripts and for the most part Lyle never did make a sentence. I am a little bit critical of that. Maybe I was too judgmental, but if you went to Princeton, you should be able to form a sentence."

Slike, who favored a verdict of first-degree murder, said such impressions never unduly influenced her evaluation of the evidence. Trial consultants say most jurors insist they focus purely on the evidence, looking for inconsistencies, and rely heavily on opening statements and closing arguments to help them interpret a case.

"Gestures, body movements, they didn't faze me at all," said Edith Foster of Los Angeles, who has served on two criminal trials. "I listened for facts. Anyone with common sense is not going to go with the way someone moves their shoulders or clenches their fingers. That isn't important."

Some experts believe that jurors focus more on nonverbal cues when confronted by testimony that taxes their understanding. Overwhelmed by very complex information or difficult terminology, a juror might be tempted to fixate on the way the person talking shuffles nervously through notes or stutters on the stand.

"Boy, we are going to see that when we get into the DNA evidence," said Vinson, a doctor of philosophy who has written a book about psychological strategies in jury persuasion. "When people are confronted in the Simpson case with information that is new to them or inconsistent with common sense, they are really going to focus on the behavior" of witnesses.

The danger is in how they interpret the clues. Vinson recalls a major antitrust suit he worked on where a witness for the plaintiff kept glancing around the courtroom. In post-trial interviews jurors said they thought the witness was being prompted by someone in the room. "That didn't happen," said Vinson, "but this witness gave the impression of being very uncomfortable and looking around, so people assumed this person was looking for help."

Research shows that most people are poor lie detectors when asked to assess truthfulness from behavior. Even professionals who are assumed to be highly skilled judges of veracity flunk as often as they succeed.

In a 1991 study published in the journal of the American Psychological Assn., professor Ekman and colleague Maureen O'Sullivan of the University of San Francisco evaluated 509 subjects, including judges, college students, psychiatrists, federal polygraphers and Secret Service agents. Each was shown videotapes of 10 people—half of whom were lying and half of whom were telling the truth about a film they were watching—and asked to identify the liars.

The only group that was significantly above average in accuracy was the Secret Service. More than half of them—53%—could pick the liars at least 70% of the time, which Ekman rated as better than chance. Judges were a distant second, with 35% scoring that well, followed by psychiatrists at 32%. Only 26% of robbery investigators and 22% of federal polygraphers hit the high accuracy range.

Ekman surmised that the Secret Service agents used nonverbal clues more effectively and were better able to interpret subtle facial changes that can signal deceit, possibly a result of the amount of time they spend scanning crowds for potential attackers. In subsequent studies, the psychology professor has found that top-rated police interrogators also performed as well as the Secret Service.

"So it is possible to detect deception from demeanor," con-

cludes Ekman, whose three decades studying the subject have included requests to spot liars at diplomatic summits and to analyze photographs of heiress Patty Hearst for clues as to whether she was a willing or reluctant bank robber.

Poker player John Tonner is a firm believer in the value of nonverbal messages. The foreman of the jury that acquitted prominent San Francisco attorney Patrick Hallinan of drug conspiracy and racketeering charges in Reno last week, Tonner is a student of "the tell"—the facial expressions and gestures that can tip off poker players to a losing hand.

Practiced at reading body language, the construction engineer quickly dismissed the prosecution's star witness as a well-rehearsed liar, in part because of eye blinking and hand movements that Tonner found phony. "You have to know what to look for and how to interpret it," the juror said.

Experience, as in the case of the federal agents, probably does count for something. But no one yet knows whether the ability to decipher liars' cues can be taught. Part of the problem for jurors and others is that lying is highly idiosyncratic.

Bella M. DePaulo, a lie-detection expert who teaches psychology at the University of Virginia in Charlottesville, said studies show that when people are telling falsehoods they tend to blink more, have more dilated pupils, rub or scratch themselves, give shorter responses that are more negative, irrelevant and general, and speak in a higher pitch. But there are no behaviors that always mean someone is lying.

"You can train someone to be better at detecting a particular person's deception" by familiarizing them with that person's clues, she said. "But that doesn't neces-

sarily generalize to someone else. Different people have different ways of lying."

"I don't think it would help a jury a lot to get training," DePaulo said. "They could be helped some, but not reliably enough."

Ekman agrees. In the courtroom version of "Truth or Consequences," juries, he says, have several strikes against them.

Guilty defendants and deceitful witnesses have months to prepare and rehearse their stories, allowing them to build self-confidence and decrease their fear of having their lies exposed.

The slow pace of justice also gives guilty suspects time to blunt any emotions associated with the crime that could blow their cover, or to rehearse their answers so many times that they begin to believe them.

An innocent defendant or truthful witness, on the other hand, could be so terrified of not being believed that a jury could read that fright or nervousness as fear of being caught, Ekman said.

Nonetheless, the lie-detection expert believes that jurors should be better instructed about how to evaluate courtroom behavior. He has proposed changing federal jury instructions to caution jurors about the limitations of nonverbal cues.

In a version of the jury instructions he drafted and sent to some judges a few years ago, he advises jurors to pay attention to facial expressions, gestures, posture and tone of voice and to "look for discrepancies between what the witness says and how the witness says it."

"But remember," he writes, "that sometimes truthful witnesses may look worried . . . and some liars can behave very convincingly."

 Article Review Form at end of book.

Why are individual testimonials not sufficient proof for the effectiveness of a therapy? How does the self-serving bias influence our judgments about the effectiveness of a course of treatment? How would you counsel people who were interested in evaluating an alternative medical treatment for themselves?

Why Bogus Therapies Seem to Work

Barry L. Beyerstein

Barry L. Beyerstein is at the Brain-Behavior Laboratory Department of Psychology; Simon Fraser University, Burnaby, British Columbia, V5A 1S6 Canada.

Abstract: *Beyerstein explains why alternative therapists and their clients, who rely on anecdotal evidence and uncontrolled observations erroneously, conclude that inert therapies work. Ten reasons that can convince intelligent, honest people that cures have been achieved when they have not are discussed.*

Nothing is more dangerous than active ignorance.

—*Goethe*

Those who sell therapies of any kind have an obligation to prove, first, that their treatments are safe and, second, that they are effective. The latter is often the more difficult task because there are many subtle ways that honest and intelligent people (both patients and therapists) can be led to think that a treatment has cured someone when it has not. This is true whether we are assessing new treatments in scientific medicine, old nostrums in folk medicine, fringe treatments in "alternative medicine," or the frankly magical panaceas of faith healers.

To distinguish causal from fortuitous improvements that might follow any intervention, a set of objective procedures has evolved for testing putative remedies. Unless a technique, ritual, drug, or surgical procedure can meet these requirements, it is ethically questionable to offer it to the public, especially if money is to change hands. Since most "alternative" therapies (i.e., ones not accepted by scientific biomedicine) fall into this category, one must ask why so many customers who would not purchase a toaster without consulting *Consumer Reports* shell out, with trusting naivete, large sums for unproven, possibly dangerous, health remedies.

For many years, critics have been raising telling doubts about fringe medical practices, but the popularity of such nostrums seems undiminished. We must wonder why entrepreneurs'

claims in this area should remain so refractory to contrary data. If an "alternative" or "complementary" therapy:

a. is implausible on a priori grounds (because its implied mechanisms or putative effects contradict well-established laws, principles, or empirical findings in physics, chemistry, or biology),

b. lacks a scientifically acceptable rationale of its own,

c. has insufficient supporting evidence derived from adequately controlled outcome research (i.e., double-blind, randomized, placebo-controlled clinical trials),

d. has failed in well-controlled clinical studies done by impartial evaluators and has been unable to rule out competing explanations for why it might seem to work in uncontrolled settings, and,

e. should seem improbable, even to the lay person, on "commonsense" grounds, why would so many well-educated people continue to sell and purchase such a treatment?

The answer, I believe, lies in a combination of vigorous marketing of unsubstantiated claims by "alternative" healers (Beyerstein and Sampson 1996), the poor level of scientific knowledge in the public at large (Kiernan 1995), and the "will to believe" so prevalent among seekers attracted to the New Age movement (Basil 1988; Gross and Levitt 1994).

The appeal of nonscientific medicine is largely a holdover from popular "counterculture" sentiments of the 1960s and 1970s. Remnants of the rebellious, "back-to-nature" leanings of that era survive as nostalgic yearnings for a return to nineteenth-century-style democratized health care (now wrapped in the banner of patients' rights) and a dislike of bureaucratic, technologic, and specialized treatment of disease (Cassileth and Brown 1988). Likewise, the allure of the "holistic" dogmas of alternative medicine is a descendant of the fascination with Eastern mysticism that emerged in the sixties and seventies. Although the philosophy and the science that underlie these holistic teachings have been severely criticized (Brandon 1985), they retain a strong appeal for those committed to belief in "mind-over-matter" cures, a systemic rather than localized view of pathology, and the all-powerful ability of nutrition to restore health (conceived of as whole-body "balance").

Many dubious health products remain on the market primarily because satisfied customers offer testimonials to their worth. Essentially, they are saying; "I tried it and I got better, so it must

be effective." But even when symptoms do improve following a treatment, this, by itself, cannot prove that the therapy was responsible.

The Illness-Disease Distinction

Although the terms *disease* and *illness* are often used interchangeably, for present purposes it is worth distinguishing between the two. I shall use disease to refer to a pathological state of the organism due to infection, tissue degeneration, trauma, toxic exposure, carcinogenesis, etc. By illness I mean the feelings of malaise, pain, disorientation, dysfunctionality, or other complaints that might accompany a disease. Our subjective reaction to the raw sensations we call symptoms is molded by cultural and psychological factors such as beliefs, suggestions, expectations, demand characteristics, self-serving biases, and self-deception. The experience of illness is also affected (often unconsciously) by a host of social and psychological payoffs that accrue to those admitted to the "sick role" by society's gatekeepers (i.e., health professionals). For certain individuals, the privileged status and benefits of the sick role are sufficient to perpetuate the experience of illness after a disease has healed, or even to create feelings of illness in the absence of disease (Alcock 1986).

Unless we can tease apart the many factors that contribute to the perception of being ill, personal testimonials offer no basis on which to judge whether a putative therapy has, in fact, cured a disease. That is why controlled clinical trials with objective physical measures are essential in evaluating therapies of any kind.

Correlation Does Not Imply Causation

Mistaking correlation for causation is the basis of most superstitious beliefs, including many in the area of alternative medicine. We have a tendency to assume that when things occur together, they must be causally connected, although obviously they need not be. For example, there is a high correlation between the consumption of diet soft drinks and obesity. Does this mean that artificial sweeteners cause people to become overweight? When we count on personal experience to test the worth of medical treatments, many factors are varying simultaneously, making it extremely difficult to determine what is cause and effect. Personal endorsements supply the bulk of the support for unorthodox health products, but they are a weak currency because of what Gilovich (1997) has called the "compared to what?" problem. Without comparison to a similar group of sufferers, treated identically except that the allegedly curative element is withheld, individual recipients can never know whether they would have recovered just as well without it.

Ten Errors and Biases

The question is, then: Why might therapists and their clients who rey on anecdotal evidence and uncontrolled observations erroneously conclude that inert therapies work? There are at least ten good reasons.

1. The Disease May Have Run Its Natural Course

Many diseases are self-limiting—providing the condition is not chronic or fatal, the body's own recuperative processes usually restore the sufferer to health. Thus, before a therapy can be acknowledged as curative, its proponents must show that the number of patients listed as improved exceeds the proportion expected to recover without any treatment at all (or that they recover reliably faster than if left untreated). Unless an unconventional therapist releases detailed records of successes and failures over a sufficiently large number of patients with the same complaint, he or she cannot claim to have exceeded the published norms for unaided recovery.

2. Many Diseases Are Cyclical

Arthritis, multiple sclerosis, allergies, and gastrointestinal complaints are examples of diseases that normally "have their ups and downs." Naturally, sufferers tend to seek therapy during the downturn of any given cycle. In this way, a bogus treatment will have repeated opportunities to coincide with upturns that would have happened anyway. Again, in the absence of appropriate control groups, consumers and vendors alike are prone to misinterpret improvement due to normal cyclical variation as a valid therapeutic effect.

3. Spontaneous Remission

Anecdotally reported cures can be due to rare but possible "spontaneous remissions." Even with cancers that are nearly always lethal, tumors occasionally disappear without further treatment. One experienced oncologist reports that he has seen twelve such events in about six thousand cases

he has treated (Silverman 1987). Alternative therapies can receive unearned acclaim for remissions of this sort because many desperate patients turn to them when they feel that they have nothing left to lose. When the "alternatives" assert that they have snatched many hopeless individuals from death's door, they rarely reveal what percentage of their apparently terminal clientele such happy exceptions represent. What is needed is statistical evidence that their "cure rates" exceed the known spontaneous remission rate and the placebo response rate (see below) for the conditions they treat.

The exact mechanisms responsible for spontaneous remissions are not well understood, but much research is being devoted to revealing and possibly harnessing processes in the immune system or elsewhere that are responsible for these unexpected turnarounds. The relatively new field of psychoneuroimmunology studies how psychological variables affect the nervous, glandular, and immune systems in ways that might affect susceptibility to and recovery from disease (Ader and Cohen 1993; Mestel 1994). If thoughts, emotions, desires, beliefs, etc., are physical states of the brain, there is nothing inherently mystical in the notion that these neural processes could affect glandular, immune, and other cellular processes throughout the body. Via the limbic system of the brain, the hypothalamic pituitary axis, and the autonomic nervous system, psychological variables can have widespread physiological effects that can have positive or negative impacts upon health. While research has confirmed that

such effects exist, it must be remembered that they are fairly small, accounting for perhaps a few percent of the variance in disease statistics.

4. The Placebo Effect

A major reason why bogus remedies are credited with subjective, and occasionally objective, improvements is the ubiquitous placebo effect (Roberts, Kewman, and Hovell 1993; Ulett 1996). The history of medicine is strewn with examples of what, with hindsight, seem like crackpot procedures that were once enthusiastically endorsed by physicians and patients alike (Skrabanek and McCormick 1990; Barrett and Jarvis 1993). Misattributions of this sort arise from the false assumption that a change in symptoms following a treatment must have been a specific consequence of that procedure. Through a combination of suggestion, belief, expectancy, cognitive reinterpretation, and diversion of attention, patients given biologically useless treatments can often experience measurable relief. Some placebo responses produce actual changes in the physical condition; others are subjective changes that make patients feel better although there has been no objective change in the underlying pathology.

Through repeated contact with valid therapeutic procedures, we all develop, much like Pavlov's dogs, conditioned responses in various physiological systems. Later, these responses can be triggered by the setting, rituals, paraphernalia, and verbal cues that signal the act of "being treated." Among other things, placebos can cause release of the body's own morphinelike pain killers, the endorphins (Ulett 1996, ch. 3). Because these learned responses can be palliative, even when a treatment itself is physiologically unrelated to the source of the complaint, putative therapies must be tested against a placebo control group—similar patients who receive a sham treatment that resembles the "real" one except that the suspected active ingredient is withheld.

It is essential that the patients in such tests be randomly assigned to their respective groups and that they be "blind" with respect to their active versus placebo status. Because the power of what psychologists call expectancy and compliance effects (see below) is so strong, the therapists must also be blind as to individual patients' group membership. Hence the term double blind—the gold standard of outcome research. Such precautions are required because barely perceptible cues, unintentionally conveyed by treatment providers who are not blinded, can bias test results. Likewise, those who assess the treatment's effects must also be blind, for there is a large literature on "experimenter bias" showing that honest and well-trained professionals can unconsciously "read in" the outcomes they expect when they attempt to assess complex phenomena (Rosenthal 1966; Chapman and Chapman 1967).

When the clinical trial is completed, the blinds can be broken to allow statistical comparison of active, placebo, and no treatment groups. Only if the improvements observed in the active treatment group exceed those in the two control groups by a statistically significant amount can the therapy claim legitimacy.

5. Some Allegedly Cured Symptoms Are Psychosomatic to Begin With

A constant difficulty in trying to measure therapeutic effectiveness is that many physical complaints can both arise from psychosocial distress and be alleviated by support and reassurance. At first glance, these symptoms (at various times called "psychosomatic," "hysterical," or "neurasthenic") resemble those of recognized medical syndromes (Shorter 1992; Merskey 1995). Although there are many "secondary gains" (psychological, social, and economic) that accrue to those who slip into "the sick role" in this way, we need not accuse them of conscious malingering to point out that their symptoms are nonetheless maintained by subtle psychosocial processes.

"Alternative" healers cater to these members of the "worried well" who are mistakenly convinced that they are ill. Their complaints are instances of somatization, the tendency to express psychological concerns in a language of symptoms like those of organic diseases (Alcock 1986; Shorter 1992). The "alternatives" offer comfort to these individuals who for psychological reasons need others to believe there are organic etiologies for their symptoms. Often with the aid of pseudoscientific diagnostic devices, fringe practitioners reinforce the somatizer's conviction that the cold-hearted, narrow-minded medical establishment, which can find nothing physically amiss, is both incompetent and unfair in refusing to acknowledge a very real organic condition. A large portion of those diagnosed with "chronic fatigue," "environmental sensitivity syndrome," and various stress disorders (not to mention many suing because of the allegedly harmful effects of silicone breast implants) look very much like classic somatizers (Stewart 1990; Huber 1991; Rosenbaum 1997).

When, through the role-governed rituals of "delivering treatment," fringe therapists supply the reassurance, sense of belonging, and existential support their clients seek, this is obviously worthwhile, but all this need not be foreign to scientific practitioners who have much more to offer besides. The downside is that catering to the desire for medical diagnoses for psychological complaints promotes pseudoscientific and magical thinking while unduly inflating the success rates of medical quacks. Saddest of all, it perpetuates the anachronistic feeling that there is something shameful or illegitimate about psychological problems.

6. Symptomatic Relief Versus Cure

Short of an outright cure, alleviating pain and discomfort is what sick people value most. Many allegedly curative treatments offered by alternative practitioners, while unable to affect the disease process itself, do make the illness more bearable, but for psychological reasons. Pain is one example. Much research shows that pain is partly a sensation like seeing or hearing and partly an emotion (Melzack 1973). It has been found repeatedly that successfully reducing the emotional component of pain leaves the sensory portion surprisingly tolerable. Thus, suffering can often be reduced by psychological means, even if the underlying pathology is untouched. Anything that can allay anxiety, redirect attention, reduce arousal, foster a sense of control, or lead to cognitive reinterpretation of symptoms can alleviate the agony component of pain. Modern pain clinics put these strategies to good use every day (Smith, Merskey, and Gross 1980). Whenever patients suffer less, this is all to the good, but we must be careful that purely symptomatic relief does not divert people from proven remedies until it is to late for them to be effective.

7. Many Consumers of Alternative Therapies Hedge Their Bets

In an attempt to appeal to a wider clientele, many unorthodox healers have begun to refer to themselves as "complementary" rather than "alternative." Instead of ministering primarily to the ideologically committed or those who have been told there is nothing more that conventional medicine can do for them, the "alternatives" have begun to advertise that they can enhance conventional biomedical treatments. They accept that orthodox practitioners can alleviate specific symptoms but contend that alternative medicine treats the real causes of disease: dubious dietary imbalances or environmental sensitivities, disrupted energy fields, or even unresolved conflicts from previous incarnations. If improvement follows the combined delivery of "complementary" and scientifically based treatments, the fringe practice often gets a disproportionate share of the credit.

8. Misdiagnosis (by Self or by a Physician)

In this era of media obsession with health, many people can be induced to think they have diseases they do not have. When these healthy folk receive the oddly unwelcome news from orthodox physicians that they have no organic signs of disease, they often gravitate to alternative practitioners who can almost always find some kind of "imbalance" to treat. If "recovery" follows, another convert is born.

Of course, scientifically trained physicians are not infallible, and a mistaken diagnosis, followed by a trip to a shrine or an alternative healer, can lead to a glowing testimonial for curing a grave condition that never existed. Other times the diagnosis may be correct but the time course, which is inherently hard to predict, might prove inaccurate. If a patient with a terminal condition undergoes alternative treatments and succumbs later than the conventional doctor predicted, the alternative procedure may receive credit for prolonging life when, in fact, there was merely an unduly pessimistic prognosis—survival was longer than the expected norm, but within the range of normal statistical variation for the disease.

9. Derivative Benefits

Alternative healers often have forceful, charismatic personalities (O'Connor 1987). To the extent that patients are swept up by the messianic aspects of alternative medicine, psychological uplift many ensue. If an enthusiastic, upbeat healer manages to elevate the patient's mood and expectations, this optimism can lead to greater compliance with, and hence effectiveness of, any orthodox treatments he or she may also be receiving. This expectant attitude can also motivate people to eat and sleep better and to exercise and socialize more. These, by themselves, could help speed natural recovery.

Psychological spinoffs of this sort can also reduce stress, which has been shown to have deleterious effects on the immune system (Mestel 1994). Removing this added burden may speed healing, even if it is not a specific effect of the therapy. As with purely symptomatic relief, this is far from a bad thing, unless it diverts the patient from more effective treatments, or the charges are exorbitant.

10. Psychological Distortion of Reality

Distortion of reality in the service of strong belief is a common occurrence (Alcock 1995). Even when they derive no objective improvements, devotees who have a strong psychological investment in alternative medicine can convince themselves they have been helped. According to cognitive dissonance theory (Festinger 1957), when experiences contradict existing attitudes, feelings, or knowledge, mental distress is produced. We tend to alleviate this discord by reinterpreting (distorting) the offending information. To have received no relief after committing time, money and "face" to an alternate course of treatment (and perhaps to the worldview of which it is a part) would create such a state of internal disharmony. Because it would be too psychologically disconcerting to admit to oneself or to others that it has all been a waste, there would be strong psychological pressure to find some redeeming value in the treatment.

Many other self-serving biases help maintain self-esteem and smooth social functioning (Beyerstein and Hadaway 1991). Because core beliefs tend to be vigorously defended by warping perception and memory, fringe practitioners and their clients are prone to misinterpret cues and remember things as they wish they had happened. Similarly, they may be selective in what they recall, overestimating their apparent successes while ignoring, downplaying, or explaining away their failures. The scientific method evolved in large part to reduce the impact of this human penchant for jumping to congenial conclusions.

An illusory feeling that one's symptoms have improved could also be due to a number of so called demand characteristics found in any therapeutic setting. In all societies, there exists the "norm of reciprocity," an implicit rule that obliges people to respond in kind when someone does them a good turn. Therapists, for the most part, sincerely believe they are helping their patients and it is only natural that patients would want to please them in return. Without patients necessarily realizing it, such obligations are sufficient to inflate their perception of how much benefit they have received. Thus,

controls for compliance effects must also be built into proper clinical trials (Adair 1973).

Finally, the job of distinguishing real from spurious causal relationships requires not only controlled observations, but also systematized abstractions from large bodies of data. Psychologists interested in judgmental biases have identified many sources of error that plague people who rely on informal reasoning processes to analyze complex events (Gilovich 1991, 1997; Schick and Vaughn 1995). Dean and colleagues (1992) showed, using examples from another popular pseudoscience, handwriting analysis, that without sophisticated statistical aids, human cognitive abilities are simply not up to the task of sifting valid relationships out of masses of interacting data. Similar difficulties would have confronted the pioneers of pre-scientific medicine and their followers, and for that reason, we cannot accept their anecdotal reports as support for their assertions.

Summary

For the reasons I have presented, individual testimonials count for very little in evaluating therapies. Because so many false leads can convince intelligent, honest people that cures have been achieved when they have not, it is essential that any putative treatment be tested under conditions that control for placebo responses, compliance effects, and judgmental errors.

Before anyone agrees to undergo any kind of treatment, he or she should be confident that it has

been validated in properly controlled clinical trials. To reduce the probability that supporting evidence has been contaminated by the foregoing biases and errors, consumers should insist that supporting evidence be published in peer-reviewed scientific journals. Any practitioner who cannot supply this kind of backing for his or her procedures is immediately suspect. Potential clients should be wary if, instead, the "evidence" consists merely of testimonials, self-published pamphlets or books, or items from the popular media. Even if supporting articles appear to have come from legitimate scientific periodicals, consumers should check to see that the journals in question are published by reputable scientific organizations. Papers extolling pseudoscience often appear in official-looking periodicals that turn out to be owned by groups with inadequate scientific credentials but with a financial stake in the questionable products. Similarly, one should discount articles from the "vanity press"—journals that accept virtually all submissions and charge the authors for publication. And finally, because any single positive outcome—even from a carefully done experiment published in a reputable journal—could always be a fluke, replication by independent research groups is the ultimate standard of proof.

If the practitioner claims persecution, is ignorant of or openly hostile to mainstream science, cannot supply a reasonable scientific rationale for his or her methods, and promises results that go well beyond those claimed by orthodox biomedicine, there is strong reason to suspect that one is dealing with a quack. Appeals to other ways of knowing or mysterious sounding "planes," "energies," "forces," or "vibrations" are other telltale signs, as is any claim to treat the whole person rather than localized pathology.

To people who are unwell, any promise of a cure is especially beguiling. As a result, false hope easily supplants common sense. In this vulnerable state, the need for hard-nosed appraisal is all the more necessary, but so often we see instead an eagerness to abandon any remaining vestiges of skepticism. Erstwhile savvy consumers, felled by disease, often insist upon less evidence to support the claims of alternative healers than they would previously have demanded from someone hawking a used car. Caveat emptor!

References

Adair, J. 1973. *The Human Subject.* Boston: Little, Brown and Co.

Ader, R., and N. Cohen. 1993. Psychoneuroimmunology: Conditioning and stress. *Annual Review of Psychology* 44: 53–85.

Alcock, J. 1986. Chronic pain and the injured worker. *Canadian Psychology* 27(2): 196–203.

———.1995. The belief engine. *Skeptical Inquirer* 19(3): 1–8.

Barrett, S., and W. Jarvis. 1993. *The Health Robbers: A Close Look at Quackery in America.* Amherst, N.Y.: Prometheus Books.

Basil, R., ed. 1988. *Not Necessarily the New Age.* Amherst, N.Y.: Prometheus Books.

Beyerstein, B., and P. Hadaway. 1991. On avoiding folly. *Journal of Drug Issues* 20(4): 689–700.

Beyerstein, B., and W. Sampson. 1996. Traditional medicine and pseudoscience in China. *Skeptical Inquirer* 20(4): 18–26.

Brandon, R. 1985. Holism in philosophy of biology. In *Examining Holistic Medicine,* edited by D. Stalker and C. Glymour. Amherst, N.Y.: Prometheus Books, 127–36.

Cassileth, B., and H. Brown. 1988. Unorthodox cancer medicine. *CA-A Cancer Journal for Clinicians* 38(3): 176–86.

Chapman, L., and J. Chapman. 1967. Genesis of popular but erroneous diagnostic observations. *Journal of Abnormal Psychology* 72: 193–204.

Dean, G., I. Kelly, D. Saklofske, and A. Furnham. 1992. Graphology and human judgment. In *The Write Stuff,* edited by B. and D. Beyerstein. Amherst, N.Y.: Prometheus Books, 342–96.

Festinger, L. 1957. *A Theory of Cognitive Dissonance.* Stanford: Stanford University Press.

Gilovich, T. 1991. *How We Know What Isn't So: The Fallibility of Human Reason in Everyday Life.* New York: Free Press/Macmillan.

———.1997. Some systematic biases of everyday judgment. *Skeptical Inquirer* 21(2): 31–5.

Gross, P., and N. Levitt. 1994. *Higher Superstition.* Baltimore: Johns Hopkins University Press.

Huber, P. 1991. *Galileo's Revenge: Junk Science in the Courtroom.* New York: Basic Books.

Kiernan, V. 1995. Survey plumbs the depths of international ignorance. *The New Scientist* (April 29): 7.

Merskey, H. 1995. *The Analysis of Hysteria: Understanding Conversion and Dissociation.* 2d ed. London: Royal College of Psychiatrists.

Melzack, R. 1973. *The Puzzle of Pain.* New York: Basic Books.

Mestel, R. 1994. Let mind talk unto body. *The New Scientist* (July 23): 26–31.

O'Connor, G. 1987. Confidence trick. *The Medical Journal of Australia* 147: 456–9.

Roberts, A., D. Kewman, and L. Hovell. 1993. The power of nonspecific effects in healing. Implications for psychosocial and biological treatments. *Clinical Psychology Review* 13: 375–91.

Rosenbaum, J. T. 1997. Lessons from litigation over silicone breast implants: A call for activism by scientists. *Science* 276 (June 6, 1997): 1524–5.

Rosenthal, R. 1966. *Experimenter Effects in Behavioral Research.* New York: Appleton-Century-Crofts.

Schick, T., and L. Vaughn. 1995. *How to Think About Weird Things: Critical Thinking for a New Age.* Mountain View, Calif.: Mayfield Publishing.

Shorter, E. 1992. *From Paralysis to Fatigue: A History of Psychosomatic Illness in the Modern Era.* New York: The Free Press.

Silverman, S. 1987. Medical "miracles": Still mysterious despite claims of believers. *Pscientific American* (July): 5–7. Newsletter of the Sacramento Skeptics Society, Sacramento, Calif.

Skrabanek, P., and J. McCormick. 1990. *Follies and Fallacies in Medicine.* Amherst, N.Y.: Prometheus Books.

Smith, W., H. Merskey, and S. Gross, eds. 1980. *Pain: Meaning and Management.* New York: SP Medical and Scientific Books.

Stalker, D., and C. Glymour, eds. 1985. *Examining Holistic Medicine.* Amherst, N.Y.: Prometheus Books.

Stewart, D. 1990. Emotional disorders misdiagnosed as physical illness: Environmental hypersensitivity, candidiasis hypersensitivity, and chronic fatigue syndrome. *Int. J. Mental Health* 19(3): 56–68.

Ulett, G. A. 1996. *Alternative Medicine or Magical Healing.* St. Louis: Warren H. Green.

 Article Review Form at end of book.

How can faulty reasoning give us an overly pessimistic view of the state of the world?

It's Not as Bad as You Think It Is

Misguided handwringing about our society's decline distracts us from the real crises

Nicholas Lehman

Nicholas Lehman is a national correspondent for The Atlantic Monthly *and a contributing editor of* The Washington Monthly.

Abstract: *The period of the 1990s is one of relative calm for the United States, with no strong external enemies and even domestic crime lessening. Yet from President Clinton to the ordinary citizen, there is a perception of social decay. An analysis of some of these alleged social problems are presented in their true light.*

One of President Clinton's main challenges in his second term is going to be trying to move the United States away from a self-conception as a nation in crisis. It's a problem partly of his own making. In his 1995 State of the Union address, for example, delivered right on the heels of the big Republican sweep in the 1994 elections, Clinton said, "[Far] more than our material riches are threatened; things far more precious to us—our children, our families, our values . . . The values that used to hold us together seem to be coming apart." That was the speech in which he called for a New Covenant that would address America's problems "above all, how can we repair the damaged bonds in our society. . . ."

In saying this, Clinton was not imposing his own eccentric views on the rest of us. He probably had been reading polls that told him such sentiments would strike a responsive chord, and even if he hadn't, many other people were painting the same picture more luridly. Newt Gingrich has a standard speech line that reads, "No civilization can survive with 12-year-olds having babies, with 15-year-olds killing each other, with 17-year-olds dying of AIDS, with 18-year-olds getting diplomas they can't read." A stream of books about the fraying of the American social fabric has been published over the last few years; the current occupant of the best-seller list in this category, whose title says it all, is Robert Bork's *Slouching Towards Gomorrah.*

It will be very difficult for us to explain to our grandchildren why the United States in the mid-1990s thought of itself in such a bleak way. Our country is as triumphant as any has ever been. We have no external enemies who pose a real threat. We are at peace. We are not in a depression or a recession. The unemployment rate is relatively low. The political system is stable. Compared to the run of American history, let alone world history, this is an unusually calm moment.

Even if you take it as a given that Americans are going to pick something to hand-wring about, pervasive social decay is not the obvious choice. All through the 1980s and up through the 1992 presidential election, the main national concern was with the economy, not the society. You would think that if social concerns came to the fore during the past five years, it would be in response to alarming social developments over that time. In fact, it has been a phenomenon floating free of reality, driven by no actual contemporary developments.

The standard litany of our social problems is, roughly: crime, drugs, illegitimacy, deteriorating schools, divorce, welfare dependency, and poverty. None of the indicators in these areas is currently rising dramatically, and several are falling—most notably, crime rates. The divorce rate peaked between 1979 and 1981 and has been declining modestly since. School completion rates are steady among whites and rising among blacks. The proportion of children born out of wedlock has been holding steady since 1990. Household median income has begun to rise, and the poverty rate has begun to fall. What the policy-work community has fixed on as the one current trend most worth being alarmed about, rising income inequality—between 1977 and 1992, average family income for the poorest fifth of Americans decreased by 17 percent while it increased for the richest fifth by 28 percent, and for the richest hundredth by 91 percent—is often written about, but almost never discussed by politicians in election campaigns in the way that social breakdown is.

What can explain the popularity of the perception of a social crisis, then? A few possibilities come to mind:

- Delayed reaction. Social trends like crime, divorce, illegitimacy, dropout rates, and drug-taking, which we identify with the culture of the 1960s, all rose most steeply during the 1970s. The reason is that cultural developments spread gradually from a few to the many: What dozens of young people in Haight-Ashbury were doing in 1965 millions of young people were doing (in watered-down form) in Omaha and Peoria 10 years later. Official social commentators didn't catch this, because in the '60s they had been focused on places like Haight-Ashbury and in the '70s they were focused on the '60s being over. Only now is the enormity of the social changes of 20 years ago sinking in among the American leadership— and these changes, after all, haven't been completely reversed, but rather have drifted a little down from the high plateau.

- Metropolitanization, especially in the Sunbelt. All the attention given to the shrinkage of American cities obscures the steady, constant growth of metropolitan areas, which now account for more than three-quarters of the American population. In the South and Southwest, metropolitan areas are growing rapidly. They tend to be populated by people from surrounding small towns and rural areas who find themselves arrived in a much more permissive culture than they have been used to. This helps explain the popularity, in Sunbelt suburbia, of Pentecostal churches, and also of the Christian Coalition,

which, because it is so good at turning out social-issue voters, has done more than any other single political force to put the perception of social breakdown on the national agenda.

- Everything seems different, and therefore disturbing. The surface feeling of American middle-class life has changed quite a lot over the last generation. The biggest change, by far, is the replacement of the upwardly mobile male breadwinner and housewife as the dominant family type by the staying-afloat family of two working parents and a child-care provider. Another important change is the exponential widening—beyond a fairly constructed, safe, wholesome band of programming material—of what's available on television, in popular recordings, and in other cultural media. Big changes by definition leave people feeling dislocated; doomsday views of the situation are an easy sell.

- The world is a ghetto. For most of the twentieth century, crime, marital instability, out-of-wedlock childbearing, drug use, and poor education have been very high in the self-contained world of the black poor, and much, much lower among whites. Over the last 25 years, the prevalence of all these phenomena has risen, from a low base, in white America—much more than it has in black America. So whites are now much more aware of them, both as problems in the ghettos and as potential problems outside the ghettos. The perception of crisis is, in a sense, simply an acknowledgment of personal risk by the white middle class.

But to understand why the feeling that our society is falling apart has taken hold is one thing. To pander to that feeling is another.

Wild rhetorical overkill is bad in and of itself. It cheapens the currency of political talk. How many 12-year-olds, really, are having babies? When there actually is a crisis, what will there be left to say that will rouse the nation, and not be discounted by a public that has been hearing inflated talk for years?

When politicians use the easy, dramatic language of social crisis, it has a strange disabling effect on the government. The biggest language guns are being hauled out, the deepest and most intimate connection to the public forged, with regard to a problem that government can't do much about. If you define the country's big problem as being insufficient health care coverage, then the connection to government action is obvious. If you define the country's big problem as "values," it's a way of signaling that the government is good and important (because it is alarmed) without making a commitment to government's doing anything, except for small, symbolic gestures like promoting the V-chip. The more central that government officials make social disarray appear to be, the less central government becomes as a problem-solving institution in the society.

Finally, universalizing any problem makes it more difficult to fix. Public schools are a good example. It isn't that "public school" doesn't work, it's that some public school systems have been allowed to deteriorate dangerously. If a finite number of schools are the problem, then it's possible to think of a solution. If schools, generally, are the problem, then we have to throw up our hands, or think in terms of squishy, impossible missions like changing the entire ethos of the society.

America's social and economic problems are heavily concentrated at the lower end of the society. The whole society isn't in crisis. Saying that it is only permits the crisis that is going on not to be solved.

 Article Review Form at end of book.

WiseGuide Wrap-Up

- Systematic research demonstrates that everyday judgment is not to be trusted completely and that we commonly make a number of predictable errors in our judgments. We can sharpen our perceptual and judgmental skills through understanding the scientific method.

- Lying is a common phenomenon in human society. The majority of the population is rarely above chance levels in detecting lies, and even 80% of professionals, such as judges and police officers, are doing no better than random guesses when evaluating lies.

- Memory is not a perfect record of events like a videotape. Rather, it is quite malleable and open to influence both from internal states, such as mood, and external states, such as another's perception of what occurred.

R.E.A.L. Sites

Site name: Committee for the Scientific Investigation of Claims of the Paranormal

URL: http://www.csicop.org/

Why is it R.E.A.L.? This is the official site of the Committee for the Scientific Investigation of Claims of the Paranormal (CSICOP). Founded by such intellectual luminaries as Carl Sagan and Isaac Asimov, CSICOP "fights back" against unscientific reports of paranormal phenomena. The flagship of the organization is their journal, the *Skeptical Inquirer,* where two of the articles in this section came from. Other topics they have covered include everything from pseudoscience to conspiracy theories, with forays into poltergeist sightings, little green men, and miracle photos. Read an article from this month's *Skeptical Inquirer.* What is the article investigating, and what conclusions does it reach? Then follow the cool surf alien to check out some of the "skeptical" Internet links.

Key topics: cognitive blases, social cognition

Site name: Exploring Nonverbal Communication

URL: http://zzyx.ucsc.edu/~archer/

Why is it R.E.A.L.? In two of the articles in this section, you read about people trying to detect deception. As you know, people are not that good at recognizing lies. One of the important domains that people use is nonverbal communication. At this web site, you can see how good you are at recognizing "body language." The site has a set of pictures that are part of a videotaped series. You are asked to determine mood from facial expression and to discern relationships among the people in the pictures. Before you go to this site, estimate how good you think you are at interpreting nonverbal communication. After trying to interpret the pictures, assess whether you were correct in your estimation.

Key topics: nonverbal communication, social cognition, deception, law

section

2

Learning Objectives

- Describe current theories of self and identity, and understand how the idea of self and identity may differ with regard to gender, race, and culture.

- Describe the important identity domains for young black women.

- Be able to explain why boosting self-esteem may not boost accomplishments.

- Be able to list and explain the causes and consequences of procrastination.

- Be able to explain how self-handicapping protects the self.

The Self

"I am an individual. I have my thoughts, and feelings, and dreams, and all of those are mine alone." We often think that we are self-created and independent, but the self develops through our interactions with other people. Consider an infant: does he or she really have an idea of himself or herself as a separate individual? How does this concept begin to form? When a child hears things like, "Aren't you a sweet little girl!" or, "What a tough little guy!" she or he begins to define a self-concept. That baby girl can say "I am sweet," but that notion reflects what others have said to and about her, and that process doesn't end when she grows up. So it is for much of what we think of as "our own." Our feelings, thoughts, and dreams all bear the mark of people and situations we have encountered in our lives. Even the very idea of an independent, autonomous self seems to be in part socially determined. Western societies, with their cultural heritage of individual effort and self-fulfillment, foster such "independent" selves, whereas Eastern societies, which place more emphasis on collective goals, are more likely to foster "interdependent" selves.

As with attitudes, the self may be said to contain cognitive elements referring to our thoughts and beliefs about ourselves; affective elements referring to our feelings about ourselves (including our self-esteem); and behavioral elements referring to how we present ourselves to the world. Because the self is such a rich and varied entity that is obviously of great interest and importance to us, it shouldn't be surprising that the self becomes intertwined in our social thinking and living. Although sometimes we try to forget the self, we obviously carry it with us at all times. The self affects everything we do, from our perceptions and judgments of others to our behavior in groups. Although, historically, research on the self has been neglected in social psychology, today this is a growing research area.

The Stephens article delves into one of the most crucial questions about the self, namely, "What is the self?" or "Who am I?" Stephens interviews a number of theorists about their research programs on the self and on identity. One common theme is that there is no single answer to "Who am I?" Rather, we are made up of many different selves. Furthermore, these researchers argue that your mental well-being rests on accepting that you have multiple selves, rather than searching for a unified self. The article also discusses some cultural differences in self and identity. After reading this article, you may have a new answer (or more likely, answers) to the question "Who am I?"

The next selection examines the task of identity formation for young black women. Shorter-Gooden and Washington cover a number of identity theories, particularly developmental identity theories. They discuss the common critique that these theories were developed using white males, and that identity formation may be different for those who are not white males. They present in-depth interviews with a number of black female college students about how they answer the question, "Who am I?" and how they see identity formation. The data collected from these interviews provide some different perspectives on our ideas of the self.

Our next article discusses a timely issue, both socially and politically: the extent to which we should be working to improve self-esteem. The dominant paradigm is that high self-esteem is responsible for success in school, work, and life, and that to improve in those areas one need only to work on boosting one's self-esteem. Psychologist Harold Stevenson explains why this approach is potentially harmful and foolish. His thesis (and that of many psychologists) is that high self-esteem is a consequence of accomplishments, not a cause.

You may be reading these articles just before your exam, and wondering for the millionth time why you put off preparing until the last minute. "The Ups and Downs of Dawdling" describes research on something we all have done and often hate ourselves for doing—procrastination. Procrastination and self-handicapping are ways the self reacts to potential successes and failures. Researchers have found that some people will adopt self-defeating behavior at the same time they are trying to succeed. Some students, for example, might stay up all night partying just before a big exam, even if they genuinely would like to do well on the test. Research on self-handicapping tells us that people engage in such behaviors in order to have ready-made excuses, should they fail. It is far less disturbing to the self to blame failure on lack of sleep than on lack of ability.

The articles in this unit, taken as a whole, provide some answers about one of the most critical aspects of your college experience—the continuing development of yourself. These researchers and theorists are examining questions you might find yourself asking about who you are, why you do things in a certain way, and who you will become. The scientific study of the self allows us to learn more than we can by self-reflection alone.

Questions

R7. How would the psychologists in the Stephens article define the word self or the word identity? How is their approach useful from a therapeutic standpoint?

R8. What did the women in the Shorter-Gooden and Washington article mean when they talked about strength? To what extent did achievement (e.g., school, work) and affiliation (e.g., relationships) make up these women's idea of self?

R9. What are some steps that Stevenson suggests to improve self-esteem? Why does he see the current self-esteem movement as worrisome?

R10. What do researchers on procrastination see as the root cause of procrastination? How does the use of procrastination develop and flourish?

How would the psychologists in this article define the word *self* or the word *identity*? How is their approach useful from a therapeutic standpoint?

To Thine Own Selves Be True

A new breed of psychologists says there's no one answer to the question "Who am I?"

Mitchell Stephens

Pick a late-20th-century city, better an American city, even better a California city, and study one of the inhabitants. Note the range of people this individual is exposed to: the different ethnic backgrounds, the different lifestyles, the different beliefs. Then observe the variety of behaviors the subject exhibits: from vegetarianism to weightlifting, or from bungee jumping to helping the homeless. And note how often and how easily these behaviors change.

Now move in closer, close enough to hear the specimen's thoughts. A jumble of voices will become audible: some bold, some whiny; some mature, some immature; some naive, some cynical. You'll pick up echoes of parents, friends and talk-show hosts; rapper-like boasts and Woody Allen-like anxieties.

Keep listening and eventually you will hear a question. Perhaps it will arrive during a session with a therapist or a heart-to-heart with a friend, perhaps in some lonely moment late at night. (The older and the more self-satisfied the subject, the longer you may have to wait.) But at some point that person will wonder: "Who am I?" And if you have been paying attention, you will understand why no good answer comes.

"Who am I?" Snuggled up behind this question is a comfortable, mostly unnoticed assumption: that we each have a kernel of identity, a self. It is a supposition that has long lain at the center of Western culture: "Know thyself," advised the Delphic oracle, classical Greece's version of self-help therapy. "To thine own self be true," Shakespeare counseled.

However, mutating lifestyles and changing intellectual currents have led a group of increasingly influential psychologists—postmodern psychologists seems to be the name that is sticking—to the conclusion that we have no single, separate, unified self. They maintain that we contain many selves and that the proper response to the suggestion "Get in touch with yourself" or "Be yourself" is "Which one?"

Hazel Rose Markus, professor of psychology at the University of Michigan, calls this "the most exciting time in psychology in decades and decades." We have begun to realize, she says, that "there isn't just one answer to the 'Who am I?' question."

Consider, as an example, the individual named Mick Jagger. The Rolling Stones' lead singer was and, if the tabloids are to be believed, remains a classic libertine, but he is also a father and, until recently at least, a family man. Jagger is a rock 'n' roller, a bohemian, whose songs and lifestyle challenge traditional standards of behavior; yet he travels in upper-class British circles, hobnobbing with dukes and princesses. Jagger can be coarse and crude, yet he knows his nonfiction and his vintages.

Which is the real Mick? His answer: all of the above. "People find it very hard to accept that you can be all these things at almost the same time," Jagger has complained.

Relax, Mick. The times seem to be catching up with you once again. This new group of psychologists starts from the assumption that there is no single Mick, just a rotating bunch of possible Micks, changing as the people you are with and the situations you are in change. And, these psychologists believe, similarly disparate groups of selves, if less wealthy and less famous, inhabit us all. Like Walt Whitman, we "contain multitudes."

Healthy multitudes. We are not talking here of those who suffer from "multiple personality disorder." That nightmarish condition (chronicled in popular books and movies) is characterized by dissociative states in which a personality "splits" into different selves with different memories, some of which appear to know nothing about the other selves. No, we are talking about healthy people, like Jagger, who don't blank out, who are quite aware of everything they are doing, but who have, quite naturally, created different selves to relate to different aspects of their multifaceted lives.

"There are people who can live very comfortably and successfully with a multiple vision of who they are," says Cal State Northridge psychology professor Edward Sampson. "And they don't go to traditional therapists unless they want to get that knocked out of them." This is not, its proponents contend, just another provocative theory. It is a response to some feelings that, in this fractured, complicated, media-saturated, post-"Ozzie and Harriet" world, are very much in the air. There is the sense that we are often, if not always, playing— at work, at our relationships, even at parenthood; the sense that each of us can switch roles as easily as we switch costumes—from business person to jock, from backpacker to sophisticate, from nurturer to sex object.

The implications of the theory are large: It's not just that we each have different sides to our personality; it's that we have no central personality in relation to which all our varied behaviors might be seen as just "sides." We are, in other words, not absolutely anything.

"The true self is dead," proclaims Walter Truett Anderson, author of *Reality Isn't What It Used to Be*, a primer on postmodernism.

If you find this somewhat difficult to swallow, you're not alone. Some psychologists consider the whole issue a waste of time. "It doesn't matter if it's one self or two or three or 5,000," scoffs Robert Zajonc, director of the Institute for Social Research at the University of Michigan and Markus' husband. Zajonc, who has spent much of his life in Europe, finds this preoccupation with the self—or selves—typically American. "I don't think of my self, as such," he says. "I may think of my schedule, my obligations, my meetings, but I don't really spend too much time asking, 'Who am I?'"

Others who do spend time asking are disturbed by the suggestion that there isn't one answer. After all, the idea that we each have a single identity, one true self—just as we each have one true nose and one true medical history—does have a certain seductiveness. Our friends and acquaintances don't seem to have much trouble dealing with each of us as if we were a constant, consistent entity. Why should we?

"People certainly are capable of experiencing themselves as having a relative unity," says Louis Sass, a Rutgers clinical psychology professor who has been critical of some of these new ideas. "They have in the past, and I doubt that has changed much."

Kenneth Gergen, a Swarthmore psychology professor whose book, *The Saturated Self: Dilemmas of Identity in Contemporary Life,* provides the best introduction to postmodern psychology, notes a similar resistance to his postmodern perspective among some of his students. " 'It's just empirically wrong,' they say, or, 'That's just your point of view.' I've had students who've complained to the deans that this idea was really so antithetical to their values that they felt it was injurious to the student body."

Gergen, who is wont to question traditional notions of truth and reality as well as identity, understands his students' disquiet. Belief in a single self is so basic to our culture, to the ways each of us has of thinking and talking about what we call "ourself," that it cannot be easily surrendered.

Gergen "himself," however, began having trouble with the "Who am I?" question, and therefore came into conflict with this language, when he was only 9. "I grew up in a family that was very educated, very cultured," Gergen says. His father was a professor and one of his brothers is David Gergen, the former Reagan media wizard, now a MacNeil/Lehrer NewsHour commentator. "I had a whole way of being in that family which was virtually required, but then I got deposited in a county school in rural North Carolina. And there was no way I could be the person I was at home in that school system, so I kind of fought to stay alive by changing my whole accent, my way of talking, my way of being."

That made two selves: the self Gergen used at home and the self he used in school.

"Then there was another transition," Gergen recalls. "This time to a city school, which had a whole different set of concerns, which again weren't the ones in my family. And then I went from that city school to Yale, which required that I leave the Southern thing behind." So Gergen had to "make" yet another identity for himself.

While in graduate school at Duke, he read the psychological literature that argued the importance to our mental well-being of maintaining a unified, centralized, coherent self. "But it just made no sense, given my experience," he explains. "Now I could either say, 'I'm very sick,' or I could say, 'This literature has got to be wrong.' " Gergen has been challenging the traditional psychological understanding of the self off and on ever since. And lately he has had lots of help.

A group of counselors and therapists, for example, has begun noting that we all must "create" other selves as we leave our families in search of friendship, success and love—and then move on to new friendships, new successes and new loves. Social psychologists have begun studying not only our "child selves," our "professional selves," our "friendship selves" and our "parent selves," but also what Hazel Markus labels our "possible selves," our "feared possible selves," our "ideal selves," our "fleeting selves," our "tentative selves" and our "chronically accessible selves."

Philosophers have pointed out that the self divides the mo-ment we start looking for it: There is the self that we're trying to find plus the self that is doing the looking, plus the self within which this game of hide and seek is being played. Even the practice of placing an alarm clock out of reach in the bedroom implies that we have at least two selves—a responsible nighttime self and a lazy morning self.

But perhaps the most interesting support for Gergen's position has come from those philosophers of mind, cognitive psychologists and biologists who investigate the workings of consciousness. When they examine the gray matter or interrogate their computer models in search of something that might pass for a self, they come up empty. It's not there.

"Our common-sense notion is of the self as a sort of inner boss, a sort of puppeteer inside the body, who is in charge," says Daniel Dennett, author of *Consciousness Explained*. "So that, for instance, when I talk my vocal apparatus is being controlled as if there was some homunculus, sitting at a mighty theater organ, making the words come out, as if my body speaks on behalf of this sort of central meaner on the inside. But as soon as you look closely at this notion of self, it seems to break down."

Dennett's research into the workings of consciousness has convinced him that there is no "homunculus" or little person, no "central meaner," no "ghostly supervisor," no "benevolent dictator," sitting there at the center of the brain, making decisions for the rest of the mind and watching consciousness like an audience might watch a movie. There is, in other words, no point of pure Dennettness, no "brain pebble," somewhere in Dennett's head that contains his identity or self. Consciousness, instead is a rather sloppy, multilayered thing in which various takes on reality, supplied by our various perceptual and cognitive organs, supersede each other.

But if there is no kernel of selfness inside our brains, why do we all seem to start with this common-sense notion of a single, separate, unified self? The answer may be that not all people do. Here Gergen's view has gotten some support from anthropology and our increasing awareness of other cultures.

"I took a trip to Japan," says Markus, "and that, as a social psychologist, is a journey that alters your world altogether. That's where I really saw great differences in the answer that gets given to the 'Who am I?' question." The Japanese, Markus learned and confirmed in subsequent research projects, do not look upon the self as being nearly as separate and self-contained as Americans do.

"Here, there's a real press to individuate yourself, to be special and unique, to separate from others, to be your own person," Markus says. "It's encoded in all our sacred texts and documents: We want independence and liberty and to be free. As Americans we're absolutely fearful of showing that we're a social or a group product in some way. We need to see ourselves as bounded wholes. But in Japan, the common view is that the individual is just a fraction. You can only be whole there when you fit in with groups."

From an anthropological or historical perspective, it is the American conception of an isolated, unified self—the conception most of us take for granted—that may be the exception. "Our view of the self has a history," says Philip Cushman, of the California

School of Professional Psychology in Berkeley. "It comes from a tradition of self-contained individualism." That I-gotta-be-me! tradition, a compulsion to do things "my way," may never have been stronger than it has been in 20th-century America.

An escape from this exaggerated individualism is, for Gergen, one of the major benefits of the theory of multiple selves. Gergen defines those various selves as "the capacities we carry within us for multiple relationships." We have, for example, selves for relating with our bosses, selves for our subordinates, selves reserved for our friends and selves that come to life only in the presence of certain someones.

These selves, despite what we like to think here in America, are not our property alone. They are not just "discovered" within us. They are "created" in our relationships with other people. It probably will take a child, or at least the thought of a child, to help you create yourself as a parent. You may never have an opportunity to create a certain romantic, moonstruck, poetry-writing self unless you pick up the scent of Mr. or Ms. Right. "You can't be a self by yourself," Markus concludes.

Our selves are the product of what Gergen calls—with a nod to the Japanese—"relatedness." And Gergen (exhibiting a hopeful self) believes that acknowledging our various selves and accepting our "relatedness" is a route to the psychologist's ever-present goal: improved mental health.

This San Diego woman was frazzled, anxious and depressed—"at times really anxious and deeply depressed," reports psychologist Maureen O'Hara. "She exhibited, in other words, typical late-20th-century symptoms."

The woman worked in the Navy, as a medic. She went home to a husband and three children. And on holidays she returned to the village in Mexico where she had been reared. Tough sailor one moment, gentle, nurturing mom the next, deferential daughter every few months—perhaps not the typical late-20th-century life, but characteristically wide-ranging and scattered.

The woman's problem, it soon became apparent, was the tension, the conflict, between her disparate roles. Which of these selves was really her? "She couldn't reconcile them," O'Hara says. She had no good answer to the "Who am I?" question. O'Hara, president of the Assn. for Humanistic Psychology, is one of those who have begun to use the ideas of postmodern psychology to treat patients. She says acceptance of multiple selves turned out to be the key to relieving that San Diego woman's anxiety and depression. "We worked for a while, and she realized she didn't have to reconcile the three worlds she lived in," O'Hara says. "She didn't have to worry about being consistent. She could honor all these different selves. The woman described it as 'allowing each personality to get out of the way of the others.' "

Sass, of Rutgers and author of the forthcoming book *Madness and Modernism,* acknowledges that there might be some "rigid" people for whom learning that they can allow themselves to express different sides of their personality might have therapeutic value. "But," he asks in a recent critique of "the postmodern turn in contemporary psychoanalysis": "What of those who suffer from problems of a different sort—for example, from feelings of emptiness, meaninglessness and unrelatedness; from the inability to

form stable relationships, or from a lack of sustaining interests or continuing goals, values and ideals?" These problems, too, as Sass notes, are "characteristic of our age." By surrendering our belief in a true self, don't we risk aggravating them?

Maybe not. Maybe it is the separate, unified self—the one that traditional psychotherapists are still trying to help us "find" or "realize"—that is causing these feelings of "emptiness, meaninglessness and unrelatedness." Maybe our feelings of inadequacy have grown with the inevitable frustrations of the effort to locate and bolster this mythical "true self." Maybe we have spent too many hours on too many couches trying to determine who we really are. Maybe by accepting, as that San Diego woman did, the idea that our identities come from our relationships, we could find a way out of the psychological desert in which some of us now wander.

The word *postmodern* has been stretched over a lot of different ideas, but the central one seems to be that our way of looking at the world is not a given, that we create what we see as "reality" through language. This view has at least as many detractors among academics as supporters. Berkeley philosopher John Searle, for example, has debated angrily with Gergen at academic conferences whether "reality" is in fact just a creation of language. "Science is based on the supposition of an independently existing reality," Searle maintains. "If you don't believe in that then you're out of business."

Gergen, however, argues that we "construct" reality through the stories—the narratives—we tell about it. Other societies, for example, have told other stories about such seemingly basic matters as mental illness, emotions, and thought—and therefore these concepts had a different "reality" for them. Our identities, too, Gergen maintains, are constructed—products of different stories we tell ourselves about ourselves.

Postmodernism is based on some difficult theories (poststructuralism, deconstruction, etc.) hatched, for the most part, in France, but somehow this new view of psychology seems most at home in America, particularly California. In an insular, homogeneous Old World town it might have been possible for people to define themselves in terms of a single belief, a single way of life, but not here. Not where we are tugged at by so many possible belief systems and lifestyles—each of which presents us with new "possible selves."

"California has always been where the idea of the possible came from," says Markus, who grew up in San Diego. "There is a bit of Hollywood in everyone in California—the sense that you can be other than who you are now, that you can kind of create yourself."

And why settle for creating just one self? Indeed, how could you settle for creating just one self in a world where even adults are encouraged to play, a world where we can trade in our one "true" nose for a shorter version, a world where we can move from one identity to another—with a change of clothes, a change of channel, an unexpected phone call—as easily as we might move from Main Street to Adventureland at Disneyland? Gergen and friends say they did not invent this new postmodern world. They are just trying to help us adjust to it. Don't agonize over consistency or authenticity, they advise. Enjoy yourselves!

But if this is indeed where we're headed, some questions must be answered. Questions about ethics and morality, to begin with. Sass, for one, is not at all sanguine about this acceptance of inconsistency and inauthenticity. "There are clearly dangers in giving up that notion of a single self," he notes. "You absolve the person of responsibility for making judgments." Imagine the excuses people might make: "Hey, it wasn't my fault. One of my other selves did it."

Absolving people of responsibility for their behavior, however, is not at all what O'Hara has in mind for postmodern psychology. Instead, she hopes these new views of identity will cause us to reopen "the ethical conversation" and produce some original ideas on how people—multiselved people—can be held "accountable to each other." The issue might not be who we really are but whether our various selves can ethically share the same body.

Gergen attempts to construct an ethics of postmodernism upon a slightly different foundation: He places his faith in the concept of "relatedness." If we become aware of the extent to which our selves are created with others, Gergen contends, perhaps we'll be more, not less, responsible in our dealings with those others—more aware of the debt we owe them, less likely to think we can "find ourself" by leaving them behind.

Perhaps. Still, the issue of how our various selves are going to deal with others' various selves in this new postmodern world remains problematic. If everybody is plural, how do we decide whom we like and whom we dislike? How, if our identities are constantly subject to change, do we know whom it is we're talking

to, whom we're taking a shine to? These questions might be combined into one question: How can two people who know all this be, gulp, in love?

"My wife and I went through this painfully at first," confesses Gergen, whose wife, Mary, is also a psychology professor. "This is a second marriage for both of us, kind of a romantic thing: We ran away from the world. So, early on in our marriage, she'd frequently ask me whether I still loved her." And Gergen, who was trying to think out some of these psychological issues, didn't know how to respond: "What exactly as a psychological event could love mean? And how could I do an introspective examination of all my interior to know whether it was still there or not?

"Finally, she said, 'Look, when I ask you whether you love me, don't go through these tortuous questions of what's really real about love and how you'd know. Just say the words meaningfully, and I'll be a lot better off.'" And that may be the key to life in the postmodern world. We will have to do our best to say words like "I love you" meaningfully—even though we sense there are dozens of "I's," not all of whom can be in agreement on anything, even though we know we'll never pin down whom "you" really might be. We will have to learn to make do, in other words, with rituals and approximations.

"I don't think we need someone to love all 93 of our selves," Markus says. "If someone just takes three or four of them real seriously, that's enough to keep most of us going on most days."

 **Article Review Form at end of book.**

What did the women in this article mean when they talked about strength? To what extent did achievement (e.g., school, work) and affiliation (e.g., relationships) make up these women's idea of self?

Young, Black, and Female

The challenge of weaving an identity

Kumea Shorter-Gooden and N. Chanell Washington

Abstract: *This is an exploratory qualitative study of the experience of identity in late adolescent African-American women. Using a semi-structured interview, 17 18- to 22-year-old community college students were interviewed about how they see their identity and about the personal salience of various identity domains—race, gender, sexual orientation, relationships, career, religious beliefs, and political beliefs. It was found that these seven ego identity domains varied in importance, with racial identity as the most salient, while the domains of gender, relationships, and career were also important sources of identity. A sense of "strength" also emerged as an important element of self-definition. Particular attention is paid to the intersection of racial and gender identity for these African-American women who must evolve a sense of self within the context of a society that devalues Blacks and women.*

Introduction

Being an African-American female adolescent and growing up in the United States poses particular challenges. Young Black females must contend with the typical adolescent developmental tasks, but they must do this in the context of a society that devalues Blacks and women (hooks, 1981; Reid, 1988). If adolescence is the time when one consolidates a sense of identity, which according to Erikson (1968) is based in part on one's ethnicity and gender, then to develop an identity that integrates a healthy sense of one's Blackness and femaleness must be demanding. Thus, a greater understanding of the identity development process in young Black women would be helpful in furthering our knowledge of the mental health challenges and successes of African-American female adolescents and adults. To this end, our focus is first on establishing the context in which African-American women live and then on exploring the issue of identity development as it relates to this group.

The context in which African-American women in the United States develop an identity is a racist and sexist one. Historically, African-American women have the distinction of being the only group that was enslaved and brought to the United States "to work, to produce, and to reproduce" (Almquist, 1995, p. 577). The legacy of racism and sexism during slavery continues today (hooks, 1981). Numerous social scientists have spoken of the continued dual oppression that Black women face because of racism and sexism (e.g. Beale, 1970; Murray, 1970; Hare and Hare, 1972; Staples, 1973; Giddings, 1984; Reid, 1988), as well as of the triple oppression (based on race, gender, and class) that this group contends with because they are disproportionately members of the lower socioeconomic statuses (e.g. Murray, 1970; Hare and Hare, 1972; Almquist, 1995). For example, the income of

Kumea Shorter-Gooden and N. Chanell Washington, Young, Black, and Female: The Challenge of Weaving an Identity. JOURNAL OF ADOLESCENCE 1996, v. 19, no. 5, October, pp. 465–475. Reprinted by permission.

Black women in the U.S. lags far behind the incomes of Anglo men, Black men, and Anglo women, even when differences in levels of education are controlled for (Horton and Smith, 1993).

The oppression of African-American women is evident not only in the economic sphere; it is evident also in the fact that they are socially devalued (hooks, 1981; Reid, 1988; Greene, 1990). Greene notes that although American society devalues all women, among women, White women are idealized and Black women are assigned a subordinate status. For example, African-American women represent the antithesis of what is considered American female beauty (Reid, 1988). In some cases, the devaluation of Black women takes the form of active assaults, as demonstrated by the fact that Black women are more often victims of criminal assault and rape than White women (Horton and Smith, 1993). At other times, however, the devaluation of African-American women takes the form of disregard or neglect. Myers (1989) points out that Black female adolescents are often ignored or invisible; both their strengths and their problems receive little attention. Although the Black community may serve to buffer African-American women from much of the impact of racism and sexism (Barnes, 1980), what has been described is the larger societal context that surrounds these women as they develop an identity.

The formation of a sense of identity, or ego identity, is seen by Erikson (1968) as the primary developmental task of the adolescent years. Identity is a self-definition which is comprised of goals, values, and beliefs to which the person is committed and which provide a sense of continuity over time. According to Erikson, identity reflects a variety of chosen commitments, but it is also integrally tied to one's ascribed characteristics, like race and gender. Marcia (1966) operationalized Erikson's identity development concepts and developed a semi-structured interview to assess participants' experience of crisis and development of commitments in the areas of occupation, and political and religious ideology—notably, all "chosen" rather than "ascribed" domains. In the past three decades, numerous empirical studies, using Marcia's framework, have been conducted on identity development and on the relationship between ego identity development and emotional well being (see reviews in Marcia, 1980 and Waterman, 1985).

Erikson's (1968) initial formulations about women's identity focused on the womb or "inner space" and the presumed centrality of the roles of wife and mother to the development of women's identity. Erikson has been critiqued widely for his male-centered view of women's identity (Franz and White, 1985). Similarly, Marcia's identity interview has been modified over the years from what is now seen as the original male-centered focus on the domains of occupation, religion, and politics to the current inclusion of questions about sexual and interpersonal attitudes, which are seen as especially important to women (Patterson et al., 1992). There has been increased attention over the years to gender and issues relevant to women in the study of ego identity, but the focus has generally been on gender differences, for example, in the identity domains that are most salient for women in contrast to men, or on alternative identity domains of importance to women (see Matteson, 1993). The experience of gender itself, or gender identity, in other words, one's concept of oneself as a woman, has been little studied. Given that being female is devalued in this society, how women handle or integrate the notion of being a woman into their identity is an important area of exploration.

Although substantial attention has been given to gender issues in ego identity development, only a few studies utilizing the Erikson/Marcia model have looked at identity in African-American adolescents (Shorter, 1978; Phinney and Tarver, 1988; Aries and Moorehead, 1989; Phinney, 1989; Phinney and Alipuria, 1990; Watson and Protinsky, 1991), and only one study (Aries and Moorehead, 1989) has focused on the connection between racial identity and other identity domains, e.g. occupation and sexual-interpersonal attitudes, such that one gets a sense of the overall ego identity of these youth. In Aries and Moorehead's study of Black junior and senior high school students, it was found that ethnic or racial identity was the most important identity domain for the teens' sense of identity. In this study, however, gender issues and differences were not highlighted.

While research on the ego identity of African-Americans has been recent and minimal, concern about Black racial identity has a long history stemming, notably, from Kenneth and Mamie Clark's doll studies of color preference in young Black children (Clark and Clark, 1947; see Cross (1991) for a review of theory and research on

Black identity). In the 1970s and 1980s, a number of models of Black racial identity were developed. William Cross's stage theory of Nigrescence has become the centerpiece for much of the subsequent research in this area (Helms, 1990). Cross (1971) theorized and found evidence for a Negro-to-Black-transformation which depicts the process of racial identity formation in the late adolescent years. More recent researchers have found that the formation of a sense of Black racial identity is an important element in the psychological development of African-American adolescents and young adults (Parham, 1989), and is positively related to emotional well-being (Parham and Helms, 1985a,b).

In work that provides a theoretical bridge between the Erikson/Marcia ego identity framework and the Black racial identity model, Phinney and her associates have made similar findings: for African-American adolescents, and perhaps especially for Black girls, ethnic/racial identity is a very salient aspect of identity (Phinney and Tarver, 1988; Phinney and Alipuria, 1990), and is related to psychological well-being (Phinney, 1989).

However, research using the Cross and Phinney models has not focused on gender issues or on specific identity challenges for girls and women. Recently, Myers and her associates (Myers *et al.*, 1991; Reynolds and Pope, 1991) developed a model of identity formation for people who are members of multiple oppressed groups, like being Black and female; however, as with the Cross and Phinney models, the focus is solely on ascribed, or group-derived, identities rather than on

ego identity in general, which reflects ascribed and chosen elements.

Thus, while there are a few studies from the Erikson/Marcia model that explore ego identity in African-American adolescents and a number of studies from the Cross and Phinney models that explore racial/ethnic identity in Black adolescents, no published studies have focused on the specific ego identity issues of African-American women (Shorter-Gooden, 1992). There is evidence that for Black female adolescents racial identity is an important source of self-definition; however little else is known. Little is known about how African-American women weave an identity comprised of attitudes and feelings about themselves as Blacks, as women, and as unique individuals. Moreover, since all of the reviewed studies are quantitative in approach, little is known about how African-American women themselves talk about and depict their identity.

Hence, this exploratory study is aimed at generating hypotheses about the ego identity of late adolescent African-American women. In addition to this general exploratory goal, we were specifically interested in investigating: (1) to what extent racial and gender identity are central components of identity, and how these two societally devalued sources of identity are dealt with in identity formation; (2) what identity domains (i.e. race, gender, sexual orientation, relationships, career, religious beliefs, political beliefs) are most salient for these women, and what the quality of their investment is in these domains; and (3) how late adolescent African-American women characterize and portray their identity.

Method

Because of the exploratory nature of the study, a qualitative interview strategy was adopted. Qualitative designs are particularly useful for exploratory research in areas where little is known (Patton, 1990). Data were collected in the spring of 1993 by the authors and a doctoral student in psychology, all of whom are African-American women. Participants were 17 African-American females between the ages of 18 and 22, who were students at a Southern California community college, where approximately one-tenth of the student body was Black. The women were recruited through the Office of Student Activities, many of them through the campus Black Student Alliance.

Data were collected in individual sessions of 40 to 75 minutes held on campus. Participants completed a brief demographic questionnaire, after which a semistructured Identity Interview, developed and piloted for this study, was administered and audiotaped. The interview began with the question "When you think about your identity, what comes to mind? What are the important aspects of your identity?" and then followed with "In what way is ____ an important aspect of your identity?" There were then specific probes about the seven domains of concern, i.e. race, gender, career, religious beliefs, political beliefs, relationships, and sexual orientation. For example, participants were asked: "Do you have religious beliefs? Are religious beliefs an important aspect of your identity? In what way?" Participants were also asked if they could think of anything else that had not yet been mentioned that was an important aspect of their identity, and what people and experiences had influenced their identity formation.

The demographic characteristics of the 17 participants were as follows: all identified as Black or African-American; however one had a mother and two had fathers of non-African origin. None were married or had children. Fifteen participants indicated that they were heterosexual; however, two did not respond to the question about sexual orientation. Half indicated they had grown up with their mother (and not with their father). Approximately two-thirds of the participants' parents had attended at least one college. Two-thirds of the participants reported they had lived their life mostly in "predominantly African-American neighborhoods," and the same proportion indicated that before attending their present college they had attended schools that were "very racially mixed." At the time of the interview, all but two were living with parent(s). Ten of the women were members of the college's Black Student Alliance.

To analyse the data, the interviews were transcribed and then coded independently by the authors as to whether or not each of the seven identity domains was an important part of self-definition for each participant. The inter-rater reliability was 93%. Next, both authors read and re-read the interview transcripts in order to: (1) examine the quality of each woman's investment in the various domains, in other words, the importance of each area; (2) examine how the different identity domains intersected; and (3) identify prominent themes and issues.

Results

When asked the somewhat ambiguous question, "When you think about your identity, what comes to mind?" eleven participants indicated being "African-American" or "Black," six said "being a woman or female," and five gave a response that included the word "strong." Those who did not volunteer responses were asked specifically "Is being Black or African-American an important aspect of your identity?" All but one participant indicated it was. For the comparable question about gender identity, all 17 indicated it was, and the following figures indicate the number of women who considered the additional areas as being important aspects of their identity: relationship identity, 14; career identity, 11; religious identity, 7; sexual orientation, 6; political identity, 4.

Although all of the women indicated that gender identity was an important aspect of identity, their comments about the ways in which gender identity was important suggest that gender identity was less salient than it appeared. Many of the women had very little to say about why gender was important. For example, one woman said: "I guess being female is important because, hmm, I'm not sure. It's hard to explain, I have to really think why it's important, I just know it is."

Several participants, however, connected their female identity with their African-American identity:

Well, in this time I think it's really hard to be an African-American woman . . . we are what you can call a double negative; we are Black and we are a woman and it's really hard . . . but I feel stronger for it. I know what I want and there's nothing that I can see that will stop me from getting where I want to go. Not my color, not my gender, not anything.

Notably, only one participant mentioned the terms "feminist" or "feminism" in her discussion of her gender identity.

Racial identity was a very important aspect of almost all of the participants' identities, as evidenced not only by the number who said it was important (all but one) but also by the lengthy discussions, in many cases, about the meaning of being African-American. However, there was variation amongst the women in how much they had examined and focused on racial identity issues. Following are excerpts from two women who appeared to have struggled actively with these issues.

I'd rather say I'm African-American than I'm Black because of the connection with the land, knowing that I come from somewhere. . . . When I think of Africa I think of these great kingdoms and stuff, so it lets me identify with that.

That is important to me because society sees African-American females as . . . always getting pregnant and all that kind of thing and being on welfare and because I go to school and I graduated and I don't have babies and . . . I think that's what makes me want to be different. Not in my color but in my whole identity, to be different.

As exemplified in the first excerpt, for some of the women Black identity had to do with a connection to African or African-American heritage and culture; however, most talked about an identity based on the need to overcome the negative aspects of being Black, as in the second excerpt. In the latter instance, being Black was about struggling against negative stereotypes; whereas in the former case it had more to do with celebrating one's ancestry. In both cases, there was a positive sense about Black identity—either because Blackness was seen as inherently positive or because struggling against society's negative views of Blacks impelled the woman to work harder to accomplish her goals.

In this sample, the exceptions were one woman who, when asked if being Black or African-American was an important aspect of her identity, said "I don't think so," and one woman who said that being Black was important but who had little else to say about this aspect of her identity: "It's who I am. It's what I see when I look in the mirror. I don't know. It's just what I think."

As mentioned, five women volunteered the word "strong" in response to the initial question about their identity. A review of the transcripts revealed that 13 of the 17 participants mentioned the term "strong," "stronger," or "strength" in their interview. In some cases these terms were used a dozen or more times throughout the interview. For example:

The *strength* is very important because it lets me define who I am and with *strength* I don't get lost in other people. I think it's important to have *strength* in order to have a true identity because if you don't, sometimes you can get caught up in relationships and lose yourself in them. . . . you're *stronger* because you're Black, because you have to struggle constantly because you're different. You have to be better than the best. You have to work harder to be the best that you can be and that's it.

Strength appears to refer to being tough, determined, and able to deal with the adversity one meets because of being Black, as well as to having a strong sense of self that is not overrun by others.

Most of the participants conveyed that they either felt they had these qualities, that they were working to develop these qualities, or that they admired these characteristics in those people who had had the most impact on their identity development. When participants referred to role models in their lives as "strong," they usually were referring to other African-American women, often their mother or another relative.

Relationship identity—identity centered around one's relationship with others—emerged as a very salient area in these women's lives. Of the 14 women who indicated that being in relationships was an important part of their identity, 12 talked about the importance of being a daughter in relationship to their parent(s), usually their mother. Notably, half of the women had grown up with their mother and not their father. Being a daughter was almost always the first relationship mentioned. Ten indicated that being a friend was an important part of their identity. Being a "girlfriend" to a male partner was indicated only twice although two women talked of the importance to their identity of becoming a wife in the future, and two spoke of the importance of becoming a mother in the future. The participants often talked at length about the significance of being in relationships. One example is:

I'm a daughter and I want to make my mother really proud of me. That's very important, you know. And every time I do something extra special it makes me stand out . . . and that makes her happy and I want to make her happy. I want to take care of her because she had a rough life.

As noted earlier, career identity was important for two-thirds of the sample. All of the women in-

dicated they had career goals, although in a couple of cases women had two possible career directions, and a few indicated that their career direction might change. Career interests varied from being a teacher, lawyer, or accountant, to working in business, in the health or mental health fields, or in the entertainment industry. The women talked about how their motivation to succeed academically and career-wise was influenced by their parents and other relatives; however, there was only one woman who talked about her specific career choice as a direct result of her family's wishes.

In all, eight, or half, of the women had an identity that included a focus on all four of the domains of race, gender, relationships, and career. All of these women also talked, at some point in the interview, about the importance of strength to their current identity or the importance of perceiving strength in role models who have impacted their identity formation.

Seven women, all of whom were Christian, identified their religious beliefs as important to their identity. For example:

. . . learning or knowing what I know [about the mistreatment of Blacks] can make you angry, can make you aggressive. It can really do some damaging things, but, being that I do have spiritual beliefs and I believe that anger shouldn't be a part of our character, it helps me to focus . . . [My] spiritual beliefs help me to channel you know, okay, put this over here, fine, it happened, or it's happening or whatever, but this is where you need to go. This is what you need to do to help the situation . . .

This woman's religious identity was integrally connected to her racial identity. For her and two other women, religious identity appeared to be the identity domain which was most important in their lives.

With regards to sexual orientation and political beliefs, six of the participants indicated that sexual orientation was an important part of their identity. The comments in response to this question were usually very limited and brief. Eight participants responded "no" to the question "Do you have political beliefs?" and only four indicated that their political beliefs were an important part of their identity.

In summary, our findings are that the self-definition of this sample of African-American women is composed of various identity domains, which vary in importance, with racial identity as the most salient and gender identity as important but less salient than racial identity. In addition, most of the women had a sense of identity based on relationships and career goals. A little less than half felt that their religious beliefs were central to their identity, and even fewer considered sexual orientation or political beliefs to be salient aspects of their identity. Also of note is that many of these women felt the quality "strength" was a central part of their identity.

Discussion

In keeping with the recent literature on African-American adolescents and young adults (Parham and Helms, 1985a, b; Phinney and Tarver, 1988; Aries and Moorehead, 1989; Parham, 1989; Phinney, 1989; Phinney and Alipuria, 1990), racial identity was a salient and central aspect of these women's self-definition. Race, more than any other area, was a source of self-definition for

these women. These women varied, however, in their experience of racial identity—in how salient it was, in how actively they had struggled with issues of racial identity, and in the content of their racial identity beliefs and attitudes. Despite these variations, in general the women seemed to have positive feelings about being Black. This suggests that while the societal context of racism may contribute to the salience of racial identity, it does not automatically mean that the resultant identity will mirror societal views, and thus be negative. The fact that a substantial number of the participants were recruited at a Black Student Alliance meeting and that all of the participants were college students at a predominantly non-Black institution are limitations of the study and may account for how important racial identity was to their sense of identity.

While gender identity was noted by all the participants as an important aspect of identity, the limited comments about gender identity and the fact that gender identity was often talked about concurrently with racial identity suggest that it is less salient than issues of race. In some ways this group, though committed to gender as a source of identity, seems rather unevolved, or foreclosed, vis à vis gender issues. A number of hypotheses arise in connection with this finding. One possibility is that these issues are addressed later on in the sequence of identity challenges. Although Erikson (1968) talks of identity formation as a late adolescent phenomenon, recent researchers are considering whether the process of identity formation is a more extended process—from early adolescence through early to middle adulthood (Josselson, 1987). Moreover,

Fujino and King (1994) speculate that women of color may develop a sense of racial identity first and a sense of gender identity later.

A second, related hypothesis is that active work around gender issues is somewhat less important for African-American women than is work around racial issues. Racial issues may demand attention for survival; however, gender exploration may not be as essential, perhaps because racism is a more potent force than sexism in Black women's lives (Giddings, 1984).

Moreover, integrating an active, conscious sense of one's Blackness with an active, conscious sense of one's womanness may be particularly challenging. As Phinney (1993) suggests, it may be difficult to integrate multiple group identities, particularly if the norms and values of the groups are inconsistent. Reid (1988) sees racial identity and gender identity as "conflicting demands" which create a "double bind" for Black women (p. 213). In this sample, it may be that the more active struggle around racial, in contrast to gender, identity issues is a reflection of difficulty during late adolescence in integrating two seemingly inharmonious identities.

Another hypothesis is that the work on gender issues has already been done by virtue of these women incorporating a basic sense of feminism from their foremothers. Scott (1991) and Robinson (1985) talk about Black women as the original feminists. And while only one interviewee used the term "feminist," their comments about themselves and their aspirations conveyed a sense that they valued themselves as people and felt they could achieve whatever they set their minds to. What did not come across was a sense of inferiority based on their gender or a sense that they needed to be taken care of or rescued by men. Perhaps a feminist sensibility, minus the lingo of feminism, is what characterizes these women. Further support for this notion is the finding of the importance of meaningful relationships with other women in these women's lives.

Relationships were, in fact, an important part of most of these women's identities, and almost all of the relationships that helped define their identity were with other women. This finding diverges sharply from Erikson's (1968) early notions that a woman's identity develops based on the identity of the male with whom she partners. And yet this finding converges with a growing body of research on ego identity in Anglo women which indicates that interpersonal concerns are important to identity formation (Patterson et al., 1992). More generally, this finding fits with a body of theory and research on women which stresses the importance of connection, in contrast to separation, in their development (Miller, 1991). The developing literature on the importance of a sense of communion or relatedness in people of African origin also helps to make sense of this finding (Myers, 1988; Akbar, 1989).

The identity domains of religious beliefs, political beliefs, and sexual orientation were of importance to a minority of the group. While religious and political commitments are chosen, sexual orientation, like race and gender, is generally an ascribed identity. All but two participants identified themselves as heterosexual and none identified as lesbian or bisexual; however, heterosexuality was not seen by most as a central

part of who they are. In a society that is predominantly heterosexual and that is biased towards heterosexuality, identity formation around being heterosexual may be of limited salience, particularly for people who are struggling with two other identities that are devalued—being Black and being female.

One of the most striking findings was the emergence of the notion of "strength," a personal characteristic or trait, as a central issue in many of these women's identities. A number of writers speak of the strength of Black women (Murray, 1970; Ladner, 1972; Robinson, 1985). Kesho Scott (1991), in a discussion of her in-depth interviews with middle-aged African-American women, emphasizes the relevance of Jacqueline Jones's (1985) comment about Black women "having nothing to fall back on: not maleness, not whiteness, not ladyhood, not anything." One hypothesis is that a sense of strength is the key to self-definition and survival when one has nothing else to fall back on—perhaps when, as a Black woman, one is forced to survive in a sexist and racist society. A sense of strength may be an important coping mechanism for African-American women.

The findings in this study should be interpreted with caution because of the limited and select college student sample. One advantage of a qualitative study with a small sample is the flexibility to investigate relatively unexplored phenomena in an open-ended manner; the disadvantage is the difficulty generalizing findings to the broader population, in this case, to other late adolescent African-American women.

However, a number of interesting hypotheses arise from this study. We suggest the following:

(1) African-American women develop a sense of strength in reaction to struggling with two ascribed identities—race and gender—that are devalued; or alternatively, the more racism and sexism an African-American woman perceives, the more likely she is to have an identity that includes a sense of strength. (2) For late adolescent African-American women, a sense of strength serves as a buffer, or mediating variable, against the challenges (or stress) of racism and sexism. (3) Late adolescent African-American women who have an identity that includes a sense of strength are psychologically healthier than those whose identity doesn't include a sense of strength. (4) Gender identity is a more central concern for adult than for adolescent African-American women. (5) African-American women who engage in active exploration around gender issues do this after they have engaged in active exploration around racial identity issues.

Furthermore, an interesting topic for research is the relationship between commitment to various identity domains and psychological functioning. For example, are those women who see relationships as a central part of their identity emotionally healthier than those who do not? Is a commitment to certain combinations of identity domains indicative of greater emotional health than a commitment to some other combinations?

Additional qualitative and quantitative studies with larger, more representative samples and with different age cohorts could shed light on these hypotheses and research questions and increase our understanding of the way in which African-American women weave an identity tapestry in the context of a racist and sexist society.

Acknowledgements

We would like to thank LaShaun Turner, Ph.D., for her assistance in conducting this study. This article is based on a presentation at the American Psychological Association Convention in Los Angeles in August 1994.

References

Akbar, N. (1989). Nigrescence and identity: Some limitations. *The Counseling Psychologist*, 17, 258–263.

Almquist, E. M. (1995). The experiences of minority women in the U.S.: Intersections of race, gender, and class. In *Women: A Feminist Perspective*, Freeman, J. (Ed.), pp. 573–606. Mountain View, California: Mayfield.

Aries, E. and Moorehead, K. (1989). The importance of ethnicity in the development of identity of Black adolescents. *Psychological Reports*, **65**, 75–82.

Barnes, E. J. (1980). The Black community as the source of positive self-concept for Black children: A theoretical perspective. In *Black Psychology*, 2nd Edn, Jones, R. L. (Ed.), pp. 106–130. New York: Harper & Row.

Beale, F. (1970). Double jeopardy: To be Black and female. In *The Black Woman*, Cade, T. (Ed.), pp. 90–100. New York: New American Library.

Clark, K. B. and Clark, M. P. (1947). Racial identification and preference in Negro children. In *Readings in Social Psychology*, Newcomb, T. M. and Hartley, E. L. (Eds), pp. 169–178. New York: Holt, Rinehart, and Winston.

Cross, W. E. (1971). The Negro-to-Black conversion experience: Towards a psychology of Black liberation. *Black World*, **20**, 13–27.

Cross. W. E. (1991). *Shades of Black—Diversity in African-American Identity*. Philadelphia: Temple University Press.

Erikson, E. (1968). *Identity: Youth and Crisis*. New York: W. W. Norton.

Franz, C. E. and White, K. M. (1985). Individuation and attachment in personality development: Extending Erikson's theory. *Journal of Personality*, **53**, 224–256.

Fujino, D. C. and King, K. R. (1994). *Toward a model of womanist identity development*. Presentation at the Annual Convention of the American Psychological Association, Los Angeles, CA.

Giddings, P. (1984). *When and Where I Enter: The Impact of Black Women on Race and Sex in America*. New York: Bantam Books.

Greene, B. (1990). What has gone before: The legacy of racism and sexism in the lives of Black mothers and daughters. *Women and Therapy*, **9**, 207–230.

Hare, N. and Hare, J. (1972). Black women 1970. In *Readings on the Psychology of Women*, Bardwick, J. M. (Ed.), pp. 178–181. New York: Harper & Row.

Helms, J. E. (1990). An overview of Black racial identity theory. In *Black and White Racial Identity—Theory, Research, and Practice*, Helms, J. E. (Ed.), pp. 9–32. New York: Greenwood.

hooks, b. (1991). *Ain't I a Woman: Black Women and Feminism*. Boston: South End Press.

Horton, C. P. and Smith, J. C. (Eds) (1993). *Statistical Record of Black America*, 2nd Edn. Detroit, Michigan: Gale Research.

Jones, J. (1985). *Labor of Love, Labor of Sorrow*. New York: Basic Books.

Josselson, R. (1987). *Finding Herself: Pathways to Identity Development in Women*. San Francisco: Jossey-Bass.

Ladner, J. A. (1972). *Tomorrow's Tomorrow: The Black Woman*. Garden City, New York: Anchor Books.

Marcia, J. (1966). Development and validation of ego identity status. *Journal of Personality and Social Psychology*, **3**, 551–558.

Marcia, J. E. (1980). Identity in adolescence. In *Handbook of Adolescent Psychology*, Adelson, J. (Ed.), pp. 159–187. New York: Wiley.

Matteson, D. R. (1993). Differences within and between genders: A challenge to the theory. In *Ego Identity—A Handbook for Psychosocial Research*, Marcia, J. E., Waterman, A. S., Matteson, D. R., Archer, S. L. and Orlofsky, J. L. (Eds), pp. 69–110. New York: Springer-Verlag.

Miller, J. B. (1991). The development of women's sense of self. In *Women's Growth in Connection: Writings from the Stone Center*, Jordan, J. V., Kaplan, A. G., Miller, J. B., Stiver, I. P. and Surrey, J. L. (Eds), pp. 11–26. New York: Guilford.

Murray, P. (1970). The liberation of Black women. In *Voices of the New Feminism*, Thompson, M. L. (Ed.), pp. 87–102. Boston: Beacon Press.

Myers, H. F. (1989). Urban stress and mental health in Afro-American youth: An epidemiological and conceptual update. In *Black Adolescents*, Jones, R. (Ed.). Berkeley, California: Cobb & Henry.

Myers, L. J. (1988). *Understanding an Afrocentric World View: Introduction to an Optimal Psychology*. Dubuque, Iowa: Kendall/Hunt.

Myers, L. J., Speight, S. L., Highlen, P. S., Cox, C. I., Reynolds, A. L., Adams, E. M. and Hanley, C. P. (1991). Identity development and worldview: Toward an optimal conceptualization. *Journal of Counseling and Development*, **70**, 54–63.

Parham, T. A. (1989). Cycles of psychological nigrescence. *The Counseling Psychologist*, **17**, 187–226.

Parham, T. A. and Helms, J. E. (1985a). Attitudes of racial identity and self-esteem of Black students: An exploratory investigation. *Journal of College Student Personnel*, **26**, 143–147.

Parham, T. A. and Helms, J. E. (1985b). Relation of racial attitudes to self-actualization and affective states of Black students. *Journal of Counseling Psychology*, **32**, 431–440.

Patterson, S. J., Sochting, I. and Marcia, J. (1992). The inner space and beyond: Women and identity. In *Adolescent Identity Formation*, Adams, G. R., Gullotta, T. P. and Montemayor, R. (Eds) pp. 9–24. Newbury Park, California: Sage.

Patton, M. Q. (1990). *Qualitative Evaluation and Research Methods*, 2nd Edn. Newbury Park, California: Sage.

Phinney, J. S. (1989). Stages of ethnic identity development in minority group adolescents. *Journal of Early Adolescence*, **9**, 34–49.

Phinney, J. S. (1993). Multiple group identities: Differentiation, conflict, and integration. In *Discussions on Ego Identity*, Kroger, J. (Ed.), pp. 47–73. Hillsdale, NJ: Lawrence Erlbaum Associates.

Phinney, J. S. and Alipuria, L. (1990). Ethnic identity in college students from four ethnic groups. *Journal of Adolescence,* **13,** 171–183.

Phinney, J. S. and Tarver, S. (1988). Ethnic identity search and commitment in Black and White eighth graders. *Journal of Early Adolescence,* **8,** 265–277.

Reid, P. T. (1988). Racism and sexism: Comparisons and conflicts. In *Eliminating Racism: Profiles in Controversy,* Katz, P. A. and Taylor, D. (Eds), pp. 203–221. NY: Plenum.

Reynolds, A. L. and Pope, R. L. (1991). The complexities of diversity: Exploring multiple oppressions. *Journal of Counseling and Development,* **70,** 174–180.

Robinson, C. R. (1985). Black women: A tradition of self-reliant strength. In *Women Changing Therapy: New Assessments, Values and Strategies in Feminist Therapy,* Robbins, J. H. and Siegel, J. R. (Eds), pp. 135–144. New York: Harrington Park Press.

Scott, K. Y. (1991). *The Habit of Surviving.* New York: Ballantine Books.

Shorter, D. L. (1978). The relationship between political activism and psycho-social development in late adolescent Black women. Unpublished doctoral dissertation, University of Maryland.

Shorter-Gooden, K. (1992). *Ethnic, gender, and ego identity development in African-American female adolescents.* Presentation at the Centennial Annual Convention of the American Psychological Association, Washington, D.C.

Staples, R. (1973). *The Black Woman in America.* Chicago: Nelson Hall.

Waterman, A. S. (1985). Identity in the context of adolescent psychology. In *Identity in Adolescence: Process and Contents,* Waterman, A. S. (Ed.), pp. 5–25. San Francisco: Jossey-Bass.

Watson, M. F. and Protinsky, H. (1991). Identity status of Black adolescents: An empirical investigation. *Adolescence,* **26,** 963–966.

 Article Review Form at end of book.

What are some steps that Stevenson suggests to improve self-esteem? Why does he see the current self-esteem movement as worrisome?

Self-Esteem

The myth of feeling good about oneself

Stevenson discusses why the idea of raising children's self-esteem as a sure means of improving their levels of achievement and solving many of the nation's social ills is a myth.

Harold W. Stevenson

Dr. Stevenson is professor of psychology, University of Michigan, Ann Arbor.

No one would argue that children thrive when they feel respected, important, and cared for by other persons, or that they falter when they lack the self-pride and self-confidence that accompanies such approval and support. However, at the hands of educators eager to encourage lagging pupils, a myth has developed that raising youngsters' self-esteem is a sure means of improving their levels of achievement and solving many of the nation's social ills.

The 1990 report of the California Task Force to Promote Personal and Social Responsibility, for instance, proposes that "Self-esteem is the likeliest candidate for a 'social vaccine,' something that empowers us to live responsibly and that inoculates us against the lure of crime, violence, substance abuse, teen pregnancy, child abuse, chronic welfare dependency, and educational failure. The lack of self-esteem is central to more personal and social ills plaguing our state and nation as we approach the end of the twentieth century."

If, indeed, self-esteem is a precondition for learning and a panacea for so many social problems, it would be foolish to disagree with proponents such as Jack Canfield, author of popular books about self-esteem, who suggests that courses enhancing it are the "major missing link to educational reform in America today," or Robert Reasoner of the California Center for Self-Esteem, who concludes that emphasis on it "may well be our only hope for a better world." This focus on the importance of self-esteem occurs so widely in current educational and popular writings that its momentum has created what some call the self-esteem movement—the practice of supplying positive feedback regardless of the quality of performance.

Efforts to convince the public of the importance of positive self-regard are not new. More than a century ago, followers of French psychotherapist Emile Coua proclaimed that "Every day in every way I am getting better and better." More recently, the power of positive thinking and positive reinforcement has been promoted by writers such as Norman Vincent Peale, Nathaniel Branden, and B. F. Skinner. A happy, productive life was assured, if only people would accentuate the positive and eliminate the negative.

By the 1960s, following the advent of the self-actualization theories of personal growth espoused by psychologists Abraham Maslow and Carl Rogers, interest in enhancing self-esteem as a path to accomplishment got under way in the nation's schools. Since then, dozens of "how-to" books have described ways for improving children's positive feelings about themselves.

If the responses of others make me feel good about myself, the argument goes, I will be motivated, convinced of my ability to learn, and launched on a path to a successful life. The theory is simple: Feeling good is a necessary predecessor of accomplishment.

Despite its current popularity, questions can be raised about the assumptions underlying the self-esteem movement. For example, what benefit does a third-grader gain in learning to copy the words, "I am Terri. I love and approve of myself," if she otherwise can not write an intelligible sentence? Would it help Terri to learn to tell herself, "I am smart," "I am a good student," or "I am me and I am enough"—all forms of the "affirmative language" espoused by Douglas Bloch and Jon Merritt in their book, *Positive Self-talk for Children?*

Does it really enhance the self-esteem of members of the fifth-grade baseball team—or improve their athletic skill—when everyone is awarded a trophy, despite the fact that the team did not win a single game in this year's schedule or show noticeable improvement throughout the season? What effect will this have on next year's efforts when this record of performance ends with apparent approval and satisfaction?

Does hearing classmates recite from a list of nice things to say to each other—such as "You brighten my day," "I'm lucky to know you," or "You're a good buddy"—convey a sincere message or one that is perceived as being artificial or "weird"?

Teaching kids to be sensitive to the feelings of others is to be lauded: providing them with trite phrases to be repeated mechanically is teaching nothing.

Every morning, hundreds of Hispanic-American children gather on their school playgrounds or in auditoriums to pledge allegiance to the flag and to hear a record announce, in both English and Spanish, phrases such as "I am special," "I am great," or "I am a very important person." The pupil echoes the phrases as they are heard. The teachers complain that nothing is changed, that the days go on the same as ever. They still have to deal with the children's problems—and with the loss of a half-hour of teaching time.

People are eager to extol the toddler for a few tentative steps and the two-year-old for simply attempting to match form with hole in a puzzle board. Self-esteem is heightened in the young child through such noncontingent love and approval. Older kids, though, are astute analysts and know when performance merits praise and when it does not. Repeating indiscriminate praise or acclaiming minimal accomplishments run the risk of transforming positive responses into meaningless jargon or hollow flattery.

Self-esteem theorists appear to have it backwards. Meaningful self-evaluation and positive self-esteem usually are the results, not the antecedents, of accomplishment. Praise is just one source of feedback; self-esteem more often comes from an awareness that the requirements of a sought-after goal have been mastered. Acquiring the knowledge and skills that enable a child to make progress toward such goals is a necessary basis for developing healthy, realistic self-esteem.

Ben, a seven-year-old who attended a family summer camp in Michigan, offers a good example of how self-esteem is built upon solid achievement. Ben is captivated by horses and visited the camp's horse barn every day. On the fourth day, he returned, excitedly exclaiming, "Know what? I got my blue M!" After telling his parents the step-by-step requirements to get the blue M, he informed them with a big smile and clenched fist, "I'm proud of myself! Yay!" The reaction of an interested counselor and the ultimate praise of his family undoubtedly were important, but the boost in Ben's self-esteem primarily came from knowing he had mastered the main requirements of beginning horsemanship.

Sports is an arena in which Americans generally have little reluctance to require hard work and persistence. Coaches do not hesitate to point out errors and mistakes as the players attempt to achieve the orderly mastery of specific goals. Children's self-esteem does not appear to suffer when they are told that they need to practice more and concentrate on the task at hand. The usual effect is renewed effort to work, practice, and learn.

In contrast, Americans are reluctant to have teachers evaluate the academic performance of their elementary school children with more than a "satisfactory" or "needs improvement." Later, parents urge high schools to adopt more lenient grading systems, worried that the children's self-esteem will plummet when they find the "satisfactory" of earlier years now has become a "C" or "D." This reluctance to place children in academic situations where mistakes can be used as part of the learning process seems to be based on a fear that low grades may be interpreted as failure or stupidity, rather than lack of studying.

Sympathetic teachers, aware of the difficulties students encounter in their everyday lives, often relinquish standards in an effort to build students' self-confidence. In doing so, they deprive youngsters of the kinds of experience that are prerequisite to later success. Students are short-changed and their prospects for later employment are placed in jeopardy when teachers fail to teach them diligence and effort can help to avoid academic problems, and when they fail to provide children with realistic feedback in meeting well-defined, challenging goals.

American students face a bleak future if they are unable to compete with their peers, both in the U.S. and other industrialized countries. The seriousness of the matter becomes evident in the results of comparative studies of academic achievement. In one, for example, 96% of Chinese and 90% of Japanese fifth-graders tested had mathematics scores higher than the average of their counterparts in the U.S. Results are not much better at the 11th-grade level: 96% of the Chinese and 92% of the Japanese received scores above American average scores. These Chinese and Japanese are among the peers with whom American youngsters must compete in the economies of the 21st century.

One might guess from the growing emphasis on self-esteem that American children generally have a negative self-image. This is not the case. In research conducted with representative samples of 11th-graders and their parents in Minnesota and Virginia, for instance, we found that Americans seem to have an unusually positive image of themselves. Participants were asked to rate the student's achievement in mathematics and general academic subjects on a seven-point scale where a rating of four was defined as average. Both students and their parents made ratings whose averages were significantly above average—that is, above four. "Above average" ratings were not limited to academic areas; the students gave themselves these ratings on a diverse array of characteristics, including how hard they studied, their intellectual ability, athletic skills, physical appearance, and how well they got along with others. Chinese and Japanese students and parents made more realistic appraisals; their average ratings conformed more closely to the average as the researchers had defined it.

Evaluations made by the Americans do not describe students plagued by self-doubt and in need of strong reassurance. Of course, there are American youngsters who have low self-esteem and who respond to this by giving up academic pursuits. Nevertheless, the principal challenge, it seems, is not so much in building up their self-esteem as in teaching them that all students are capable of raising their levels of performance if they are willing to work hard. We asked several thousand American and East Asian students to tell us what was most important for doing well in school. The most common response of the East Asian students was "studying." The U.S. students said "a good teacher." The difference in locus of responsibility reflected in these answers well may reveal the consequence of a "feel good" approach. It indeed is harder to study than to listen, but it takes study in order to learn.

What conclusions can be drawn? First, it is through progress and accomplishment that students develop the confidence which underlies solid self-esteem. Second, meeting challenging goals and receiving accurate feedback provides a sense of competence that leads to a healthy, realistic basis for feeling good about oneself. There is no evidence that adopting ever-higher standards as they learn and requiring students to work harder will lower their positive feelings about their abilities.

Having kids tell themselves, like Stuart Smalley's frequent self-affirmation on "Saturday Night Live," "I'm good enough. I'm smart enough. And doggonit, people like me" may be comforting for the moment, but we delude ourselves if we think a "feel good" approach will solve the problems of educating America's children and protecting the nation from social ills.

Praise and award certificates—the currency of the self-esteem movement—are cheap. More tangible types of reform that rely on redesigning institutions such as schools are expensive, difficult, and time-consuming. Even so, Americans must be as hard-headed and as clear as their competitors in realizing that an effective educational system and successful programs for children and youth are fundamental to a nation's health and progress. Feeling good is fine; it is even better when people have something to feel good about.

 Article Review Form at end of book.

What do researchers on procrastination see as the root cause of procrastination? How does the use of procrastination develop and flourish?

The Ups and Downs of Dawdling

Don't worry about missing those deadlines: It's never too late to be really, really late.

Mark Wheeler

Am on deadline. I am thinking. Totally, totally focused. I am hungry. My fingers are poised on the keyboard, waiting for the command from my mind, itself awash with thoughts. Strategizing. Who to quote? Who to paraphrase? What to eat? Let's see, what university is this psychologist from; I know I wrote it down somewhere—what's that buzzing? Here it is, Case Western Reserve. Okay, write this down: "Her research reveals"—it's a fly; I hate flies. No, don't write that. "Her work suggests"—ahh, hit the window, huh? Whatsa matter, fella, little problem identifying transparent solids? "Her research suggests"—look at this, there's so much dust on this monitor I can write my name on it—ah-choo, oh great, now I'm catching a cold. I gotta eat something.

So (cough), are you the dawdling kid? The type who tends to tarry? Or are you more the merry procrastinator, one who truly enjoys that extra free time of utter irresponsibility before compressing the angst of hard work into the fewest possible remaining hours?

If you're the kind of person who gets the irrepressible urge to change the litter box (cough) right when you're up against a deadline, then you may wish to heed the results of Dianne Tice's recent study, scheduled for publication in the journal *Psychological Science*. It's entitled "Longitudinal Study of Procrastination, Performance, Stress, and Health: The Agonies and Ecstasies of Dawdling."

Tice, who teachers psychology at Case Western Reserve University in Cleveland, found that procrastination indeed has its short-term rewards, but long-term bad things can take their toll, especially on one's health. In addition, despite the rallying cry of all committed procrastinators—"I do my best work under pressure!"—their best just ain't good enough when measured against the work of those namby-pamby kiss-kiss Goody Twoshoes who start their projects right away and finish them on time or even—gasp—early.

Procrastination, Tice's work shows, is like attaching a generic KICK ME sign to your derriere in terms of the negative impact it can have on your entire life. Tice conducted two studies, the first with 44 students, the second with 58. Both groups were enrolled in her health psychology course, for which two exams, an optional final, and a term paper were required. At the start of the semester, the due date for the term paper was announced, and students were told that if they could not meet the deadline they could have an automatic extension to a specific later date. Now, to me, an automatic extension is akin to waving a campaign contribution in front of a sitting president, but who am I to judge? (Sneeze.) The students were guaranteed anonymity, and none of the results were looked at until final grades were posted.

Four weeks into the semester during the first study, the students were asked to take a test called Lay's General Procrastination Scale. The Lay scale was invented by Canadian psychologist Clarry Lay of York University in Ontario, and it asks people to fess up to how frequently they put things off. The test consists of a series of statements such as "I usually make decisions as soon as possible" and offers a range of five comments that run from "Not true for me" to "True for me." (I looked at the test. Now, right off the bat I have a problem with at least three statements: "A letter may sit for days after I write it before I mail it"; "In preparing for deadlines, I often waste time by doing other things"; and "I often have a task finished sooner than necessary." To these I'd like to insist on adding at least three optional answers: "Who has time to write letters?" "I prefer to think of it as necessary prep work"; and "Ha, ha, ha, ha, ha!").

After the courses were completed, Tice compiled the results and, sure enough, found a correlation between shirkers and bad things: self-professed procrastinators, it seemed, did indeed turn their papers in later and received significantly lower grades—an average of three-quarters of a grade lower than their nonprocrastinating counterparts (cough, sniff). Anyone who didn't turn in a paper received an automatic "Incomplete" for a grade, good until the middle of the following semester before the grade reverted to an F. Tice swears that, sure enough, one student waited until 3 P.M. of the last day before calling to find out what she needed to do to avoid failing.

Her student footdraggers did get some good news, at least early on (ahchoo!). The results seemed to suggest that, health-wise, lollygaggers had the right idea: they were having a swell time, enjoying life, catching a few Cleveland rays, visiting Milwaukee, and in short doing anything except what they were supposed to be doing. Meanwhile, the fuddy-duddies who were getting down to business were already—poor babies—showing mild signs of stress and ill health.

"Then, with the second study group," says Tice, "I measured health effects at the end of the semester." Sure enough, it became clear that virtue did indeed have its rewards. With deadline looming and a lack of progress staring them in the face, the procrastinators' stress levels started to soar. Their insouciant attitude typically collapsed into higher rates of headaches, stomachaches, colds, and more trips to the student health clinic as well as, I'd guess, the bathroom, compared with those proboscis-to-the-grind-stone types who had worked steadily from the start (cough).

Now, I know what you're thinking—everybody puts things off now and then. James Thurber ("It is better to have loafed and lost than never to have loafed at all") was obviously a member of the back-burner set. Harold Brodkey took 27 years to publish his first novel. Scarlett O'Hara maintained a "What, me worry?" attitude toward thinking about Tara. And who hasn't put off making a dental appointment, figuring income tax, or, say, having a prostate exam (cough, cough, cough, cough, cough).

Yet despite the obvious effects on health, procrastinators do not often change their ways. The reason is simple—sometimes procrastination works. "What makes procrastination habitual is that for many people, it does work most of the time, and it makes them feel good," Tice says. For example, if a student pulls an all-nighter and gets a good grade, "it reinforces the behavior. That's a huge relief and sense of accomplishment."

What makes nonprocrastinators so—let's just bring it out into the open, shall we?—annoying, is that they have little tolerance for their counterparts. Such futzes, they sniff, need to learn time-management techniques. Or they simply need to get off their lazy whatevers and take care of business. But Joseph Ferrari, a psychologist at De Paul University in Chicago who has collaborated with Tice on procrastination studies, says that the tomorrow types aren't by nature lazy.

"To tell a procrastinator to, as the commercial goes, 'Just do it,' is like telling a person who's clinically depressed to 'Hey! Cheer up!,' " he says. And time management? Please. "Like most people, true procrastinators will make a list of things to do, but they never get beyond the list—they just keep reshuffling the items."

Ferrari rattles off fun facts about procrastinators: "Low self-esteem, low self-confidence, tendency toward perfectionism . . ." In other words, procrastination is a bad way to be, and a lot of people—some 20 percent of the adult population—apparently revel in it.

"There are two main forms of procrastination," says Tice. "One involves things that aren't important to you and are also nonthreatening, like mowing the lawn. The other, though, is something you really want to do well but that brings a lot of anxiety along with it." And procrastinators don't postpone that anxiety by doing something fun, says Tice. "Because they feel guilty, they use their nervous energy to do something else that's useful but nonessential and not fun." (Nonessential? Rotating the tires on my car? On schedule?!)

What procrastination comes down to, both Tice and Ferrari say, is fear. "Many procrastinators have a fear of failure and a fear of success," says Tice. The first is understandable, but the second? Even the most hard-core procrastinators would find success satisfying, right? Wrong, says Ferrari.

"If you succeed," he says, "that raises the expectation that you should succeed again. That can be very stressful and unnerving. The research now suggests that procrastinators use procrastination as a self-handicapping strategy to protect their self-esteem. Because if they do poorly, they can attribute it to the handicap that 'I didn't have enough time.' But if they overcome the handicap and succeed, so much the better."

Poppycock, a representative of the punctually challenged community would cry, if I ever got around to it. Perhaps stalling is a result of natural selection. While our forebears were evolving, a little lingering along with wariness might have been a good thing. After all, over the next rise in yonder dale might be something hairy and toothy that wanted to eat you. Better to hang back and let Mr. Protohuman go-getter get up and go first.

Indeed, not everyone agrees that procrastination is such a bad thing. I'm sure that Les Waas, president of the Pennsylvania-based Procrastinators Club of America (motto: "We're behind you all the way"), is a strong be-

liever in the benefits of putting everything off.

The 40-year-old club is 14,000 members strong, but Waas's old joke is that the other 750,000 members just haven't gotten around to joining yet. The members generally don't stay very busy by not doing much. Now and again they'll have their annual Christmas party in June. They may or may not give out awards to racehorses that finish last, and it's a cold day you-know-where when they send out their newsletter, titled Last Month's Newsletter. "We keep issuing the same one," says Waas. "The news isn't new but nobody cares." Sometimes they publicly protest promptness prejudice—two years ago it was against a restaurant chain because it offered early-bird specials. New members are welcome to join, but beware—"If you fill the application out properly and get it back on time," says Waas, "you can forget about becoming a member."

I know Waas said these things, but I confess I didn't get this information firsthand, because I never quite got around to calling him. (Hey, I've been sick.) Several newspapers did, though, and in one piece in the *Chicago Tribune* last year, Waas was quoted as saying, "There's hardly anything that can't be postponed. Even your death can be put off if you don't drink or smoke and you eat right and exercise. Every time you do anything, you are putting something else off."

Can't argue with that. Truly words to live by, and proof positive that procrastinators don't just stall willy-nilly; the big P is a philosophical way of life.

When I finally did get around to calling Waas, he was late for a meeting but happy to take a few minutes to talk to me

anyway. "We see procrastination as a positive attitude toward life," he says. "It saves a lot of time—if you have two weeks to do something, it will take you two weeks. If you have one day, it will take you one day, thereby freeing up the other 13 to do something else."

The opposite of a procrastinator is an anti-crastinator, says Waas. "They rush through life, never taking time to smell the flowers, and they have a tendency to die young. A good procrastinator is always the last one to arrive at an event, so he never has to wait in lines or get stuck in traffic. It's much less stressful."

At the time of our conversation, Waas was not busy preparing for Procrastination Week, which is scheduled annually for the first week in March. Waas figures they'll celebrate it sometime in the second or third week. Because he had time to chat, I ran the results of Tice's study by him for his reaction.

"Well, I'm a fairly healthy guy, and most of the members I know seem to be better off healthwise," he says. "Most of our members, it should be noted, aren't losers. They're mostly professional people, better educated, and when we do have a meeting, which is rare, everybody seems to enjoy themselves. It's obvious that we are people who enjoy life."

Making light and placing a positive spin on procrastination does not amuse the killjoy Ferrari, though, who says he's spent most of his career dispelling the myth that procrastination is fun. "My problem with the mainstream press is that they have always seen the subject as funny when it's not. This is a psychological problem with serious consequences."

Society, he says, reinforces the problem. Take the holiday season: "At Christmas, the closer to December 25 it gets, the more department stores have sales. It just reinforces procrastination." Ideally, says Ferrari, "it would be better to increase prices as the holiday draws near to punish the last-minute shopper."

Since neither Tice nor Ferrari is a clinical psychologist, they were hesitant to give advice on how to break the hold-the-phone habit. Independently, though, both did mention one common and often successful antistalling strategy. "Every big task can be broken down into a series of smaller tasks," says Tice, "and once you've achieved the completion of a small task, reward yourself. The reward can provide a little motivation to move on to the next small step."

A sound strategy, perhaps, but what's going to cause the procrastinator to actually carry out that first small task? I suppose I should think about that some more, but I really don't feel well. I think I need to go lie down.

 Article Review Form at end of book.

WiseGuide Wrap-Up

- The idea of the self as a single, unified entity is especially prevalent in twentieth-century America. It may be more accurate to see oneself as having many related selves that fit into the appropriate situations and relationships.

- An important identity domain for women is their relationships with other people. Black women also see themselves in relation to other people, but an important domain seems to be that of individual strength, a need to overcome the difficulties they face by being black and being a woman.

- Self-esteem can best be understood as something that is built up through accomplishments and recognition of hard work. There is little evidence that improving self-esteem will improve one's proclivity to work and one's accomplishments.

- Individuals who fear failing at an important task may use self-handicapping to protect themselves from failure (and sometimes from success). One commonly used form of self-handicapping is procrastination. Ultimately, self-handicapping has a negative effect in that the individual does not reach his or her potential.

R.E.A.L. Sites

This list provides a print preview of typical **coursewise** R.E.A.L. sites. (There are over 100 such sites at the **courselinks**™ site.) The danger in printing URLs is that web sites can change overnight. As we went to press, these sites were functional using the URLs provided. If you come across one that isn't, please let us know via email to: webmaster@coursewise.com. Use your Passport to access the most current list of R.E.A.L. sites at the **courselinks**™ site.

Site name: Cyberia Shrink's Tests, Tests, Tests

URL: http://www.queendom.com/tests.html

Why is it R.E.A.L.? A favorite activity of modern society is to take magazine quizzes that tell you about the "true" you. Some of these quizzes may be valid, but often, they are made up just for that magazine article and have little real meaning. This site gathers together a number of reputable online psychological tests. You can take tests on such topics as self-esteem, attributional style, locus-of-control, and emotional intelligence, to name but a few. The site provides an instant score and verbal feedback. As the introduction to this site proclaims, "Psychological tests cannot solve your problems, but they may help you get to know yourself better." Go to this site and take one psychological test. Do you think the results are an accurate representation of your personality?

Key topics: attribution, self-concept, self-esteem, self-help

Site name: Procrastination Research Group

URL: http://www.carleton.ca/~tpychyl/

Why is it R.E.A.L.? This is the web page of the Procrastination Research Group, which is composed of undergraduate and graduate psychology students and their faculty advisor at Carleton University. Their site discusses the history of the word *procrastination,* and it presents research that an undergraduate student did to determine which intervention strategies are most helpful at preventing procrastination. Go to the site and read these techniques. Do you think any could work for you? They also have a number of online studies on procrastination you can take part in—just don't wait too long. . . .

Key topics: self-help, self-handicapping, motivation

section

3

Learning Objectives

- Understand what an attitude is and how attitudes influence behavior.

- Understand short-term and long-term influences on attitudes.

- Understand how advertisers seek to change people's attitudes by using a variety of persuasion techniques.

- Recognize the ability of advertising to influence attitudes.

- Understand how cognitive dissonance can be used to change someone's attitudes and behavior.

Attitudes and Persuasion

 **WiseGuide Intro**

Humans are opinionated creatures. Many of us can barely restrain the urge to tell others what we think about any number of topics. Some of the most spirited and emotional arguments take place between people with differing attitudes about religion, politics, or even food. An attitude is a general evaluative orientation toward an object—a sense that something is good or bad, right or wrong, positive or negative, favorable or unfavorable. These objects can be concrete and specific, such as a type of car or tennis shoe, or something abstract, like equality. Of course, many of our most important attitudes concern other people: our family and friends—and our enemies.

It's hard to imagine making it through a day without relying on these inner judgments about the people and things in our world. At one time many social psychologists were skeptical that attitudes were really all that important in social life, but we now know that our attitudes provide guidance for our behavior, as well as help express our individual values and beliefs. This shouldn't really come as a surprise; the multi-billion-dollar advertising industry is based on the premise that changing consumers' attitudes can affect their purchasing behavior. Our system of government depends upon citizens regularly expressing their attitudes about politicians and policies, through the ballot box and other means.

But what's really behind attitudes? And how do attitudes change? Why do some attempts at persuasion (attitude change) succeed while others fail? The readings in this section tackle some of these basic questions about attitudes and attitude change.

Our democratic system of government demands that citizens express their political attitudes through voting and other forms of participation. Yet scholars of political attitudes have noticed some troubling trends in citizens' attitudes toward the major political parties, politicians, and government in general. Seymour Martin Lipset's article presents evidence about increasingly cynical political attitudes among citizens in several democracies, including the United States. Lipset traces these changed attitudes to certain social and economic trends as well as specific historical events.

Our next article was written by Gloria Steinem to explain to readers why *Ms.* magazine no longer accepts advertising. We are afforded an inside look at how the advertising industry operates in the publishing world, and how ubiquitous its presence is. I think you will be surprised, as I was, to find out how many pages of popular magazines are dedicated to advertising and to discover how carefully these ads are placed with reference to stories. In this article you see persuasion—the art and science of attitude change—in action.

Questions

R11. What are the sources of citizens' hostile attitudes toward government? Are these sources primarily *cognitive* (belief-based) or *affective* (emotion-based)? How do such general attitudes about government influence political behavior?

R12. Why do advertisers try to exert editorial control at magazines? How do advertisers help to reinforce stereotypes?

R13. Is advertising effective at changing people's attitudes? What are some of the needs that cigarette advertisers appeal to?

R14. How do you induce cognitive dissonance in someone? How can you influence people by pointing out their hypocrisy?

"Hooked on Tobacco" also discusses how advertisers influence our attitudes. In particular, the article focuses on how teenagers develop attitudes toward smoking. The article discusses the types of persuasion techniques the cigarette advertisers use to generate positive attitudes toward smoking by presenting an attractive image of smokers. Peer influence on attitudes toward smoking is also discussed.

Our final article by Christopher Shea talks about a different method of inducing attitude change. Researcher Elliot Aronson is interested in how to influence people to have safe-sex attitudes, and then to act in accordance with these attitudes by using condoms. He uses cognitive dissonance as a method first to change attitudes and then to make behavior consistent with those attitudes. The basic idea behind this method is to make people aware of when they are being hypocritical. This makes them uncomfortable, and in order to reduce that unpleasant feeling, they feel compelled to change their attitudes.

What are the sources of citizens' hostile attitudes toward government? Are these sources primarily *cognitive* (belief-based) or *affective* (emotion-based)? How do such general attitudes about government influence political behavior?

America Today
Malaise and resiliency

Seymour Martin Lipset

Dr. Lipset is Hazel Professor of Public Policy at George Mason University.

Ironically, the victory of the democracies in the Cold War has been followed by a decline in their major democratic institutions. One of the most disturbing trends has been a widespread falloff in the strength of political parties. As Joseph Schumpeter noted in his classic Capitalism, Socialism and Democracy, the masses' principal tool for affecting the composition and policies of government is their ability to choose among organized alternatives—that is, parties. In the more established democracies, institutionalized political parties are becoming increasingly fragile. Electorates around the world have become much more volatile, less loyal to particular parties, and more prone to shift among them. And yet, as Schumpeter and Stein Rokkan emphasized, strong partisan loyalties that can survive political disasters are a necessary condition for stable democracy.

The demise of parties has in fact been a frequent occurrence in emerging democracies, whose new organizations necessarily lack a loyal base. The Federalist Party, one of the first parties to appear in the United States, lost power in 1800 and soon ceased to be a major contender for presidential office. Similar developments have been seen in post-Franco Spain and postcommunist Poland, where Solidarity, which once claimed ten million members, is now a shadow of its former self. Even older, more established democratic systems are not immune. In Canada, the formerly dominant Conservative Party captured only 16 percent of the vote and two seats in the parliamentary elections of 1993. In Italy, a series of scandals has nearly eliminated the two parties that dominated most postwar administrations, the Christian Democrats and the Socialists.

The weakening of parties is but one indicator that even well-established democracies are currently facing difficulties. Across the developed world, opinion polls show that citizenries are increasingly distrustful of their political leaders and institutions. When asked about their level of confidence in government, large majorities in almost every country report that they have "none," "little," or "a fair amount." Those who report a high degree of trust generally constitute a small minority.

The United States provides a striking example of this universal breakdown of respect for authority. Opinion surveys indicate that confidence in U.S. political institutions has declined precipitously and steadily since the mid-1960s. The Louis Harris Poll, which has investigated the subject since 1966, reported in 1994 the lowest level of confidence ever in political leaders. Those expressing "a great deal" of confidence in the executive branch of government constituted only 12 percent of a national sample in 1994, as compared to 24 percent in 1981 and 41 percent in 1966. Trust in Congress was even lower, with only 8 percent strongly positive in 1994, as compared to 16 percent in 1981 and 42 percent in 1966.

A study undertaken by the University of Michigan's Survey Research Center has been asking: "Would you say that the government is pretty much run by a few big interests looking out for themselves, or that it is run for the benefit of all the people?" In 1964, 29

Seymour Martin Lipset, from "Malaise and Resiliency in America," JOURNAL OF DEMOCRACY, July 1995, pp. 4–18. © 1995. Helen Dwight Reid Educational Foundation.

percent of respondents said it was run for the benefit of a few big interests. By 1980, the proportion so replying had increased to 70 percent; in 1992, fully four-fifths of respondents expressed this cynical view. A Gallup poll conducted for the Times Mirror organization in 1994 found that 66 percent of a national sample agreed with the statement "Government is almost always wasteful and inefficient." A similar percentage felt that "most elected officials don't care what people like me think" up from 47 percent in 1987, and 33 percent in the 1960s.

Such doubts about government have manifested themselves in numerous ways, including a decline in voter participation. At one time, the United States could boast that the overwhelming majority of eligible voters cast ballots. The situation changed after World War I, with the figure dropping to around 50 percent, partly as a result of women gaining the vote. It reached a post-World War II high of close to two-thirds in 1964 before dropping again. The 1980s and early 1990s saw a new wave of decline to just over 50 percent; the United States now has the lowest rate of voter participation in national elections of all the established democracies except Switzerland. Even fewer voters take part in lower-level contests and primaries. Reporting on the midterm primaries in 1994, the Committee for the Study of the American Electorate noted that only 18 percent of the voting-age population cast ballots, as compared to 24 percent in 1974 and 33 percent in 1966.

Third Parties

The United States is also experiencing an erosion of support for the traditional two-party system.

In a 1994 Gallup poll, for the first time in polling history a majority of those interviewed—53 percent—expressed interest in seeing a third major party. By March 1995—following the Republican capture of Congress—the proportion in favor had increased to 57 percent. Evidence that this sentiment is not simply symbolic is provided by the support that Ross Perot obtained in the 1992 presidential election and still enjoys. Perot secured the highest percentage of the vote ever attained by a third-party candidate, with the exception of Theodore Roosevelt in 1912. (Roosevelt, however, was a dissident Republican, preferred in the 12 primaries of that year by most of his party's supporters.) When participants in surveys conducted in 1994 and 1995 were asked for whom they would vote if the election were held today—Clinton, a named Republican, or Ross Perot—Perot was chosen by between one-sixth and one-fifth of respondents. An April 1995 CNN/Gallup poll found that 20 percent of respondents preferred Perot to Clinton or Republican senator Robert Dole.

A Gallup poll conducted for Times Mirror in early 1995 (following the first hundred days of the Republican-controlled Congress) indicated no improvement in, and possibly a worsening of, the American public's "spirits about the state of the nation." An April 1995 Hart-Teeter survey showed that the percentage who believed that "things in the nation . . . are off on the wrong track" had increased to 50 percent—up from 42 percent in November 1994—while those answering that the nation is headed in the right direction had declined to 32 percent, from 37 percent. The Times Mirror report on reactions to the Gingrich-led Congress notes:

A change in power in Washington usually causes more Americans to say, for at least a short period of time, that the country is headed in the right direction. Not so in the current Times Mirror survey, which found almost three out of four (74 percent) respondents dissatisfied with the way things are going in the country today, slightly higher than a year ago (71 percent in March 1994). Moreover, of 22 problem areas on which respondents were polled, majorities or pluralities say the nation was losing ground on fully 18 of them.

The Legacy of the 1960s

This erosion of trust in American government is troubling. In a July 1979 television address, then-President Jimmy Carter characterized it as a "fundamental threat to American democracy," a "crisis of confidence . . . that strikes at the very heart and soul and spirit of our national will." He pointed to a growing disrespect for government, churches, schools, the news media, and other institutions and emphasized that "the gap between our citizens and our government has never been so wide." That gap has widened since Carter's speech.

Opinion polls indicate a dramatic decline in confidence beginning during the mid-1960s, a time characterized by widespread protest, and continuing to the present. The catalyst was a combination of public reaction to the Vietnam War and the general discontent expressed by various social movements—initially linked to the antiwar struggles but then concerned with race relations, the status of women, and the environment—that criticized America for not living up to its democratic and egalitarian promise. Previously, organized protest in Western democratic society had been driven largely by the traditionally underprivileged strata, but the movements of the 1960s were instigated mainly by more affluent groups—university students, professionals, and middle-class women. The civil rights campaigns led by Martin Luther King, Jr., were the main exception.

After the Vietnam War ended, mass protest declined—indeed, almost vanished. Yet, as noted above, public-opinion surveys and electoral behavior revealed that a large proportion of Americans continued to feel frustrated with their political leaders and institutions. Events in the following decade, including the economic down-swing of the early 1970s and the Watergate scandal, intensified the disdain for political leadership. The Carter years, marked by economic stagnation, high rates of inflation and unemployment, and the Iran hostage crisis, did not help.

A temporary hiatus in the downward trend in public confidence occurred in the 1980s, when the economic growth and prosperity that characterized most of Ronald Reagan's term in office resulted (ironically, given Reagan's antagonism to statism) in an increase in trust in government. The improvement was minor, however, and attitudes toward other major institutions—for example, business and labor—were unaffected. In any case, the Reagan blip ended with the eruption of the Iron-contra scandal in November 1986. The downward trend has continued under President Bush and Clinton, interrupted by an upswing after the Gulf War in early 1991 that proved to be very short-lived.

Perhaps even more significant are reports from the National Opinion Research Center (NORC) indicating a decline in interpersonal trust. In response to the question "Some say that most people can be trusted, while others say that you can't be too careful in dealing with people. Which do you believe?" the proportion reporting that most people can be trusted dropped by more than a third between 1970 and 1993, from 58 percent to 37 percent.

Discontent

Why is there so much malaise among the American people? The events of the 1960s are not enough to explain why feelings of discontent have persisted—or, more accurately, increased—or why the growing distrust has extended to inter-personal relations. Politicians tend to blame the media, and I suspect that to a considerable degree they are right. American presidents since George Washington have complained about their press coverage. Thomas Jefferson, Andrew Jackson, Abraham Lincoln, and Franklin D. Roosevelt all perceived—accurately—that the press was largely antagonistic toward the administration. Those on the left, from Jefferson to Roosevelt and Harry S. Truman, believed that the owners of the major media outlets were conservatives and controlled what their papers wrote about them. Since Lyndon Johnson, presidents have identified media bias as reflecting the views of journalists rather than owners, and as liberal rather than conservative. There is little doubt that the predominantly leftist views of reporters affect the way the news is presented. But this is not the main reason for the media's emphasis on the failings of elites and institutions. The fact is that good news is not news; bad news is. A plane that lands does not constitute a story: a plane that crashes does. Politicians characterized by honesty, personal integrity,

and a good family life are dull. Sexually promiscuous and corrupt political figures are interesting. In short, the press looks for failings. The desire to identify and exaggerate scandals among political, social, and economic elites has always characterized open societies.

There is a new factor that I think has been responsible for perpetuating and extending the decline of trust: the shift from print media to television as the major source of news. Television has a much greater impact on the viewer than newspapers or magazines have on the reader. The transition from print to broadcast media began in the 1960s. The Vietnam War was the first televised war; for the first time, people could witness the spilling of blood from their own living rooms. The strong public reaction to the prolonged war was to a considerable extent a function of pictorial reportage. Since then, the domination of the camera has continued to grow. News of the world's problems now reaches people almost immediately and in what appears to be an unbiased manner. Television encourages viewers to believe that they are directly witnessing events as they unfold.

There have been other important changes as well. Norman Ornstein has noted that the increase in reportage on scandals and corruption in government and other political institutions is linked to greater disclosure. Sweeping reform of the political process, in conjunction with the rise of the computer, has resulted in a dramatic increase in information that has been grist for investigative journalism. Playing just as strong a role in undermining trust in leaders has been the enormous growth in "prosecutorial zeal," flowing in part from "the reform-era creation of a Public Integrity

Section in the Justice Department, which defines its success by the volume of prosecution of public officials." As a result, Ornstein reports, "between 1975 and 1989, the number of federal officials indicted on charges of public corruption increased by a staggering 1,211 percent, whereas the number of non-federal public officials indicted doubled during the same period." There has clearly been more bad news available to report, as well as a more effective medium through which to transmit it.

These developments may account for the growth of distrust not only in institutions, but also in people. Polling data indicate that a large segment of the public sees moral order crumbling and is disturbed by reports of higher rates of illegitimate births, more permissive sexual morals, and evidence of increased drug use and crime. The changes brought by elections seemingly have no lasting effect on trust in institutions.

Governmental Gridlock

All of these developments have intensified the problem of "gridlock" in American politics. Gridlock, or the inability of political institutions to react quickly, is not a new phenomenon but flows in large part from the basic structure of the U.S. government. The Founding Fathers were mostly classical liberals who feared and disliked the power of the state. They sought to limit the powers of the executive and make it difficult for political leaders to be effective. As all Americans know, the authors of the Constitution established a polity characterized by checks and balances. The president is chosen by the people, not by a parliament. There are two al-

most equal legislative bodies, the Senate and the House of Representatives, which are elected separately and for varying terms. The members of a fourth body, the Supreme Court, are appointed for life terms to interpret legislation and mediate relations among the elected branches of government. The Founding Fathers succeeded in making it difficult to enact major reforms. If they were to return to Washington today, they would recognize our government as the one they envisioned, although, like most Americans, they might be unhappy with some of the effects. One of the most important consequences of the separation of powers is a weak party and governmental system, one in which the executive branch has little control over the legislature.

Gridlock

The system differs greatly from that of parliamentary countries such as Britain and Canada, which have disciplined legislative parties. A prime minister with an effective parliamentary majority is much more powerful than an American president; he can secure the enactment of the legislation that he and his cabinet support in a short period of time. In the United States, presidents may propose, but—as they quickly learn—Congress disposes. With the relatively weak party discipline of the United States, gridlock occurs even when the president and both congressional bodies nominally belong to the same party. Franklin D. Roosevelt was overwhelmingly reelected in 1936 with an enlarged Democratic majority in Congress, yet that Congress rejected much of the legislation Roosevelt proposed during his second term. Jimmy Carter

and Bill Clinton both learned that they had to campaign to try to get Democratic majorities to pass the legislation they wanted. Each failed on his major issue, Carter on oil and energy, Clinton on health care. Undisciplined congressional parties are not a recent phenomenon, although in pre–World War II days presidents and party leaders exerted greater influence over members of Congress.

Gridlock has become especially pronounced as a result of the 1994 elections, which gave Congress to the Republicans, with the Democrats still controlling the White House. Yet such situations, although deplored by almost all political scientists, are what most Americans prefer. The Wall Street Journal/NBC News poll conducted by Hart and Teeter reported that in 14 surveys carried out between September 1986 and June 1994, majorities or pluralities said that it is "better to have different political parties controlling the Congress and the presidency to prevent either one from going too far" than to have the "same political party control both . . . so they can work together." Clearly, Americans want government to be self-limiting. They continue to adhere to the country's antistatist tradition, as enunciated by Jefferson's dictum that the government which governs least governs best. In 1994, a majority of American voters opted for the only major antistatist party in the Western world, the Republicans.

Beyond the phenomenon of gridlock, it is certain that the decline of patronage, the growth of a merit-based civil service, and the increasing reliance on primary elections as a means of nominating candidates have further weakened party organizations. In the past, party nominees were designated by conventions of the party faithfully interested in securing patronage, rewards, jobs, and contracts from elected officeholders. Today, candidates rarely turn to the party organizations. Rather, the road to a nomination via the primaries consists of the formation of committees of friends and potential supporters and, most important, the raising of money from people with similar political objectives, whether for ideological reasons or for the benefit of special interests.

Political theorist Robert Dahl contends that the decrease in Americans' confidence in government reflects a "fragmentation" of the political process. By this he means a decline of party organization, both inside and outside the government, accompanied by an increase in the sheer number of interest groups and lobbies, and the growing lack of accountability of political leaders that has resulted.

Paradoxically, the growing disdain for government may also reflect the American people's increasing dependence on government since the 1930s. Most people in the advanced democracies, even in the United States, have come to rely on the state to solve most of society's problems and to provide jobs, security for the aged, health care, and good schools. Socialism and communism may have collapsed, but heavy reliance on what Dahl describes as an increasingly complex and incomprehensible government has not. We expect much from the state, and we turn against elected officials when they fail to provide what we want. Declining confidence in government makes it even more difficult for the political leaders to enact new programs and deal with

problems that the public would like to see resolved, such as health care. It also encourages antistatist protest—both moderate, as in the case of the Perot movement, and extreme, as in the example of the "militias" linked to the bombing of the federal building in Oklahoma City in April 1995.

The Changing Campaign

The diminished influence of party organizations and leaders—what Americans once called "machines" and "bosses"—has increased the importance of money in American elections. With the emergence of television as the prime campaign medium, candidates, including incumbents, need large sums. Close to 60 percent of congressional campaign budgets now go toward broadcasting, as compared to 17 percent in the 1950s. Candidates must hire campaign managers, consultants, pollsters, and speech writers, and buy television time in two contests, the primary and the general election. The increased significance of television has not only made money more important in politics, but also changed the nature of campaigns. Television presses candidates to speak simply and in few words, leading to a decline in the discussion of issues. The length of "sound bites," or statements by candidates presented on television, has decreased dramatically. Thomas Patterson reports that by 1988 the typical sound bite presented in newscasts was less than ten seconds long. The print media have followed television's lead in reducing the space devoted to presenting candidates' views. Hence the need for nominees to spend ever greater sums of money to project their message.

Ironically, this increased need for funds has been accompanied by major reforms in campaign laws. Restrictions on contributions imposed in the 1960s have made the collection of money much more difficult. Because wealthy supporters can no longer make large individual contributions, special interests—armed with funds collected from many different individuals—are in a stronger position to influence politicians than they were in the past. This increased influence of interest groups, particularly their ability to get Congress to defeat certain measures, has resulted in the intensification of the natural tendency toward gridlock.

Interest Groups

The failure of the 1994 Clinton proposals for health-care reform illustrates the increased impact of money on American policy making. A complex plan proposed by the president's task force on health-care reform was obstructed by myriad organizations and interests, including insurance groups and business organizations. Other interest groups, such as labor unions, heavily lobbied Congress for Clinton's health plan. Hospitals and universities campaigned both for and against as well. The result was gridlock.

As the health-care episode shows, members of Congress must be responsive not only to their constituencies, but also to fund-raisers and lobbyists. The weakening of parties, the ever-growing need to raise campaign funds, and the greater influence of government on the economy have all contributed to the enhancement of the role of the lobbyist. Over the past 20 years, the number of lobbyists doubled from roughly 3,500 to 7,000. Lobbyists, of course, are not simply those representing corporations or other monied private interests: public-interest lobbies such as environmental and civil rights groups as well as feminist organizations all exert pressure.

Organized political influence operates somewhat differently in the United States than in other democratic countries. Lobbying of individual representatives or legislators is much less important in parliamentary countries than in the United States, since MPs in Toronto or Liverpool or Hamburg must support cabinet policy. Those seeking to pass or defeat legislation in such systems must apply pressure on the cabinet or national party leaders.

American election research conducted by Paul Lazarsfeld and Angus Campbell in the 1940s and 1950s documented the importance of major structural cleavages like class, region, religion, and ethnicity in determining where voters stood. Increased education and higher rates of social and geographic mobility, however, have reduced the importance of these factors. Correlations between class and party voting have dropped in the United States as well as in other countries. The great decline in the proportion of the American work force belonging to trade unions, from 33 percent in 1955 to 16 percent today, has contributed to the reduction of the importance of class in politics. At the same time, a number of issues less related to socioeconomic status, such as the environment and abortion, have acquired increased salience. The rise of feminism has also played a role, shifting some more-educated, socially liberal women to the left and economically underprivi-

leged, religious, and morally conservative women to the right. With increased assimilation and higher rates of intermarriage, ethnicity and religion have become less important groupings, particularly white Protestants, and the most recent immigrant groupings, particularly Latinos, still maintain communal political ties. It is clear, however, that such cleavages have become less relevant as rallying points of political engagement for citizens.

Civic Engagement

A more debatable source of decline in democratic loyalties and participation has recently been suggested by Robert Putnam. He contends that the traditional networks that have brought together Americans with common views and interests, helping to sustain political parties and political participation, have lost strength over the past few decades. His analysis derives from Alexis de Tocqueville's classic work *Democracy in America*, which emphasized the role of the many voluntary associations that were interposed between citizenry and the state in America. Tocqueville observed that these structures promoted independence, communication, limited government, community participation, political skills, and leadership. He was particularly impressed by religion, which was much stronger in the United States than in many other countries, was not supported by the state, and fostered a myriad of voluntary groups. Tocqueville also emphasized the importance of the institutions of civil society in the creation and maintenance of democratic cultural norms.

Following Tocqueville's logic, Putnam suggests that a

major reason for the decline in civic virtue and political activism in the United States is a weakening of the institutions of civil society. According to Putnam, participation in public life—or, to use his term, "civic engagement"—has fallen precipitously over the past three decades, as indicated by declining membership in many types of civic associations, from religious groups to women's clubs and bowling leagues. These changes are important, because "researchers in such fields as education, urban poverty, unemployment, the control of crime and drug abuse, and even health have discovered that successful outcomes are more likely in civically engaged communities."

Putnam explores several possible explanations for the drop in associational membership, including the movement of women into the labor force, the decline in the size and stability of the family, and high rates of geographic mobility. He particularly emphasizes the impact of television, noting that the increase in time spent watching television has "dwarfed all other changes in the way Americans pass their days and nights." Other technological developments have also contributed to the individualization of the use of leisure time. For example, changes in the ways people listen to music—development of the cassette tape, the compact disc, and the Walkman—have helped "privatize" Americans and reduce their interpersonal contacts outside of work.

News Media

The timing of the decline of trust in institutions corresponds with that of changes in exposure to the media. NORC found that the proportion of the population watching television for an hour a day or less decreased from 37 percent in 1964 to 27 percent in 1978 to 22 percent in 1989, before rising slightly to 25 percent in 1993. Those looking at the tube for four hours or more each day climbed from 19 percent in 1964 to 28 percent in 1993. At the same time, the proportion reading a newspaper every day fell from 73 percent in 1967 to 46 percent in 1993. Gallup polls report a drop in the percentage of people indicating that they "read a daily newspaper yesterday" from 71 percent in 1965 to 45 percent in 1995. Meanwhile, the proportion of "watched news on TV yesterday" increased from 55 percent in 1965 to 61 percent in 1995.

While the positing of a relationship between declining levels of associational membership and the fall off in political participation is logical, a close look at the evidence suggests that civil society remains relatively healthy in the United States. Comparative survey data, for example, still confirm Tocqueville's conclusion that Americans are more civically engaged than most other people in the world. According to the World Values Survey of 1990, the United States has considerably higher rates of membership in voluntary organizations than any other nation. Eighty-two percent of Americans belong to at least one of 16 types of voluntary organizations, as compared to 53 percent of Germans, 39 percent of the French, 36 percent of Italians, and 36 percent of the Japanese. Moreover, Americans have the highest rates of membership in almost all of the 16 types of organizations, with trade unions being the main exception. With regard to charitable or social-service activities, 49 percent of Americans

reported volunteering in 1990–91, as compared to 13 percent of Germans and 19 percent of the French. A higher percentage—73 percent—contributed money to such causes, as compared to 43 to 44 percent of the French and Germans; American contributors also gave much more per capita. The proportion of the adult population in the United States that volunteers for community-service activities climbed in Gallup polls from 27 percent in 1977 to 54 percent in 1989, before falling to 46 percent in 1994.

Religious Groups

Americans are clearly the most religiously committed people in Christendom, with the exception of a few countries like Ireland and Poland, where religion and nationalism are inter-twined. But there is conflicting information about trends. With regard to membership in church-affiliated groups, NORC reports a drop from 42 percent in 1974 to 35 percent in 1993, with the greatest part of the decline occurring in the late 1970s. Gallup, on the other hand, reports that membership in churches and synagogues has remained steady at about two-thirds, and that the rate of weekly church attendance has fluctuated only slightly, with the figure for 1994 (38 percent) almost identical to those for 1950 (39 percent) and 1987 (40 percent).

Certain civic groups like the National Organization of Women, the Sierra Club, and the American Association of Retired Persons have also grown, as Putnam reports. The latter increased from 400,000 dues-paying members in 1960 to 33 million in 1993. Yet as Jeffrey Berry notes, and Putnam agrees, they have a "cheap membership" being essentially lobby-

ing and mailing-list groups rather than the type of associations, described by Tocqueville, that promote civic engagement.

Between 1974 and 1993, NORC regularly inquired about the interpersonal relations of Americans using three different questions concerning frequency of visits with relatives, neighbors, and friends. The percentage of Americans reporting that they visited with neighbors "daily to several times a month" decreased from 44 percent in 1974 to 33.5 percent in 1993. During the same interval, the percentage spending time regularly with relatives fell much less, from 57 percent to 52 percent; the percentage seeing friends regularly actually increased, from 40 percent to 45 percent.

Data on participation in informal groups are obviously relevant here. Robert Wuthnow's 1990 study of the informal small-groups movement, based on a Gallup poll, personal interviews, and in-depth case studies, found that 40 percent of Americans over the age of 18 participate regularly in a small group in which they find mutual caring and support. The main reasons given for joining these groups are "to gain a feeling of community" and "to find spirituality." In accordance with these groups' pragmatic focus, entry and exit requirements are minimal and few demands are made of members. Despite the flexibility of these "rules," three-fourths of the groups have existed for more than five years, and most have lasted longer than the current membership has been involved. Nearly half of the participants have been members of small groups for five or more years. Wuthnow's conclusion is that, although these groups make participants feel good, they do not challenge members to make significant commitments to others or to the large community.

The thesis that the vitality of civil society, as reflected by the level of participation in voluntary organizations, is linked to the strength of democracy is nearly two centuries old. It implies, as Putnam suggests, that the two should move in tandem. Much of the available evidence on trends supports Putnam's conclusion that Americans' involvement in voluntary organizations has declined. Yet there are enough data to the contrary to warrant the Scottish verdict of "not proven"— to which I would add "but probable." Clearly, more research in this area is needed.

The Survival of the American Dream

Given the bad news about attitudes toward governance in the United States—feelings that have persisted or intensified since Newt Gingrich became House Speaker—what accounts for the continued stability of the American political system? Why are we not witnessing mass unrest or grievous forms of opposition? Why is the major protest movement—that led by Ross Perot—basically centrist, even conservative, with respect to economic and social policy? Part of the answer lies in the continued, though perhaps somewhat diminished, strength of American civic culture. As detailed above, volunteering for charitable causes, some types of organizational membership, and religious activities have increased or remained constant, and the United States remains ahead of other nations in its level of citizen participation in volun-

tary institutions. Perhaps even more important is the evidence that most Americans are not unhappy about their personal lives or prospects: in fact, they show considerable optimism about the future. They still view the United States as a country that rewards personal integrity and hard work, as a nation that—government and politics aside—still "works."

The American Dream is still alive, even if the government and other institutions are seen as corrupt and inefficient. A 1994 survey-based study conducted for the Hudson Institute found that over four-fifths of Americans, or 81 percent, agree with the statement, "I am optimistic about my personal future." Three-quarters, or 74 percent, agreed with the statement "In America, if you work hard, you can be anything you want to be." Not surprisingly, when asked to choose between "having the opportunity to succeed" and "having security from failing," over three-quarters, or 76 percent, opted for the former, with only one-fifth preferring security.

A 1994 Gallup poll for Times Mirror yielded similar results. Over two-thirds of respondents, or 67 percent, said that they expected their financial situation to improve "a lot" or "some"; only 14 percent said it would get worse. Large majorities rejected the statement "Success in life is pretty much determined by forces outside our control." Most affirmed the traditional American laissez-faire ideology, with 88 percent agreeing with the statement "I admire people who get rich by working hard," and 85 percent agreeing that "poor people have become too dependent on government assistance programs." Perhaps more significant, 78 per-

cent endorsed the view "The strength of this country today is mostly based on the success of American business."

Income Inequality

Such views persist despite the hard evidence that income inequality is increasing and is greater in the United States than in most European nations and Japan. The explanation for this pattern may lie in America's cultural emphasis on meritocracy and upward mobility. And greater proportions, in fact, do rise into the more privileged sectors in the United States than elsewhere. Given the strength of the aspiration to do so, it is not surprising that Americans are more disposed to approve of high salaries for "stars" in entertainment, athletics, and the market in general—that is, for achievers at every level. Comparative survey research indicates that Americans are much more approving of sizeable income differences than both Europeans and the Japanese. Support for the overall system is also reinforced by a relatively low unemployment rate—currently between 5 and 6 percent. There is certainly some unhappiness about the economy and income distribution in the United States, which reinforces other sources of political malaise, but is much less pronounced than elsewhere.

Clearly, the American political system—though distrusted and ineffective in dealing with major social problems—is in no real danger. Most Americans remain highly patriotic and religious, believe that they are living in the best society in the world, and think that their country, in spite of its problems, still offers them opportunity and good prospects for economic security. Although the effects of the Great Depression of the 1930s were worse in the United States than in most of Europe, America came out of it with its party system, state institutions, and material values intact. The polity will no doubt survive the current wave of political malaise as well.

What Is to Be Done?

The United States does exhibit major symptoms of decline that cannot be ignored. There has been a definite falloff in political participation, in popular confidence in the political system and other major institutions, and in adherence to the traditional party system, as well as a weakening of some of the voluntary institutions of civil society and—perhaps most important of all—of trust in one another. The rise of television and other new technologies appears to be exacerbating the difficulties.

Political parties constitute a crucial civic institution. Their increasing weakness, in combination with the inherent vulnerabilities of the internally conflicted American political system, is producing an image of governmental impotence or "gridlock." Paradoxically, as government has become bigger, absorbing old institutions and

taking on new roles, it has become less effective. Citizens feel (and in fact are) more dependent on a government that they trust less, and their distrust has rendered government less capable. Moreover, there is no consensus regarding how American political institutions should be reformed.

What is to be done? Or, rather, what can be done? Obviously, there is no simple answer. Yet we can identify a general direction. One option is the strengthening of political parties—that is, the re-creation of machines. While no one would advocate a return to patronage politics, the expansion of nomination primaries, the election of presidential convention delegates through proportional representation, and the restriction of campaign donations have all served to undermine parties. "Progressive" campaign reforms have forced candidates and officeholders to devote much of their time to fund-raising, which in turn has made them more dependent on those who can mobilize contributions, generally interest groups. Primaries have had similar effects and have strengthened the influence of dedicated ideological extremists.

Realistically, however, it is extremely doubtful that policies enhancing party organization will be adopted. Government funding of campaigns may be increased.

Dependence on expensive television coverage may be reduced by adopting the practice followed in Britain and some other countries of limiting or outlawing paid political spots and requiring the stations to give free time to all candidates. But most of the negative forces cited here are unlikely to be reversed by purposeful social action. Perhaps the cycle of malaise that was initiated by reactions to the Vietnam War and reinforced by subsequent scandals, economic downturns, and a series of ineffective presidents will be broken by a new, more charismatic leader who presides over a prosperous economy. Such an outcome, however, is not in the hands of the electorate or the analysts.

Tocqueville was indeed correct in stressing the importance of the voluntary institutions of civil society. That base, as we have seen, is still relatively strong in the United States. Americans remain more active in voluntary associations and more willing to contribute to nongovernmental organizations than citizens in any other country. Voluntarism seemingly is the reverse of statism. Election results and opinion polls indicate that Americans are the most antistatist people in the world, as well as the strongest exponents of the independent sector.

 Article Review Form at end of book.

Why do advertisers try to exert editorial control at magazines? How do advertisers help to reinforce stereotypes?

Sex, Lies and Advertising

Suppose archaeologists of the future dug up women's magazines and used them to judge American women. What would they think of us—and what can we do about it?

Gloria Steinem

Gloria Steinem was a founding editor of Ms. *in 1972 and is now its consulting editor. She is also at work on* The Bedside Book of Self-Esteem *for Little Brown.*

About three years ago, as *glasnost* was beginning, and *Ms.* seemed to be ending, I was invited to a press lunch for a Soviet official. He entertained us with anecdotes about new problems of democracy in his country. Local Communist leaders were being criticized in their media for the first time, he explained, and they were angry.

"So I'll have to ask my American friends," he finished pointedly, "how more *subtly* to control the press." In the silence that followed, I said, "Advertising."

The reporters laughed, but later, one of them took me aside: How *dare* I suggest that freedom of the press was limited? How dare I imply that his newsweekly could be influenced by ads?

I explained that I was thinking of advertising's media-wide influence on most of what we read. Even newsmagazines use "soft" cover stories to sell ads, confuse readers with "advertorials," and occasionally self-censor on subjects known to be a problem with big advertisers.

But, I also explained, I was thinking especially of women's magazines. There, it isn't just a little content that's devoted to attracting ads, it's almost all of it. That's why advertisers—not readers—have always been the problem for *Ms.* As the only women's magazine that didn't supply what the ad world euphemistically describes as "supportive editorial atmosphere" or "complementary copy" (for instance, articles that praise food/fashion/beauty subjects to "support" and "complement" food/fashion/beauty ads), *Ms.* could never attract enough advertising to break even.

"Oh, *women's* magazines," the journalist said with contempt. "Everybody knows they're catalogs—but who cares? They have nothing to do with journalism."

I can't tell you how many times I've had this argument in 25 years of working for many kinds of publications. Except as money-making machines—"cash cows" as they are so elegantly called in the trade—women's magazines are rarely taken seriously. Though changes being made by women have been called more far-reaching than the industrial revolution—and though many editors try hard to reflect some of them in the few pages left to them after all the ad-related subjects have been covered—the magazines serving the female half of this country are still far below the journalistic and ethical standards of news and general interest publications. Most depressing of all, this doesn't even rate an exposé.

If *Time* and *Newsweek* had to lavish praise on cars in general and credit General Motors in particular to get GM ads, there would be a scandal—maybe a criminal investigation. When women's magazines from *Seventeen* to *Lear's* praise beauty products in general and credit Revlon in particular to get ads, it's just business as usual.

Gloria Steinem, "Sex, Lies, and Advertising," MS. July/August 1990, p. 18. Reprinted by permission of the author.

When *Ms.* began, we didn't consider *not* taking ads. The most important reason was keeping the price of a feminist magazine low enough for most women to afford. But the second and almost equal reason was providing a forum where women and advertisers could talk to each other and improve advertising itself. After all, it was (and still is) as potent a source of information in this country as news or TV and movie dramas.

We decided to proceed in two stages. First, we would convince makers of "people products" used by both men and women but advertised mostly to men—cars, credit cards, insurance, sound equipment, financial services, and the like—that their ads should be placed in a women's magazine. Since they were accustomed to the division between editorial and advertising in news and general interest magazines, this would allow our editorial content to be free and diverse. Second, we would add the best ads for whatever traditional "women's products" (clothes, shampoo, fragrance, food, and so on) that surveys showed *Ms.* readers used. But we would ask them to come in *without* the usual quid pro quo of "complementary copy."

We knew the second step might be harder. Food advertisers have always demanded that women's magazines publish recipes and articles on entertaining (preferably ones that name their products) in return for their ads; clothing advertisers expect to be surrounded by fashion spreads (especially ones that credit their designers); and shampoo, fragrance, and beauty products in general usually insist on positive

editorial coverage of beauty subjects, plus photo credits besides. That's why women's magazines look the way they do. But if we could break this link between ads and editorial content, then we wanted good ads for "women's products" too.

By playing their part in this unprecedented mix of *all* the things our readers need and use, advertisers also would be rewarded: ads for products like cars and mutual funds would find a new growth market; the best ads for women's products would no longer be lost in oceans of ads for the same category; and both would have access to a laboratory of smart and caring readers whose response would help create effective ads for other media as well.

I thought then that our main problem would be the imagery in ads themselves. Carmakers were still draping blondes in evening gowns over the hoods like ornaments. Authority figures were almost always male, even in ads for products that only women used. Sadistic, he-man campaigns even won industry praise. (For instance, *Advertising Age* had hailed the infamous Silva Thin cigarette theme, "How to Get a Woman's Attention: Ignore Her," as "brilliant.") Even in medical journals, tranquilizer ads showed depressed housewives standing beside piles of dirty dishes and promised to get them back to work.

Obviously, *Ms.* would have to avoid such ads and seek out the best ones—but this didn't seem impossible. *The New Yorker* has been selecting ads for aesthetic reasons for years, a practice that only seemed to make advertisers more eager to be in its pages. *Ebony* and *Essence* were asking for ads with positive black images,

and though their struggle was hard, they weren't being called unreasonable.

Clearly, what *Ms.* needed was a very special publisher and ad sales staff. I could think of only one woman with experience on the business side of magazines—Patricia Carbine, who recently had become a vice president of *McCall's* as well as its editor in chief—and the reason I knew her name was a good omen. She had been managing editor at *Look* (really *the* editor, but its owner refused to put a female name at the top of his masthead) when I was writing a column there. After I did an early interview with Cesar Chavez, then just emerging as a leader of migrant labor, and the publisher turned it down because he was worried about ads from Sunkist, Pat was the one who intervened. As I learned later, she had told the publisher she would resign if the interview wasn't published. Mainly because *Look* couldn't afford to lose Pat, it *was* published (and the ads from Sunkist never arrived).

Though I barely knew this women, she had done two things I always remembered: put her job on the line in a way that editors often talk about but rarely do, and been so loyal to her colleagues that she never told me or anyone outside *Look* that she had done so.

Fortunately, Pat did agree to leave *McCall's* and take a huge cut in salary to become publisher of *Ms.* She became responsible for training and inspiring generations of young women who joined the *Ms.* ad sales force, many of whom went on to become "firsts" at the top of publishing. When *Ms.* first started, however, there were so few women with experience selling space that Pat and I made the rounds of ad agencies ourselves. Later, the fact that *Ms.* was asking companies to do business in a different way meant our saleswomen had to make many times the usual number of calls—first to convince agencies and then client companies besides—and to present endless amounts of research. I was often asked to do a final ad presentation, or see some higher decision-maker, or speak to women employees so executives could see the interest of women they worked with. That's why I spent more time persuading advertisers than editing or writing for *Ms.* and why I ended up with an unsentimental education in the seamy underside of publishing that few writers see (and even fewer magazines can publish).

I ended up with an unsentimental education in the seamy underside of publishing that few writers see and even fewer magazines can publish.

Let me take you with us through some experiences, just as they happened:

• Cheered on by early support from Volkswagen and one or two other car companies, we scrape together time and money to put on a major reception in Detroit. We know U.S. carmakers firmly believe that women choose the upholstery, not the car, but we are armed with statistics and reader mail to prove the contrary: a car is an important purchase for women, one that symbolizes mobility and freedom.

But almost nobody comes. We are left with many pounds of shrimp on the table, and quite a lot of egg on our face. We blame ourselves for not guessing that there would be a baseball pennant play-off on the same day, but executives go out of their way to explain they wouldn't have come anyway. Thus begins ten years of knocking on hostile doors, presenting endless documentation, and hiring full-time saleswomen in Detroit; all necessary before *Ms.* gets any real results.

This long saga has a semi-happy ending: foreign and, later, domestic carmakers eventually provided *Ms.* with enough advertising to make cars one of our top sources of ad revenue. Slowly, Detroit began to take the women's market seriously enough to put car ads in other women's magazines, too, thus freeing a few pages from the hothouse of fashion-beauty-food ads.

But long after the figures showed a third, even a half, of many car models being bought by women, U.S. makers continued to be uncomfortable addressing women. Unlike foreign carmakers, Detroit never quite learned the secret of creating intelligent ads that exclude no one, and then placing them in women's magazines to overcome past exclusion. (*Ms.* readers were so grateful for a routine Honda ad featuring rack and pinion steering, for instance, that they sent fan mail.) Even now, Detroit continues to ask, "Should we make special ads for women?" Perhaps that's why foreign cars still have a disproportionate share of the U.S. women's market.

• In the *Ms.* Gazette, we do a brief report on a congressional hearing into chemicals used in hair dyes that are absorbed through the skin and may be carcinogenic. Newspapers report this too, but Clairol, a Bristol-Myers subsidiary that makes dozens of products—a few of which have just begun to advertise in *Ms.*—is outraged. Not at newspapers or newsmagazines, just at us. It's bad enough that *Ms.* is the only women's magazine refusing to provide the usual "complementary" articles and beauty photos, but to criticize one of their categories—*that* is going too far.

We offer to publish a letter from Clairol telling its side of the story. In an excess of solicitousness, we even put this letter in the Gazette, not in Letters to the Editors where it belongs. Nonetheless—and in spite of surveys that show *Ms.* readers are active women who use more of almost everything Clairol makes than do the readers of any other women's magazine—*Ms.* gets almost none of these ads for the rest of its natural life.

Meanwhile, Clairol changes its hair coloring formula, apparently in response to the hearings we reported.

• Our saleswomen set out early to attract ads for consumer electronics: sound equipment, calculators, computers, VCRs, and the like. We know that our readers are determined to be included in the technological revolution. We know from reader surveys that *Ms.* readers are buying this stuff in numbers as high as those of magazines like *Playboy;* or "men 18 to 34," the prime targets of the consumer electronics industry. Moreover, unlike traditional women's products that our readers buy but don't need to read articles about, these are subjects they want covered in our pages. There actually *is* a supportive editorial atmosphere.

"But women don't understand technology," say executives at the end of ad presentations. "Maybe not," we respond, "but neither do men—and we all buy it."

"If women *do* buy it," say the decision-makers, "they're asking their husbands and boyfriends what to buy first." We produce letters from *Ms.* readers saying how turned off they are when salesmen say things like "Let me know when your husband can come in."

After several years of this, we get a few ads for compact sound systems. Some of them from JVC, whose vice president, Harry Elias, is trying to convince his Japanese bosses that there is something called a women's market. At his invitation, I find myself speaking at huge trade shows in Chicago and Las Vegas, trying to persuade JVC dealers that showrooms don't have to be locker rooms where women are made to feel unwelcome. But as it turns out the shows themselves are part of the problem. In Las Vegas, the only women around the technology displays are seminude models serving champagne. In Chicago, the big attraction is Marilyn Chambers, who followed Linda Lovelace of *Deep Throat* fame as Chuck Traynor's captive and/or employee. VCRs are being demonstrated with her porn videos.

In the end, we get ads for a car stereo now and then, but no VCRs; some IBM personal computers, but no Apple or Japanese ones. We notice that office magazines like *Working Woman* and *Savvy* don't benefit as much as they should from office equipment ads either. In the electronics world, women and technology seem mutually exclusive. It remains a decade behind even Detroit.

• Because we get letters from little girls who love toy trains, and who ask our help in changing ads

and box-top photos that feature little boys only, we try to get toy-train ads from Lionel. It turns out that Lionel executives *have* been concerned about little girls. They made a pink train, and were surprised when it didn't sell.

Lionel bows to consumer pressure with a photograph of a boy *and* a girl—but only on some of their boxes. They fear that, if trains are associated with girls, they will be devalued in the minds of boys. Needless to say, *Ms.* gets no train ads, and little girls remain a mostly unexplored market. By 1986, Lionel is put up for sale.

But for different reasons, we haven't had much luck with other kinds of toys either. In spite of many articles on child-rearing; an annual listing of nonsexist, multi-racial toys by Letty Cottin Pogrebin; stories for Free Children, a regular feature also edited by Letty; and other prizewinning features for or about children, we get virtually no toy ads. Generations of *Ms.* saleswomen explain to toy manufacturers that a larger proportion of *Ms.* readers have

preschool children than do the readers of other women's magazines, but this industry can't believe feminists have or care about children.

• When *Ms.* begins, the staff decides not to accept ads for feminine hygiene sprays or cigarettes: they are damaging and carry no appropriate health warnings. Though we don't think we should tell our readers what to do, we do think we should provide facts so they can decide for themselves. Since the antismoking lobby has been pressing for health warnings on cigarette ads, we decide to take them only as they comply.

Philip Morris is among the first to do so. One of its brands, Virginia Slims, is also sponsoring women's tennis and the first national polls of women's opinions. On the other hand, the Virginia Slims theme, "You've come a long way, baby," has more than a "baby" problem. It makes smoking a symbol of progress for women.

We explain to Philip Morris that this slogan won't do well in our pages, but they are convinced its success with some women means it will work with *all* women. Finally, we agree to publish an ad for a Virginia Slims calendar as a test. The letters from readers are critical—and smart. For instance: Would you show a black man picking cotton, the same man in a Cardin suit, and symbolize the antislavery and civil rights movements by smoking? Of course not. But instead of honoring the test results, the Philip Morris people seem angry to be proven wrong. They take away ads for *all* their many brands.

This costs *Ms.* about $250,000 the first year. After five years, we can no longer keep track. Occasionally, a new set of executives listens to *Ms.* saleswomen, but because we won't take Virginia Slims, not one Philip Morris product returns to our pages for the next 16 years.

Gradually, we also realize our naiveté in thinking we *could* decide against taking cigarette ads. They became a disproportionate support of magazines the moment they were banned on television, and few magazines could compete and survive without them; certainly not *Ms.*, which lacks so many other categories. By the time statistics in the 1980s showed that women's rate of lung cancer was approaching men's, the necessity of taking cigarette ads has become a kind of prison.

• General Mills, Pillsbury, Carnation, DelMonte, Dole, Kraft, Stouffer, Hormel, Nabisco: you name the food giant, we try it. But no matter how desirable the *Ms.* readership, our lack of recipes is lethal.

We explain to them that placing food ads *only* next to recipes associates food with work. For many women, it is a negative that works *against* the ads. Why not place food ads in diverse media without recipes (thus reaching more men, who are now a third of the shoppers in supermarkets anyway), and leave the recipes to specialty magazines like *Gourmet* (a third of whose readers are also men)?

When women's magazines from *Lear's* to *Seventeen* praise beauty products in order to get ads, it's just business as usual.

These arguments elicit interest, but except for an occasional ad for a convenience food, instant coffee, diet drinks, yogurt, or such extras as avocados and almonds, this mainstay of the publishing industry stays closed to us. Period.

• Traditionally, wines and liquors didn't advertise to women: men were thought to make the brand decisions, even if women did the buying. But after endless presentations, we begin to make a dent in this category. Thanks to the unconventional Michel Roux of Carillon Importers (distributors of Grand Marnier, Absolut Vodka, and others), who assumes that food and drink have no gender, some ads are leaving their men's club.

Beermakers are still selling masculinity. It takes *Ms.* fully eight years to get its first beer ad (Michelob). In general, however, liquor ads are less stereotyped in their imagery—and far less controlling of the editorial content around them—than are women's

products. But given the underrepresentation of other categories, these very facts tend to create a disproportionate number of alcohol ads in the pages of *Ms.* This in turn dismays readers worried about women and alcoholism.

• We hear in 1980 that women in the Soviet Union have been producing feminist *samizdat* (underground, self-published books) and circulating them throughout the country. As punishment, four of the leaders have been exiled. Though we are operating on our usual shoestring, we solicit individual contributions to send Robin Morgan to interview these women in Vienna.

The result is an exclusive cover story that includes the first news of a populist peace movement against the Afghanistan occupation, a prediction of *glasnost* to come, and a grass-roots, intimate interview of Soviet women's lives. From the popular press to women's studies courses, the response is great. The story wins a Front Page award.

Nonetheless, this journalistic coup undoes years of efforts to get an ad schedule from Revlon. Why? Because the Soviet women on our cover *are not wearing makeup.*

• Four years of research and presentations go into convincing airlines that women now make travel choices and business trips. United, the first airline to advertise in *Ms.*, is so impressed with the response from our readers that one of its executives appears in a film for our ad presentations. As usual, good ads get great results.

But we have problems unrelated to such results. For instance:

because American Airlines flight attendants include among their labor demands the stipulation that they could choose to have their last names preceded by "Ms." on their name tags—in a long-delayed revolt against the standard, "I am your pilot, Captain Rothgart, and this is your flight attendant, Cindy Sue"— American officials seem to hold the magazine responsible. We get no ads.

There is still a different problem at Eastern. A vice president cancels subscriptions for thousands of copies on Eastern flights. Why? Because he is offended by ads for lesbian poetry journals in the *Ms.* Classified. A "family airline," as he explains to me coldly on the phone, has to "draw the line somewhere."

It's obvious that *Ms.* can't exclude lesbians and serve women. We've been trying to make that point ever since our first issue included an article by and about lesbians, and both Suzanne Levine, our managing editor, and I were lectured by such heavy hitters as Ed Kosner, then editor of *Newsweek* (and now of *New York Magazine*), who insisted that *Ms.* should "position" itself *against* lesbians. But our advertisers have paid to reach a guaranteed number of readers, and soliciting new subscriptions to compensate for Eastern would cost $150,000, plus rebating money in the meantime.

Like almost everything ad-related, this presents an elaborate organizing problem. After days of searching for sympathetic members of the Eastern board, Frank Thomas, president of the Ford Foundation, kindly offers to call Roswell Gilpatrick, a director of Eastern. I talk with Mr. Gilpatrick, who calls Frank Borman, then the president of Eastern. Frank Borman calls me to say that his airline is not in the business of censoring magazines: *Ms.* will be returned to Eastern flights.

• Women's access to insurance and credit is vital, but with the exception of Equitable and a few other ad pioneers, such financial services address men. For almost a decade after the Equal Credit Opportunity Act passes in 1974, we try to convince American Express that women are a growth market—but nothing works.

Finally, a former professor of Russian named Jerry Welsh becomes head of marketing. He assumes that women should be cardholders, and persuades his colleagues to feature women in a campaign. Thanks to this 1980s series, the growth rate for female cardholders surpasses that for men.

For this article, I asked Jerry Welsh if he would explain why American Express waited so long. "Sure," he said, "they were afraid of having a 'pink' card."

• Women of color read *Ms.* in disproportionate numbers. This is a source of pride to *Ms.* staffers, who are also more racially representative than the editors of other women's magazines. But this reality is obscured by ads filled with enough white women to make a reader snowblind.

Pat Carbine remembers mostly "astonishment" when she requested African American, Hispanic, Asian, and other diverse images. Marcia Ann Gillespie, a *Ms.* editor who was previously the editor in chief of *Essence*, witnesses ad bias a sec-ond time: having tried for *Essence* to get white advertisers to use black images (Revlon did so eventually, but L'Oréal, Lauder, Chanel, and other companies never did), she sees similar problems getting integrated ads for an integrated magazine. Indeed, the ad world often creates black and Hispanic ads only for black and Hispanic media. In an exact parallel of the fear that marketing a product to women will endanger its appeal to men, the response is usually, "But your [white] readers won't identify."

In fact, those we are able to get—for instance, a Max Factor ad made for *Essence* that Linda Wachner gives us after she becomes president—are praised by white readers, too. But there are pathetically few such images.

• By the end of 1986, production and mailing costs have risen astronomically, ad income is flat, and competition for ads is stiffer than ever. The 60/40 preponderance of edit over ads that we promised to readers becomes 50/50: children's stories, most poetry, and some fiction are casualties of less space; in order to get variety into limited pages, the length (and sometimes the depth) of articles suffers; and, though we do refuse most of the ads that would look like a parody in our pages, we get so worn down that some slip through. (See this issue's No Comment.)* Still, readers perform miracles. Though we haven't been able to afford a subscription mailing in two years, they maintain our guaranteed circulation of 450,000.

*Does not appear in this publication.

> **It turns out Lionel executives *have* been concerned about little girls. They made a pink train and were surprised when it didn't sell.**

Nonetheless, media reports on *Ms.* often insist that our unprofitability must be due to reader disinterest. The myth that advertisers simply follow readers is very strong. Not one reporter notes that other comparable magazines our size (say, *Vanity Fair* or *The Atlantic*) have been losing more money in one year than *Ms.* has lost in 16 years. No matter how much never-to-be-recovered cash is poured into starting a magazine or keeping one going, appearances seem to be all that matter. (Which is why we haven't been able to explain our fragile state in public. Nothing causes ad-flight like the smell of nonsuccess.)

My healthy response is anger. My not-so-healthy response is constant worry. Also an obsession with finding one more rescue. There is hardly a night when I don't wake up with sweaty palms and pounding heart, scared that we won't be able to pay the printer or the post office; scared most of all that closing our doors will hurt the women's movement.

Out of chutzpah and desperation, I arrange a lunch with Leonard Lauder, president of Estée Lauder. With the exception of Clinique (the brainchild of Carol Phillips), none of Lauder's hundreds of products has been advertised in *Ms.* A year's schedule of ads for just three or four of them could save us. Indeed, as the scion of a family-owned company whose ad practices are followed by the beauty industry, he is one of the few men who could liberate many pages in all women's magazines just by changing his mind about "complementary copy."

Over a lunch that costs more than we can pay for some articles, I explain the need for his leadership. I also lay out the record of *Ms.*: more literary and journalistic

prizes won, more new issues introduced into the mainstream, new writers discovered, and impact on society than any other magazine; more articles that became books, stores that became movies, ideas that became television series, and newly advertised products that became profitable; and, most important for him, a place for his ads to reach women who aren't reachable through any other women's magazine. Indeed, if there is one constant characteristic of the ever-changing *Ms.* readership, it is their impact as leaders. Whether it's waiting until later to have first babies, or pioneering PABA as sun protection in cosmetics, *whatever* they are doing today, a third to a half of American women will be doing three to five years from now. It's never failed.

But, he says, *Ms.* readers are not *our* women. They're not interested in things like fragrance and blush-on. If they were, *Ms.* would write articles about them.

On the contrary, I explain, surveys show they are more likely to buy such things than the readers of, say, *Cosmopolitan* or *Vogue*. They're good customers because they're out in the world enough to need several sets of everything: home, work, purse, travel, gym, and so on. They just don't need to read articles about these things. Would he ask a men's magazine to publish monthly columns on how to shave before he advertised Aramis products (his line for men)?

He concedes that beauty features are often concocted more for advertisers than readers. But *Ms.* isn't appropriate for his ads anyway, he explains. Why? Because Estée Lauder is selling "a kept–woman mentality."

I can't quite believe this. Sixty percent of the users of his products are salaried, and gener-

ally resemble *Ms.* readers. Besides, his company has the appeal of having been started by a creative and hardworking woman, his mother, Estée Lauder.

That doesn't matter, he says. He knows his customers, and they would *like* to be kept women. That's why he will never advertise in *Ms.*

In November 1987, by a vote of the Ms. Foundation for Education and Communication (*Ms.*'s owner and publisher, the media subsidiary of the Ms. Foundation for Women), *Ms.* was sold to a company whose officers, Australian feminists Sandra Yates and Anne Summers, raised the investment money in their country that *Ms.* couldn't find in its own. They also started *Sassy* for teenage women.

In their two-year tenure, circulation was raised to 550,000 by investment in circulation mailings, and, to the dismay of some readers, editorial features on clothes and new products made a more traditional bid for ads. Nonetheless, ad pages fell below previous levels. In addition, *Sassy*, whose fresh voice and sexual frankness were an unprecedented success with young readers, was targeted by two mothers from Indiana who began, as one of them put it, "calling every Christian organization I could think of." In response to this controversy, several crucial advertisers pulled out.

Such links between ads and editorial content was a problem in Australia, too, but to a lesser degree. "Our readers pay two times more for their magazines," Anne explained, "so advertisers have less power to threaten a magazine's viability."

"I was shocked," said Sandra Yates, with characteristic directness. "In Australia, we think you have freedom of the press—but you don't."

Since Anne and Sandra had not met their budget's projections for ad revenue, their investors forced a sale. In October 1989, *Ms.* and *Sassy* were bought by Dale Lang, owner of *Working Mother, Working Woman,* and one of the few independent publishing companies left among the conglomerates. In response to a request from the original *Ms.* staff—as well as to reader letters urging that *Ms.* continue, plus his own belief that *Ms.* would benefit his other magazines by blazing a trail—he agreed to try the ad-free, reader-supported *Ms.* you hold now and to give us complete editorial control.

II.

Do you think, as I once did, that advertisers make decisions based on solid research? Well, think again. "Broadly speaking," says Joseph Smith of Oxtoby-Smith, Inc., a consumer research firm, "there is no persuasive evidence that the editorial context of an ad matters."

Advertisers who demand such "complementary copy," even in the absence of respectable studies, clearly are operating under a double standard. The same food companies place ads in *People* with no recipes. Cosmetics companies support *The New Yorker* with no regular beauty columns. So where does this habit of controlling the content of women's magazines come from?

Tradition. Ever since *Ladies Magazine* debuted in Boston in 1828, editorial copy directed to women has been informed by something other than its readers' wishes. There were no ads then, but in an age when married women were legal minors with no right to their own money, there

was another revenue source to be kept in mind: husbands. "Husbands may rest assured," wrote editor Sarah Josepha Hale, "that nothing found in these pages shall cause her [his wife] to be less assiduous in preparing for his reception or encourage her to 'usurp station' or encroach upon prerogatives of men."

Hale went on to become the editor of *Godey's Lady's Book,* a magazine featuring "fashion plates": engravings of dresses for readers to take to their seamstresses or copy themselves. Hale added "how to" articles, which set the tone for women's service magazines for years to come: how to write politely, avoid sunburn, and—in no fewer than 1,200 words—how to maintain a goose quill pen. She advocated education for women but avoided controversy. Just as most women's magazines now avoid politics, poll their readers on issues like abortion but rarely take a stand, and praise socially approved lifestyles. Hale saw to it that *Godey's* avoided the hot topics of its day: slavery, abolition, and women's suffrage.

What definitively turned women's magazines into catalogs, however, were two events: Ellen Butterick's invention of the clothing pattern in 1863 and the mass manufacture of patent medicines containing everything from colored water to cocaine. For the first time, readers could purchase what magazines encouraged them to want. As such magazines became more profitable, they also began to attract men as editors. (Most women's magazines continued to have men as top editors until the feminist 1970s.) Edward Bok, who became editor of *The Ladies' Home Journal* in 1889, discovered the power of advertisers when he rejected ads for patent medicines

and found that other advertisers canceled in retribution. In the early 20th century, *Good Housekeeping* started its Institute to "test and approve" products. Its Seal of Approval became the grandfather of current "value added" programs that offer advertisers such bonuses as product sampling and department store promotions.

By the time suffragists finally won the vote in 1920, women's magazines had become too entrenched as catalogs to help women learn how to use it. The main function was to create a desire for products, teach how to use products, and make products a crucial part of gaining social approval, pleasing a husband, and performing as a homemaker. Some unrelated articles and short stores were included to persuade women to pay for these catalogs. But articles were neither consumerist nor rebellious. Even fiction was usually subject to formula: if a woman had any sexual life outside marriage, she was supposed to come to a bad end.

In 1965, Helen Gurley Brown began to change part of that formula by bringing "the sexual revolution" to women's magazines—but in an ad-oriented way. Attracting multiple men required even more consumerism, as the Cosmo Girl made clear, than finding one husband.

In response to the workplace revolution of the 1970s, traditional women's magazines—that is, "trade books" for women working at home—were joined by *Savvy, Working Woman,* and other trade books for women working in offices. But by keeping the fashion/beauty/entertaining articles necessary to get traditional ads and then adding career articles besides, they inadvertently produced the antifeminist stereotype of Super Woman. The male-imitative, dress-for-success woman carrying a briefcase became the media image of a woman worker, even though a blue-collar woman's salary was often higher than her glorified secretarial sister's, and though women at a real briefcase level are statistically rare. Needless to say, these dress-for-success women were also thin, white, and beautiful.

By the time suffragists had won the vote, women's magazines were too entrenched as catalogs to help women use political power.

In recent years, advertisers' control over the editorial content of women's magazines has become so institutionalized that it is written into "insertion orders" or dictated to ad salespeople as official policy. The following are recent typical orders to women's magazines:

- Dow Cleaning Products stipulates that ads for its Vivid and Spray 'n Wash products should be adjacent to "children or fashion editorial"; ads for Bathroom Cleaner should be next to "home furnishing/family" features; and so on for other brands. "If a magazine fails for 1/2 the brands or more," the Dow order warns, "it will be omitted from further consideration."

- Bristol-Myers, the parent of Clairol, Windex, Drano, Bufferin, and much more, stipulates that ads be placed next to "a full page of compatible editorial."

- S.C. Johnson & Son, makers of Johnson Wax, lawn and laundry products, insect sprays, hair sprays, and so on, orders that its ads *"should not be opposite extremely controversial features or materials antithetical to*

the nature/copy of the advertised product." (Italics theirs.)

- Maidenform, manufacturer of bras and other apparel, leaves a blank for the particular product and states: "The creative concept of the _____ campaign, and the very nature of the product itself appeal to the positive emotions of the reader/consumer. Therefore, it is imperative that all editorial adjacencies reflect that same positive tone. The editorial must not be negative in content or lend itself contrary to the _____ product imagery/message (e.g., *editorial relating to illness, disillusionment, large size fashion, etc.*)." (Italics mine.)

- The De Beers diamond company, a big seller of engagement rings, prohibits magazines from placing its ads with "adjacencies to hard news or anti/love-romance themed editorial."

- Procter & Gamble, one of this country's most powerful and diversified advertisers, stands out in the memory of Anne Summers and Sandra Yates (no mean feat in this context): its products were not to be placed in *any* issue that included *any* material on gun control, abortion, the occult, cults, or the disparagement of religion. Caution was also demanded in any issue covering sex or drugs, even for educational purposes.

Those are the most obvious chains around women's magazines. There are also rules so clear they needn't be written down: for instance, an overall "look" compatible with beauty and fashion

ads. Even "real" nonmodel women photographed for a woman's magazine are usually made up, dressed in credited clothes, and retouched out of all reality. When editors do include articles on less-than-cheerful subjects (for instance, domestic violence), they tend to keep them short and unillustrated. The point is to be "upbeat." Just as women in the street are asked, "Why don't you smile, honey?" women's magazines acquire an institutional smile.

Within the text itself, praise for advertisers' products has become so ritualized that fields like "beauty writing" have been invented. One of its frequent practitioners explained seriously that "It's a difficult art. How many new adjectives can you find? How much greater can you make a lipstick sound? The FDA restricts what companies can say on labels, but we create illusion. And ad agencies are on the phone all the time pushing you to get their product in. A lot of them keep the business based on how many editorial clippings they produce every month. The worst are products," like Lauder's as the writer confirmed, "with their own name involved. It's all ego."

Often, editorial becomes one giant ad. Last November, for instance, *Lear's* featured an elegant woman executive on the cover. On the contents page, we learned she was wearing Guerlain makeup and Samsara, a new fragrance by Guerlain. Inside were full-page ads for Samsara and Guerlain antiwrinkle cream. In the cover profile, we learned that this executive was responsible for launching Samsara and is Guerlain's director of public relations. When the *Columbia Journalism Review* did one of the few articles to include women's magazines in coverage of the influence of ads, editor Frances Lear was quoted as defending her magazine because "this kind of thing is done all the time."

Often, advertisers also plunge odd-shaped ads into the text, no matter what the cost to the readers. At *Woman's Day,* a magazine originally founded by a supermarket chain, editor in chief Ellen Levine said, "The day the copy had to rag around a chicken leg was not a happy one."

Advertisers are also adamant about where in a magazine their ads appear. When Revlon was not placed as the first beauty ad in one Hearst magazine, for instance, Revlon pulled its ads from *all* Hearst magazines. Ruth Whitney, editor in chief of *Glamour,* attributes some of these demands to "ad agencies wanting to prove to a client that they've squeezed the last drop of blood out of a magazine." She also is, she says, "sick and tired of hearing that women's magazines are controlled by cigarette ads." Relatively speaking, she's right. To be as censoring as are many advertisers for women's products, tobacco companies would have to demand articles in praise of smoking and expect glamorous photos of beautiful women smoking their brands.

I don't mean to imply that the editors I quote here share my objections to ads: most assume that women's magazines have to be the way they are. But it's also true that only former editors can be completely honest. "Most of the pressure came in the form of direct product mentions," explains Sey Chassler, who was editor in chief of *Redbook* from the sixties to the eighties. "We got threats from the big guys, the Revlons, blackmail threats. They wouldn't run ads unless we credited them.

"But it's not fair to single out the beauty advertisers because these pressures came from everybody. Advertisers want to know two things: What are you going to charge me? What *else* are you going to do for me? It's a holdup. For instance, management felt that fiction took up too much space. They couldn't put any advertising in that. For the last ten years, the number of fiction entries into the National Magazine Awards has declined.

"And pressures are getting worse. More magazines are more bottom-line oriented because they have been taken over by companies with no interest in publishing.

"I also think advertisers do this to women's magazines especially," he concluded, "because of the general disrespect they have for women."

Even media experts who don't give a damn about women's magazines are alarmed by the spread of this ad-edit linkage. In a climate *The Wall Street Journal* describes as an acknowledged Depression for media, women's products are increasingly able to take their low standards wherever they go. For instance: newsweeklies publish uncritical stories on fashion and fitness. *The New York Times Magazine* recently ran an article on "firming creams," complete with mentions of advertisers. *Vanity Fair* published a profile of one major advertiser, Ralph Lauren, illustrated

It's been three years away from the grindstone of ad pressures. . . . I'm just realizing how edges got smoothed down—in spite of all our resistance.

by the same photographer who does his ads, and turned the lifestyle of another, Calvin Klein, into a cover story. Even the outrageous *Spy* has toned down since it began to go after fashion ads.

And just to make us really worry, films and books, the last media that go directly to the public without having to attract ads first, are in danger, too. Producers are beginning to depend on payments for displaying products in movies, and books are now being commissioned by companies like Federal Express.

But the truth is that women's products—like women's magazines—have never been the subjects of much serious reporting anyway. News and general interest publications, including the "style" or "living" sections of newspapers, write about food and clothing as cooking and fashion, and almost never evaluate such products by brand name. Though chemical additives, pesticides, and animal fats are major health risks in the United States, and clothes, shoddy or not, absorb more consumer dollars than cars, this lack of information is serious. So is ignoring the contents of beauty products that are absorbed into our bodies through our skins, and that have profit margins so big they would make a loan shark blush.

III.

What could women's magazines be like if they were as free as books? as realistic as newspapers? as creative as films? as diverse as women's lives? We don't know.

But we'll only find out if we take women's magazines seriously. If readers were to act in a concerted way to change traditional practices of *all* women's magazines and the marketing of *all* women's products, we could do it. After all, they are operating on our consumer dollars; money that we now control. You and I could:

- write to editors and publishers (with copies to advertisers) that we're willing to pay *more* for magazines with editorial independence, but will *not* continue to pay for those that are just editorial extensions of ads;

- write to advertisers (with copies to editors and publishers) that we want fiction, political reporting, consumer reporting—whatever is, or is not, supported by their ads;

- put as much energy into breaking advertiser's control over content as into changing the images in ads, or protesting ads for harmful products like cigarettes;

- support only those women's magazines and products that take *us* seriously as readers and consumers.

Those of us in the magazine world can also use the carrot-and-stick technique. For instance: pointing out that, if magazines were a regulated medium like television, the demands of advertisers would be against FCC rules.

Payola and extortion could be punished. As it is, there are probably illegalities. A magazine's postal rates are determined by the ratio of ad to edit pates, and the former costs more than the latter. So much for the stick.

The carrot means appealing to enlightened self-interest. For instance: there are many studies showing that the greatest factor in determining an ad's effectiveness is the credibility of its surroundings. The "higher the rating of editorial believability," concluded a 1987 survey by the *Journal of Advertising Research*, "the higher the rating of the advertising." Thus, an impenetrable wall between edit and ads would also be in the best interest of advertisers.

Unfortunately, few agencies or clients hear such arguments. Editors often maintain the false purity of refusing to talk to them at all. Instead, they see ad salespeople who know little about editorial, are trained in business as usual, and are usually paid by commission. Editors might also band together to take on controversy. That happened once when all the major women's magazines did articles in the same month on the Equal Rights Amendment. It could happen again.

It's almost three years away from life between the grindstones of advertising pressures and readers'

needs. I'm just beginning to realize how edges got smoothed down—in spite of all our resistance.

I remember feeling put upon when I changed "Porsche" to "car" in a piece about Nazi imagery in German pornography by Andrea Dworkin—feeling sure Andrea would understand that Volkswagen, the distributor of Porsche and one of our few supportive advertisers, asked only to be far away from Nazi subjects. It's taken me all this time to realize that Andrea was the one with a right to feel put upon.

Even as I write this, I get a call from a writer for *Elle*, who is doing a whole article on where women part their hair. Why, she wants to know, do I part mine in the middle?

It's all so familiar. A writer trying to make something of a nothing assignment; an editor laboring to think of new ways to attract ads; readers assuming that other women must want this ridiculous stuff; more women suffering for lack of information, insight creativity, and laughter that could be on these same pages.

I ask you: Can't we do better than this?

 Article Review Form at end of book.

Is advertising effective at changing people's attitudes? What are some of the needs that cigarette advertisers appeal to?

Hooked on Tobacco

The teen epidemic

The cigarette industry needs kids to smoke. It's getting plenty. But parents—and the rest of us—can fight back.

Consumers Union

Over the past three decades, the number of smokers in the U.S. has slowly but steadily declined. It's been a true public-health success story: For millions of ex-smokers, the drive for self-preservation has proved stronger than the addictive power of nicotine and the persuasive power of the tobacco industry. But now that progressive trend may come to a halt.The drop in the nation's smoking rate is leveling off, and for a chilling reason: As adult smokers quit, there's a steady supply of teenagers stepping up to replace them.

Every day, 3000 American teen-agers reach adulthood as confirmed cigarette smokers. That's roughly equal to the number of adults who give up smoking or die from the diseases it causes. Most teens started when they were legally too young to smoke; kids under 18 smoke an estimated 17 billion of the 500 billion cigarettes sold each year in

the U.S. Teens are the primary source of new smokers; after they turn 20, almost no one starts.

"Since the first Surgeon General's report in 1964, the public health movement has been very successful in convincing adults not to start smoking," says John Pierce, an epidemiologist at the University of California, San Diego. "But we've had very little impact on kids."

Today, about one in three high school seniors say they smoked in the past month, and about one in five smoke daily. That's particularly alarming because, unlike the teens of 30 or 40 years ago, these new smokers know full well how dangerous cigarettes are; they've been hearing for years that tobacco is addictive and deadly.

Antitobacco and public-health advocates have tried to adapt their messages to teens, using school programs and aggressive ad campaigns. But they have little to show for their efforts. In California, for instance, a $600-million antismoking cam-

paign cut the overall smoking rate by an impressive 30 percent. Yet it couldn't make a dent in the teenage smoking rate—even though nearly $150-million of the money went directly into school programs, and much of the general campaign was targeted at adolescents.

The voices of medical reason are up against forces that can overcome teen-agers' fear of disease and death—at least long enough for the teens to become addicted to nicotine. The tobacco industry has waged a relentless campaign to recruit smokers; in spite of being banned from the airwaves cigarettes are advertised more heavily than any product except cars.

Despite the industry's protests that it has no such intentions, the campaign has clearly snared kids, not only with the infamous Joe Camel, but also with a host of other print advertising, merchandising strategies, and even direct-mail campaigns. Add in the power of peer pressure and the willingness of store owners to sell cigarettes to minors, and it's no wonder that so many teens are hooked.

There is much at stake here. A significant drop in teen-age smoking would cut deep into the tobacco industry's main source of new customers. But from a public-health standpoint, keeping kids away from cigarettes is the single most effective way to fight the nation's leading preventable cause of death.

Everybody's Doing It

"I was 14, at summer sleep-away camp, with all these girls my age who were from New York City. They all smoked and I thought they looked so cool. Smoking was one of my first rebellious acts, you know? All these really cool girls were doing it.

That's how it started for a suburban Connecticut teen-ager we'll call Allison M. (because she believes her parents don't know she smokes). At first it was an occasional thing. By senior year she was up to a pack a day. Now an 18-year-old college freshman and finally buying her *Marlboro Lights* legally, she knows she's addicted, although she never thought that would happen. "I don't think I could quit right now," she says. "I don't want to have to go without a cigarette. I get so irritable if I can't have one when I want to."

Allison's story is typical, says the University of California's John Pierce. "The overriding thing is the image of being cool. They all think they're not going to get addicted, that they can stop—but they can't."

Of course, teens are growing up in a culture that's long been permeated with attractive images of smokers and cigarettes. Hollywood does it's share, but it's cigarette makers who have so thoroughly wallpapered our world that their ads and logos are inescapable. The images they emphasize—in magazines popular with teen-agers, on the billboards they see at sporting events and on the way to school, on the sides of buses, and in the doorways of convenience stores—resonate perfectly with the psychological and social needs of adolescents:

Social acceptance. Cigarette ads play to the craving for popularity. *Newport* ads invariably feature confident-looking young couples having fun together, often with an erotic subtext. *Camel* ads call Joe a "smooth character"; with his saxophone, his panache, his Ray-Bans, and his trendy wardrobe, he looks it. (At a high school we visited, one boy who apparently had absorbed the ads' message volunteered that *Camels* were popular among kids because "they're the strongest and smoothest.")

Personal independence. One of the main developmental tasks of adolescence is to assert independence from one's parents by constructing one's own identity. *Marlboro* has successfully exploited that need for years with its cowboy alone on the range. A *Virginia Slims* campaign last spring said the cigarette was "as free-spirited as you."

Weight control. This theme plays into many teen-age girls' preoccupation with thin figures. *Mistys* are "slim and

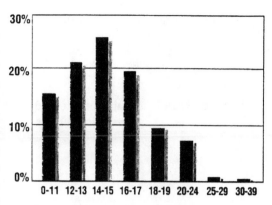

Source: U.S. Centers for Disease Control and Prevention.

When smokers start. Nearly every smoker began as a teen-ager. For a group of people in their 30s who had been daily smokers at some point—or still were—this graph shows their age when they first smoked.

sassy." A *Virginia Slims* ad says, "If I ran the world, calories wouldn't count." The models in the advertisements are extremely thin, wearing fashionable clothes. Even the cigarettes themselves are extra-slender. Fashion and celebrity magazines that help promote an ultra-slim beauty ideal carry plenty of cigarette advertising but rarely speak out editorially about the dangers of smoking.

An advertising executive who had worked on the *Marlboro* account was quoted in the 1994 edition of the annual U.S. Surgeon General's report, which for the first time focused on teen-age smoking. "When all the garbage is stripped away, successful cigarette advertising involves showing the kind of people most people would like to be, doing the things most people would like to do, and smoking up a storm. I don't know any way of doing this that doesn't tempt young people to smoke."

T-Shirts and Tattoos

Ads are just a small part of the tobacco industry's campaign.

Ad Dollars and Teen Smokers

Cigarette makers say their ads are aimed at adults, not kids. But the more money spent on print and outdoor advertising for a particular brand, the more popular it is among underage smokers. Adult smoking preferences don't follow spending quite as closely.

Cigarette Brand	Major-Market Ad Costs, in Millions	Market Share Ages 12–18	Market Share U.S. Overall
Marlboro	$75.6	60%	24%
Camel	42.9	13	4
Newport	34.5	13	5
Kool	20.5	1	3
Winston	17.6	1	7

Sources: Maxwell Consumer Report, Competitive Media Reporting, U.S. Centers for Disease Control and Prevention. All figures are for 1993.

Cigarette makers spend nearly half their marketing money on so-called "value added" promotions like coupons and premiums. Some you can pick up right at the store with your cigarettes. With two packs you get a flashlight or can holder. With four you get a baseball cap. With five you get a T-shirt.

Cigarette makers also rely heavily on catalog promotions. Customers amass bar-codes or certificates—"Camel Cash" is the best-known example—to trade for merchandise. *Marlboro* has sent vans around to convenience-store parking lots so customers can redeem their "Marlboro miles" on the spot. Many products in the catalogs would appeal to adolescents. A *Virginia Slims* "V-wear" catalog last year featured temporary tattoos. A "Camel Cash" catalog included a suede baseball jacket, a beach towel, and a charm bracelet.

Though the catalog order forms require customers to state that they're over 21, these products do find their way into the hands of minors. John Slade, a physician at the University of Medicine and Dentistry of New Jersey who studies tobacco marketing, conducted a nationwide phone survey of chil-

dren age 12 to 17. He found that 11 percent owned at least one promotional item.

Mail-order promotions have enabled tobacco companies to build enormous direct-mail lists of smokers. Slade's poll found that 7.6 percent of teen-agers had received cigarette companies' mail addressed directly to them. Extrapolating to the entire U.S. population this age, Slade estimates that there are 1.6 million teen-agers' names on the companies' mailing lists.

Who's the Target?

Cigarette marketers have a dilemma. Their industry code says they must aim their sales pitch at adults—but market research shows that nearly all smokers start smoking, and become loyal to a specific brand, before adulthood.

The companies insist their marketing efforts don't intentionally target teen-agers. The $5-billion they spend every year on advertising and promotion, they say, is intended to promote their brands among adults who already smoke.

But the tobacco companies' intent hardly matters. There's

abundant evidence that, whether or not the companies plan it, children of all ages are paying close attention to their messages.

Nothing captures this issue as well as R.J. Reynolds's Joe Camel. In 1991, University of Georgia researcher Paul Fischer found that 30 percent of 3-year-olds, and 91 percent of 6-year-olds, could match the Joe Camel cartoon character with the cigarette it was promoting. At the same time, Joseph DiFranza, a physician at the University of Massachusetts who researches tobacco promotion, found that nearly 98 percent of high-school students recognized the character, versus 72 percent of adults. (We saw this for ourselves when we visited a 10th-grade health class and showed students a Joe Camel advertisement. Only one of them said he had no idea who the character was—a boy who had immigrated from Sri Lanka two weeks earlier.)

R.J. Reynolds denied targeting children with the Joe Camel character and hired Richard Mizersky, a University of Florida marketing researcher, to repeat the Fischer study. Like Fischer, he found high recognition rates. But he also asked the children whether they liked cigarettes, and found that "there's clearly no link between recognition and liking." While 41 percent of 3-year-olds said they liked cigarettes, less than 4 percent of the 6-year-olds said so.

Other researchers, however, point out that the response to a straight-forward question like Mizersky's may not predict behavior. Even if young children tell a researcher they don't like cigarettes, they are likely to change their minds many times before adolescence.

Persuaded to Buy?

If you ask teen-agers, they will insist that they could never, ever be influenced by an ad. "I personally don't think advertising had that much bearing on me," Allison M. says. "I can't believe that seeing Joe Camel on a billboard will make a 15-year-old think, 'Oh, Joe Camel smokes cigarettes so I should too.' "

But Slade says this attitude is to be expected. "Advertising at its best leaves impressions and influences people without their noticing it," he says. "It doesn't surprise me that's what people say. But look at what they do."

In fact, there is abundant evidence that cigarette advertising effectively reaches kids before they're even out of middle school, shaping their perceptions and behavior. Several studies have found that adolescents consistently overestimate the number of people who smoke—thinking that smoking is more socially acceptable than it is—and that youngsters exposed to the most advertising overestimate the number the most. When kids begin to experiment with smoking, they experiment with the most heavily advertised brands.

That certainly appears to have been the case with *Camels*. Here is what's known. In 1986, the brand's market share among 17-to-24-years-olds was less than 3 percent. In 1988, Joe Camel was introduced. By 1989, the market share among underage smokers was 8 percent. By 1993, the share among underage smokers had risen to 13 percent.

Similar effects have been seen before. John Pierce, of the University of California, has used decades' worth of Federal health-interview data to reconstruct the change in cigarette brand shares

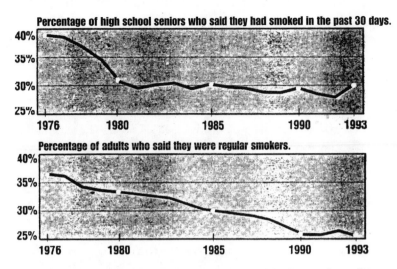

Percentage of high school seniors who said they had smoked in the past 30 days.

Percentage of adults who said they were regular smokers.

Where new smokers come from.   The smoking rate among adults, having dropped for years, has leveled off now. The adult smokers who quit or die are being replaced by a steady supply of young people who began smoking in their teens. Sources: U.S. Centers for Disease Control and Prevention; 'Monitoring the Future,' University of Michigan.

over time, and found they consistently correlate with ad campaigns. For example, the percentage of teen-age girls who started smoking regularly rose sharply in the late 1960s with the introduction of *Virginia Slims*, the first cigarette brand designed and marketed specifically for women. During the same period, the rate for boys didn't change.

Peer Influence

What's happening, Pierce thinks, is that "advertising makes people susceptible" to experimenting with smoking. "But once they're susceptible, advertising doesn't make them want to experiment. Exposure to peers does."

Based on polling of California schoolchildren, Pierce and his colleagues have developed a "smiling susceptibility" scale that captures this process. The first rung on the scale is awareness of ads—which is all but universal. The next steps include believing the ads promote smoking's benefits, having a favorite ad, having a favorite brand, and either owning a cigarette pro-

motional item or being willing to wear one. Kids who score highest on the scale are four times as likely as the lowest-scoring kids to say they might try a cigarette if one of their best friends offered it.

Many studies have established that having a circle of smoking friends powerfully predisposes children to experiment with smoking. Based on interviews with some 5000 Californians aged 12 to 17, Pierce found that teen-agers who had best friends of both sexes who smoked were 13 times as likely to have smoked within the past month as youngsters without smoking fiends. By contrast, having a smoking family member didn't even double the likelihood of a youngster's smoking.

Fortunately, four out of five people make it through high school without becoming daily smokers. Those who do start smoking, research has shown, tend to share certain risk factors: low socioeconomic status, poor school achievement, excessive rebelliousness and risk-taking, low self-esteem, dropping out of school, and not planning on college.

Cherry-Flavored Tobacco Bits: Another Marketing Triumph

Most kids have tried smoking tobacco. But few of them sucked on it—until after the "smokeless tobacco" industry launched an aggressive, 20-year campaign to attract new customers. The promotional effort—the U.S. Surgeon General said in a report last year—succeeded in greatly increasing the product's use among the young.

Most smokeless tobacco is snuff, which users tuck next to their gums. In 1970, snuff was an old man's habit. Federal surveys found that 3.4 percent of men over 65 habitually "dipped," compared with fewer than 1 percent of young men aged 18 to 24. Then ads and promotions from U.S. Tobacco—which dominates the snuff market—started associating the product with rodeos, rock stars and monster trucks. Like cigarette manufacturers, snuff makers vehemently deny marketing their products to underage users. But some ads appeared to "target male adolescents," the Surgeon General said, "by providing explicit instructions for use (sometimes delivered by well-known professional athletes) and by suggesting that the product could be used without adult detection."

By 1991, use of snuff had risen more than 10 times among young men—to 7.5 percent—while actually declining by about one-third among male senior citizens. It's illegal to sell snuff to anyone under 18. But among teen-aged boys, its use is now nearly as common as that of cigarettes. By their last year in high school, half have tried it and one in five are current users. Many users say they first tried it in elementary school. Few girls have tried it.

The way snuff is packaged and formulated helps new users to gradually take up the habit and advance to products with stronger tastes and higher nicotine absorption, the Surgeon General said. U.S. Tobacco's product line includes Skoal Bandits, mint-flavored tobacco wrapped in teabag-like pouches that keep the fragments from floating around in the mouth. Then comes Skoal Long Cut, a loose, coarse-cut product somewhat stronger in taste and nicotine, available in such flavors as winter-green and cherry. The company's best-selling product is the fine-cut, nicotine-laden Copenhagen.

Addiction is common. The nicotine readily enters the bloodstream through the mouth's mucous membranes, and users who try to quit suffer withdrawal symptoms just as severe as a smoker's.

Bathing your mouth daily in an alkaline tobacco solution has health consequences far more immediate than those from smoking cigarettes. The most serious is oral cancer. Studies have found precancerous patches of tissue in the mouths of about half of current teen-age users; with continued tobacco use, about one in 20 such lesions will become cancerous within five years. Smokeless tobacco is also terrible for the gums: They become inflamed and recede. About one-third of teen-age users develop that condition. For these reasons, in 1986 the Surgeon General's report concluded that there was "no safe use" of smokeless tobacco.

None of this appears to apply to African-American teenagers, however. In a cultural shift that has caught public-health authorities by surprise, the smoking rate among black teens, which once matched that of white teens, has dropped steadily since 1976. The percentage of black high-school seniors who smoke daily is now just 4 percent, compared with 23 percent among whites. Health researchers are furiously seeking an explanation. "We want to bottle it, so we can sustain it for black teens and pass it along to white teens," says Michael Eriksen, director of the U.S. Centers for Disease Control and Prevention's Office on Smoking and Health.

Easy to Buy

Teens primed by ads and surrounded by friends who smoke just need a ready source of cigarettes to allow them to progress to outright addiction. No problem.

Although every state outlaws the sale of tobacco products to anyone under 18, study after study has documented that those laws go almost completely unenforced. Some stores are careful not to sell to underage teens, but not enough; "I can count on one hand the number of times I've been carded for a cigarette," says Allison. The youngest smokers often say they buy their cigarettes from vending machines.

Under public pressure, cigarette makers and the Tobacco Institute have attempted to address the problem in several ways; for example, they give tobacco retailers stickers to post by the cash register reminding teenagers that they can't legally buy cigarettes. But the stickers don't appear to make clerks less willing to sell to teens. Joseph DiFranza, the University of Massachusetts researcher, took five underage teenagers to 156 central Massachusetts stores. They were able to buy cigarettes at 137 stores, including six of the seven displaying the sticker.

What Should Be Done

According to the latest data, half of all lifelong smokers will die prematurely—an average of eight years early. For that reason alone, halting the teen-age smoking epidemic must be a public-health priority. But how?

Last year, an expert panel of the National Academy of Sciences addressed the question and recommended three major strategies: Banning nearly all cigarette advertising and promotion, raising cigarette taxes to make smoking less affordable, and enforcing the laws against selling to teens.

Advertising

Ideally, we'd like to see Congress ban *all* cigarette advertising and also all promotional uses of cigarette-brand logos. Many tobacco-control activists have sought such a ban for years, and it often gains majority support in public opinion polls. A challenge on First Amendment grounds would be likely but many legal scholars believe the Supreme Court would uphold such a restriction.

The tobacco industry argues that teen smoking rates haven't changed much in countries that have enacted such bans. But the most comprehensive review ever done on the subject, by new Zealand health officials in 1989, found that teen-age smoking rate declined faster in countries with stricter ad bans.

Advertising bans would be more effective, too, if marketers didn't find so many ways to evade them. Canada banned ads, but left one loophole: Companies could still sponsor cultural and sporting events. The companies do, and make sure that every poster, advertisement, billboard, or program contains a large image of the brand's logo and name. In European countries, companies barred from advertising their cigarettes simply advertise clothing, matches, or cigarette lighters that bear their logo.

Given the present political realities in Washington, a national ban on cigarette advertising is unlikely. But states and communities can and should take their own steps to reduce teen-age smoking, through both law enforcement and taxation.

Restricting Sales

In 1992, Congress enacted the Synar Amendment, which requires states to put teeth into their laws against selling cigarettes to minors—or lose much-needed Federal money for drug and alcohol treatment. However, the amendment itself has gone unenforced for nearly three years, awaiting clearance of the regulations by the Office of Management and Budget. In the meantime, any real progress on enforcing sales laws has occurred at the local level.

In communities where police rigorously enforce the law, sales and teen smoking drop. In Solano County, California, intensive enforcement of sales laws reduced the percentage of stores selling to minors from 72 percent to 21 percent.

One obvious problem is the extra work this can impose on police. To get around that, some communities have licensed tobacco retailers in the same way liquor stores are licensed. The licensing fees pay for enforcement. License laws provide a strong incentive for retailers to card young-looking customers; if they're not careful, they could lose their license and thus lose to the lucrative adult trade as well.

In the year and a half after Woodridge, Ill., began licensing cigarette retailers, surveys found the proportion of seventh- and eighth-graders who reported experimenting with cigarettes fell from 46 percent to 23 percent, and the proportion of daily smokers fell from 16 percent to 5 percent. Over that same period, compliance checks found that the proportion of stores willing to sell to minors fell from 70 percent to 3 percent.

But restricting store sales will be nearly meaningless if teens are still able to buy cigarettes from vending machines. We think the machines should be banned, as they already are in some communities.

Taxes

In 1982, Canada boosted cigarette taxes to among the highest in the world. Teen-age smokers turned out to be unwilling or unable to pay $4 or more for a pack of cigarettes; the youth smoking rate dropped from 40 percent in 1981 to just 16 percent 10 years later. "For the teen market, price sensitivity is extremely high," says David Mair, associate director of the Canadian Council on Smoking and Health. "For every 10 percent increase in price, there's a 13 percent reduction in consumption."

Unfortunately, Canada also learned that when you lower the price, teen smoking goes up. Under political pressure from the tobacco industry, Canadian lawmakers rolled back the tax in February 1994 and prices dropped again. By the end of last year, teen-age smoking rates had already climbed back up to 19 percent.

How to Help a Teen

Adolescents start smoking for many intermingled reasons. Some factors that seem to fortify children against tobacco experimentation—self-esteem, academic achievement, skills for dealing with peer influence, and a close parent-child relationship—are built up slowly from toddlerhood on; they can't be provided overnight when a child reaches the high-risk age of 12 or 13. Still, if you're looking for ideas, here are several steps you can try to help your children shun cigarettes:

- **Talk.** Children whose parents don't talk to them regularly are at greater risk for experimenting with cigarettes. Make a point of discussing your children's lives and feelings. Make sure you know their friends (and the friends' parents). That will help you find out whether any of the friends is trying out smoking, so you can talk about it with your own child.

- **Help them decode ads.** Ideally, begin as early as the fourth or fifth grade, when children may first become susceptible to the images in cigarette ads. Urge them to identify seductive images.

- **Make your feelings clear.** Children who understand the depth of their parents' opposition to it are less likely to smoke.

- **Give them a reality check.** Point out perhaps while walking past office workers smoking in doors and alleys—that, despite the ads, the vast majority of adults do not smoke and no longer even tolerate the practice in public.

- **Emphasize health.** Kids are notoriously unconcerned about getting sick. Tell them anyway: Teen-age smokers have weaker lungs, cough more, and suffer worse upper-respiratory infections. Young athletes don't perform as well if they smoke. And the more years a person smokes, the greater is the risk of lung cancer in middle age.

- **Emphasize addiction.** Nicotine is so addictive that some experts compare it to heroin. And, once hooked, kids find it just as hard to kick the habit as adults do.Trouble is, there's no way to predict which kids will become addicted. So it's best not even to experiment.

- **Help them say no.** This technique is used in many formal substance-abuse prevention courses in school but can easily be adapted at home. As best you can, play the part of an admired friend or acquaintance trying to get your teen-ager to try a cigarette.

Help your child work out ways to turn down the offer.

- **Don't smoke.** If you are a smoker and are unable or unwilling to quit, at least explain to your children that you are in the grip of a fearsome addiction—and hide your cigarettes. Smoke less in front of your children and make their rooms smoke-free zones.

- **Impose consequences.** If, in spite of your efforts, you find your child experimenting with cigarettes, do not treat it as a minor "kids-will-be-kids" infraction. Treat it as what it is: an act that puts your child at very high risk of developing a life-threatening addiction. Impose whatever sanctions your family uses for a major misdeed—and don't back down.

 Article Review Form at end of book.

How do you induce cognitive dissonance in someone? How can you influence people by pointing out their hypocrisy?

A University of California Psychologist Investigates New Approaches to Changing Human Behavior

Scholar's research on safe-sex campaigns suggests people will modify actions to avoid being viewed as hypocrites.

Christopher Shea

Students at the University of California at Santa Cruz often gather signatures to save the redwoods or protect dolphins. But try to get them to trim even a few minutes off their luxurious, half-hour showers during one of central California's frequent water shortages? Forget it.

A few years ago, after sternly worded signs in shower rooms failed to do the trick, a psychology professor sent graduate assistants with waterproof stopwatches to do some snooping. They found that some students, perversely, were taking *longer* showers than before.

There's a lesson here for sex education, too, says the psychology professor, Elliot Aronson. Warnings about condom use can be counter productive. The professor, author of several influential social-psychology textbooks, thinks he has found the best way yet to get students to use condoms consistently. He adopts the same technique that helped him persuade students to shorten their showers: By making them see that they are hypocrites.

His work draws on a condition called cognitive dissonance. People want to think of themselves as holding a consistent set of views, and they want to believe they act in a way that reflect those views. When forced to confront their own inconsistencies, however, they become uncomfortable—physically agitated, in fact. This discomfort can be used to get them to modify their behavior or thoughts.

"In effect, what our research does is rub people's noses in their own hypocrisy, and that's painful to confront," Dr. Aronson says. "Most of us engage in hypocritical behavior all the time, because we can blind ourselves to it. But if someone comes along and forces you to look at it, you can no longer shrug it off."

Christopher Shea, "A University of California Psychologist Investigates New Approaches to Changing Human Behavior," THE CHRONICLE OF HIGHER EDUCATION, June 20, 1997, p. A15. Copyright 1997, The Chronicle of Higher Education. Reprinted with permission.

Reshaping Sex Education

The work has the potential to reshape sex education. But it has yet to make inroads into programs, even at his own university. The situation is a textbook example of how difficult it can be to transfer the lessons of academic research to the real world, he says. It's also, perhaps, a sign of the low esteem in which many people hold social psychology, one of the "softest" of sciences.

Dr. Aronson discussed his work last month at the annual meeting of the American Psychological Society in Washington, where people lined up afterward to ask how they might apply his findings.

But first, the long showers: In an experiment, he asked some students if they would be willing to sign a petition telling their fellow students why they should give up some sudsing time. The petition was then mounted on eye-catching posters around the campus. His snooping assistants found that the students who had made this public commitment were privately curtailing their showers, on average, to a minimally soothing three and a half minutes. Other students, told about the water problem but not asked to sign the petition, didn't change their shower habits much.

Many colleges have given students a "common sense" rationale for condoms: Use them or die. But social psychologists know that fear can lead to denial, which is what has happened with condoms. Virtually all sexually active students know the safe-sex rules backwards and forwards, but surveys find that fewer than 30 percent of them use condoms every time they should. Not wanting to associate sex with death, they concoct reasons that the warning can't possibly apply to them.

'Health and Persuasion'

Dr. Aronson thought that this gap between belief and practice was ready-made for social-psychology experiments. His first idea, however, was not to use cognitive dissonance, but to "eroticize" condoms. If students associated them with romance rather than disease, he reasoned, that might be enough to overcome their resistance. He hired two attractive actors to film a sensitive love scene, prominently featuring a condom. But he found that students who viewed a screening of his foray into what he calls "soft-core pornography" were no more likely to report using condoms than were students in control groups.

If the eroticization technique had been effective, a few racy television ads might have worked wonders. Acquainting students with their own hypocrisy was more complicated.

Dr. Aronson put out ads asking for sexually active students willing to take part in an experiment on "health and persuasion." He got 32 men and 40 women and told them they were going to help design an AIDS-prevention program to be used in high schools.

Some of the students were asked to make videotapes, starring themselves, explaining the dangers of AIDS and the benefits of condoms. They were role models, they were told. To help them with the project, the experimenters provided all of the grim facts they'd heard a million times.

After their videotaped presentation, some of the students were put into groups and asked to brainstorm about why people don't use condoms when they should. They were encouraged to talk about specific times that they hadn't followed their own rules.

Dr. Aronson had his eye on students in the "induced-hypocrisy" group, those who had publicly linked themselves with the message of safe sex and were then forced to talk about times they hadn't practiced what they had now so publicly preached. (Other groups just made the videos or just brainstormed.)

The effects were striking. Dr. Aronson give the students a chance to buy condoms after the experiment was over, and far more of those in the induced-hypocrisy group did so.

Even more striking, in follow-up interviews three months after the experiment, 92 percent of the students in the hypocrisy group said they had been using condoms without fail. Only about 55 percent of those who had made the videotapes but skipped the second part of the process were using condoms faithfully.

Of the students who had only brain-stormed, 71 percent were using condoms, as were 75 percent of those in another group, who had merely received safe-sex information. "Because of self-reporting, we can't be sure of those numbers," Dr. Aronson says. "They are probably exaggerated. But we can be sure of the relative difference."

The professor believes that this experiment can be adapted for sex education classes. Maybe, he suggests, teachers could make students talk in groups about the value of safe sex, then make them look closely at what they actually do. The sequence is important: Rubbing their noses in the hypocrisy is the key. Talking about what they ought to do isn't enough.

Trying to Spread the Word

In his more theoretical work, Dr. Aronson has tried to revive interest in cognitive dissonance. First identified in the 1950s, the idea spurred the realization that more goes into decisions than a simple weighing of rewards and punishments. The term even seeped into public discourse, though few psychologists use it anymore.

He has presented his findings to a Santa Cruz committee on AIDS awareness and has knocked on the doors of local high schools. So far, not much response. "People have been listening politely and then going their own way," he says. "I'm at my best when I'm in the library. I'm less good at giving our research away."

One problem with trying to spread the word, Dr. Aronson says, is that all of us are amateur social psychologists, with our own ideas about how to get people to change their minds. But in sex education, at least, not enough attention has been given to the psychological complexity of getting people to do something that is not particularly appealing to them, he argues.

"You can get people to switch from Colgate to Crest without much effort," he says, "but it requires a lot more wisdom and understanding of how the human mind works to get someone who has never brushed his teeth to start doing it regularly."

 Article Review Form at end of book.

WiseGuide Wrap-Up

- Attitudes derive from beliefs, feelings, and behaviors. Attitudes can be shaped by personal experiences and information from the mass media, advertisers, and so on. Long-term social and economic trends, along with memorable historical events, can all contribute to significant changes in public attitudes.

- There is no single best way to persuade people to change their attitudes. A wide variety of persuasion techniques can be used to change attitudes.

- Persuasion campaigns appeal to an individual's perceived needs. For instance, cigarette manufacturers appeal to a young person's need to be independent, to be socially accepted, to find a romantic partner, and to be thin.

- Advertising can have a strong impact on attitude formation and change, particularly in children. One can be persuaded to see the world in a certain way, and then to act accordingly. Advertisements help to reinforce current social stereotypes, such as girls not wanting to play with trains.

- Cognitive dissonance seems to be an effective technique for inducing attitude and behavior change in safe-sex programs. It works by using people's dislike of appearing hypocritical. They are first led to agree publicly with the idea of safe-sex practices, and then to discuss their own practices (which fall short of the ideal). They notice this discrepancy and alter their behavior to reduce it. This method could be used in many public health campaigns.

R.E.A.L. Sites

This list provides a print preview of typical **coursewise** R.E.A.L. sites. (There are over 100 such sites at the **courselinks**™ site.) The danger in printing URLs is that web sites can change overnight. As we went to press, these sites were functional using the URLs provided. If you come across one that isn't, please let us know via email to: webmaster@coursewise.com. Use your Passport to access the most current list of R.E.A.L. sites at the **courselinks**™ site.

Site name: Steve's Primer of Practical Persuasion and Influence

URL: http://www.as.wvu.edu/~sbb/comm221/primer.htm

Why is it R.E.A.L.? This page covers all of the basics of attitude theory and then some not-so-basic parts. You will find discussions of attitude-behavior consistency, inoculation, reactance, classical conditioning, and many other topics. The best thing about the site is that each of the topic areas is illustrated with vivid examples that demonstrate attitude theory in everyday life. Go to the site and read one of the topic areas. Can you come up with another example of this topic from your own life?

Key topics: attitudes, persuasion, decision making, politics

Site name: Social Influence: The Science of Persuasion and Compliance

URL: http://www.public.asu.edu/~kelton/

Why is it R.E.A.L.? This large and impressive web site is devoted to social influence. Social influence is the science of influence, persuasion, and compliance. Knowledge of it can help you when you need to move someone to adopt a new attitude, belief, or action. It can also help you resist the influence attempts of others. This web site is designed to help you become a more persuasive person and to help you better recognize influence attempts when you encounter them. See if you find a technique that a salesperson has used on you.

Key topics: persuasion, advertising, attitudes, conformity

section 4

Learning Objectives

- Describe the Milgram experiments and discuss the implications of the results.

- Discuss the ethical issues raised by the Milgram experiments.

- Explain why individual personalities are less important than situational circumstances in determining a cult member's behavior.

- Provide specific examples of the techniques used by cult leaders to increase conformity and compliance.

- Discuss how powerful conformity, compliance, and obedience pressures are, and identify ways to resist them.

Conformity, Compliance, and Obedience

 **WiseGuide Intro**

In Section 2 on the self, we took up the question of how other people shape our sense of who we are. In reality, of course, other people affect more than just our sense of self: they influence our everyday beliefs, attitudes, and behavior in a number of obvious and subtle ways. Achieving our goals often means somehow getting others to do what they normally would not do. Sometimes the target of social influence goes along knowingly and willingly. College students, for example, generally do what their professors ask, even if they don't always like it. Some kinds of voluntary compliance seem bizarre to us, however. Why, for example, would seemingly rational people abandon their lives to join a cult? At other times, of course, cooperation comes quite unwillingly and only after some kind of coercion.

In this section, we will consider three separate kinds of influence. In *conformity*, no one asks you to do something, but you go along because everyone else is doing it. In *compliance*, someone asks you to do something, or suggests that you do something in a manner persuasive enough that you do it voluntarily. In *obedience*, someone orders you to do something, and has the power to inflict real or imagined punishment if you do not. Sometimes, successful influence attempts to incorporate all three of these processes. For instance, if I suddenly order my class to put down their books and stand on their chairs, some will do so out of obedience alone, some because they trust me, and many just because everyone else is doing it.

Influence tactics and dynamics are at the heart of some of the most notorious and disturbing events in human history. The Nazi Holocaust, the violence on the killing fields of Cambodia, the mass suicide of the People's Temple cult in Guyana, the ethnic slaughter in Rwanda: none of these could have taken place without the mobilization of mass action through the "weapons" of social influence. Yet social influence is endemic to ordinary life, too. In Section 3 on attitudes and persuasion, we considered how advertisers seek to change your attitudes toward their products. Getting you to make a purchase, however, could hinge on something as simple as a salesperson touching your elbow or informing you that he has a cousin who went to the same college as you!

89

The first article by Alan Elms provides a fascinating first-person account of what are probably the most famous experiments in the history of social psychology: the studies of obedience conducted by Stanley Milgram. Elms was one of Milgram's graduate student assistants, and vividly describes the range of emotions experienced by both subjects and researchers. There is also a thoughtful discussion of the ethical issues raised by these experiments that psychologists have discussed for the last thirty years. Finally, Elms comments on the state of obedience research since the Milgram experiments.

The article by Zimbardo provides a basic overview of the psychology of cults. He discusses a number of reasons why a person might join a cult, and why it may not be such a crazy thing to do, after all. The article by Miller about Rio DiAngelo illustrates some of the general principles that Zimbardo describes. Rio DiAngelo is a survivor of the Heaven's Gate cult, a group that committed mass suicide in March 1997. He explains why he joined the group and how he found happiness there. This article also includes some material from the Heaven's Gate web site and their notebooks, which provides a rare glimpse into the type of mind-control techniques used in cults.

? Questions ?

R15. What was the driving force behind Milgram's experiments? What are the arguments for and against conducting these studies? Explain why the experiments provided a good representation of real life.

R16. According to Zimbardo, what are some of the conditions that make a person vulnerable to cults? Can you think of any additional vulnerabilities? Why are cults appealing to a wide range of people? What are the persuasion techniques of cults, and how do they differ from ordinary persuasion techniques?

R17. What were some of the ways that the Heaven's Gate cult removed people's individuality and encouraged them to become one with the group? Why do you think the cult was so appealing to Rio DiAngelo?

What was the driving force behind Milgram's experiments? What are the arguments for and against conducting these studies? Explain why the experiments provided a good representation of real life.

Obedience in Retrospect

Alan C. Elms

Abstract: *Milgram's original paradigm for studying obedience to authority is briefly described, and the main results are summarized. Personal observations of the conduct of the initial studies give added context for interpreting the results. Psychologists' reactions to the Milgram experiments are discussed in terms of (1) rejecting the research on ethical grounds, (2) explaining away the results as expressions of trivial phenomena, (3) subsuming obedience to destructive authority under other explanatory rubrics, and (4) endorsing or rejecting the results in terms of their perceived social relevance or irrelevance.*

The problem of obedience to authority may well be the crucial issue of our time. The experiments you took part in represent the first efforts to understand this phenomenon in an objective, scientific manner. (Stanley Milgram, *Report to Memory Project Subjects,* 1962b)

Introduction

Obedience to destructive authority was indeed a crucial social issue in 1962. The Holocaust had ended less than two decades earlier. Adolph Eichmann recently had been sentenced to death for expediting it, despite his plea that he had just been "following orders." American military advisers were being ordered to Vietnam in increasing numbers to forestall Communist control of Southeast Asia. Whether destructive obedience could reasonably be described as *the* crucial issue of the time is a judgment call; surely other issues offered competition for that status. But there can be little argument that Stanley Milgram's experiments were indeed "the first efforts to understand this phenomenon in an objective, scientific manner."

Milgram was not seeking to develop a grand theory of obedience. His main concern was with the phenomenon itself. He advised his graduate students that as they began their own research, "First decide what questions you want to answer." For him those first questions were typically substantive, not theoretical. He also told his students he sought to collect data that would still be of interest 100 years later, whatever theoretical interpretations might be made of the data. For his data on obedience, we are a third of the way through that 100 years. Those data remain of high interest indeed, offering continual challenges to our theories and to our confidence as psychologists that we really understand important aspects of human social behavior.

Milgram eventually proposed his own theoretical interpretations. But what most people still remember are the data themselves, the sheer numbers of research volunteers who obeyed every order to the very end. Before Milgram, creative writers had incorporated striking incidents of obedience into novels, poems, and screenplays. Historians had written factual accounts of remarkably obedient individuals and groups. Psychologists had developed F- and other scales to measure inclinations toward authoritar-

Quotations from unpublished correspondence of Stanley Milgram are used by permission of Alexandra Milgram.

Correspondence regarding this article should be addressed to Alan C. Elms, Department of Psychology, University of California, Davis, California 95616-8686.

Alan C. Elms, "Obedience in Retrospect," JOURNAL OF SOCIAL ISSUES, Vol. 51(3), 21–31, Fall 1995. Reprinted by permission of Blackwell Publishers.

ian tyranny and subservience. Milgram instead established a realistic laboratory setting where actual obedience and its circumstances might be closely studied.

The Obedience Paradigm

For those who have forgotten the details, and for the few who have never read them, here is the basic situation that Milgram devised. First, he advertised in the New Haven (Connecticut) daily newspaper and through direct mail for volunteers for a study of memory and learning. Volunteers were promised $4.00 for an hour of their time, plus 50 cents carfare. (At the time, $4 was well above minimum wage for an hour of work; 50 cents would have paid for a round-trip bus ride to and from most areas of New Haven.) Most of those who volunteered were scheduled by telephone to come at a given time to a laboratory on the Yale University campus.

In the basic experiments, two volunteers arrived at the laboratory at about the same time. Both were invited into the lab by the experimenter. The experimenter explained that one volunteer would be assigned the role of teacher and the other would become the learner. The teacher would administer an electric shock to the learner whenever the learner made an error, and each additional shock would be 15 volts higher than the previous one. By drawing slips of paper from a hat, one volunteer became the teacher. His first task was to help strap the arms of the other volunteer to the arms of a chair, so the electrodes from the shock generator would not fall off accidentally. The teacher was given a sample 45 volt electric shock from the shock generator, a level strong enough to be

distinctly unpleasant. Then the experimenter asked the teacher to begin teaching the learner a list of word pairs. The learner did fairly well at first, then began to make frequent errors. Soon the teacher found himself administering higher and higher shock levels, according to the experimenter's instructions. (Male pronouns are used here because most volunteers were male; in only one experimental condition out of 24 were female subjects used.)

After a few shocks the learner began to object to the procedure. After more shocks and more objections, he loudly refused to participate further in the learning task, and stopped responding. If the teacher stopped giving him electric shocks at this point, the experimenter ordered the teacher to continue, and to administer stronger and stronger shocks for each failure to respond—all the way to the end of the graded series of levers, whose final labels were "Intense Shock," "Extreme Intensity Shock," "Danger Severe Shock," and "XXX," along with voltage levels up to 450 volts. In the first experimental condition, the teacher was separated from the learner by a soundproofed wall; the learner could communicate his distress only by kicking on the wall. In subsequent conditions, teachers could hear the learner's voice through a speaker system, or sat near the learner in the same room while the learning task proceeded, or sat next to the learner and had to force his hand down onto a shock grid if he refused to accept the shocks voluntarily.

Teachers were not told several important pieces of information until their participation in the experiment was finished. Number one, the experiment was a study of obedience to authority, not a study of memory and learning.

Number two, the volunteer who assumed the role of learner was actually an experimental confederate. Number three, the only shock that anyone ever got was the 45 volt sample shock given to each teacher; the shock generator was not wired to give any shocks to the learner. Number four, the learner's kicks against the wall, his screams, his refusals to continue, were all carefully scripted and rehearsed, as were the experimenter's orders to the teacher. A number of variables could be (and were) added to the research design in different conditions (see Miller, Collins, & Brief, this issue), but these aspects were constant.

Observations from the Inside

The basic series of obedience experiments took place in the summer of 1961. Milgram was at that time a very junior assistant professor, 27 years old, with no professional publications yet in print. I had just finished my first year of graduate school when he hired me to be his research assistant for the summer. Stanley sent me a letter on June 27, a week before I was scheduled to return to New Haven from a brief summer vacation:

Matters have been proceeding apace on the project. The apparatus is almost done and looks thoroughly professional; just a few small but important pieces remain to be built. It may turn out that you will build them, but that depends on factors at present unknown.

The advertisement was placed in the *New Haven Register* and yielded a disappointingly low response. There is no immediate crisis, however, since we do have about 300 qualified applicants. But before long, in your role of Solicitor General, you will have to think of ways to deliver more people to the laboratory. This is a very important practical aspect of the research. I will admit it bears some resemblance to Mr. Eichmann's position, but *you* at least should have no misconceptions of what *we* do with our daily quota. We give them a chance to resist the commands of malevolent authority and assert their alliance with morality.

. . . . The goal this summer is to run from 250–300 subjects in nine or ten experimental conditions. Only if this is accomplished can the summer be considered a success. Let me know if there is something I have overlooked.

The summer was a success by any reasonable standards, if not fully by Milgram's. He had not overlooked anything procedural; even at that early stage in his career, he was already the most well-organized researcher I have ever encountered. But he had hardly come close to anticipating the degree to which his subjects would yield to the commands of malevolent authority, or how readily they would abrogate their alliance with morality. Milgram knew he would get *some* obedience; in a pilot study the previous winter, he had found Yale undergraduates disturbingly willing to shock their victims. But he recognized that Yale undergraduates were a special sample in many ways; that the prototype shock generator was rather crude and perhaps not altogether convincing; and that the simulated victim's displays of pain were fairly easy to ignore. For the main experiments, Milgram auditioned and rehearsed a victim whose cries of agony were truly piercing. He recruited a larger and diverse sample of nonstudent adults from the New Haven area, ranging from blue-collar workers to professionals and from 20 to 50 years in age. He constructed a professional-looking shock generator and purchased other high-quality equipment, including a 20-pen Esterline Angus Event Recorder that registered the duration and latency of each "shock" administration to the nearest hundredth of a second. He had decided that his main dependent variable would be the mean shock level at which subjects refused to go further in each experimental condition, but he wanted to be able to examine more subtle differences in their performance as well.

In early August the curtains went up on the first official obedience experiment. (More accurately, the curtains were drawn aside; Yale's new Social Interaction Laboratory, on temporary loan from the Sociology Department, was enclosed by two-way mirrors and heavy soundproofing curtains.) Would subjects be convinced of the reality of the learning-and-memory experiment, the shock generator, the victim's suffering? They were. Would subjects obey the experimenter? They did. How far would they go? On and on up the sequence of shock levels. Would any subjects go all the way to the end of the shock board? Yes indeed.

Behind the two-way mirrors, Stanley Milgram and I (as well as occasional visitors) watched each early subject with fascination and with our own share of tension. Stanley had made broad predictions concerning the relative amounts of obedience in different conditions, but we paid little attention to the gradual confirmation of those predictions. Instead we tried to predict the behavior of each new subject, based on his initial demeanor and the little we knew about his background. We were gratified when any subject resisted authority. Sometimes it was quiet resistance, sometimes noisy, but it was exciting each time it happened. As more and more subjects obeyed every command, we felt at first dismayed, then cynically confirmed in our bleakest views of humanity. We were distressed when some volunteers wept, appalled when others laughed as they administered shock after shock. The experimenter gave each subject a standard debriefing at the end of the hour, to minimize any continuing stress and to show that the "victim" had not been injured by the "shocks." When a subject appeared especially stressed, Milgram often moved out from behind the curtains to do an especially thorough job of reassurance and stress reduction. When a subject did something truly unexpected during the experiment— an especially resolute show of resistance, for instance, or a long laughing jag—Milgram would join the experimenter in giving the subject a detailed cross-examination about why he had displayed such behavior. For us as well as for the subjects, the situation quickly became more than an artificially structured experiment. Instead it presented slice after slice of real life, with moral decisions made and unmade every evening.

The Most Prominent Results

As matters turned out, Milgram did not need equipment sensitive enough to measure shock intervals in hundredths of a second. By the end of the second run of 40 subjects, if not before, his main dependent variable had become simply the percentage of subjects who obeyed the experimenter's commands all the way to the end of the shock series, contrasted with the percentage who disobeyed by quitting at *any* point in the whole long sequence of shock levels. In the first condition, a substantial majority of subjects (26 out of 40, or 65%) obeyed completely. That was the condition with minimal feedback from the learner—a few vigorous kicks on the wall. But wouldn't obedience drop substantially if the teacher could actually hear the learner screaming and demanding to be set free? It didn't. Twenty-five out of 40 were fully obedient in this second condition. Even when Milgram tried to encourage disobedience by having the learner claim a preexisting heart condition ("It's bothering me now!"), obedience remained at a high level: 26 of 40 subjects again (Milgram, 1974, pp. 56–57). Putting the victim in the same room and near the teacher reduced obedience somewhat, but 40% still obeyed fully. Indeed, even when teachers were ordered to press the hand of the screaming victim down onto a shock plate to complete the electrical circuit, a majority did so at least twice before quitting, and 30% obeyed in this fashion to the end of the shock board (Milgram, 1974, p. 35).

Milgram ran approximately a thousand subjects through various obedience conditions in less than a year. (The National Science Foundation, which financed the research, got its money's worth from two grants totaling about $60,000.) Each subject was run through the procedure individually, then was subjected to both immediate and follow-up questionnaires of various kinds. Milgram looked at the effects not only of the victim's physical proximity to the subject but of the experimenter's proximity, the amount of group support either for obedience or for defiance, and

the learning experiment's apparent institutional backing. He made a variety of interesting findings—enough to fill a book, and more. But the data that carried the greatest impact, on other psychologists and on the general public, came from those first few experimental conditions: two-thirds of a sample of average Americans were willing to shock an innocent victim until the poor man was screaming for his life, and to go on shocking him well after he had lapsed into a perhaps unconscious silence, all at the command of a single experimenter with no apparent means of enforcing his orders.

Reactions to the Research

Once these data appeared in professional psychological journals (after initial resistance from editors), they were rather quickly disseminated through newspaper and magazine stories, editorials, sermons, and other popular media. With few exceptions, the nonprofessional citations of the experiments emphasized their social relevance: Milgram had revealed in ordinary Americans the potential for behavior comparable to that of the Nazis during the European Holocaust. (According to a *TV Guide* ad for a docudrama with William Shatner as a fictionalized Milgram, the research revealed "A world of evil so terrifying no one dares penetrate its secret. Until now!" [August 21, 1976, p. A-86.])

Psychologists responded in more diverse ways. Authors eager to enliven their introductory and social psychology textbooks soon made the obedience experiments a staple ingredient (see Miller, this

issue).* Other psychologists seemed to regard Milgram's results as a challenge of one sort or another: conceptual, ethical, theoretical, political. The obedience studies were related, historically and procedurally, to earlier studies of social influence, but they did not fit readily into current theoretical models or research trends. Because of their rapidly achieved visibility inside and outside the field, they were soon treated as fair game for elucidation or attack by psychologists with a multitude of orientations.

Ethical Concerns

One type of response to the disturbing results of the obedience studies was to shift attention from the amounts of obedience Milgram obtained to the ethics of putting subjects through such a stressful experience. The first substantial published critique of Milgram's studies focused on the presumed psychic damage wreaked on his subjects by their ordeal (Baumrind, 1964). Milgram was not altogether surprised by such criticism; similar concerns had been expressed by several Yale faculty members during or soon after the experiments, and ethical questions had been raised about the research when Milgram first applied for American Psychological Association membership. But he was disappointed that his critics did not recognize the care he had put into responding to his subjects' high stress levels immediately after their participation, as well as into checking on any lingering effects over time (Milgram, 1964). Milgram was a pioneer in the debriefing procedures that are now a matter of course in psychological experiments on human subjects—

* Does not appear in this publication.

debriefing in the sense not only of questioning the subject about his or her perception of the experiment, but of providing the subject with information and encouragement that will counteract any reactions to participation that might damage the subject's self-esteem. As Milgram told me later,

My membership application to APA was held up for one year while they investigated the ethicality of the obedience experiment. In the end, they gave me a clean bill of health and admitted me to membership. Whenever any group has seriously considered the merits and problems of the experiment, they have concluded that it was an ethical experiment. Nonetheless, isolated individuals still feel strongly enough to attack it. (Personal communication, July 3, 1969)

One consequence of those individual attacks was a set of stringent federal regulations that made it virtually impossible ever again to conduct a close replication of the Milgram studies at any U.S. educational or research institution.

Many social scientists who have considered the ethics of the obedience studies in print have taken a neutral position or have come down on the side of Milgram. But outside the field, a similar perception of appropriate research and debriefing procedures is not widespread. When I participated in a conference on social science research ethics at the Kennedy Institute of Ethics 18 years after the obedience research was completed, several philosophers and professional ethicists devoted a large part of their energies to what struck me as rather crude Milgram bashing. The research scientists at the conference were not so inclined, but they had to work hard to communicate the virtues of a set of studies that had raised important issues about both the bad and the good in human nature (Beauchamp, Faden, Wallce, & Walters, 1982).

Questions of Belief

Among other early commentaries on the research, several psychologists argued that the results were not credible because the subjects did not believe they were actually harming the victim (e.g., Orne & Holland, 1968). Milgram's own data, showing that during the experiment a very high percentage of subjects believed the victim was receiving extremely painful shocks (1974, pp. 171–174, were ignored or dismissed as attempts by the subjects to give Milgram the answers he wanted. Researchers' descriptions of many subjects' visible signs of high stress were also ignored, or were assumed to be evidence merely of the subjects' enthusiastic play acting. Even a filmed record of several actual subjects (Milgram, 1965a), displaying either great stress or extraordinary improvisational acting ability, did not convince psychologists who took this dismissive position. Some critics may have assumed that the four subjects shown at length in the film, plus several others who appeared more briefly, were the most convincingly emotional subjects Milgram could find among his thousand participants. In fact, Milgram chose all of them from the 14 subjects who happened to be "selected in the normal manner for recruitment" during the two days he brought movie cameras to the laboratory (Milgram, 1965c, p. 5).

Theoretical Alternatives

Many social psychologists have accepted the ethical appropriateness of Milgram's procedures and the believability of the experimental context. Even they, however, have often redirected attention away from the specific phenomenon of destructive obedience by subsuming it under a broader theoretical approach or alternative hypothetical constructs.

Milgram was slow to offer a comprehensive theoretical account of his own. His definitions of obedience to authority, from his first to his final writings on the subject, drew upon no theoretical assumptions. Rather, they were commonsense or dictionary definitions: "Every power system implies a structure of command and action in response to the command" (Milgram, 1961, p. 2); "If Y follows the command of X we shall say that he has obeyed X; if he fails to carry out the command of X, we shall say that he has disobeyed X" (Milgram, 1965b, p. 58); "[I]t is only the man dwelling in isolation who is not forced to respond, through defiance or submission, to the commands of others"(Milgram, 1974, p. 1). In his grant proposals he referred to "internal restraints" or "internal resistances" that were pitted against the acceptance of authoritative commands, but he did not specify the nature of these internal processes (Milgram, 1961, p.3; Milgram, 1962a, p. 1). He raised the possibility of predispositional factors and of "highly complex, and possibly, idiosyncratic motive structures" (1962a, p. 17), but in the research itself he directed his efforts mainly toward identifying situational factors that increased or decreased obedience.

In his most extensive early discussion of his results (Milgram, 1965b, largely written in 1962), he cited such midlevel hypothetical constructs as "empathic cues," "denial and narrowing of the cognitive field," and a varying "sense of *relatedness* between his [the subject's] own actions and the consequences of those actions for the victim" (pp. 61–63; his italics).

Though it took Milgram less than a year to run all his subjects and not much longer than that to write several papers on the results, he worked on his book about obedience for over five years. He attributed the slowness of the book's writing in part to his becoming engaged in other sorts of research. But much of his struggle with the book appears to have centered on the difficulty of developing a general theory of obedience. The principle theoretical concepts he advanced in the book, including the agentic state (Milgram, 1974, pp. 133–134) and the evolution of a potential for obedience in humans (pp. 123–125), impressed many readers rather less than the results themselves—a reaction that both frustrated and pleased the data-centric Milgram. Though he had collected demographic information on all participants and had supported my collection of personality data from subsamples of obedient and disobedient subjects (Elms & Milgram, 1965), he gave short shrift to such data in his book, concluding that "It is hard to relate performance to personality because we really do not know very much about how to measure personality" (p. 205).

Others have usefully discussed the interaction of personality and situational variables in the obedience situations (e.g., Blass, 1991). A majority of the alternative explanations, however, have stressed cognitive processes, emphasizing ways in which the subject processed information about the situation that might have justified his obedience or strengthened his resistance. Milgram viewed such alternative explanations with interest, but took steps to rule out certain of them experimentally. One of the most obvious of these alternatives was the idea that subjects might be so awed by Yale University and so certain of its virtue that they would do anything they were told within those august halls, regardless of any general proclivity toward destructive obedience. Even before this environment-based explanation of his subjects' obedience was first offered in print, Milgram had largely vitiated it by moving the experiments from the awe-inspiring Interaction Laboratory to a rather less impressive basement facility and then to the intentionally unimpressive office of a fly-by-night company in industrial Bridgeport, Connecticut. He got essentially the same results in all three locations. A number of alternative or additional explanations of Milgram's results remain as operable hypotheses, but none has decisively carried the day. Their very diversity ensures that the larger audience for the research will continue to be concerned primarily about the subjects' disturbing behavior rather than about the internal processes that may have produced it.

The Question of Relevance

Finally among ways in which psychologists have responded to Milgram's findings are arguments concerning the social relevance of the experiments. Many psychologists, at least in their textbooks, have embraced his findings as being highly relevant to important social phenomena, including destructive obedience not only in totalitarian states but among American soldiers, Bosnian combatants, and suicidal religious cults. But others (including some who also argued that the research was unethical or experientially unconvincing) have denied any real social relevance. Even if subjects believed they were really shocking the victim, these psychologists say, they knew the situation must not be as bad as it appeared, because somebody would have stopped them if it was. Or the subjects were in a situation where the experimenter accepted responsibility for the effects of their behavior, so their behavior is not really relevant to real-world situations where blame is less readily transferred to another individual. Or some other rationale is advanced, presumably peculiar to the Milgram obedience situation, that somehow does not translate into real-world social dynamics. Milgram rightly dismissed all such explanations that had been advanced up to the time of his final writings, and very likely would have dismissed all subsequent ones, for two simple reasons: Any effective authority figure in the real world always finds ways to justify imposing his or her will on underlings. The underlings who obey authoritative commands in the real world always find rationales for their obedience. In most prominent real-world cases of destructive obedience that have been compared (or discompared) to the Milgram studies, the authorities were able to call upon a social rationale for their commands that was at least as strong as or stronger than that available to any psychological experimenter. In addition, they were often able to promise their followers much greater rewards for obedience and punishments for disobedience.

Stanley Milgram's research on obedience tapped into psychological processes that ranked as neither new nor extreme in the history of human behavior. A "crucial issue of our time," perhaps *the* crucial issue, obedience unfortunately remains. Though Milgram was proud that his studies were "the first efforts to understand this phenomenon in an objective, scientific manner," he did not want them to be the last. This issue of the *Journal of Social Issues* gives strong evidence that the efforts of other researchers to expand upon his groundbreaking work will continue unabated.

References

Baumrind, D. (1964). Some thoughts on ethics of research: After reading Milgram's "Behavioral Study of Obedience." *American Psychologist, 19*, 421–423

Beauchamp, T. L., Faden, R. R., Wallace, R.J., Jr., & Walters, L. (Eds.). (1982). *Ethical issues in social science research.* Baltimore, MD: Johns Hopkins University Press.

Blass, T. (1991). Understanding behavior in the Milgram obedience experiment: The role of personality, situations, and their interactions. *Journal of Personality and Social Psychology, 60*, 398–413.

Elms, A.C., & Milgram, S. (1965). Personality characteristics associated with obedience and defiance toward authoritative command. *Journal of Experimental Research in Personality, 1*, 282–289.

Milgram, S. (1961). *Dynamics of obedience: Experiments in social psychology.* Application for National Science Foundation research grant, Yale University.

Milgram, S. (1962a). *Obedience to authority: Experiments in social psychology.* Application for National Science Foundation grant renewal, Yale University.

Milgram, S. (1962b). *Report to Memory Project subjects.* Unpublished manuscript, Yale University.

Milgram, S. (1964). Issues in the study of obedience: A reply to Baumrind. *American Psychologist, 19*, 848–852.

Milgram, S. (1965a). *Obedience* [Film]. (Available from the Pennsylvania State University Audio-visual Services.)

Milgram, S. (1965b). Some conditions of obedience and disobedience to authority. *Human Relations, 18*, 57–76.

Milgram, S. (1965c). Study notes for "Obedience." (Distributed by the New York University Film Library.)

Milgram, S. (1974). *Obedience to authority.* New York: Harper & Row.

Orne, M.T., & Holland, C. C. (1968). On the ecological validity of laboratory deceptions. *International Journal of Psychiatry, 6*, 282–293.

Alan C. Elms, while a graduate student at Yale University, worked with Stanley Milgram on the first obedience studies and earned his Ph.D. under the direction of Irving L. Janis. Dr. Elms did laboratory studies of role-play induced attitude change and interview studies of right- and left-wing political activists before he focused his work on psychobiography. He has written *Social Psychology and Social Relevance* (1972), *Personality in Politics* (1976), and *Uncovering Lives: The Uneasy Alliance of Biography and Psychology* (1994). He has taught at Southern Methodist University, has been a visiting scholar at Trinity College, Dublin, and at Harvard University, and has been a faculty member at the University of California, Davis, since 1967.

 **Article Review Form at end of book.**

According to Zimbardo, what are some of the conditions that make a person vulnerable to cults? Can you think of any additional vulnerabilities? Why are cults appealing to a wide range of people? What are the persuasion techniques of cults, and how do they differ from ordinary persuasion techniques?

What Messages Are Behind Today's Cults?

Cults are coming. Are they crazy or bearing critical messages?

Philip Zimbardo, PhD

Philip G. Zimbardo, PhD, is professor of psychology at Stanford University and a former APA president. He has interviewed and worked closely with survivors of Peoples Temple and their family members, as well as former members of the Unification Church, Scientology, Synanon, Churches of Christ and other cults.

How do we make sense of the mass suicide of 21 female and 18 male members of the Heaven's Gate extra-terrestrial "cult" on March 23? Typical explanations of all such strange, unexpected behavior involve a "rush to the dispositional," locating the problem in defective personalities of the actors. Those whose behavior violates our expectations about what is normal and appropriate are dismissed as kooks, weirdos, gullible, stupid, evil or masochistic deviants.

Similar characterizations were evident in the media and public's reaction to other mass suicides in The Order of the Solar Temple in Europe and Canada, murder-suicide deaths ordered by Rev. Jim Jones of his Peoples Temple members, as well as of the recent flaming deaths of David Koresh's Branch Davidians and the gassing of Japanese citizens by followers of the Aum Shinrikyo group. And there will be more of the same in the coming years as cults proliferate in the United States and world wide in anticipation of the millennium.

Avoiding the Stereotypes

Such pseudo-explanations are really moralistic judgments; framed with the wisdom of hind-sight, they miss the mark. They start at the wrong end of the inquiry. Instead, our search for meaning should begin at the beginning. "What was so appealing about this group that so many people were recruited/seduced into joining it voluntarily?" We want to know also, "What needs was this group fulfilling that were not being met by traditional society?"

Such alternative framings shift the analytical focus from condemning the actors, mindlessly blaming the victims, defining them as different from us, to searching for a common ground in the forces that shape all human behavior. By acknowledging our own vulnerability to the operation of the powerful, often subtle situational forces that controlled their actions, we can begin to find ways to prevent or combat that power from exerting its similar, sometimes sinister, influence on us and our kin.

Any stereotyped collective personality analysis of the Heaven's Gate members proves inadequate when tallied against the resumes of individual members. They represented a wide range of demographic backgrounds, ages, talents, interests and careers prior to committing themselves to a new ideology embodied in the totally regimented, obedient lifestyle that would end with an eternal transformation. Comparable individual diversity has been evident among the members of many different cult groups I've studied over the past several decades. What is common are the recruiting promises, influence agendas and group's coercive influence power that compromise the personal exercise of free will and critical thinking. On the basis of my investigations and the psychological research of colleagues, we can argue the following propositions, some of which will be elaborated:

- No one ever joins a "cult." People join interesting groups that promise to fulfill their pressing needs. They become "cults" when they are seen as deceptive, defective, dangerous, or as opposing basic values of their society.

- Cults represent each society's "default values," filling in its missing functions. The cult epidemic is diagnostic of where and how society is failing its citizens.

- If you don't stand for something, you'll fall for anything. As basic human values are being strained, distorted and lost in our rapidly evolving culture, illusions and promissory notes are too readily believed and bought—without reality validation or credit checks.

- Whatever any member of a cult has done, you and I could be recruited or seduced into doing—under the right or wrong conditions. The majority of "normal, average, intelligent" individuals can be led to engage in immoral, illegal, irrational, aggressive and self destructive actions that are contrary to their values or personality—when manipulated situational conditions exert their power over individual dispositions.

- Cult methods of recruiting, indoctrinating and influencing their members are not exotic forms of mind control, but only more intensely applied mundane tactics of social influence practiced daily by all compliance professionals and societal agents of influence.

The Appeal

What is the appeal of cults? Imagine being part of a group in which you will find instant friendship, a caring family, respect for your contributions, an identity, safety, security, simplicity, and an organized daily agenda. You will learn new skills, have a respected position, gain personal insight, improve your personality and intelligence. There is no crime or violence and your healthy lifestyle means there is no illness.

Your leader may promise not only to heal any sickness and foretell the future, but give you the gift of immortality, if you are a true believer. In addition, your group's ideology represents a unique spiritual/religious agenda (in other cults it is political, social or personal enhancement) that if followed, will enhance the Human Condition somewhere in the world or cosmos.

Who would fall for such appeals? Most of us, if they were made by someone we trusted, in a setting that was familiar, and especially if we had unfulfilled needs.

Much cult recruitment is done by family, friends, neighbors, co-workers, teachers and highly trained professional recruiters. They recruit not on the streets or airports, but in contexts that are "home bases" for the potential recruit; at schools, in the home, coffee houses, on the job, at sports events, lectures, churches, or drop-in dinners and free personal assessment workshops. The Heaven's Gate group made us aware that recruiting is now also active over the Internet and across the World Wide Web.

In a 1980 study where we (C. Hartley and I) surveyed and interviewed more than 1,000 randomly selected high school students in the greater San Francisco Bay Area, 54 percent reported they had at least one active recruiting attempt by someone they identified with a cult, and 40 percent said they had experienced three to five such contacts. And that was long before electronic cult recruiting could be a new allure for a generation of youngsters growing up as web surfers.

What makes any of us especially vulnerable to cult appeals? Someone is in a transitional phase in life: moved to a new city or country, lost a job, dropped out of school, parents divorced, romantic relationship broken, gave up traditional religion as personally irrelevant. Add to the recipe, all those who find their work tedious and trivial, education abstractly meaningless, social life absent or inconsistent, family remote or dysfunctional, friends too busy to find time for you and trust in government eroded.

Cults promise to fulfill most of those personal individual's needs and also to compensate for a litany of societal failures: to make their slice of the world safe, healthy, caring, predictable and controllable. They will eliminate the increasing feelings of isolation and alienation being created by mobility, technology, competition, meritocracy, incivility, and dehumanized living and working conditions in our society.

In general, cult leaders offer simple solutions to the increasingly complex world problems we all face daily. They offer the simple path to happiness, to success, to salvation by following their simple rules, simple group regimentation and simple total lifestyle. Ultimately, each new member contributes to the power of the leader by trading his or her freedom for the illusion of security and reflected glory that group membership holds out.

It seems like a "win-win" trade for those whose freedom is without power to make a difference in their lives. This may be especially so for the shy among us. Shyness among adults is now escalating to epidemic proportions, according to recent research by Dr. B. Carducci in Indiana and my research team in California. More than 50 percent of college-aged adults report being chronically shy (lacking social skills, low self-esteem, awkward in many social encounters). As with the rise in cult membership, a public health model is essential for understanding how societal pathology is implicated in contributing to the rise in shyness among adults and children in America.

A Society in Transition

Our society is in a curious transitional phase; as science and technology make remarkable advances, antiscientific values and beliefs in the paranormal and occult abound, family values are stridently promoted in Congress and pulpits, yet divorce is rising along with spouse and child abuse, fear of nuclear annihilation in superpower wars is replaced by fears of crime in our streets and drugs in our schools, and the economic gap grows exponentially between the rich and

powerful and our legions of poor and powerless.

Such change and confusion create intellectual chaos that makes it difficult for many citizens to believe in anything, to trust anyone, to stand for anything substantial.

On such shifting sands of time and resolve, the cult leader stands firm with simple directions for what to think and feel, and how to act. "Follow me, I know the path to sanity, security and salvation," proclaims Marshall Applewhite, with other cult leaders chanting the same lyric in that celestial chorus. And many will follow.

What makes cults dangerous? It depends in part on the kind of cult since they come in many sizes, purposes and disguises. Some cults are in the business of power and money. They need members to give money, work for free, beg and recruit new members. They won't go the deathly route of the Heaven's Gaters; their danger lies in deception, mindless devotion, and failure to deliver on the recruiting promises.

Danger also comes in the form of insisting on contributions of exorbitant amounts of money (tithing, signing over life insurance, social security or property, and fees for personal testing and training).

Add exhausting labor as another danger (spending all one's waking time begging for money, recruiting new members or doing menial service for little or no remuneration). Most cult groups demand that members sever ties with former family and friends which creates total dependence on the group for self identity, recognition, social reinforcement. Unquestioning obedience to the leader and following arbitrary rules and regulations eliminates independent, critical

thinking, and the exercise of free will. Such cerebral straightjacketing is a terrible danger that can lead in turn to the ultimate twin dangers of committing suicide upon command or destroying the cult's enemies.

Potential for the worst abuse is found in "total situations" where the group is physically and socially isolated from the outside community. The accompanying total milieu and informational control permits idiosyncratic and paranoid thinking to flourish and be shared without limits. The madness of any leader then becomes normalized as members embrace it, and the folly of one becomes folie à deux, and finally, with three or more adherents, it becomes a constitutionally protected belief system that is an ideology defended to the death.

A remarkable thing about cult mind control is that it's so ordinary in the tactics and strategies of social influence employed. They are variants of well-known social psychological principles of compliance, conformity, persuasion, dissonance, reactance, framing, emotional manipulation, and others that are used on all of us daily to entice us: to buy, to try, to donate, to vote, to join, to change, to believe, to love, to hate the enemy.

Cult mind control is not different in kind from these everyday varieties, but in its greater intensity, persistence, duration, and scope. One difference is in its greater efforts to block quitting the group, by imposing high exit costs, replete with induced phobias of harm, failure, and personal isolation.

What's the Solution?

Heaven's Gate mass suicides have made cults front page news. While their number and ritually methodical formula are unusual, cults are not. They exist as part of the frayed edges of our society and have vital messages for us to reflect upon if we want to prevent such tragedies or our children and neighbors from joining such destructive groups that are on the near horizon.

The solution? Simple. All we have to do is to create an alternative, "perfect cult." We need to work together to find ways to make our society actually deliver on many of those cult promises, to co-opt their appeal, without their deception, distortion and potentiol for destruction.

No man or woman is an island unto itself, nor a space traveller without an earthly control center. Finding that center, spreading that continent of connections, enriching that core of common humanity should be our first priority as we learn and share a vital lesson from the tragedy of Heaven' Gate.

 Article Review Form at end of book.

What were some of the ways that the Heaven's Gate cult removed people's individuality and encouraged them to become one with the group? Why do you think the cult was so appealing to Rio DiAngelo?

Secrets of the Cult

Rio DiAngelo tells inside story of Heaven's Gate cult

He stayed behind to bear witness. Rio DiAngelo is the last insider, the survivor who knows what really happened in the weird world of Heaven's Gate. The exclusive, untold story of the suicide sect.

Mark Miller

Abstract: *DiAngelo left Heaven's Gate two months before the mass suicide in March 1997. He considers himself still a member, and kept in contact with the "Class," as he refers to the cult. He does not call it mass suicide, but explains that no one wanted to be left behind when their leader Do shed his "vehicle."*

For Rio DiAngelo, the first premonition came last November. The members of Heaven's Gate had learned not to take their leader's predictions too literally, and their guru, Marshall Herff Applewhite, better known to his followers as "Do" was usually careful to hedge. But this time he seemed quite specific. The arrival of the comet Hale-Bopp was the sign they had been waiting for. The Earth would be "spaded over." The chariot would swing low in late March, when the comet burned brightest. Deliverance was near.

Along about January, Rio began to get a "disturbing feeling." DiAngelo, whose real name is Richard Ford, was a relative neophyte. Many members had been with Do since the 1970s; DiAngelo had arrived only three years before. He decided that he had to leave "the class" as he calls the group, because he "had a task to do." Perhaps sensing the end was near, he took a job at a Web-page design firm in the real world. He insists there was no plan for mass suicide. Still, he knew there was a "procedure" that would allow true believers to shed their "containers." He also knew that some members had gone to Mexico to buy phenobarbital, a barbiturate fatal in large doses.

DiAngelo was the last to leave before the others left for good. In eight hours of exclusive interviews with *Newsweek,* DiAngelo described his mind-bending three-year odyssey inside a cult obsessed with castration and the cosmos—and how he found the rotting bodies in a ritzy suburb of San Diego, DiAngelo, who considers himself a soul in an earth-bound body ("my vehicle"), regards himself as a member, not an "ex-member," of Heaven's Gate, which he describes as "an advanced class for higher education," not a cult. "I lost 39 of my closest brothers and sisters, my friends," says DiAngelo. "And even though I'm trying to have control of this vehicle, it still disturbs me." DiAngelo hopes to join his brothers and sisters one day, though suicide, he hastens to add, "is not part of my plan."

First comes his moment of fame. DiAngelo is a living witness—to the repression and subtle mind control that permeated the suicide cult. His tale helps explain the eerie culture of Heaven's Gate, the lethal mix of New Age dreaming, extraordinary self-denial and sci-fi soaked paranoia that led to the mass self-annihilation in Rancho Santa Fe. Last week DiAngelo sold the made-for-TV-movie rights to ABC (he won't say for how much) and this week he will be interviewed on "Prime Time Live" by Diane Sawyer. He says he does not feel like a celebrity but rather "an instrument of clarification." He believes that his departed comrades would be "proud" of all the media hoopla. "They are laughing," says DiAngelo. "They really wanted the whole world to know this information but couldn't get it out. No one would listen. I think they would be happy."

Still, DiAngelo himself seems a little ambivalent about his own role. Returning to the world, he says, "was a slap in the face." On the other hand, he seemed to be enjoying himself as he ordered a big dinner (including wine) at a luxury hotel suite. What DiAngelo says is sometimes out of this world, but his manner is usually cool and self-contained. He learned from a master manipulator; he was molded by a regimen that made virtually every choice for its members, from their highest aspirations to their tastes in pop culture. Members of Heaven's Gate were allowed to watch TV—but they sat in assigned seats and were offered an odd blend of low- and highbrow fare. They loved "Star Trek." A PBS documentary on Thomas Jefferson was on the approved list; "GoldenEye," with Pierce Brosnan as Agent 007, was a no-

no. If an actor or actress evoked sensuous feelings in a member of the "class," the class member was supposed to turn away.

Rio DiAngelo, or "Neody," as he was known within the group, is a seeker and a survivor. He drifted into the cult for the usual depressing reasons—broken family, bad relationships, a fascination with UFOs. But he escaped its final solution because he kept a sense of detachment and an instinct for self-preservation. He may be Do's "messenger," but he was never completely his pawn.

There is a story DiAngelo tells about his wretched childhood that is unintentionally revealing. He recalls his mother, whom he describes as violent and unstable, coming to hit him as a little boy. "You want to have this wonderful image of your mom, and all of a sudden, Mom turns into this rage. It's just like this doesn't look like Mom, this is somebody else." Most little boys would have cringed in horror. DiAngelo says he just laughed, or, as he put it, "the little vehicle would make her even angrier, and she'd scream, 'Don't laugh at me!'"

DiAngelo refers to his childhood in southern California in the 1950s and '60s as "boot camp." His father walked out when he was 3, and he bounced back and forth between his grandmother's and his mother's care, if it can be called that. He was sent to various churches and schools, but never stayed long in any particular one. He became, not surprisingly, a searcher. He tried to be a hippie, a musician, an artist. He experimented with Eastern religion and read books on UFOs. He got married and had a child. Nothing filled the emptiness. Divorced, he drifted back home to live with his mother and her latest husband. He took strange pleasure in pho-

tographing their ashtrays, stacked high with old butts.

Then in January 1994, Rio, who had just turned 40, went to a hotel in Marina Del Rey to hear about a "last chance to advance beyond human." He listened as nine androgynous figures in loose clothes and short haircuts described the Earth as a "garden to grow souls to prepare them to advance to a higher level." Rio felt "an overwhelming desire, a compulsion to be part of this." He believed his true soul had matched with and entered his earthbound "vehicle." It was "like, OK, Monty, door number two, bam," recalled DiAngelo.

The only catch was that the cult wasn't taking new members. "They tried to talk me out of it," said DiAngelo. Two of the cult "overseers," "Srrody" and "Jwnody," told him the rules: no drinking, smoking or sex. Every member was "homeless by choice." Still, DiAngelo pleaded to be accepted. In the real world, as he put it, "I had nothing."

He did have an apartment in L.A. and a girlfriend but he gave those up, along with his credit cards. There wasn't much of a bank account to worry about; business as a freelance scene painter was poor. Saying goodbye to his 11-year-old son, whom he had every other weekend, was harder. He explained that he was going off to learn how to get into heaven. "I think he understood," recalled DiAngelo, his eyes misting.

DiAngelo cut off his ponytail and shucked his name. Cult members are known by a three-letter prefix followed by "doti" or "ody" (a play on the founders, Do and Ti). DiAngelo picked "Neody" because "I felt new." Different names are chosen to deal with the outside world. Richard Ford became Rio DiAngelo—the river of angels. Neody hit the road with Srrody and Jwnody and the crew. "We went coast to coast. If it wasn't every state, it sure felt like it." Rising before dawn, handing out literature to skeptical earthlings, foraging for food, DiAngelo lost all sense of time. He finally found himself living in a warehouse in San Clemente on the California coast. For about three months the group drank nothing but "master cleanser"—a concoction of lemonade, cayenne pepper and maple syrup—to rinse out their "vehicles" bloated by fast food. Then it was off to a Utah ski resort—bartering cooking and cleaning for room and board. Money was tight—funneled into the commune from odd jobs and the occasional trust-fund check.

DiAngelo heard "wonderful stories" about Do, their leader, but he did not actually see the sainted one until he had been in the cult for a month. One night, while they were camping in the desert outside Phoenix, Arix., Do suddenly appeared in the light of the campfire, flanked by two disciples. "He was very security-minded," said DiAngelo. "With a lot of new students he had to be very careful." It was only a year after the Branch Davidians had died in the Waco conflagration, and Do feared that he was a target of the FBI. The leader often lived apart from his followers, though usually close by. DiAngelo was told that Do did not like the "vibrations" of new members who were "still trying to control their anger and the lusts."

"Getting control of the vehicle" was the goal of the class. At the Next Level, there is no gender. Thus it was necessary to "reprogram." The problem as DiAngelo explains it, was that "the vehicle has a mind of its own." Sensuality "is the strongest addiction there

is. It doesn't matter if it's male-female, female-female, male to male, female to dog. You think about it and it changes your whole vibration." Sexual partners weren't even necessary. "You can do it yourself, and you can do it for free."

DiAngelo says he gradually tamed his own sensual addiction, though "dreams are tough to control." But for others sexual temptation was too much. Before DiAngelo joined up, two members had quietly gone to Mexico to be castrated. The others increasingly talked about getting "neutered." Finally, about a year ago, Do himself decided to lead the way. "He did it to his own vehicle just to make sure. He protected us in every way," says DiAngelo. Do had trouble finding a doctor willing to perform the operation, however; most wanted him to see a psychiatrist. The one he got "goofed," as DiAngelo put it. Do healed very slowly. Still, five others eagerly followed. "They couldn't stop smiling and giggling," says DiAngelo. "They were excited about it."

DiAngelo chose not to follow his master's example. "Everything is freedom of choice," he explained. "It's very rights-oriented." Under the strict regimen of the cult, however, members did not have many choices to make. Most decisions were made by the cult's hierarchy. At the top—in heaven—there was Ti, the former nurse and astrologer Bonnie Nettles, who had run off with Do in the 1970s and ascended to a Higher Level in 1985 after her vehicle was broken by liver cancer. Cult members believe her mind was so powerful it "short-circuited her vehicle." Do would have celestial conversations with Ti, about everything from the daily chores to the

group's ultimate destination. Do in turn would pass messages on to the "overseers"—a cadre of longtime cult members—who would instruct the class. Members did nothing alone; each had a "check partner" to guard against backsliding.

There were "procedures" for everything, meticulously recorded in longhand in a three-ring binder. "If you needed something," DiAngelo said, "you wouldn't go to the store. You'd write the Individual Needs Department." To guard against overweening pride and self-confidence, members were taught to be conditional in their language. The proper way to approach the "overseer" for "individual needs" was: "I may be wrong, but it seems that my deodorant is running out."

By the time DiAngelo arrived, Do had abandoned his cruder mind-control games. Followers were no longer required to report to headquarters every 12 minutes around the clock or to wear helmets (exhaustion set in, and the headgear was too hot). Still, there was always a "sense of urgency" about becoming "non-human" because there was no telling when the spaceship would arrive to take them all away. "You can't be thinking like a human, you can't be thinking are you going to have sex or you've got to shave or you have angry thoughts or raging hormones. You've got to be ready."

But ready for what, exactly? The precise method of departure was the source of some confusion. It was clear that Earth was becoming increasingly inhospitable. The messages posted by Heaven's Gate on the Internet were being greeted by scorn and derision. Do was fearful that the Feds might attack at any moment. For a time, he seemed to welcome a final showdown. On the video shelf next to "The Sound of Music" were conspiracy-theory videos about Waco and the IRS. In 1995, the cult built a fortress with cement and old tires in the New Mexico desert and bought weapons—at least five handguns and two rifles with sniper scopes. A few members who knew how to handle guns tried to teach the others how to shoot, but the enthusiasm for gunplay, and perhaps the skill level, was low among Do's gentle flock. Do himself finally received a message from Ti indicating that a shootout with the Luciferians was not the right Last Exit.

How then to reach the Higher Level? There was always the promise and hope of the spaceship's swooping down from heaven. From time to time, the group would go out into the middle of the desert and stay until dark, "just kind of hoping and praying that Ti would know we were here, and come and get us," says DiAngelo. Some would be disappointed when the heavens stared back blankly, but for most, the seances were "fun," says DiAngelo.

Sex may have been forbidden, but fun was not. "We loved having a good time and would have a good time as often as possible." Heaven's Gate was full of "fun-loving people, very flexible and open-minded." There were expeditions to UFO museums and the movies—carefully chosen by Do, of course—and, from time to time, feasts. While sex wasn't essential to the vehicle, eating ("consuming") was. So why not enjoy a little cake and ice cream? (San Diego police found seven quarts of Starbuck's Java Chip ice cream in the refrigerator of the so-called Mansion of Death.)

As Hale-Bopp drew closer last winter, the class seemed to have more and more time. By now the group had settled into the villa in Rancho Santa Fe and begun to earn good money from cyberspace as Web-page designers. In late February, the entire class traveled to Las Vegas and stayed in the Stratosphere Hotel. They went to Cirque du Soleil and carefully recorded their winnings at the slot machines and gaming tables ($58.91), as well as the money spent on water ($2.28) and on tickets for rides, including a free-fall contraption called the Big Shot ($123). In the weeks to come, there would be trips to Sea World and to see "Star Wars."

But by then, DiAngelo's "disturbing feeling" had prodded him to directly approach Do, something he had never done before. Members could communicate with Do only in writing; DiAngelo asked for a private meeting. "I told him I felt I had something to do outside the class, like a task." He told Do that he "didn't want to leave the class at all," but that he had been offered a fulltime job on the outside working for InterAct Entertainment, a company that often used Higher Source, the cult's Web-page design outfit. After reflection, Do summoned DiAngelo. "He told me that he had talked to Ti just now, and he felt like it might be part of a plan, and that I didn't understand and that he didn't understand." There was an inkling, however. DiAngelo had been chosen earlier to write a film script about the group's story. He had been volunteered by his partner, Otis Paceman (a play on "Oti Spaceman"), because of his experience in "the film industry" (which was limited mostly to building props for a theme park).

Later, DiAngelo would realize that he had been sent forth to tell the story of Heaven's Gate.

DiAngelo insists he had no real foreboding of mass suicide. Do talked of his followers' "leaving their vehicles"—but only by their own choice. Do himself would never give the order. Naturally, said DiAngelo, no one wanted to be left behind if Do himself exited. "It's like you didn't want to go anyplace without your dad," he said.

Out on his own, DiAngelo stayed in touch with the group by e-mail. But on the Monday after Palm Sunday, his messages vanished into a void, which he found "odd." Then, on Tuesday, he received a FedEx package at work. He says he knew instantly who the package was from—and what had happened. Curiously, he didn't open the package until he had returned home that evening. One glance at the letter within confirmed his suspicions: "By the time you read this, we will have exited our vehicles," it read.

In the morning he matter-of-factly announced to his boss, Nick Matzorkis, that the cult members were dead. Not quite believing him, Matzorkis drove DiAngelo to the house in Rancho Santa Fe. DiAngelo had come prepared. He took out a bottle of cologne, splashed it on a shirt, and held it over his nose. Still, "the smell could knock you over," he said. There were his "brothers and sisters," or at least their abandoned vehicles, lying peacefully in their Nikes beneath the purple shrouds. Their bags were packed with clothes and other essentials, including lip balm, and their pockets were filled with 85 bills and rolls of quarters. Ever since a member of the cult had been hassled by police for vagrancy, the "monks," as they called themselves to outsiders, carried money and IDs. "It was spooky and weird," says DiAngelo, who had brought a video camera "to keep the facts accurate."

Their deaths were "not suicide," says DiAngelo, because their souls live on at the Next Level. He has "no doubt" that everyone went "on their own." As for him, "I don't think I'm ready to make that leap right now. I would like to go to the Next Level but quite frankly I don't think I'm ready yet." Had he stayed in the "class," he says he would have declined to "exit his vehicle."

Though he is the last insider, Rio DiAngelo is not the only survivor. A man who goes by the name of "Rkk" told *Newsweek* that he, too, had received a FedEx package containing master tapes of Do's farewell message and the goodbyes of his former "crew mates." Rkk describes himself as the cult's prodigal son. For more than 20 years, he floated in and out of the class, leaving when he could not master his sexual urges. He quit at the end of last year ("I didn't get the control of my vehicle that was required to stay") but stayed in touch via e-mail. Rkk says he would have gone through with the suicide "in a microsecond. I'm tired of this stupid planet. I don't know how my exit's going to happen, but I hope it happens soon."

DiAngelo has more temporal desires. In addition to "demystifying" the cult for the media, he says he and InterAct have been "entrusted" with the Higher Source Web-site company. He wants to "preserve the dignity and quality that they had always provided." He added that he would "welcome new clients." He has long since lost touch with his mother and his siblings; his ex-wife, he says, reminded him of his

mother. His son is a different matter. At the beginning of last week, DiAngelo told a friend that he didn't plan to see his son, who was the child of his "vehicle," not him. But by midweek in his interview with *Newsweek*, he seemed to be wavering, and by Friday, after talking to his lawyer, he said that he did plan to "see the child of the vehicle."

Then there is DiAngelo's old girlfriend. Desperate after his 1988 divorce, DiAngelo had tried a "very-high-class dating service." He met someone with "style, class and beauty." He was "kind of thrown by this feeling, like, 'Gee, is this really the one?'" The two had problems, but, says DiAngelo, "the vehicle is still in love with this woman today." Will he call? He "hopes to talk to her," he said. There are many roads to heaven's gate.

On the Road with the Lost Tribe

Richard Ford, a.k.a. Rio DiAngelo, the last to leave Heaven's Gate, traveled across the United States after he joined in 1994. Highlights from his strange odyssey to Rancho Santa Fe:

1. Seeing a January 1994 story in *L.A. Weekly*—Last chance to advance beyond human—Ford goes to hear the group's message at a Marina del Rey, Calif. hotel. Later, his effort to join the group is rebuffed.

2. Ford persists and meets the group at an Anaheim, Calif. hotel. The conditions for joining the group are spelled out: no sex or drugs. And new members must bid a final farewell to family, friends and possessions.

3. Ford meets the cult's leader, Do, while camping with the

group near Phoenix. Ford is captivated by him. The initiate takes the names Neody, for use inside the group, and Rio DiAngelo, for use with outsiders.

4. Traveling across the United States, staying in each place only briefly to hold meetings, the group heads to Maine.

5. Back in California in late 1994, the group stays for three months in a warehouse in San Clemente. Drinking a cayenne, lemonade and maple-syrup brew called "master cleanser," they try to purge their "vehicles" of the junk food they had consumed on the road.

6. In late spring 1995, Rio and the group stay at ski lodge in Utah, trading cleaning and cooking for free rooms.

7. Sometime in 1996, Rio and the cult members come to the end of the trail in the house in Rancho Santa Fe.

The Rules They Lived By

Life was rigorous inside Heaven's Gate. To maintain the purity of their "vehicles"—or bodies—true believers learned to be strikingly self-effacing, denying their own desires and deferring to their comrades.

Major Offenses

- Deceit: (a) Doing an act "on the sly." (b) Lying to my teachers or any of my classmates. (c) Keeping an offense to myself, not exposing it the same day.

- Sensuality—permitting arousal in thought or in action (not nipping it in the bud).

- Breaking any instruction or procedure knowingly.

Lesser Offenses [a selection]

- Taking any action without using my check partner.
- Trusting my own judgment— or using my own mind.
- Responding defensively to my classmates or teachers.
- Criticizing or finding fault with my classmates or teachers.
- Staying in my own head, having private thoughts.
- Putting myself first, wanting my own way, rebelliousness-selfishness.
- Inappropriately offering suggestions, second-guessing, or jumping ahead of my teachers.
- Exaggerating vehicular symptoms.
- Picking or choosing certain tasks.
- Having likes or dislikes.
- Permitting lack of control over emotions to the point that it interferes with my work or rest or is a distraction to others.
- Desiring attention or approval—wanting to be seen as good.
- Engaging in familiarity, casualness, gossip, lack of restraint with others.
- Being too aggressive or pushy.
- Exercising poor control of thoughts running through my head, being easily distracted.
- Being vain about my appearance, vibrating femininity or masculinity in any way.
- Having inappropriate curiosity.

Source: Heaven's Gate Web site.

One Last Spree Before the End

In their final months, cult members indulged in some very earthly pleasures. Entries from their detailed ledgers:

Jan. 17, 1997 Some members of the cult attend a UFO conference in Laughlin, Nev. While there, they shell out $740.06 on hotels, books, tapes and UFO magazines.

Feb. 24 After buying a $1,100 motor home, the entire group of 59 travels to the Stratosphere Hotel amusement park in Las Vegas. They ride the Big Shot (a free-fall ride) and the High Roller roller coaster. They also win $58.91 gambling. Later they attend the Cirque du Soleil, charging $2,661 worth of tickets.

March 5 Cult members go to a theater to see "Star Wars." They later watch the sequels, too.

March 5–8 Some followers embark on a bus trip to Santa Rosa, Calif., and to Gold Beach, Ore., the place where Applewhite first found his calling in the wilderness. They continue on to Ashland, Ore., and Sacramento, Calif., running up more than $2,000 in hotel bills. Later in the month several members take a road trip to Tijuana. (Mexico is where the phenobarbital was bought.)

March 11 The cult takes a trip to the San Diego Wild Animal Park. Members spend $8 to feed the animals and $81.94 on ice cream. Tickets total $664.95.

March 12 Do's followers set out on another outing, this time to Sea World to see Shamu the whale. The price of admission: $1,092.

March 13 Time for another flick, at a total cost of $258 for tickets.

March 19 After taping their farewell suicide messages, everybody goes out to a pizza joint, ringing up $417 worth of pie. Then they take in another movie, "Secrets & Lies," spending $146 for tickets and $75 on soda.

March 20 Followers dig in at the Red Oak Steak House. The tab comes to $549.90.

March 21 The last lunch. The entire cult dines at a favorite haunt, Marie Callender's restaurant in Carlsbad, Calif. Every member orders a chicken pot pie and a slice of cheesecake, for a bill of $351. On the same day, two cult members report finding six cents. It is the last ledger entry.

March 22 The first suicides apparently begin as the cult serves up poisoned pudding and applesauce.

 Article Review Form at end of book.

- Milgram's experiments generated increased discussion about the ethics of causing distress to experimental subjects and prompted the formation of the American Psychological Association's ethical guidelines for researchers, which are still in use today.

- Situational forces are often more powerful than we realize in determining our behavior. This is evidenced by the behavior we see in cults and in the sometimes blind obedience to destructive authority.

- Certain situations make one vulnerable to finding a cult or cultlike group appealing. These include being in a transitional life-phase (e.g., losing a job, dropping out of school), not having a network of friends and family, and feeling purposeless and without goals.

R.E.A.L. Sites

This list provides a print preview of typical **coursewise** R.E.A.L. sites. (There are over 100 such sites at the **courselinks**™ site.) The danger in printing URLs is that web sites can change overnight. As we went to press, these sites were functional using the URLs provided. If you come across one that isn't, please let us know via email to: webmaster@coursewise.com. Use your Passport to access the most current list of R.E.A.L. sites at the **courselinks**™ site.

Site name: American Family Foundation Cult Group Information

URL: http://www.csj.org/

Why is it R.E.A.L.? This is a top-rated web site that covers information about cults, cultic groups, mind control, cult abuse, and psychological manipulation. It describes known cults and the methods they use to attract members. You will also hear stories from cult survivors much like those in the article in this section, and find out what you can do if someone you know seems to be involved with a cult. Read about some cult mind-control techniques. What principles of conformity do they employ?

Key topics: conformity, group behavior, persuasion, self-help

Site name: Social Psychology Class Paper

URL: http://www.student.richmond.edu/~nberkebi/social1.html

Why is it R.E.A.L.? At this web address is a hypertext web paper written by a University of Richmond student for her social psychology class. It is entitled "The Fundamental Attribution Error and Obedience as Factors in Perceiving Military Personnel and Behavior." As you might guess, it examines the dynamics of obedience in the military. The paper begins with a discussion of war atrocities and how civilians perceive those responsible for such atrocities. It extends the discussion of obedience from the article in this section. This site is also an excellent example of how students can make use of the web in their coursework. Read her paper and see if you agree with the conclusions she reaches.

Key topics: conformity, attribution

section

5

Learning Objectives

- Discuss the reasons that people belong to groups.

- Explain social loafing, the free rider, and the sucker effect. Discuss the conditions that make these particularly likely to occur.

- Describe the steps that lead to groupthink.

- Understand ways to make groups more productive and less likely to make poor decisions.

- Understand the process behind group identification.

- Discuss how group identification can lead to intergroup conflict.

Group Dynamics

 **WiseGuide Intro**

Every person belongs to a large number of different social groups. We can place a person within a group, or category, on the basis of his or her gender, nationality, race, age, occupation, schools attended, and on and on. Humans will probably always affiliate and associate with social groups. Attaching ourselves to a particular group can provide lots of practical benefits, and even give our self-esteem a boost. It is probably also true that we will always use other people's social categories as a cue to guide our judgments of and behaviors toward those people. This section and the section that follows explore these two sides to group life. This section on group dynamics examines the social and personal forces that bring humans together into groups, and explores how groups function and, occasionally, falter. The next section, "Stereotypes and Prejudice," looks at how members of one group think about and act toward members of another group.

As a student or a businessperson, you will inevitably have to work on some sort of group project. If you are like many people, these types of projects make you anxious. How will you be able to get the work done, yet maintain the relationships within the group? How can you make sure everyone is putting in their fair share of the effort? What sort of leadership can help the group work most effectively? Both social and organizational psychologists tackle these problems of small-group functioning.

Many decisions today are made by groups (usually called committees). It is therefore critical to know how the decision-making process is affected by group dynamics. Although it may seem that a committee of two or more people would produce better decisions than a single person working alone, social psychological research shows us that groups often make worse decisions than individuals. A notorious example of the results of poor group decision-making was the explosion of the space shuttle *Challenger* in 1986. A number of people jointly decided that it was safe to launch the shuttle, only to see it self-destruct just seconds after takeoff. "Groupthink" is a characteristic of some groups that can lead to bad decisions. Social psychologists have attempted to identify the symptoms of groupthink and to develop ways of preventing its harmful effects on group decisions. Since many of you will sometimes be in a decision-making group, whether it be a jury or a board of directors, knowing how to maximize group decision-making can be extremely valuable.

Membership in certain groups (e.g., gender) is something we have little or no control over, while belonging to other groups, such as a professional organization, can be a mark of achievement. What does membership in a group offer that can be so appealing to us? Do groups simply provide a set of practical benefits, or are there less tangible social and psychological rewards that draw us to groups?

Our first article discusses how pervasive groups are in American society. Murphy became fascinated with the preponderance of groups while looking something up in the Encyclopedia of Associations, which had 23,000 entries! He talked with people in three groups about what their groups do and why they belong. From a psychological standpoint, this article is interesting because it allows us to see what causes groups to form and how important group membership is for people.

The second article, by Shepperd, talks about groups we don't necessarily choose to belong to—work groups. His research examines ways in which people can ensure that everyone does an equal amount of work and there are no "free riders." It is a good discussion of how some of these negative intragroup dynamics work, and it provides practical information you can use in your next group project.

Our third article is rather lengthy, but in it, C. P. Neck provides a clear description of how groupthink works. He carefully lays out all of the conditions necessary for groupthink and provides examples of these conditions. He then applies those conditions to a decision made by NBC to give "The Tonight Show" to Jay Leno rather than David Letterman to demonstrate that groupthink is not inevitable.

In our final article, Russell Hardin discusses the individual and social origins of ethnic conflict, focusing on the violent clashes in East Africa between the Hutu and Tutsi and in the former Yugoslavia among the Serbs, Croats, and Muslims. Hardin argues that it is shortsighted to view these conflicts merely as some kind of irrational mob action. Rather, according to Hardin, such conflicts should be seen as an extreme end-product of what the economist Mancur Olson called "the logic of collective action."

? Questions ?

R18. Why do people join groups? What needs do groups fulfill? Must groups have a mission?

R19. What type of situation is most likely to produce a free rider? How is social loafing both an individual and a group phenomenon? What are the major issues yet to be examined in explaining social loafing?

R20. How does one come to a diagnosis of groupthink for a decision? What are the new variables the author proposes as important to understanding when groupthink will result in a bad decision?

R21. According to Hardin, what are some of the individual and collective forces that create a sense of individual loyalty to and identification with a group? Why does in-group identification sometimes turn into violent intergroup conflict?

Why do people join groups? What needs do groups fulfill? Must groups have a mission?

Busy, Busy, Busy

The work ethic in America extends to our spare time

Cullen Murphy

In search of a telephone number and an address recently, I flipped through a new edition of the three-volume *Encyclopedia of Associations*; when next I looked up, an hour or so had gone by. With its 23,000 densely crafted entries, the *Encyclopedia of Associations* is an absorbing and indispensable reference work. It is also a monument to America as the world's leading nation of joiners. We like to think of this country, of course, as one of rugged individualists, and perhaps it is. But it is also a place where people need only the flimsiest hint of a shared interest to clump together like iron filings on a magnet. As Tocqueville and other observers have noted, there seems to be no activity, endeavor, condition, passion, peeve, or state of mind in America which lacks an institutional base to rally the faithful and carry the torch.

My own accomplishments in this respect have been very modest. At a young age I was a member of a fan club built around the Blackhawks comic-book series, my secret identity (I can now re-veal) being that of "André." I have for some years been a member of the American Automobile Association, but the only meetings I attend involve tow trucks. In looking through the encyclopedia, I came to understand that my appreciation of America as a nation of joiners was extremely limited and largely abstract. I realized that I had little idea of the vast number of ways in which Americans, workaday demands behind them, deploy their energies and their time.

I decided to spend a day calling up some of the associations listed in the encyclopedia. My criteria for selection came down mostly to curiosity.

An advocate, I learned, can be found for almost anything, and advocacy is one of three broad categories into which the associations I encountered tend to fall. Joe Ann Ricca, who was until recently the president of the American branch of the Richard III Society, answered the phone at her office in Hackensack. She was quick to come to the defense of the generally vilified British monarch. Ricca contends that Richard's evil reputation was largely the creation of Tudor pro-pagandists. (Henry VII, Richard's successor, burned the work of everyone who had anything good to say.) She pointed out that x-ray analyses of various portraits of Richard III show them to have been overpainted in order to magnify the size of the hump on his back. She questioned the implication of Richard in the famous murder, in 1483, of the two princes in the Tower, his young nephews and rivals for the throne, arguing that there are other plausible suspects, and that it is even possible that the princes escaped to the Continent. The Ricardians, 650 strong, publish a journal and sponsor scholarly research. They believe that they may at last have turned the tide.

Seaver Leslie, an artist who lives in Wiscasset, Maine, believes that another tide may have turned. Leslie founded and for nearly two decades has been the director of Americans for Customary Weights and Measures. As the name suggests, the purpose of the group, which has 1,500 members, is to halt the encroachments in the United States of the metric system. The group's P.O. box number in Wiscasset is 5280, which is, of

Cullen Murphy, Busy, Busy, Busy: The Work Ethic in America Extends to Our Spare Time, THE ATLANTIC MONTHLY, June 1994, p. 24. Reprinted by permission of the author.

course, the number of feet in a mile. Its newsletter, *Footprint,* appears twice yearly, on the summer and winter solstices. Leslie observed during our conversation that traditional measures—the inch, the foot, the mile, the furlong—are all somehow derived from human proportions or human activity. The furlong, for example, was the distance a ploughman could walk from home and still be within earshot. Can it be coincidence, Leslie asked, that the rungs on ladders the world around, from culture to culture, are all a foot apart? Traditional measures, he said, "touch the poetic soul of every individual in America." In contrast, when it comes to metric, people can't even agree on which syllable to stress in the word "kilometer." Leslie's free time is spent lobbying for the repeal of Public Law 100-418, the Omnibus Trade and Competitiveness Act of 1988, which enshrined the metric system as the preferred system of weights and measures for U.S. trade and commerce and required the U.S. government to begin using the metric system in all its operations. He noted that metric has been beaten back three times—in the 1870s, the 1920s, and the 1970s—and is confident it will be beaten back again.

On the other side of this issue is the American National Metric Council, an association based in Bethesda, Maryland, with 150 members, most of them corporate. The council's president is John Deam, who in his professional life is the director of business operations for a company that designs laser-based measuring instruments. Deam, of course, holds Public Law 100-418 in high regard, and believes that once private industry comes around, the public will follow inexorably. He

notes in metric's defense that it is easy to comprehend the relationship of, say, centimeters to meters, whereas there is no such orderly relationship between feet and miles, or between inches and yards. He wonders what it says about this nation that at a time of an increasingly integrated world economy the United States stands alone among industrialized nations in its reserve toward the metric system. But Deam is heartened by some recent developments. Since last January, for example, the General Services Administration has been accepting new specifications for federal buildings only in metric units. For the record, the American National Metric Council does have an official position on the pronunciation of "kilometer": accent on the first syllable, not the second—a position, I suspect, that will be as congenial to many Americans as the metric system itself. Asked, by the way, whether he uses a yardstick at home, Deam replied, "I'm afraid I do."

A second category of associations is for those who might loosely be called contestants. I spoke with Tom Cabot, of Hermann, Missouri, who is the president of the National Organization of Mall Walkers, a group established "to give national recognition to people who walk in malls for exercise." The organization sells log books so that its 1,000 members, most of whom are women above the age of fifty-five, can record their mileage, and it awards patches and pins to those who achieve certain distances. Cabot, who sells sports medallions and Christmas ornaments for a living, explained that mall walking resembles the German tradition of outdoor "Volks marching." In 1979, Cabot helped organize the American

Volkssport Association, and sought to recruit the people he saw walking in malls. He founded the Mall Walkers because "I couldn't get them outside."

In Scranton, Pennsylvania, Bob O'Leary picked up the phone at the American Armwrestling Association. O'Leary, a distributor of nutritional supplements, is the executive chairman of the association, which has 2,000 members and is affiliated with the World Arm-wrestling Federation, headquarters in Calcutta. (Arm wrestling is India's second most popular sport, after soccer.) O'Leary explained that there are two styles of arm wrestling, stand-up and seated, and that arm wrestlers are known as "pullers." Arm-wrestling tournaments are held somewhere in America every week of the year. Any major issues facing the arm-wrestling community? "Drug testing at national events," O'Leary said. Also, a lot of effort has gone into lobbying for arm wrestling's inclusion as an Olympic sport—"obviously long overdue."

Larry Kahn, of the North American Tiddlywinks Association, in Silver Spring, Maryland, explains that most of the 100 dues-paying "winkers" in his group are men, and that most have a background in mathematics or computers. In the United States major tiddlywinks tournaments are held four or five times a year. NATWA has a sister organization known as ETWA, in England; of English winkers Kahn observes, "They're even nerdier than we are." Like participants in many other sports and games, winkers have developed a distinctive jargon. They may say, for instance, "I can't pot my nurdled wink, so I'll piddle you free and you can boondock a red." Tiddlywinks apparently enjoyed something of an efflorescence in the United States in the late 1960s and the 1970s, after which it entered a period of mild decline. Kahn blames this on the nation's having experienced a time of cynical economic opportunism and creeping spiritual discontent, which together eroded the bedrock of silliness upon which the edifice of tiddlywinks is erected. Or so I inferred. Actually, what he said when asked about the cause of the decline was simply, "Reagan."

Finally, there are the collectors. The world headquarters of the International Sand Collectors Society is located in Old Greenwich, Connecticut, and I spoke with its president, William S. Diefenbach, a retired management consultant. Diefenbach explained that the membership was held together, as it were, by "a common bond of sand." Sand from the beaches of Normandy, sand from Mount St. Helen's, sand from the Channel Tunnel, sand from the sand traps of famous golf courses. (A golf-course division of the society is in the planning stages.) The society has 400 members, Diefenbach said; General Norman Schwarzkopf, the commander of Operation Desert Storm, was granted honorary membership (which he accepted). Asked about activities, Diefenbach said, "We recently had a sand swap"—the first such event in the United States. Diefenbach puts out a newsletter, *The Sand Paper*, which among other things describes "the surpluses and needs of individual members." The members clearly don't want for projects to keep them occupied. Some items from the newsletter: "Bert Brim sent a supplement to his catalog of Ocean Beach Sands, bringing the number

up to 830." "Angela Maure is back from holiday in Egypt, and offers you: Desert al Rayum, Hurghada, the Valley of the Kings (Kramak and Hatschepsut), and the small island of Magawish." Warren Hatch has made a superb 58 minute VHS tape of 42 sands seen through a scope at 10 and 20X.

The man who answered the phone at the number listed for the International Carnivorous Plant Society was Leo Song, its business manager and also the manager of the greenhouse at California State University, in Fullerton. He explained that the purpose of the society, which has 700 members, is "to provide information that concerns carnivorous plants, from care and culture to taxonomy, nomenclature, political action, and the dissemination of new hybrid names." Asked what draws people to collecting carnivorous plants, Song said, "When you think about plants eating bugs, it kind of turns the tables." Asked about the disturbing reputation of the Venus's flytrap, Song called it ridiculous. "With the plants we've discovered so far," he said, "you don't have to worry about your cat getting eaten—even with genetic engineering." He added, though, that when people ask him if dangerously carnivorous plants do exist, he always tells them, "Well, there are areas out there that haven't been explored."

Danny Perez, an electrician in Norwalk, California, would surely agree. Perez, too, is a collector, in a way. He heads the Center for Bigfoot Studies, whose purpose is to obtain a specimen of the large, shy, primatelike creature that is believed by some to inhabit the northern woods. He was inspired to take up the cause, to which he devotes all his spare

time, by the movie *The Legend of Boggy Creek*, a documentary about Bigfoot, that he saw at the age of ten. Apparently the Bigfoot community, which consists of several hundred people, is divided on strategy, the division being between the "take-it-alive" camp and the "shoot-to-kill" camp. Perez favors the first approach. He conceded, however, that the second would be "a lot safer."

All told, I got in touch with about twenty-five associations, and at day's end it was hard to shake the feeling that compared with the lives of the people I had been talking to, my own was rudderless. Lifting my sights, I also began to wonder whether there must not exist an umbrella association to which people who run associations can belong—an organization that offers advice on, say, publicity and fund-raising, or on holding conventions, and that perhaps lobbies the government for various kinds of tax exemptions. In the Washington, D.C., phone book I found something called the Association of Societies and Associations, but despite repeated attempts was unable to speak with anyone there. Were the lines being tied up by urgent calls from the American Fancy Rat and Mouse Association? Professional Psychics United? The U.S. Amateur Tug of War Association? The Marx Brothers Study Unit? The Flying Funeral Directors of America?

What I know is that according to the taped message, "all of our staff are busy." I don't doubt it for a second.

 Article Review Form at end of book.

What type of situation is most likely to produce a free rider? How is social loafing both an individual and a group phenomenon? What are the major issues yet to be examined in explaining social loafing?

Remedying Motivation and Productivity Loss in Collective Settings

James A. Shepperd

James A. Shepperd is an Associate Professor in the Department of Psychology at the University of Florida. Address correspondence to James A. Shepperd, Department of Psychology, University of Florida, Gainesville, FL 32611; e-mail: shepperd @webb.psych.ufl.edu.

Perhaps the most annoying thing about working in a group or other setting in which efforts are pooled to form a collective product is that not all individuals contribute equally. There always seem to be some people who loaf or choose to free ride on the efforts of other people. Over the past two decades, this irksome aspect of groups has captured the attention of researchers in psychology, sociology, management, economics, and political science. The guiding questions underlying the research are why do people exert less effort in collective settings, and what can be done about the reduction in effort.

Sources of and Solutions to Low Effort in Collective Settings

The problem of low effort in collective settings has been characterized as a social disease,[1] and researchers have rallied their efforts to find a cure. The cures or remedies proposed include making individual contributions identifiable, unique, or difficult; increasing group identity and group cohesiveness; increasing personal involvement in the task; making the task more attractive; and rewarding contributors, to name a few.

Recently, I proposed a model for understanding the problem of low effort in groups and other collective settings.[2] The model, based on expectancy theory, conceptualizes low effort as a problem of low motivation arising when individuals perceive their contributions to the collective as unrewarded,

unneeded, or too costly. The model further specifies that productivity loss in collectives can be remedied by (a) providing incentives for contributing, (b) making contributions indispensable, and (c) decreasing the cost of contributing. The first and third solutions affect the *value* associated with contributing, whereas the second solution affects the *expectancy* that personal contributions are consequential.

The first source of low productivity (contributions are unrewarded) results when contributors derive no benefit from contributing, either because personal contributions are unidentifiable (thus, individuals cannot enjoy the proper rewards for a good performance) or because the behavior or its outcome is not valued (i.e., the contributors do not care if the collective goal is realized). The solution is to provide an incentive for contributing. The incentive need not be a material one, such as money or bonuses. Because people are generally concerned with achieving a positive evaluation (or avoiding a negative evaluation), merely the prospect of evaluation is sufficient to remedy low productivity.[3] Moreover, the evaluation need not be external. To the extent that individuals are concerned with evaluating themselves favorably, merely the opportunity for self-evaluation is sufficient to eliminate low motivation and productivity.[4]

The second source of low productivity (contributions are unnecessary) results when contributors perceive no contingency between their contributions and achieving the collective goal. That is, contributors believe that the collective product (e.g., winning a tug-of-war match, building a house, writing a group report) will be achieved regardless of whether they work hard or not. Thus, personal contributions are perceived as dispensable, leading individuals to free ride on the contributions of other people. The solution to this second source of low motivation and productivity is to make individuals perceive their contributions as indispensable, for example, by decreasing the redundancy of contributions or by dividing the task so that each contributor provides something unique and essential.

The third source of low productivity (contributions are too costly) results when contributors regard the material or psychological costs of contributing to exceed any benefit that might be attained from achieving the collective product. The material costs refer to the depletion of resources that are diverted from some other, more profitable venture. The psychological costs refer to a feeling of exploitation that arises from the perception that other people are

free riding on one's own efforts, enjoying the benefits of a good collective performance (e.g., an A on a group project in a course) while personally contributing little. Generally, people are loathe to be exploited in this way and will even refrain from contributing themselves to avoid this psychological cost, even though holding back may mean that the collective outcome is not achieved. The costs can be thought of as disincentives to contributing that undermine achieving the collective goal. The solution is to decrease or eliminate the material and psychological costs of contributing. The material costs can be reduced by making the task easier or less taxing on personal resources. The psychological costs can be reduced by changing the task from a collective one to an individual one (e.g., paying workers for piecework rather than hourly) or by ensuring that free riding will be punished.

What We Know

Over the past two decades, we have made tremendous progress in our understanding of low motivation and productivity in collective settings. In this section, I discuss several of the most notable advances in knowledge.

Cognitive Versus Physical Tasks

Although the initial research on social loafing, the free-riding effect, and the sucker effect examined productivity loss on physical tasks, subsequent research has demonstrated that the same processes operate with cognitive tasks. Indeed, in the laboratory, productivity loss has been shown on physical tasks such as pulling a tug-of-war rope, clapping and

cheering, swimming in a relay race, pumping air, and wrapping gum, as well as on cognitive tasks such as evaluating written work, detecting blips on a screen, solving mazes, making paper moons, and generating uses for objects.

A Group Versus Individual Phenomenon

The problem of low motivation and productivity in collective settings traditionally is regarded as a group phenomenon. Most textbooks in introductory and social psychology and in management and organizational behavior discuss the topic in a chapter or section of a chapter on groups. However, it is misleading to regard low motivation in collective settings solely as a group phenomenon or one that occurs only when individuals pool their efforts. Perceiving contributions as unrewarded, unneeded, or too costly is an intrapsychic phenomenon that can occur among people working individually. Specifically, if an individual working on a solo project sees no benefit to working hard, perceives no contingency between his or her efforts and achieving a desired outcome, or perceives the cost of success as too high, exceeding any benefit that might be derived from a successful performance, then he or she will withhold effort.

Nevertheless, settings in which individuals combine their efforts to form a group or collective product seem particularly likely to foster these conditions. When efforts are pooled, individual contributions often cannot be monitored or identified, thus removing the incentive (or sanction) that often accompanies evaluation. The result is greater social loafing. Likewise, when efforts are pooled, the responsibility for achieving a good group performance is shared. The necessity of any one individual's efforts is reduced, increasing the perceived dispensability of contributions and, as a result, increasing the likelihood of free riding. Finally, when efforts are pooled, the possibility arises that other people will free ride on one's own efforts. Consequently, individuals will decrease their own contributions to avoid being exploited by others.

Cultural Differences

Cross-cultural studies of motivation and productivity loss in collective settings are rare. Nevertheless, studies comparing Japanese and Chinese with Americans suggest that free riding and social loafing are universal (albeit, perhaps more prevalent among Japanese and Americans than among Chinese). However, when structural changes in the collective systems increase the prospect that other people will free ride, there are cultural differences in how individuals respond. If permitted, Japanese are more likely than Americans to withdraw from the situation.[5] This difference appears to be attributable to differences between the two cultures in how collective systems are maintained. Japanese typically maintain collective systems externally through mutual monitoring and sanctioning. When structural changes remove the ability to monitor and sanction, Japanese prefer to withdraw from the situation rather than risk being victim of another person's free riding. Americans, by contrast, maintain collective systems internally by instilling feelings of duty and obligation. They generally are less affected by changes that remove the ability to monitor and sanction, believing that other people, like themselves, will continue to contribute to the collective from a sense of obligation or duty.

Low Productivity as a Social Dilemma

The problem of low motivation and productivity in collective settings can be conceptualized as a social dilemma. A social dilemma is any situation in which individuals face a conflict between their own selfish interests and the interests of the collective. The most familiar example is Hardin's "The Tragedy of the Commons," which illustrates the conflict that exists when a number of shepherds graze their herds on a common pasture.[6] Although each shepherd derives greater profit from increasing his or her herd size, if every shepherd increases the size of his or her herd, the pasture will be damaged from overgrazing. Thus, the behavior that is most beneficial for the individual shepherd (i.e., increasing the size of his or her herd) is harmful for the community as a whole should every shepherd act similarly.

In collective settings, the collective or group goal can be thought of as the commons. It is in the best interest of each individual member to withhold contributions and free ride, forcing others to work hard to achieve the goal. However, if all people withhold effort, then the collective goal will not be achieved and presumably everyone will suffer. The feature distinguishing research on productivity loss and the larger literature on social dilemmas is the commodity that influences the collective welfare. Investigations of social dilemmas typically focus on the problem of overtaxing some finite public resource, such as the commons, or the problem of providing some public good, such as public television. Investigations of productivity loss in performance groups, by contrast, focus on factors that influence the amount of effort individuals contribute to some collective venture. More generally, this body of research is concerned primarily with the loss in motivation and subsequent reduction in productivity among individuals working collectively compared with individuals working alone.

Evaluation and Creativity

Although making contributions identifiable and thus able to be evaluated is an effective strategy for eliminating social loafing, it has a serious liability. The prospect of evaluation increases the quantity of contributing, but has a deleterious effect on the quality of contributions. Specifically, on tasks that require creativity, anticipated evaluation (either external or self-evaluation) can produce decrements in performance, leading to less creativity than when no evaluation is anticipated.[7]

The Effects of Norms and Roles

There is growing evidence that norms exercise a strong influence over the amount of effort individuals contribute in a collective setting. Some norms can lead individuals to withhold effort. Such is the case, for example, with antiproduction norms that carry sanctions for "rate-busters," people whose high efforts can make other contributors look bad by comparison. Other norms can lead to either decreases or increases in effort, depending on the nature of the situation. For example, the equity norm holds that payoffs or rewards should be distributed in proportion to contributions. Accordingly, if individuals believe that their rewards for contributing will exceed their efforts, they will contribute more to reestablish equity. However, should they believe that their rewards for contributing will fall short of their efforts, perhaps because other people are rewarded equally for contributing less, then they will withhold effort to reestablish equity.[8]

What We Don't Know

Although we have progressed in our understanding of why people exert less effort when efforts are pooled, when loafing and free riding are most likely to occur, and what can be done in response, there remain several unanswered questions. In this section, I explain just a few of the unresolved issues in the study of motivation and productivity loss in collective settings.

- *The effects of group characteristics.* There is considerable evidence demonstrating the benefit of providing internal incentives for good individual performances. However, few studies have examined the utility of providing incentives (either internal or external) for a good collective performance. Consequently, it is unclear just how effective incentives for a good collective performance will be. In addition, it is unclear whether group characteristics such as group cohesiveness and group identity can function as incentives that increase members' productivity. Specifically, are cohesive groups more productive than noncohesive groups? Are group members with high group identity less likely to loaf

than group members with low group identity?

- *Is dispensability independent from value?* Altering the perceived dispensability to contributing can also affect the perceived value of contributions, and vice versa. Specifically, the more a given individual's contributions are regarded as indispensable, the more the contributions will be valued. If a given team member's efforts are unnecessary to winning a tug-of-war match, his or her contributions may not be valued much. However, if high efforts from all team members are essential to winning the match, the value of each individual's contributions will be high. This observation raises the question of whether the value associated with contributing and the perceived indispensability of contributions operate independently. It is possible that perceived dispensability of contributing affects motivation and productivity by influencing the perceived value of the contributions.

- *Reducing the psychological costs.* Little research has examined the effects of the psychological costs of contributing on motivation and how the costs associated with contributing might be reduced. The most effective solution, changing the task from a collective one to an individual one, requires partitioning the collective goal into individual sections. With the goal partitioned into sections, individuals can no longer fall prey to the free-riding attempts of others. Each individual can enjoy the fruits (as well as suffer the consequences) of his or her personal contributions.

Unfortunately, outside the psychology laboratory, it often is not possible or not feasible to partition the public good into individual sections. Many tasks, such as building a house, producing a group project, and winning a team sport, require that efforts be combined. Alternative solutions, such as promising that free riders will be punished, will be effective only so far as contributors believe that the people who control the rewards and punishments can identify which group members did what. Clearly, strategies for reducing the psychological costs of contributing are sorely needed.

Summary

The tendency for people to loaf or free ride on the contributions of other people, although commonplace, is not an inevitable consequence of working in a group. We now know that the lower productivity found among individuals pooling their contributions relative to individuals working alone is largely a problem of low motivation resulting from the perception that contributions are unrewarded, unneeded, or too costly. Moreover, research by psychologists and other social scientists has revealed that managers, coaches, teachers, and other group leaders can elicit high effort from group and team members provided there is an incentive to contribute, members of the collective perceive their contributions as indispensable, and the costs of contributing do not exceed any benefit that might be derived from a good collective performance.

Notes

1. B. Latané, K. Williams, and S. Harkins, Many hands make light the work: The causes and consequences of social loafing, *Journal of Personality and Social Psychology, 37,* 822–832 (1979).
2. J. A. Shepperd, Productivity loss in performance groups: A motivation analysis, *Psychological Bulletin, 113,* 67–81 (1993).
3. S. Harkins and J. Jackson, The role of evaluation in eliminating social loafing, *Personality and Social Psychology Bulletin, 11,* 457–465 (1985).
4. S. G. Harkins and K. Szymanski, Social loafing and self-evaluation with an objective standard, *Journal of Experimental Social Psychology, 24,* 354–365 (1988).
5. T. Yamagishi, Exit from the group as an individualistic solution to the free rider problem in the United States and Japan, *Journal of Experimental Social Psychology, 24,* 530–542 (1988).
6. G. J. Hardin, The tragedy of the commons, *Science, 162,* 1243–1248 (1968).
7. K. Szymanski and S. G. Harkins, Self-evaluation and creativity, *Personality and Social Psychology Bulletin, 18,* 259–265 (1992).
8. N. L. Kerr, Norms in social dilemmas, in *Social Dilemmas: Social Psychological Perspectives,* D. Schroeder, Ed. (Praeger, New York, in press).

Recommended Reading

Shepperd, J. A. (1993). Productivity loss in performance groups: A motivation analysis. *Psychological Bulletin, 113,* 67–81.

Williams, K., Karau, S., and Bourgeois, M. (1993). Working on collective tasks: Social loafing and social compensation. In *Group Motivation: Social Psychology Perspectives,* M. A. Hogg and D. Abrams, Eds. (Harvester/Wheatsheaf, New York).

 Article Review Form at end of book.

How does one come to a diagnosis of groupthink for a decision?
What are the new variables the author proposes as important to
understanding when groupthink will result in a bad decision?

Letterman or Leno

A groupthink analysis of successive decisions made by the National Broadcasting Company (NBC)

Christopher P. Neck

Abstract: *Groupthink decisions are based on group culture or in-group desire for unanimity, are often found to be unrealistic responses to situations and are therefore defective. Conditions that lead to groupthink include insulation of the group, social and ideological homogeneity, leader preference and lack of methodical procedures. Such context lead to defects that include lack of information on alternatives due to poor research and bias on data selection. However, groupthink can be avoided as shown in the National Broadcasting Co. senior executives' decision on Jay Leno and David Letterman.*

Introduction

In 1972, Irving Janis coined the term "groupthink" as "a mode of thinking that people engage in when they are deeply involved in a cohesive in-group . . . members' striving for unanimity override their motivation to realistically appraise alternative courses of action . . . a deterioration of mental efficiency, reality testing, and moral judgment that results from in-group pressures"[1, p. 9]. Support for the occurrence of this phenomenon was based on his historical case analysis of the decision-making activities of governmental policy-making groups that resulted in either major "fiascos" or outstanding successes.

Since the origination of groupthink, additional case studies have appeared in the literature that involve the retrospective applications of actual group decision-making situations to Janis' groupthink framework[2]. More specifically, groupthink has been used to explain highly consequential decision-making settings such as the Iran hostage rescue mission[3], the Kent State Gymnasium controversy[4], the Space Shuttle Challenger launch[5], and the jury deliberations in the trial of US v. John DeLorean[6]. Although these analyses provide support for the occurrence and/or avoidance of the groupthink phenomenon, this case study approach to the groupthink research still falls short of completely addressing this decision-making process, owing to one glaring omission. All of these studies that followed Janis' work were situations involving a single decision executed by a group in which groupthink did or did not occur. Consequently, the groupthink literature is missing case studies that examine successive decisions made by the same decision-making group. Surely, we can learn as much, if not more, about decision-making by examining consecutive decisions made by the same group, thus examining a group over a period of time rather than just studying a single decision-making process of a group. In fact, this omission was partly committed by Janis as six of the seven policy-making groups that he analyzed involved an examination of a single decision-making situation[2]. A clearer understanding of groupthink could be facilitated by a case study that examines multiple decisions made by the same group over a period of time in

C. P. Neck, "Letterman or Leno: A Groupthink Analysis of Successive Decisions Made by the National Broadcasting Company (NBC)."
JOURNAL OF MANAGERIAL PSYCHOLOGY, 11(8), 3–18. Reprinted with permission.

which the decision-making group is susceptible to groupthink and describes the factors that seem to account for why defective decision making does or does not occur in each separate decision-making context. Considering that most of the important and highly consequential decisions affecting organizations today are made in groups, a better understanding of the groupthink phenomenon could be quite beneficial[6].

The purpose of this paper is to enhance the literature by providing a modern and business-oriented case analysis of highly consequential successive decisions made by the same group—in which the conditions for groupthink were prevalent in each decision, yet the phenomenon was avoided by the group in the later decision. In short, this case analysis involves a group of senior executives of the National Broadcasting Company (NBC) and their decisions relating to NBC's flagship late-night television show, The Tonight Show, the most profitable television show ever[7]. Specifically, the first decision facing the NBC executive group was determining the successor to Johnny Carson, the 30-year host of The Tonight Show, once he retired. The second decision confronting the NBC management team involved determining what to do with one of their other late-night stars, David Letterman, since they did not decide in their first decision to offer him the The Tonight Show hosting job. Thanks to the work of William Carter[7] in which he interviewed many of the primary players related to these decisions, information concerning these two successive decisions made by the same group of NBC executives is available for analysis as consecutive group decisions possibly susceptible to group-

think. These interviews were quite extensive in that several hundred interviews were conducted with more than 100 people connected with the television business and the programming of late-night television. Each individual was interviewed at least once and most were interviewed several times[7].

Before delving into the details of this management team's decision-making processes, a brief overview of Janis'[2] framework is provided. Then, the successive decisions of the NBC executives are analyzed in terms of the groupthink phenomenon. Finally, an enhanced groupthink framework based on the evidence obtained from our case study will be presented and discussed.

Groupthink: An Overview

The major thrust of Janis' model is that the presence of a number of specific antecedent conditions increases the probability that the group will demonstrate symptoms representative of groupthink[2]. Additionally, these symptoms will lead to observable defects in the group's decision-making processes that might result in poor quality decisions[8].

Antecedent Conditions

According to Janis, antecedent conditions are the observable causes of groupthink. In other words, they are the conditions "that produce, elicit, or facilitate the occurrence of the syndrome" [2, p. 176]. The primary antecedent condition necessary for groupthink is a highly cohesive group. As Janis states:

. . . Only when a group of policy-makers is moderately or highly cohesive can we expect the groupthink syndrome to emerge as

the members are working collectively on one or another of their important policy decisions[2, p. 176].

Group cohesiveness is often defined as "the result of all the forces acting on the members to remain in the group"[9]. Similarly, Janis argues that "the more amiability and esprit de corps among the members of an in-group of policy-makers, the greater the danger that independent critical thinking will be replaced by groupthink . . ."[2, p. 245].

However, it is important to note that cohesiveness is a necessary but insufficient condition for groupthink to pervade a decision-making group. Janis postulated a number of secondary conditions necessary for groupthink to occur. Some of these secondary conditions related to the structural or administrative faults of the organization. These include:

- insulation of the group;
- leader preference for a certain decision;
- lack of norms requiring methodical procedures;
- homogeneity of members' social background and ideology.

The remaining conditions are related to the decision-making context and include:

- high stress from external threats with low hope of a better solution than the leader's;
- low self-esteem temporarily induced by the group's perception of recent failures, excessive difficulties on current decision-making tasks, and moral dilemmas (i.e., apparent lack of feasible alternatives except ones that violate ethical standards)[2].

Symptoms of Groupthink

The existence of the antecedent conditions produces the "observables" or symptoms of groupthink. Janis argued that eight symptoms were evident in the fiascoes studied and serve as the primary means of identifying the occurrence of groupthink. The symptoms include:

1. an illusion of invulnerability;

2. an unquestioned belief in the group's inherent morality;

3. collective efforts to rationalize;

4. stereotyped views of enemy leaders as evil, weak, or stupid;

5. self-censorship of deviations from the group consensus;

6. a shared illusion of unanimity;

7. direct pressure on any member who expresses strong arguments against any of the group's stereotypes;

8. the emergence of self-appointed mind guards to protect or screen the group from adverse information[2].

Decision-Making Defects

When a group displays the symptoms listed above, the group may exhibit specific defects in the decision-making process. Janis states "whenever a policy-making group displays most of the symptoms of groupthink, we can expect to find that the group also displays symptoms of defective decision making"[2, p. 175]. The defects in the decision-making process that result from groupthink are:

- incomplete survey of alternatives;

- incomplete survey of objectives;

- failure to examine risks of preferred choice;

- failure to reappraise initially rejected alternatives;

- poor information search;

- selective bias in processing information at hand;

- failure to work out contingency plans.

Janis hypothesized that the more frequently a group exhibits these defects, the worse will be the quality of the decisions[1].

NBC Executive Group

The successive decisions made by the group of NBC executives regarding the late night television programming issue appear to be prime examples of cases where many of the antecedent conditions necessary for groupthink to occur were present. Before examining these separate decision-making processes, a brief overview of the members of the NBC management group is provided. These members include: Robert Wright, the president of NBC; Warren Littlefield, the head of NBC programming; and John Agoglia, executive vice president of NBC. Within this group, the highest ranking official was Bob Wright (Littlefield and Agoglia reported to him), and he was ultimately responsible for the decisions made.

Also, it is important to provide an overview of the two primary players affected by these decisions, Jay Leno and David Letterman. Leno was the permanent guest host for The Tonight Show from 1987–1992. Letterman was the host of the television programme that followed The Tonight Show on NBC, Late Night. This programme was quite successful for NBC. As Carter remarked:

. . . Letterman was first called refreshing and later brilliant . . . Emmy Awards rolled in. Dollars

followed. Letterman's audience grew modestly, but steadily, up toward 4 million viewers a night. And these were highly prized viewers: mostly young, mostly male, mostly people who were not being reached by many other television shows . . .[7, p. 30].

Within the entertainment industry, speculation existed regarding both men as candidates for the next The Tonight Show host.

It has been suggested that the groupthink framework can be a useful method for studying a decision-making group[6, 10]. Thus, the actual decisions by the NBC executive group regarding NBC's late night programming will now be analyzed in terms of the groupthink framework. During this analysis, various excerpts from Carter's interviews are utilized to illustrate various analytical points. However, it should be noted that these excerpts are only samples of a larger body of data that supports the arguments proposed in this manuscript (see [7] for a more extensive analysis of the interviews with key individuals surrounding these decisions by NBC executives). Consequently, this analysis is not solely based on these selected quotations but rather on the entire text of the interview data.

Decision One: The Successor to Johnny Carson

As mentioned earlier, the first decision that will be analyzed in terms of groupthink involved the NBC group's decision of deciding who would replace the 30-year host of the show, Johnny Carson, once he decided to retire. (Johnny Carson announced his retirement on May 23, 1991—one week after this first decision by the NBC management group.) The outcome of this decision was the selection of Jay Leno as the new

The Tonight Show host. This decision to select Leno over Letterman proved to be disastrous for NBC because Letterman accepted a contract to bring his late night show to another network (CBS) to compete head to head with NBC's The Tonight Show.

Letterman's show won the competition in terms of both ratings and advertising dollars. But more importantly, NBC lost its reign of being the pinnacle in late-night television[7].

Highly Consequential Decision

Although Janis did not directly include a "highly consequential decision" as an antecedent condition, it has been suggested that it should be included in an analysis of groupthink because all the decision-making situations that Janis[2] examined were of a highly consequential nature[6]. The highly consequential nature of this first decision to NBC was clearly evidenced by what the continued success of The Tonight Show (which was contingent on an effective host) meant to the network. As Carter states:

. . . The show poured out cash, many years grossing more than $100 million and providing as much as 15 to 20 percent of the profits recorded by the entire network. For NBC, Carson was the key to the mint . . .[7, p. 17]. . . . Almost thirty years into his nightly role as the nation's chief cultural color commentator, Carson was the single biggest money generator in television history . . .[7, p. 3].

Obviously, the continued success of The Tonight Show was, in money terms, very crucial to NBC. And, determining the next host was a very consequential decision for the NBC executives because the host was a large component towards the show's success[7].

Group Cohesion

As stated earlier, the primary condition necessary for the occurrence of groupthink is a highly cohesive group. Cohesiveness involves an esprit de corps among the members, where members like each other and feel a part of a close-knit group. The NBC executive group was very cohesive. One factor contributing to this was that they were the chief decision makers for NBC who were stationed on the West Coast (Burbank, California)—that is, they were isolated from the other executives at the headquarters of NBC in New York City. This isolation forced the three members to work closely together on important projects and to stand behind each other so their message could be heard at the headquarters in New York City.

Insulation of Group

This condition refers to a situation when "the cohesive decision-making group is insulated from the judgment of qualified associates"[2, p. 249]. As stated above, the geographical location of the group created a situation of insulation from other aspects of the television network. Also, the evidence of the group's insulation from expert judgment occurs in the fact that the group never contacted the outgoing 30-year host about his opinion on a suitable replacement. As Carter argues: "To the astonishment of many of The Tonight Show staff, NBC had never seen fit to consult Carson about the naming of a successor . . ."[7, p. 79].

Leader Preference for a Certain Decision

Janis argues that this groupthink condition implies that "the leader does not feel constrained by any

organizational tradition to avoid pushing for his own preferred policies"[2]. This antecedent condition did seem to exist with this NBC executive group. The top level NBC executive within the group, Robert Wright, actively voiced his opinion. He felt "that NBC had established over thirty years an audience that expected certain things, and Jay Leno looked like the perfect successor to that, while David Letterman remained the ideal performer for the 12:30 show"[7, p. 63].

Methodical Procedures

This antecedent condition applies to lack of methodical procedures for instituting information search and objective appraisals of the consequences of the main alternatives[2]. The NBC executive group did not seem to use definite procedures to ensure that all aspects of the issue were discussed. Interview data appear to support this contention, in that at no time were specific procedures for decision making mentioned by the NBC executive group members[7].

Homogeneity of Members' Backgrounds

Janis describes this antecedent condition in terms of "lack of disparity in social background and ideology among the members makes it easier for them to concur on whatever proposals are put forth"[2, p. 250]. The members of the NBC group appeared to be a fairly homogeneous group. All were male, white, and were executives for NBC.

High Stress from External Threats

It has been suggested that the symptoms of groupthink will be most pronounced when high stress from external threats is present[2]. In terms of reaching a decision, the members of the NBC management team seemed to perceive external pressure from the press, other television networks, and Jay Leno's manager (Helen Kushnick). In terms of the former, with rumors circulating within the television industry that Johnny Carson would be retiring soon, the NBC executives were being constantly bombarded by reporters asking them who was going to be the next host of The Tonight Show. As Carter reveals the words of several NBC personnel:

. . . The press reaction would be a roaring fire, besieging offices on each coast for information

. . . All the reporters were yelling the same question: "Who's getting Johnny's job?"[7, p. 9].

Similarly, the group members felt pressure from another television network, CBS. Specifically, CBS had offered a contract to Jay Leno for a late-night show on CBS for about $6 million a year. This increased the pressure among the NBC executive group. Carter indicates the pressured situation felt by the top executive in the NBC group:

. . . He couldn't hand The Tonight Show to Leno while Carson still occupied it; but if he didn't, he might lose Leno to CBS. And whenever the show did change hands, Letterman would have to be factored into any resolution . . .[7, p. 38].

Finally, the NBC group perceived pressure from Helen Kushnick, Jay Leno's manager. Evidence of this is provided by Carter:

. . . As Jay's Tonight spots improved and he started to get more and more favorable press, she [Helen Kushnick] began to turn the heat on NBC— lightly at first, but full blast was soon to come . . .[7, p. 47]. . . . In mid-April, she had had enough. She called

Agoglia with a simple message: "I want Jay signed"[7, p. 62].

Temporary Low Self-Esteem

The rationale for this antecedent condition is that a lowering of self-esteem constitutes an internal source of stress that is induced by various factors, including the group's perception of recent failures. It seemed that the NBC executives' self-esteem was lowered because of the failures that the members had experienced in the past with a key factor in this decision-making process, David Letterman. As Robert Wright said: ". . . I tried, but Dave made it difficult. He did not encourage anyone to just drop in and see him. . ."[7, p. 60].

Supportingly, another NBC executive remarked:

. . . When you tried with Dave, he made you feel stupid. It was: Leave me alone but love me. You got to the point where you would think: If I go in there to see him, it's going to be so awkward . . .[7, p. 60].

To summarize the analysis thus far, the primary groupthink antecedent condition of high group cohesion existed as well as six of the six secondary antecedent conditions. Janis argues that the more of the antecedent conditions that are present, the greater number of groupthink symptoms will occur and thus, the greater the chances of defective decision making[2]. Thus, based on the number of antecedent conditions present in the NBC executive group's decision involving the successor of Johnny Carson, it should be expected that groupthink symptoms would emerge and decision-making defects should occur. Accordingly, this analysis yields information that supports this contention— that is, groupthink symptoms and

decision-making defects did indeed occur during this first decision.

Symptoms of Groupthink in Decision One

Most of the symptoms of groupthink relate to three broad areas: overestimation by the group, the closed-mindedness of the group, and pressures within the group towards uniformity[2]. Overestimation refers to the group's miscalculation of their judgement[2]. It appears that the NBC management group overestimated the abilities of Jay Leno and the lack of ability in David Letterman. As Carter states:

Littlefield believed that Leno had an accessibility that the audience embraced, and that even though the 11:30 show was considered a late-night franchise, this audience really was broad-based. When push came to shove for Warren Littlefield, Jay Leno was just more broad-based than David Letterman . . .[7, p. 64].

The general symptom of closed-mindedness of the group describes the condition where the group collectively espouse their own views at the expense of not considering alternative opinions[2]. Additionally, groups displaying this symptom exhibit stereotypical views of those outside their group with a competing opinion. Closed-mindedness seems to permeate this group, as evidenced by their stereotypical views of David Letterman. Carter remarks:

. . . Littlefield thought that Letterman's penchant for what he called "ambushing the guest" would never play with the broad-based audience that came to the set at 11:30. Whether Dave was really nasty to his guests or just funny with them wasn't an issue that Warren Littlefield or John Agoglia had to commission special research to determine; they didn't even have to watch the show to see if it was true . . .[7, p. 64] . . . Littlefield and Agoglia had that image of the nasty Dave branded into their memories. They argued for Jay as the broad-based comedian who could play to the big crowd at the earlier hour, where Dave simply couldn't . . .[7, p. 161].

Additionally, the closed mindedness of the group was reinforced by an NBC executive outside the group:

. . . But another long time NBC executive who was regularly involved in the late-night lineup said Agoglia was only part of an overall management style that saw everything as "just business," never considering the implications of any action they were taking . . .[7, p. 54].

The final groupthink symptom classification involves pressures within the group towards uniformity. Evidence did not appear in Carter's interviews to suggest that there was direct overt pressure to conform within the group. Thus, this symptom did not emerge directly. However, since no one in the group voiced opinions inconsistent with the leader's view, this may suggest that pressures were operating within the group to suppress divergent views. The later discussion of decision-making defects supports this contention.

Thus, the atmosphere within this decision-making context was primarily one of closed-mindedness and overestimation of the group. According to Janis, when a group displays these primary groupthink symptoms, the group may exhibit specific defects in the decision-making process[2]. Indeed, the NBC executive group experienced many of the defects posited in the groupthink framework.

Decision-Making Defects

Given that the earlier analysis of the groupthink symptoms indicated that the group evidenced closed mindedness and overestimation, then it seems logical that the "concurrence seeking tendency" did occur among the NBC executives and thus the defects resulted.

For example, an examination of the primary defects postulated by Janis[2] reveals their presence in the executive's decision making:

- **Incomplete survey of alternatives.** The overall tone of the group that failed to encourage divergent viewpoints seemed to ensure that alternative solutions and discussion of objectives were not discussed. This narrow-focused atmosphere was supported by Carter's analysis:

  . . . Before the deal with Jay Leno was closed, NBC's executives held no discussions about whether David Letterman should still be considered for The Tonight Show . . . [7, p. 63].

- **Failure to examine risks of preferred choice.** The NBC team appeared to be lackadaisical in their examination of the risks of selecting their preferred choice, Jay Leno, as host of The Tonight Show. This is reinforced by an NBC executive external to the NBC executive group making this decision:

  . . . I always felt it was never being talked out . . . It sounds so fundamental, but I always felt people weren't getting in a room and saying: Well, what if? What if Dave is unhappy about this deal?[7, p. 54].

- **Poor information search.** The NBC executive group's information search could be

described as inadequate. One example of this poor information involved the omission of a critical source of information regarding the decision. This is described by Carter:

. . . To the astonishment of many on The Tonight Show staff, NBC had never seen fit to consult Carson about the naming of his successor, and he never volunteered an opinion . . .[7, p. 79]

- **Selective bias in processing information at hand.** This decision defect can be described as a bias in terms of the way the group members perceive and view information and/or bias in terms of the information that the group focuses on. This defect was exhibited as evidenced in the analysis by Carter: ". . . The network's executives were apparently choosing not to know things they could have known . . ."[7, p. 110].

In support, a senior NBC executive not within the management group remarked: ". . . An enormous amount of avoidance techniques were being employed . . ."[7, p. 110].

Thus, the interview data suggest that this decision-making group exhibited the major decision-making defects of groupthink. In short, the NBC executive group: incompletely surveyed alternatives; failed to examine the risks of the preferred choice; inadequately searched for information; and processed selective information in a biased manner.

In summary, analysis of this first decision suggests the following conclusions. All of the groupthink antecedent conditions were present in the decision-making group. The members did not engage in behaviors designed to examine alternatives critically and the leaders' suggested solution was promoted. These behaviors were evidence that the antecedent conditions resulted in the concurrence seeking groupthink symptoms that led to a defective decision-making process. Furthermore, the emergence of groupthink symptoms and decision-making defects provides support for the implied causal link between symptoms and defects proposed by Janis—where there are symptoms, the decision-making defects do occur.

Decision Two: What to Do with David Letterman

After the first issue was decided and, thus, Jay Leno was chosen as the new The Tonight Show host, the NBC executive group had to confront another critical decision—that is, what to do with NBC's valuable talent, David Letterman. Subsequent to NBC's decision to choose Leno over Letterman for The Tonight Show hosting job, Letterman was offered a contract from CBS to host a late-night show, directly in competition with Leno's show. The contract was a three-year deal that guaranteed Letterman a yearly salary of $12.5 million[7]. NBC had 30 business days to match the offer or lose Letterman to CBS. The decision that NBC group (composed again of Wright, Littlefield, and Agoglia) had to make was whether or not to match the offer or let Letterman go to CBS. We will briefly analyze this decision by the same decision-making group in terms of the groupthink framework.

Antecedent Conditions

Carter's interviews revealed that all of the antecedent conditions were groupthink present—with

the exception of two: leader preference for a certain decision; and insulation of the group from experts. (Note in the first decision, all of the antecedents were present.) First, the leader of the group this time did not push his preference for the decision. Carter provides further insight:

. . . On and on the argument went, with Bob Wright maintaining a scrupulously neutral position, never tipping his hand, just asking for opinions around the table . . .[7, p. 202].

Consequently, the leader in this decision-making situation not only did not voice his preferred solution but also encouraged all members to speak up with concerns, questions, and new information.

Second, with this decision (unlike the first one), the group did not insulate itself from the judgment of qualified individuals external to the group. Carter adds:

. . . In the meantime with only days before he was to sit down with Letterman . . . Wright decided to look for help from some unscientific consultants. He started calling people whose opinions he valued . . . On Sunday, just a day before his scheduled meeting with Letterman, Wright made another call, one he had previously resisted making. He called his friend, Johnny Carson . . .[7, p. 167].

Symptoms

Once again, the group in the second decision seemed to exhibit the primary groupthink symptoms. First, they again: seemed to overestimate Leno's ability and underestimate Letterman; exhibited closed-minded actions; and covertly exerted pressures towards uniformity. In terms of the first two symptoms of overestimation, Carter reveals:

. . . The Leno team kept its own drumbeat in Bob Wright's ear; Jay is going to win . . . Forget about what was being written in the press about Jay being stodgy and not as freewheeling and funny as he used to be . . .[7, p. 161].

The second symptom of closed-mindedness is displayed via the stereotypical perceptions of Letterman and the media still within the group. Carter remarks:

. . . The media, as the pro-Leno forces saw it, were part of the enemy. Most of them were based in New York anyway—Letterman country—and newspaper writers never had the same taste as people . . .[7, p. 161].

Additional support for the group's continued closed-minded, stereotypical views are provided:

. . . Wright told the pro-Leno executives that Letterman could change his approach . . . But Littlefield and Agoglia dismissed the possibility. Dave's not capable of a change that drastic . . .[7, p. 161].

To summarize the analysis of this second decision, thus far, four of the six antecedent conditions existed as well as the primary groupthink symptoms. Thus, based on Janis' framework[2], the symptoms present in the second decision of the NBC group, should result in the occurrence of decision-making defects. However, this analysis of the second decision yields information that goes against this contention—that is, groupthink decision-making defects did not occur despite the display of concurrence-seeking symptoms.

Defects

As stated previously, the group did not exhibit during this second decision any of the decision-making defects specified in the groupthink framework. For instance, an examination of the primary defects reveals their absence in the executives' second decision:

- **Incomplete survey of alternatives.** The tone of the group meetings provides support for the thorough nature of the group's analysis of the situation:

. . . Every meeting with his [Wright's] executive staff kicked up the familiar questions: Could NBC afford to lose Letterman? Would Letterman's style of comedy work at 11:30? Was Leno over his shaky period and would his show improve? Were Leno's strong ratings for real? What would happen to NBC's forty-year dominance of late night if Letterman went head-to-head with Leno[7, p. 157]?

- Additional support for the contention that the group this time canvassed all of its alternatives is provided by Carter: ". . . Wright was prepared to offer Letterman all kinds of options beyond staying in his 12:30 show . . ."[7, p. 162].

- **Failure to examine risks of preferred choice.** Evidence suggests that during this second decision, the NBC group paid close attention to the risks associated with the preferred alternatives. Robert Wright's reaction to the group's comment that Jay Leno would win in a head-to-head competition with Letterman supports this contention. As Wright admonishes:

. . . That's a hell of a risk to take . . . If we don't have to take that risk, I would rather not . . . We already have plenty of risks in prime time. We don't have to test a theory to see whether 11:30 can withstand two big stars going against the same audience, when we've been there by ourselves for thirty years. That isn't a risk high

on my lists of risks . . .[7, pp. 161–2].

- **Poor information search.** The detailed nature of the NBC executive group's information search was evident in the behavior of the members during group discussions of this second decision. As Carter observes:

. . . Wright decided to try to see if a special research study could clear away some of the smoke . . . he told Eric Cardinal, the executive in charge of research in Burbank, to set up some competitive studies between Leno and Letterman . . .[7, p. 158].

Thus, it can be concluded that this decision-making group, during this second decision, substantially met Janis' primary criteria of sound decision making[2]—and thus avoided the major decision-making defects of groupthink. In short, the group members: thoroughly canvassed a wide range of alternatives; carefully weighed the costs and risks associated with various courses of action; and searched for relevant information necessary to make a sound decision.

Discussion

A comparison of the case studies of the successive decisions made by the same group of NBC executives indicates that in both decision-making situations, the group exhibited all of the symptoms of groupthink. However, in the later decision, the group did not succumb to groupthink, and thus to defective decision making; whereas, in the first decision groupthink and the corresponding defects did indeed result. Further, all of the antecedent conditions existed within the group

during the first decision-making process; but only four of the six conditions were present during the later decision-making situation. Finally, in the second decision, the leader strongly encouraged members to voice their opinions—which did not occur in the first decision. Consequently, this analysis suggests that the key to understanding why the same group succumbed to groupthink in one situation but not in another lies in the absence of the two antecedent conditions—insulation of the group and the leader stating his decision preference; and the presence of the leader behavior—of not encouraging the airing of member opinions. However, given the fact that all of the symptoms also emerged in the second decision, this suggests a different sequence of these two antecedent variables other than that proposed by Janis within the groupthink framework[2].

Specifically, this suggests that insulation of the group and promotion of leader decision preference are not antecedents to symptoms but rather moderators between symptoms and decision-making defects. Additionally, this suggests that the leader behavior of encouraging members' views also moderates symptoms and defects. In explaining the use of a moderator variable, Baron and Kenny state that this type of variable is introduced when a relation holds in one setting but not in another [11]. The analysis of these two NBC decisions suggests that the presence of group insulation and the leader behaviors of not making known his/her preferred solution and encouraging opinions explains why, within the same group, groupthink occurs during one decision-making situation and is prevented in another.

Thus, in group decision-making situations in which many of the symptoms of groupthink exist, the factors that may determine whether or not the group will exhibit decision defects will be whether or not the group prevents itself from being insulated from qualified experts and if the leader does not voice his preferred solution and encourages members' opinions. This relationship is portrayed graphically in Figure 1.*

Impact on Prescriptions for Prevention

The revised model suggests that more specific prescriptions for prevention of groupthink can be made. First, group members need to be aware of the impact that insulation from outside experts can have on the quality of its decision-making process. When the group is insulated, the greater the likelihood that the group will fail to consider important information and alternative solutions to the problem at hand. Second, the type of leadership suggested here is not just one that sits back and simply does not make known his or her preferred solution. Additionally, the leader must be one that requires all members to speak up with concerns, questions, and new information. Further, the leadership style required to avoid groupthink is not a laissez-faire leader or non-involved participative leader. This leader is active in directing the activities of the group but does not make known a preferred solution. The group still must develop and evaluate alternative courses of action but under the direct influence of a leader who forces critical appraisal of alternatives and who solicits multiple opinions. In fact, other groupthink research supports this contention that these types of leader behaviors may facilitate groupthink prevention[12].

Much additional research is necessary to test the revised framework. First, laboratory research is needed to understand how various leadership behaviors affect the development of groupthink. Second, the impact of a group's insulation from qualified experts on decision-making effectiveness needs to be investigated. Finally, research that tests the revised framework with real decision-making groups will be needed to refine new prescriptions for preventing groupthink.

Conclusion

This paper has reviewed the basic tenets of groupthink and examined successive decisions by the same NBC executive group. The analysis (based on interviews with individuals internal and external to the group) revealed that the factors that explained why groupthink occurred in one decision-making situation but not in another consecutive decision were insulation of the group from qualified experts and specific leadership behaviors (stating preferred decision choice, and not encouraging member opinions). These two variables, insulation and leadership behaviors, are proposed as moderators of the relationship between groupthink symptoms and decision-making defects. These two moderators lead to new prescriptions for the prevention of groupthink. Much additional research is needed to test the degree to which the revised framework can be used to guide prescriptions for groupthink prevention.

*Does not appear in this publication.

References

1. Janis, I. L., *Victims of Groupthink,* Houghton Mifflin, Boston, MA, 1972.
2. Janis, I. L., *Groupthink,* Houghton Mifflin, Boston, MA, 1982.
3. Smith, S., "Groupthink and the hostage rescue mission," *British Journal of Political Science,* Vol. 15, 1984, pp. 117–23.
4. Hensley, T., and Griffin, G., "Victims of groupthink: the Kent State University board of trustees and the 1977 gymnasium controversy," *The Journal of Conflict Resolution,* Vol. 30, 1986, pp. 497–531.
5. Moorhead, G., Ference, R., and Neck, C. P., "Group decision fiascoes continue: Space shuttle Challenger and a revised groupthink framework," *Human Relations,* Vol. 44, 1991, pp. 539–50.
6. Neck, C. P., and Moorhead, G., "Jury deliberations in the trial of U.S. v. John DeLorean: A Case analysis of groupthink avoidance and an enhanced framework," *Human Relations,* Vol. 45, 1992, pp. 1077–90.
7. Carter, W. J., *The Late Shift: Letterman, Leno, and the Network Battle for the Night,* Hyperion, New York, NY, 1994.
8. Moorhead, G., and Montanari, J., "An empirical investigation of the groupthink phenomenon," *Human Relations,* Vol. 39, 1986, pp. 399–410.
9. Festinger, L., "A theory of social comparison processes," *Human Relations,* Vol. 7, 1954, pp. 117–140.
10. Manz, C. C., and Sims, H. P. Jr, "The potential for groupthink in autonomous work groups," *Human Relations,* Vol. 35, 1982, pp. 773–84.
11. Baron, R., and Kenny, D., "The moderator-mediator variable distinction in social psychological research: Conceptual, strategic, and statistical considerations," *Journal of Personality Social Psychology,* Vol. 51, 1986, pp. 1173–82.
12. Neck, C. P., and Moorhead, G., "Groupthink remodeled: The importance of leadership, time pressures, and methodical decision-making procedures," *Human Relations,* Vol. 48, 1995, pp. 537–57.

Article Review Form at end of book.

According to Hardin, what are some of the individual and collective forces that create a sense of individual loyalty to and identification with a group? Why does in-group identification sometimes turn into violent intergroup conflict?

Contested Community

Russell Hardin

Abstract: *The psychology of group identification is complex. Conflict, individual interests and incentives, the potential for violence in ethnic identification and other aspects are discussed. African-American ghetto slang and Bosnia are among examples used.*

In a widely known joke, a Jewish man is cast ashore on a desert island, where he remains for five years. One day, the captain of a passing ship notices two impressive buildings on what is supposed to be an uninhabited desert island. He anchors and goes ashore. There are two beautiful synagogues on the beach, about half a mile apart, but no one is to be seen. The captain and his crew enter one of the synagogues, where they find the lone man. Told that the man built the two synagogues himself, the captain is in awe. "But they're so beautiful. How did you do it?" The man shrugs and says that, after all, he's been there with nothing else to do for five years. "But why did you build two?" the captain asks. "In this one, I worship," the man says. "That one I wouldn't go near."

The joke is funny because it is about the charms of group identification. It also represents the seeming irrationality of such identification. What I wish to discuss is how such identification can turn sour and produce ugly, often violent results. A tale about Hutu versus Tutsi, or Serb versus Muslim, or Jewish versus Arabic identifications would not be so funny.

Group identification and the norms of exclusion that groups sometimes develop are often thought to be primordial—that is, alas, the view of the New York Times in recent years. Or they are thought to be extra-rational in some other sense. Although there may be primordial instincts for identification and for violence, many of the primordialist arguments about ethnic conflict are silly. For example, Robert Kaplan asserts that the psychology of Yugoslavs is hideously different from our own, that it includes deep currents of ethnic hatred and memories of awful events from six centuries past, and that it controls contemporary relations between Croats, Muslims, and Serbs (*New York Times Book Review*, April 18, 1993). Kaplan evidently believes that knowledge is inheritable through Lamarckian laws. I wish it were—then at least I might be able to speak French much better and ancient Anglo-Saxon English and Gaelic as well. Unfortunately, however, I might then be torn by ethnic hatred of myself as French, hatred of myself as English, and hatred of myself as Irish. I would be a mess. Many parties in Yugoslavia would share this fate, since they are not historically as distinct as the rabid nationalists there maintain they are.

In what follows, I wish to understand group identification and norms of exclusion in large part as the distorted result of individual self-interest. To a rational-choice theorist, this sounds superficially implausible. In 1965, the economist Mancur Olson published his very influential book *The Logic of Collective Action*. The central argument of that book was that a large group, political or otherwise, cannot generally succeed merely because its members share an interest in success for the group. If a group is to succeed, it will have to find incentives that can be tailored to individual members, typically incentives having nothing to do with the larger interest of the group. An irony, long noticed in the social sciences, of Olson's argument is that it appeared just at the beginning of a remarkable era of large-group organizations. The civil rights movement was big before Olson's book saw its way into print, and the antiwar movement was looming on the near horizon. Nearly three decades after Olson concluded that it is irrational for most members of large interest groups to contribute to their groups' goals, uncounted numbers of ethnic and other groups seem to be motivating their members to extraordinary actions.

What happened to Olson's argument? Was it wrong? No, I think it was generally right. For example, consider the large group of us who would like to elect someone to Congress, say the group of 93,000 people who went to the polls in November 1994 to reelect Sam Gejdenson in Connecticut. In one of the narrowest congressional elections ever, he won by four votes, so any one individual vote was of no avail. Even the votes of five or a hundred people put together might have been of no avail, because Congress could have chosen to seat his opponent on some claim that the votes were miscounted (Newt Gingrich's rise to leadership might be dated from his leading a walkout from the House of Representatives when a Democrat who had lost the official count was seated over his Republican opponent). Such a claim is almost certainly valid when there are 186,000 votes to be counted. The chance that one person's vote actually matters in a typical large-scale election is probably less than the chance that that person will be killed in an accident on the way to or from the polls. Therefore, unless a person is going to be rewarded with a job by the winning candidate, it can-

not be in his or her interest to vote. If one votes, either it is for moral or expressive or other reasons—or it is because one radically misjudges one's personal interests in the matter. In any case, voting is, again, not in the individual voter's interest.

If the dangers of voting outweigh the benefits, how much more so must the dangers of the strong ethnic identification that leads one to join in ethnic violence outweigh the personal benefits? Prima facie, it would seem that such strong ethnic identification is not rational in the narrow sense of being in the individual's interest. Against this prima facie conclusion, I wish to argue that ethnic identification and the violence that sometimes follows from it can be seen as individually rational in large part. This involves several explanatory tasks: first, to give an account of norms of exclusion, which requires an account of the interest that members of a group have in abiding by the group's norms; second, to give an account of why exclusive groups fall into conflict and even violence with each other; and finally, to attempt to normative assessment of claims for the rightness and goodness of group identification, as in the contemporary literature on communitarianism.

The Nature of Norms of Exclusion

It would be odd to claim that much of the activity we see in current violent conflicts and in milder ethnic hostilities is not extra-rational in some ways, to varying degrees across individuals and groups. But norms of exclusion are largely socially, not biologically or genetically, constructed. Hence, our problem in understanding them is to under-

stand the social processes that produce them. Understanding can benefit from analyzing norms of exclusion of many varieties, not only those of ethnic exclusion. I will not detail the range of such norms here, but note that they include the norms of the duel in Renaissance through nineteenth-century Europe; the norms of the vendetta as practiced in many times and places, including Corsica, medieval Iceland, and Montenegro; the norms of Jewish guilt; the norms of ghetto slang and contemporary rap; and the norms of academic disciplines.

Understanding the norms of exclusion can also benefit from analyzing the very different incentive structure of many universalistic norms. For example, there are the norms of keeping promises, telling the truth, marital fidelity, civic duty to vote in elections, Catholic guilt, and many others. It is instructive to note that the force of many universalistic norms depends on their being naturally reinforced by interest, as is true of the norm of keeping promises, or on their being distorted into forms that make them more nearly norms of exclusion. Norms for collective action are otherwise generally very weak. For example, the norm of civic duty to vote is not a very powerful norm, as suggested by the U.S. national elections in November 1994, when it motivated no more than 38 percent of America's eligible voters.

As an example of norms of difference, which are generally norms of exclusion, consider one fairly astonishing norm that has arisen in the United States within the lifetimes of most adult Americans: the use of the term "nigger" as a term of endearment and honor among American blacks. I grew up in Texas during the civil rights movement, and the word "nigger" still stirs so much revulsion in me that I was hesitant even to write in it this context. The odd fact is that I could not speak it in any ordinary context. But American blacks can not only use it, they can exult in using it.

How did that happen? In outline, the story is as follows: The meanings and uses of words are merely conventions of language. Conventions forcefully govern our behavior when they are widely adopted. For example, the convention of driving on the right is enforced with the threat of lethal consequences. Few conventions are so powerful as this remarkable example of an ideal-type that has, as Robert Merton says, a concrete instance. But linguistic norms are also forceful. If one speaks English in relevantly wrong ways, one's prospects are diminished. If one speaks only French in Anglophone Canada or in the United States, one's prospects are also diminished. The black teenagers who call each other "nigger" and who talk and gesture in rap or the cool pose cannot beneficially transport their slang and style to the worlds of universities, banks, and politics beyond the local community. Yet the black teenager who holds out against ghetto slang and style is apt to be shunned within that local community. As Shawn Hunt, an academically gifted Brooklyn teenager, told the *New York Times*, (April 25, 1993) he uses "straight-up-and-down English" in the larger world, but he can't do that in his neighborhood. His friends "wouldn't take too good to that," he says.

Note the difference between the simple driving convention and the conventions of ghetto slang and style. Typically, no one wishes to violate the driving convention. But Shawn Hunt regularly wishes to violate the norms of ghetto slang. He also wishes to follow those norms much of the time. Why? If he follows those norms in his community, he is rewarded with comfortable relations with many people, with inclusion in their activities, which are among Shawn's pleasures. If he violates those norms at other times, he is rewarded in very different ways—he could earn a college degree that would open many desirable opportunities to him. The norm of ghetto slang is an exclusive norm. The threat of shunning gives black teenagers strong incentive to use it; the promise of other opportunities gives them strong incentive not to use it.

To generalize Shawn Hunt's interests, recall Thomas Wolfe's pair of theses in *You Can't Go Home Again*. Wolfe was educated at Harvard, and then he returned to his home in Asheville, North Carolina. There he discovered two related things. First, one cannot really go back "home" because after the pleasures of cosmopolitan life, it will hardly be home any longer. And second, one who does try to go back home is not really welcome—without, perhaps, giving up much of the learning and suppressing the tastes developed abroad. Wolfe clearly appreciated the benefits, the comforts of home. He characterized a town as "coiling in a thousand fumes of homely smoke, now winking into a thousand points of friendly light its glorious small design, its aching passionate assurances of walls, warmth, comfort, food, and love." Hence, in his view, the costs of separation were real and potentially large. (Incidentally, one might recognize the phrase George Bush took from Wolfe, the "thousand points of light" of his 1988 presidential campaign.)

The other thesis in Wolfe's pair is that one may have learned or changed too much to find the comforts of home as pleasing as they once had been. Wolfe saw that the comforts of home may be as appealing as they are in part because of ignorance of the alternatives. The full process is as follows: The comforts induce staying at home, which secures ignorance by pruning vistas, which maintains tastes for the comforts of home. That is a demoralizing chain of relationships. Those like Wolfe can break that chain only at the price of permanent disquiet.

Shawn Hunt may be the talented person who can switch from one style of speech to another to fit his milieu. I have an old friend in Texas who talks with everyone in their style—he is a spectacular mimic. And he gains from his talent. He told me I should do likewise if I wanted to get mechanics, salespeople, and others to take my interests to heart. Alas, I lack the talent. I am stuck in one style. Many of Shawn Hunt's fellow teenagers must have my liability, and they are essentially at the fringes of their neighborhood groups. Eventually, they may be shunned, or they may have to content themselves with severe reduction of external opportunities. Like me, they cannot have it both ways.

On this account, a ghetto teenager such as Shawn Hunt must choose from interest in large part. The norm of exclusion that governs behavior in his group imposes considerations of his interest on him. The norm requires more than an explanation of his behavior, however. It requires an answer to the question, "Why do people shun violators of a norm of group identification?" Is that also a matter of interest? If talking straight-up-and-down English makes his friends uncomfortable, if Shawn is unreliable because he begins to absent himself from their activities while he studies, then those friends may soon prefer not to have him around. They may stop seeking him out, and they may shun him enough to make him as uncomfortable as he makes them. People at the fringe of the group are at risk.

Now back to "nigger." How did the slang develop? We tend to look for specific causal accounts in explaining social results. But here it may be more instructive to see the structure of a result than to find the exact historical progression that led to it. For example, by spontaneous choices and developments over many decades, Americans would be driving their buggies and wagons to the right of each other when they met. Once enough others did that, everyone else had the incentive to do likewise. The English and the Swedes just as spontaneously wound up driving left. There was no inherently compelling a priori reason to choose one particular rule over the other. But there was compelling reason to follow either one once it developed into a convention. Young blacks might have adopted many forms of slang that would serve to exclude whites from their community. That they wound up with "nigger," rap, and the cool pose is less interesting than that they are compelled by such norms of exclusion.

We could try to tell the story of how "nigger" became honorific. Older southern blacks sometimes admonished black children, "You ain't nothin' but a nigger, and don't you forget it." Stokeley Carmichael and others transformed this into a challenge: "In this country you ain't nothin' but niggers, and don't you forget it." From this, it was a short step to using "nigger" as an honorific identification. It was a remarkable trick—but millions of such tricks are turned every day. What made this trick a new linguistic convention was that it was soon used by many blacks. Countless other terms of exclusion must have been used. But in the competition for novelty and impact, "nigger" may have had unusual advantages. In the end, it came to common usage just as driving on the right had earlier.

Typical norms of ethnic exclusion have many of the qualities of ghetto slang. They are social conventions, not a priori or natural distinctions. And they are reinforced through the interested actions of relevant group members, especially through the shunning of those who waver at the fringes of the group. Sometimes they are specifically exacerbated by potential leaders, as Slobodan Milosevic and Radovan Karadzic deliberately pushed for Serbian superiority and Croatian, Muslim, and Turkish inferiority and even moral repugnance. Milosevic wanted to become leader and then to reinforce his position. He acted very much in his own interest. And he made it the interest of many Serbs to follow his lead.

The Serbs who lived in Sarajevo, an international city with a heavily intermarried population of Croats, Serbs, and Muslims, were clearly at the fringes of the nation of Serbs that Milosevic cultivated. They did not readily identify with the hypernationalist Serbs. They have paid the price of being at the fringes. In November 1993, after eighteen months of Serbian siege of Sarajevo, winter was coming on and the urban amenities of water, electricity, and stores with food were destroyed. Many Serbs finally gave up and left Sarajevo.

One young Serbian man tried to cross the Serbian military line with his family. His parents, wife, and children were allowed to pass, but he was detained by the local commander. "You stayed with the balija [Serbian slang for "Muslims"] for eighteen months," the commander said. "Okay, let's see how you feel about the balija now. You can go to the front lines and kill a balija, then maybe we'll let you go (*New York Times*, November 14, 1993)."

Similarly, many young Croatian men in Mostar in Bosnia found that either they could leave their homes altogether or they could identify with fellow Bosnian Croats altogether by joining in the murderous attacks on Muslim civilians. Like Shawn Hunt, who could not talk either way on demand, they had to make a choice. Several hundred eventually chose to stay or to return home and joined a civilian unit of killers, who stalk Muslims and shoot them. They shoot men, women, and children, and they make sure their victims are dead lest they rise and shoot the killers in the back as they leave.

The atrocities of Yugoslavs in Bosnia apparently do not match the atrocities of Hutu and Tutsi in Rwanda and Burundi. These countries were set up by their former colonial supervisor, Belgium, which pulled out without creating any institutional structure for self-governance. As in other newly independent Belgian colonies, the result was immediate civil war, which has de facto never ended. After more than three decades of violent conflict, some groups have concluded that the only way to gain control is to kill everyone on the other side. Expulsion of most of the Tutsi from Rwanda thirty years ago has merely produced a new generation of people in dreadful refugee camps. These are people for whom armed struggle inside Rwanda must have been more attractive, despite its risk of death, than continued life in the camps. As in the case of the Serbian refugee from Sarajevo, who was at the fringes of the group of those who rabidly identify as Serbians, suspect Hutu and Tutsi have been at grave risk. Intermarried Hutu men in Rwanda reputedly slaughtered their Tutsi wives. Perhaps they did not even need the injunction to kill a balija to establish their identification. They knew where they stood, and they knew they had to escape from the fringes of disloyalty.

Many commentators have noted the Serbians have been especially hard on cities and the monuments of civilization. They have shelled, dynamited, and bulldozed mosques and civic buildings, and they have razed whole cities. Bogdan Bogdanovic, a Serbian architect, accuses Milosevic of wanting to destroy civilization in Yugoslavia. He is probably partly right. But the Serbian urge is, rather, more precisely, to purge the kind of cosmopolitan thought that is naturally hostile to the creation of exclusive communities. Milosevic wants ignorance, the ignorance that underlies his account of the history of Yugoslavia, the ignorance that makes it possible for one to believe in the implausible myths of Serbian greatness and Croatian, Muslim, and Turkish depravity. With those beliefs, narrow identification with Serbia is more readily possible. On some accounts, the most rabid Serbs are from small towns and rural areas in which there are no Croatians or Muslims. They come from exclusive communities, and they are uncomfortable with cities and other peoples.

Group Identification and Group Conflict

I have spoken of identification rather than of identity. The latter term suggests that there is an objective basis to the identities that people profess. But it is at worst an open question whether identifications are socially constructed, as I think they are. And it is identification, a subjective fact, that affects motivation. Croatians, Muslims, and Serbs have only minor differences in objective identity, yet the strength of their identifications is so great that they are murdering each other. Their differences, nominally, are that they have mostly different religions, although until four years ago theirs was a strikingly irreligious society. Genetically, they are not distinct; what differences they have are the result of geographical separation over many centuries. Muslims are merely Serbs whose forbears converted to Islam—unless their later forebears converted back to Orthodoxy or to Catholicism. They all speak the same language, although Serbs use a different alphabet. Using the same language has caused the hyper-nationalists a lot of grief, because they are intent on forcing through differences in their common language to justify their claims of group difference.

Hutu and Tutsi may have more distinctive objective differences, although intermarriage has produced a very large number of people who are mixed. More-over, the precolonial terminology of Hutu and Tutsi reflected class membership, not an ethnic identity. A Hutu could rise in class and become Tutsi. The objective measures of identity of many, perhaps most, people in the United States are so complex that the notion of ethnic identity hardly makes sense for them. Identification

might nevertheless be strong, and many identify as, for example, African or English despite having insufficient genetic ground for the identification.

In any case, again, it is identification, not identity, that creates conflict. And this is the second issue I wish to address. What are the sources of conflict between groups? One might suppose the conflict is somehow external to the groups, that it is merely a problem for them. Or, alternatively, one might suppose it is something that is created by the groups. In very large part, it is clearly created by the groups in the following sense: If we have identified as a group, then, under certain circumstances, we may individually expect to prosper more from our group's prospering than from our own success in grasping individual opportunities. There are two classes of goods that we, as a group or as individuals, might seek. First there are distributional goods, such as money, farmland, and so forth. And second, there are positional goods, such as jobs in the government or the army.

European aristocrats were governed by the dueling norm, which did not apply to others. That they lived up to the norm kept them distinct as a class through the several centuries in which they were displaced economically by the rising bourgeoisie. Through much of that time, they had privileged access to positions in the state and in the army. In precolonial times, the Tutsi held all positions of authority in the nominal governments of what eventually became Rwanda and Burundi, but there was less privilege than one might suppose because Hutu could become Tutsi. In postcolonial times, Hutus seized control of Rwanda and established privileged access to state jobs, especially in the military and the police.

In Rwanda and in many other nations, including arguably some of the newly independent former Soviet republics, government was itself the most valuable resource for anyone who wanted to prosper. A person's odds of getting one of the good positions in government, however, would be greatly enhanced if members of other groups could be excluded from holding them. The mere fact of ethnic identification therefore creates a conflict of interest. This is not necessarily true in every case of multiple ethnic groups. For example, if the economy is booming, one's best prospects might well depend more on individual performance than on ostensible identity. But in bad economic times, or in nations in which the government controls most of the economic opportunities, conflict of interest between ethnic groups is virtually defined.

The conflicts in formerly socialist nations and in the quasi-socialist nations of Africa are exacerbated by the government's coincidental role in the economy. If there were less government involvement, there might be greater inequality between individuals but less inequality between groups—and less violence between groups. It may be one of the great tragedies of history that so many nations became independent during the high tide of the belief that the Soviet Union had a better way—with centralized control of all opportunities.

Normative Questions about Norms of Exclusion

People commonly think their norms are more than merely a sta-

tistician's norms of typical behavior. They think their norms are right, that other norms would be wrong. Philosophers and social scientists under the sway of David Hume and Max Weber think such a conclusion is wrong because, in Hume's words, it is the derivation of an "ought" from an "is"—or in Weber's words, it is a violation of the fact-value distinction. Anthropologists and many others, however, know that ordinary people commonly do infer values from mere facts. What is, is assumed to be good. We have norm X. Therefore norm X is right. This is a kind of group solipsism.

Contemporary communitarian philosophers hold a somewhat milder position: A group's norms are good for that group. And moreover, we have no way to deduce what would be generally good norms; we have only norms that are, in fact, derived within groups. The communitarian philosophers are not quite relativists about value. They do not hold that every group's views are right. A group's views are only right for it—and perhaps only in a functional sense, the way our driving to the right is good for us. Or they hold what is essentially an epistemological position, as Richard Rorty does: Rorty does not say that a group's values are right for it; he merely says that, from within their own community, members cannot judge the practices of another's community. We are stuck with group solipsism for epistemological reasons.

Many actual communitarians, such as Milosevic's Serbs or Rwanda's Hutus, hold a very different view. They think their norms are right, pure and simple. Rorth, Charles Taylor, and many others are philosophical communitarians, or even merely episte-

mological communitarians. They are hostile to traditional ethics, which has almost invariably been universalistic. In a universalistic ethics, what is right for one is right for another under relevantly similar circumstances. Strangely, however, many of the antiuniversalistic philosophical communitarians hold a universalistic view of their own: They think community is good. Actual communitarians typically hold no such view. They think merely that their community is good. In defending their community, they may be willing to obliterate other communities.

It is sometimes argued of various values that their truth is somehow correlated with the strength with which they are held. Consider this view in the light of differences between universalistic norms and norms of exclusion. Many universalistic norms have as their object the overcoming of self-interest. For example, the norm of civic duty that often leads people to vote is a motivation that runs against self-interest. Most people have no interest in taking half an hour or more out of the day just to vote when they can be virtually certain that their vote will not make any difference to the outcome. Norms of exclusion typically are quite different. They are reinforced by self-interest. Shawn Hunt speaks ghetto slang with his neighborhood friends because he loses if he doesn't. Only if he is at the fringe of his group do his interests begin to run against the group's norms, and then he violates the norm.

Universalistic norms typically have motivational force from moral or public-spirited concern, but they run contrary to self-interest. Norms of group exclusion probably have motivational force from moral or public-spirited concern, and they also have motivational force from self-interest. They are doubly supported. Not surprisingly, therefore, they are generally more strongly held than are universalistic norms. There is a class of exceptions to this claim: the norms that are enforced in the context of essentially one-on-one relationships, not in large-group relationships of collective action. For example, I have a clear interest in keeping most of my promises, because most of them are made to individuals with whom I have an interest in a continuing relationship. Politicians who make promises to the larger public still have some of that interest, but much less so. Therefore, their promises are less credible and less likely to be fulfilled.

But, generally, it is true that large-scale universalistic norms are less effective than communal norms of exclusion. This claim sounds counter-intuitive to many people, but it is little more complex than the claim that having interest and normative values push in the same direction is more effective than having them work against each other. It is not in the end surprising, therefore, that people assert their group's norms of exclusion with great, even intolerably great, force. That they do so, however, is no test of the rightness of those norms. Commitment is a matter of fact; rightness is a matter of value. Strength of commitment does not imply degree of rightness. For example, commitment does not make vengeful murder right, no matter how intensely it is desired and believed to be right.

In sum, epistemological communitarianism implies two striking conclusions: First, we should give consideration to community members. In particular, we should acknowledge the extent to which communities can constrain knowledge to produce behavior that we might otherwise wrongly attribute to especially evil or vicious personal character. Second, we should give strong consideration to the contingent sources of support for various communal values and norms. Often we will find that we can explain these in ways that lead us to conclude they have no moral standing. These two conclusions together imply that normative communitarianism is misguided.

More generally, we should conclude that group organization and individual commitment to group purposes are not proof of the rightness or goodness of what the group wants or achieves. Indeed, we should often become suspicious of group success in mobilizing individuals just because individual incentives typically run counter to group action. We should look to the incentives that produce group commitment to determine what their character is. These may be perverse and destructive. In seeking larger shares of their societies' goods, groups often destroy much of those goods, making virtually everyone worse off. For the present generation, they gain not the spoils of victory, but the spoliation of their lives.

Successful collective action may sometimes be a wonderful achievement. But it may also be a dreadful achievement, the source of great harm, even to those who succeed in the collective action. In the widespread mobilization of the imagined communities of the ethnic groups of our time, the harms seem to grotesquely outweigh any plausible benefits.

Despite the occasional good that it may do, group solipsist ethnic assertion is one of the great disasters of modern civilization.

Edward Said fears "that you cannot both 'belong' and concern yourself with [others] who do not belong" (Blaming the Victim, p. 178). As in the major cases of ethnic identification in our time, to belong means to lessen concern for those who are excluded or, worse, to be overtly hostile to them. The dreadful lesson of these conflicts seems to be that individuals have an immediate interest in doing things that lead to their own shackling and to the suppression of others. They can have an interest in reducing themselves to something less than human, to a standard pawn in a large strategic game, plausibly played by thugs. They give up their claim to personal identity by giving themselves over fully to trivializing identification, in which, as Henry Louis Gates writes, "your tale is subordinated to an overarching narrative" (New Yorker, March 7, 1994). Individuals acting in groups bolstered by norms of exclusion can transcend the negative logic of collective action—but all too often only at the cost of degradation of self and other.

Related Articles/ Suggested Further Readings

Russell Hardin. *One for All: The Logic of Group Conflict.* Princeton: Princeton University Press, 1995.

Rene Lemarchand. *Burundi: Ethnocide as Discourse and Practice.* Cambridge: Cambridge University Press, 1994.

Mancur Olson, Jr. *The Logic of Collective Action.* Cambridge, Mass.: Harvard University Press, 1965.

 Article Review Form at end of book.

WiseGuide Wrap-Up

- People are in groups that serve a wide variety of needs. Groups may be purely social, or very instrumental. Groups provide a way for people to be with similar others, to mobilize social action, to find support, and to support their self-esteem. Groups also find ways of enforcing group loyalty and preventing defection.

- In many groups social loafing occurs; that is, some members do very little work and take advantage of the others' efforts. Social loafing is particularly likely when members feel that their contributions are unneeded, unrewarded, or come at too high a personal cost. Incentives can reduce the likelihood of social loafing.

- Groupthink is a risk of group decision-making. Characteristics of group leaders may moderate the effects of groupthink, as does reducing the degree to which group members are insulated from other opinions.

- Group identification is often a social construction. Identifying with a group seems to be important to people's self-concept. Group indentification can sometimes lead to conflict when resources become scarce.

R.E.A.L. Sites

This list provides a print preview of typical **coursewise** R.E.A.L. sites. (There are over 100 such sites at the **courselinks**™ site.) The danger in printing URLs is that web sites can change overnight. As we went to press, these sites were functional using the URLs provided. If you come across one that isn't, please let us know via email to: webmaster@coursewise.com. Use your Passport to access the most current list of R.E.A.L. sites at the **courselinks**™ site.

Site name: Self-Directed Work Teams

URL: http://users.ids.net/~brim/sdwtt.html

Why is it R.E.A.L.? You may think that group projects are only something you do in a college classroom, but that is not at all true. In the world of business, more and more companies, such as car-maker Saturn and overnight delivery service Federal Express, are turning to Self-Directed Work Teams (SDWT). This collaborative model can produce faster, higher quality products than can the traditional boss-worker model. The catch: People often have not learned how to work well on group projects—whether it be in the classroom or the workplace. This site provides many annotated links to web sites that discuss research on group work, how to improve teamwork, examples of SDWT projects, and more. Go to this site and find one tip that you can use in your next group project.

Key topics: group behavior, workplace

section

6

Learning Objectives

- Understand the problems of detecting discrimination and how to correct for these problems.

- Explain the process by which stereotypes affect those who are stereotyped, and how it impairs their performance.

- Understand the concept of "aversive racism" and how it is manifested.

- Discuss some ways, according to psychological research, that you can recognize and limit the impact of prejudice and stereotyping.

Stereotypes and Prejudice

 **WiseGuide Intro**

Sometimes membership in a particular category can tell us a lot about an individual. A person's religion, for example, certainly provides us with useful information about the person's spiritual outlook, although it might not tell us much about his or her politics. Many social categories, however, such as "male" or "Hispanic," are so broad and diverse that they tell us little if anything about any particular group member's beliefs, ambitions, or abilities. Still, many people insist that even such broad groups as men and women are fundamentally different from one another—just look at the popularity of books and magazine articles that play up the allegedly enormous differences in the ways that men and women think, talk, and act.

If we believe that social groups differ significantly from one another, then we are likely to use a person's group membership as a cue that tells us something about that person's characteristics. The effects of this cue-taking can be fairly benign, but when our impressions of others are guided by false, overgeneralized, or negative *stereotypes,* the result can be misunderstanding, prejudice, or discriminatory treatment. Even fairly positive stereotypes, if relied on too much, can make us overlook a person's unique, individual qualities.

What makes a person think about or treat another person on the basis of a stereotype? Why are some stereotypes so persistent, even when they are false? What are the social costs of negative stereotyping and the individual costs to the person who is stereotyped? The articles in this section address the sometimes darker side of group-based social thinking and behavior.

The article by Rutte and colleagues examines the factors that make it more likely that we will correctly perceive discrimination. The authors note that everyone agrees that people with better qualifications should be paid more, regardless of their gender, yet males consistently make more money than females do, even when they are equally qualified. The authors suggest that people do believe in equal pay for equal work, but that salary inequities between men and women can be difficult to detect.

The second article, by Signorielli, McLeod, and Healy, examines how the mass media reinforce and perpetuate gender stereotypes. A number of studies have demonstrated that the images of men and women in movies, TV, and magazines are quite stereotypical. Many people assume, however, that traditional gender stereotypes on TV went out with "Leave It to Beaver," and that young people today don't see the same kinds of sexist messages their parents did. MTV portrays itself as representing youthful, contemporary, forward-looking ideals, yet Signorielli finds that the images of men and women portrayed in advertisements broadcast on MTV are just as stereotypical as those that appeared a generation ago.

The article by Woo talks about a program of research conducted by Claude Steele and his colleagues. You may have read about this research elsewhere, as it has appeared in a number of popular magazines and newspapers in the last year or two. One of the reasons that people find

R22. According to Rutte and colleagues, when do people have difficulty detecting that discrimination is occurring?

R23. What are some of the main components of the stereotypic female that MTV advertisers provide their viewers? Do you think the stereotype is any different in the ads than it is in the videos?

R24. How do researchers think that stereotype vulnerability interferes with performance? What are two ways that you can reduce the possibility of stereotype threat to someone?

R25. How might people who don't believe that they hold negative stereotypes nevertheless behave in a discriminatory fashion? What are the three ways that affirmative action programs detect the presence of "aversive racism"?

R26. What are some of the specific suggestions for reducing prejudice and stereotyping of another person? Which of these do you think would work on a college campus?

Steele's work so exciting is that it helps to explain how stereotypes may negatively affect the performance of stereotyped group members. For instance, there is a commonly held stereotype that women are bad at math. Dr. Steele investigated whether it was true that women were bad at math, or that their concern about these low expectations distracted them from doing well at math. Steele finds convincing evidence that the performance of both women and minorities may suffer greatly when they feel threatened by negative stereotypes. The article concludes with a discussion of a successful intervention program that Dr. Steele designed at the University of Michigan.

In our next article, John Dovidio discusses how psychological research helps make the case for continuing affirmative action programs. While it often appears that overt racism and sexism have declined in the United States in the last forty years, women and minorities are still disadvantaged compared to men and whites in many ways, including occupational prestige and income. Dovidio's research helps explain the discrepancy between perceived levels of discrimination in our society and actual levels. His program of research has looked at a phenomenon he calls "aversive racism," which is an uncomfortable, contradictory blend of negative feelings toward minorities and egalitarian ideals. Dovidio argues that many people do not like to admit (even to themselves) that they have negative attitudes toward minorities, but that such attitudes play out in subtle forms of discriminatory behavior. This type of racism may be especially damaging because it is less obvious at first glance than overt, hostile racism.

Our last article is a synopsis of some of what we have already learned about prejudice and discrimination. Farrington specifically talks about racism as it occurs in high schools, and about some ways that individuals can resist stereotyping others. Although some of the suggestions may seem simplistic, the advice is based on a body of research findings over the years. One important point that this article makes is to remind us that we can do something about prejudice and discrimination and that we should be encouraged—not discouraged—by the research that psychologists do on this topic.

According to Rutte and colleagues, when do people have difficulty detecting that discrimination is occurring?

Organization of Information and the Detection of Gender Discrimination

Christel G. Rutte,[1] Kristina A. Diekmann,[2] Jeffrey T. Polzer,[2] Faye J. Crosby,[2] and David M. Messick[2]

1University of Nijmegen, The Netherlands, and 2J.L. Kellogg Graduate School of Management, Northwestern University

One of the basic tenets of organizational fairness is that people who have equal qualifications and do equal work should have equal rewards (Sheppard, Lewicki, & Minton, 1992). Yet in many organizations, women are compensated less than exactly comparable men (for a summary of recent studies, see Crosby, in press). There are several possible explanations for the persistence of this phenomenon. One is that male employees resist changes for fear that true equity would jeopardize their salary levels. This motivational explanation is based on the assumption that men are motivated to main-

tain discriminatory practices (Cordova, 1992). An alternative, cognitive explanation is that inequities persist because salary discrimination is difficult to detect. It is the latter possibility that is explored in the present report.

To correct discrimination, people must first notice it. What type of evidence would lead to the conclusion that someone's salary is inappropriately low? We suggest that clear evidence would be provided by a violation of what we call *ordinal equity.* Ordinal equity characterizes a group if the ranking of the members by qualifications and the ranking by salaries result in the same ordering of people. In a comparison of two people, ordinal equity means that the more qualified person gets a higher salary. Ordinal equity is not concerned with the magnitudes of the differences. Ordinal *in*equity results when an employee who has better qualifications than another employee earns a lower salary than that other employee.

Consider the following example: Firm X has two branches, both of which have male and female employees. Further assume that there are only two relevant qualifications for salary determination in this firm: seniority (measured by the number of years with the firm) and level (a numerical organizational assignment, with a higher number indicating a higher level). Suppose that the mean qualifications and salaries for the two branches of the firm are as given in Table 1. Within each branch of Firm X, women, on average, show better qualifications than men, yet have lower salaries. Salary discrimination within the firm is conspicuous within each sublevel of the organization because intrabranch comparisons exhibit ordinal inequity.

Now suppose that in another company, Firm Y, the mean qualifications and salaries for men and

Christel G. Rutte, Diekmann, Kristina A., Polzer, Jeffrey T., Crosby, Faye J., Messick, David M., Organization of Information and the Detection of Gender Discrimination. PSYCHOLOGICAL SCIENCE 1994, v5, n4, July, pp. 226–231. Copyright © 1994 American Psychological Society. Reprinted with the permission of Cambridge University Press.

women are the same as in Firm X, except that the numbers for women are exchanged between the two branches, as shown in Table 1. The actual numbers in Firm Y are precisely the same as in Firm X, but in Firm Y there is no ordinal inequity. In Branch A, women are more qualified than men and earn a higher salary. In Branch B, men are more qualified and earn more than female employees. In Firm Y, the evidence for unfairness is less conspicuous than in Firm X because there is no ordinal inequity.

Note that Firm X and Firm Y are identical in terms of the overall mean salaries and qualifications of their female managers and also of their male managers. In both firms, if we average across Branches A and B and assume equal numbers of managers in the branches, the male managers earn a mean salary of $45,000 while the female managers earn a mean salary of $42,000. Given that the female managers (at either firm) are somewhat better qualified than the male managers, ordinal inequity is evident at the level of the firm for both Firm X and Firm Y. The current experiment extends previous research by varying the level at which discrimination is apparent—a lower level, like the branch, or the firm.

As our example shows, even when inequities are not conspicuous at the local level (e.g., within a branch of a firm), they can be made more apparent when the information from a number of sources is aggregated. Prior research confirms this claim. Several experiments have shown that the format in which information is presented plays an important role in the detection of discrimination (Clayton & Crosby, 1986; Crosby

& Clayton, 1986; Crosby, Cordova, & Jaskar, in press). In these studies, subjects confronted information that concerned the qualifications and salaries of male and female managers in an organization; this information was either in aggregate form (all the information in a single, large table) or in piecemeal form (information concerning the different departments of the organization on separate pages). Results from these studies indicate that people are less likely to detect discrimination when information is presented as individual cases (i.e., piecemeal form). Yet when the individual cases are aggregated so that idiosyncratic differences in qualifications can be averaged, people identify discrimination correctly (Cordova, 1992; Twiss, Tabb, & Crosby, 1989).

In our experiment, information of the sort displayed in Table 1 was presented to subjects who were then asked to judge the fairness of the salaries of the employees of a hypothetical firm, Company Z, having 10 departments. In all cases, Company Z was in fact discriminating against one group (women or men) in favor of the other group (men or women) in terms of salaries. We manipulated conspicuousness such that when discrimination was conspicuous, 9 of the 10 departments displayed ordinal inequity. In the inconspicuous condition, although the qualifications and salaries were the same, they were rearranged so that none of the departments displayed ordinal inequity. We also manipulated format such that subjects saw either the entire aggregated table of qualifications and salaries for male and female employees for every department or saw the

same information in piecemeal form, one department at a time.

We had three concrete hypotheses about the impact of the organization of the information. First, we expected salary discrimination to be more easily detected when it was conspicuous (i.e., when there was ordinal inequity within the departments) than when it was inconspicuous (i.e., when there was ordinal equity within the departments). Second, we expected salary discrimination would be more easily detected when the information was presented in aggregate form than when it was presented piecemeal. Third, we expected that the conspicuousness of the discrimination would have less of an impact when the information was presented in aggregate form than when the information was presented piecemeal. In the aggregate conditions, subjects could easily make both intradepartmental and interdepartmental comparisons. They could also more easily estimate the mean qualifications and the mean salaries (which are identical in all conditions) to detect discrimination on an organizational level. The piecemeal condition made the estimation of average data more difficult, and made interdepartmental comparisons more difficult than intradepartmental comparisons.

Finally, we speculated as to whether gender would make a difference. Hence, we included gender of the target of discrimination and gender of subjects as independent variables. If gender identification were evoked by the task (Messick & Mackie, 1989), people might be especially sensitive to bias against their own gender. To find out, we varied the materials so that half of the time

Branch	Men			Women		
	Years	Level	Salary	Years	Level	Salary
			Firm X			
A	10	12	$40,000	11	12	$37,000
B	12	14	$50,000	12	16	$47,000
			Firm Y			
A	10	12	$40,000	12	16	$47,000
B	12	14	$50,000	11	12	$37,000

Table 1 Hypothetical Examples of Salary Discrimination

females received a lower salary than comparably qualified males and half of the time the reverse was true.

Method

Subjects were 95 male and 41 female M.B.A. students enrolled in four different organizational behavior courses at the Kellogg Graduate School of Management. The experiment was conducted as a classroom exercise, although subjects could opt not to participate. Before receiving the materials, subjects were told that the exercise concerned compensation issues and that its purpose and relevance would be revealed upon completion of the exercise. Subjects within each of the four classes were assigned randomly to one of either experimental conditions.

A 2 × 2 × 2 × 2 factorial design was used: the design crossed conspicuousness (conspicuous vs. inconspicuous inequity), format (aggregate vs. piecemeal), gender of the target (whether discrimination was against male or female managers), and gender of the subject. Subjects were given information concerning the average salary, level, and years with the firm of male and female managers in 10 departments of Company Z.

Subjects were told that "there are two 'input' variables (level in the firm and years of employment in the firm) which determine the appropriate salaries. For each and every department, these two input variables, and only these input variables, are supposed to determine salary." Subjects were also told that the firm had 18 levels, of which 10 were managerial, and that an employee at a higher level should receive a higher salary. Similarly, more years of employment should lead to a higher salary.

To determine the precise numbers to use for salary, level, and years for each of the 10 departments, we used the following regression equation:

salary = 4(*level*) + 1.5(*years*) + *bias*.

This equation reflected our belief that level is more important than mere seniority. For the advantaged managers, the average bias was + $4,000; for the disadvantaged managers, it was −$4,000. See Table 2 for the data created from this equation. Level and seniority are positively correlated, as they would be in real organizations.

The first independent variable, conspicuousness, concerned whether each department's data were characterized by ordinal inequity (conspicuous) or ordinal

equity (inconspicuous). Subjects in the conspicuous condition received their information as presented in Table 2: The disadvantaged managers had higher qualifications but lower salaries than the advantaged managers in a given department. This ordinal inequity was found within 9 of the 10 departments. Subjects in the inconspicuous condition were presented with information that was characterized by ordinal equity in all departments. These subjects received the same information contained in Table 2, except that the five bottom rows for advantaged managers were switched with the five top rows. The information concerning disadvantaged managers remained unchanged.

The second independent variable, format, consisted of two levels (aggregate vs. piecemeal). Subjects in the aggregate format condition received all the information for the 10 departments in aggregate form (i.e., on one page). Subjects in the piecemeal condition received this same information one department at a time (i.e., one department per page). Thus, subjects in both conditions received exactly the same departmental information, but this information was more conveniently arranged in the aggregate condition. Once subjects reviewed the departmental information (either the single page, in the aggregate condition, or 10 pages, in the piecemeal condition) and turned to the questions, they could not turn back to the departmental information.

The third factor concerned the gender of the target of discrimination. Subjects received information in which either female

Table 2 · Base Information About Levels, Years, and Salaries in Company Z

Department	Average Female Managers			Average Male Managers		
	Level	Years	Salary	Level	Years	Salary
A	9	6	$41,000	8	5	$44,000
B	10	9	$49,000	9	8	$52,000
C	11	8	$52,000	11	5	$55,000
D	12	8	$56,000	12	7	$63,000
E	12	16	$68,000	12	14	$73,000
F	12	20	$74,000	12	10	$67,000
G	13	15	$70,000	12	13	$71,000
H	13	19	$76,000	13	17	$83,000
I	14	17	$78,000	13	16	$80,000
J	14	20	$81,000	14	19	$89,000

managers were disadvantaged (i.e., were more qualified, but received lower salaries) relative to male managers or male managers were disadvantaged relative to female managers. The target of discrimination was manipulated simply by reversing the gender labels on the materials presented to subjects. When females were the target of discrimination, the information was presented as in Table 2. When males were the target, the labels of this table were switched such that the left-hand label read "Average male managers" and the right-hand label read "Average female managers."

Data for the fourth independent variable, gender of the subject, were collected at the end of the questionnaire.

Subjects were instructed to study the information presented to them without using a calculator. Once they completed their examination of the departmental information, they were instructed to turn to the next page, which asked them to respond to two key questions. The first was, "Please rate your perception of the fairness of the relative pay for male and female managers at Company Z." A 9-point rating scale (1 = very unfair, 9 = very fair) followed. The second key question asked, "In how many of the 10 departments was there pay inequity?" This question was followed by the integers from 0 through 10. We asked this question to determine whether the manipulated variables would affect the accurate detection of discrimination. Finally, subjects were asked to recall, without turning back to the stimulus information, the average salary, level, and years for both male and female managers at Company Z.

Results

Preliminary analyses revealed no significant differences between the four classes. The data were combined, and the dependent variables were submitted to four-way analyses of variance. The correlation between the two major dependent variables, perceived fairness and estimated number of unfair departments, was −.67. We analyzed these variables separately because they measure different quantities.

For the perceived fairness judgments, there was a significant main effect for conspicuousness, $F(1, 120) = 24.89$, $p < .001$. As predicted, subjects in the conspicuous condition rated relative pay as significantly less fair ($M = 2.94$) than subjects in the inconspicuous condition ($M = 4.65$). There was also a significant main effect for gender of the target, $F(1, 120) = 9.25$, $p < .01$. When female managers were the target of unfairness, subjects rated the relative pay as significantly less fair ($M = 3.25$) than when male managers were the target of unfairness ($M = 4.31$). We did not find the predicted main effect for format.

For the estimated number of departments with pay inequity, there was a significant main effect for conspicuousness, $F(1, 118) = 62.57$, $p < .001$. Subjects in the inconspicuous condition reported significantly fewer departments with pay inequity ($M = 4.20$) than subjects in the conspicuous condition ($M = 7.55$).

There was also a significant conspicuousness-by-format interaction for this dependent variable, $F(1, 118) = 8.66$, $p < .01$. The means underlying this interaction are presented in Table 3. The pattern of this interaction was as anticipated: The conspicuousness variable had a larger impact when the materials were presented piecemeal than when they were in aggregate format.

Finally, there was a significant interaction between gender of the target and subject gender, $F(1, 118) = 4.82$, $p < 0.05$. As is evident in Table 4, this interaction reflects a gender bias: Each gender detected more departments having discrimination when that gender was the target of discrimination. In comparison to male subjects, female subjects detected more departments with pay inequity when females were the target of discrimination, and the converse was true for men.

In order to determine whether subjects in the aggregate and piecemeal conditions based their fairness judgments on different information, we performed regression analyses in which we regressed each subject's fairness judgment against five variables: (1) gender of subject; (2) the subject's estimated number of departments with pay inequity; (3) the difference in recalled years of service between female and male managers; (4) the difference in recalled level between female and male managers; and (5) the difference in recalled salary between female and male managers. The latter three difference measures were corrected for target conditions: When the target of discrimination was male, the difference scores were multiplied by –1, and when the target was female, the difference scores were multiplied by +1. This correction is necessary because the information about male and female managers in the male-target condition is reversed relative to the female-target condition.

We expected that, in the piecemeal condition, subjects might base their fairness judgments only on the estimated number of discriminating departments because mean levels of qualifications and salaries would be relatively inaccessible. These additional factors would be relatively more accessible in the aggregate condition, and therefore might influence the fairness judgments in that condition. We expected the relationship between salary difference and rated fairness to be positive (the larger the

| Table 3 | Mean Number of Departments Estimated to Display Pay Inequity as a Function of Conspicuousness and Format | | |

	Conspicuousness	
Format	Conspicuous	Inconspicuous
Aggregate	6.79	4.43
	n = 34	n = 30
	s.d. = 2.64	s.d. = 2.61
Piecemeal	8.28	4.00
	n = 35	n = 35
	s.d. = 1.95	s.d. = 2.58

Note. The total number of departments in the firm was 10, so the possible numbers ranged from 0 to 10.

| Table 4 | Mean Number of Departments Estimated to Display Pay Inequity as a Function of Subject Gender and Target Gender | | |

	Subject Gender	
Target Gender	Female	Male
Female	7.09	5.43
	n = 22	n = 46
	s.d. = 2.69	s.d. = 3.06
Male	5.00	6.21
	n = 18	n = 48
	s.d. = 2.93	s.d. = 3.00

Note. The total number of departments in the firm was 10, so the possible numbers ranged from 0 to 10.

recalled salary difference favoring the more qualified group, the more fair), and the other relationships to be negative (e.g., the more departments displaying discrimination, the less fair; the greater women's level over men's, given the fixed salary difference, the less fair).

The results of the two regression analyses can be found in Table 5. The only significant predictor of fairness judgments of subjects in the piecemeal condition was reported number of departments with pay inequity. The more departments subjects reported as having inequity, the lower the rating of fairness. In the aggregate condition, there were three significant predictors of fairness judgments: the number of departments reported as having

pay inequity; the recalled difference in level between male and female managers; and the recalled difference in salary between male and female managers. The higher the number of departments subjects perceived as having pay inequity, the more negative the difference in salaries, and the more positive the difference in level, the lower were subjects' ratings of fairness. These findings suggest that subjects in the piecemeal condition used only the estimated number of discriminating departments in making their fairness judgments. In the aggregate condition, subjects appear to have based their fairness judgments on the estimated differences in salaries and levels in addition to the number of discriminating departments. One-tailed tests of the

Table 5

Table 5 Results of Regression Analyses on Fairness Judgments for Aggregate and Piecemeal Conditions

Variable	Aggregate Condition			Piecemeal Condition		
	beta	t	p <	beta	t	p <
Gender of subject	0.088	0.845	n.s.	−0.016	−0.159	n.s.
Number of departments with pay inequity	−0.547	−5.213	.001	−0.711	−7.403	.001
Difference in salary	0.301	2.664	.01	0.091	0.954	n.s.
Difference in level	−0.312	−2.835	.007	0.054	0.531	n.s.
Difference in years	−0.085	−0.826	n.s.	−0.014	−0.141	n.s.
Constant		11.744	.001		14.010	.001

Note. For the aggregate condition, multiple $R = .74$, $R^2 = .55$, $F = 11.77$, $p < .001$. For the piecemeal condition, multiple $R = .71$, $R^2 = .51$, $F = 12.34$, $p < .001$.

greater extremity of the regression coefficients in the aggregate condition than in the piecemeal condition produced a significant result for salaries ($t[106] = 2.42$, $p < .01$) and a marginal value for levels ($t[106] = 1.50$, $p < .07$).

Discussion

These findings support the notion that the organization of information regarding qualifications and salaries influences the detection of salary discrimination. Subjects perceived more unfairness regarding men's and women's salaries and a greater number of departments that displayed salary discrimination when the materials contained ordinal inequity than when they did not.

These findings extend previous research in that they draw attention to the unit or level at which discrimination can be easily observed. When discrimination is conspicuous at the department level, more unfairness is perceived than when discrimination is inconspicuous (i.e., when there is ordinal equity), regardless of format. Moreover, in estimating the number of discriminating departments—one of the

cues to unfairness—subjects may be more accurate in the piecemeal than in the aggregate condition. Subjects in the conspicuous-aggregate condition estimated that 6.79 departments discriminated, while subjects in the conspicuous-piecemeal condition estimated that 8.28 departments discriminated. (Nine of the 10 departments in Table 2 showed ordinal inequity. The exception was Department F, in which women were more qualified and had higher salaries.) When the data are presented piecemeal and the discrimination is conspicuous, subjects merely have to keep a running count of the departments characterized by ordinal inequity to accumulate evidence of unfairness.

This fact may be partly responsible for our failure to find the predicted main effect for format. Unlike previous studies (see Clayton & Crosby, 1986; Crosby & Clayton, 1986; Crosby et al., in press) in which one gender's qualifications were not uniformly superior to the other's, in this study, the qualifications of the more qualified gender were at least as good as the qualifications of the other gender on both attributes and better on at least one.

The data in the conspicuous-piecemeal condition leave little doubt about discrimination at the department and the firm levels.

In the conspicuous-aggregate condition, in contrast, having all the data in a single table seems to have done two things. First, it disrupted the simple counting of departments. Second, the regression analysis suggests that the aggregate format provided cross-departmental data, making mean levels and salaries available to influence the fairness judgment. The first of these factors might reduce the perceived unfairness, whereas the second might tend to increase it. This is a possible reason why we failed to find a main effect for format and to replicate the format-by-conspicuousness interaction with the fairness judgments.

Our finding of a main effect of target gender for perceived-fairness judgments—discrimination against women is judged as more unfair than precisely the same discrimination against men—parallels the finding by Rodin, Price, Bryson, and Sanchez (1990) that discrimination against weaker members of society is viewed as more indicative of prejudice than the same discrimination against stronger members of society. Rodin et al. used several different groupings—blacks and whites, men and women, gays and straights, for instance—and their vignettes were simpler than the material our subjects read. Nevertheless, our results support their asymmetry hypothesis, the proposal that discrimination against the weaker group is more indicative of prejudice and more unfair than discrimination against the stronger group.

Also of interest is the finding that in estimating the number of departments that discriminated, subjects were especially sensitive to discrimination against their own gender. While the focus of this experiment was on the impact of the organization and presentation of information about discrimination, this own-gender sensitivity reminds us that the processing of information about unfairness may have egocentric or ethnocentric components as well (Clayton & Crosby, 1986). When it is our (gender's) metaphorical ox that is being gored, we see more departments involved than when it is the other's.

Our results support the position that the perception of discrimination is influenced by the way in which relevant information is presented and processed. In this study, the global magnitude of the discrimination, as measured by the bias term in the regression equation, was constant. Nevertheless, discrimination was less easily detected when the qualifications and salaries within a department were equitable, in an ordinal sense, than when they were not. An important implication of our findings is that seemingly innocuous compensation patterns—that is, those characterized by ordinal equity—can obscure serious gender discrimination.

References

Clayton, S., & Crosby, F. J. (1986). Postscript: The nature of connections. *Journal of Social Issues, 42,* 189–194.

Cordova, D. I. (1992). Cognitive limitations and affirmative action: The effects of aggregate versus sequential data in the perception of discrimination. *Social Justice Research, 5,* 101–116.

Crosby, F. J. (in press). Understanding affirmative action. *Basic and Applied Social Psychology.*

Crosby, F. J., & Clayton, S. (1986). Introduction: The search for connections. *Journal of Social Issues, 42,* 1–10.

Crosby, F. J., Cordova, D. I., & Jaskar, K. (In press). On the failure to see oneself as disadvantaged: Cognitive and emotional components. In M. Hogg & D. Abrams (Eds.), *Group motivation: Social psychological perspectives.* London: Harvester-Wheatshef.

Messick, D. M., & Mackie, D. M. (1989). Intergroup relations. *Annual Review of Psychology, 40,* 45–81.

Rodin, M. J., Price, J. M., Bryson, J. B., & Sanchez, F. J. (1990). Asymmetry in prejudice attribution. *Journal of Experimental Social Psychology, 26,* 481–504.

Sheppard, B. H., Lewicki, R. J., & Minton, J. W. (1992). *Organizational justice.* New York: Lexington.

Twiss, C., Tabb, S., & Crosby, F. J. (1989). Affirmative action and aggregate data: The importance of patterns in the perception of discrimination. In F. A. Blanchard & F. J. Crosby (Eds.), *Affirmative action in perspective* (pp. 159–167). New York: Springer-Verlag.

 Article Review Form at end of book.

What are some of the main components of the stereotypic female that MTV advertisers provide their viewers? Do you think the stereotype is any different in the ads than it is in the videos?

Gender Stereotypes in MTV Commercials

The beat goes on

Nancy Signorielli
Douglas McLeod
Elaine Healy

This study examines gender portrayals and stereotyping in a sample of commercials on MTV. The findings revealed that characters in MTV commercials, like those in music videos, are stereotyped. Female characters appeared less frequently, had more beautiful bodies, were more physically attractive, wore more sexy and skimpy clothing, and were more often the object of another's gaze than their male counterparts.

Over the past 20 years, content analyses of television and its advertising have found that women are underrepresented and portrayed in stereotypical ways (Signorielli, 1985a). This study examines gender stereotyping in a genre not previously investigated: MTV commercials.

MTV commercials have been proclaimed as trendsetters in commercial advertising (Dalton, 1985; Gershon & Gantz, 1992). Despite their innovative contributions to advertising style, MTV commercials may have patterns of gender stereotyping found in other commercials. MTV has immense appeal for adolescents and young adults and has joined the other mass media as an influential agent of socialization. Advertisers have been drawn to MTV in order to associate their products with a medium on the cutting edge of the youth culture.

Gender Roles and Television Content

Studies have consistently found that commercials are stereotyped by gender (Courtney & Whipple, 1983; Signorielli, 1985a). Research conducted over the past 25 years has revealed that commercials in prime-time and weekend daytime children's programs rarely use a woman's voice as a voice-over. Moreover, men are presented as authoritative, even for products used primarily by women (Bretl & Cantor, 1988; Dominick & Rauch, 1972; Lovdal, 1989; O'Donnell & O'Donnell, 1978). While men and women are more equally represented (in terms of numbers) in prime-time commercials, women are very underrepresented in commercials aired during children's programs (Doolittle & Pepper, 1975; Riffe, Goldson, Saxton, & Yu, 1989).

Some recent studies (Bretl & Cantor, 1988; Ferrante, Haynes, & Kingsley, 1988; Lovdal, 1989) have examined voice-overs, occupation of major characters, product spokespersons, and general product categories, comparing findings

Signorielli, N., McLeod, D., Healy, E. (1994). Gender Stereotypes in MTV Commercials: the Beat Goes On, JOURNAL OF BROADCASTING AND ELECTRONIC MEDIA, 38 (1), 91–101. Reprinted by permission.

from recent samples of commercials with those of studies conducted in the 1970s. In short, these analyses found little overall change in the presentation of men and women in commercials aired during the prime-time hours.

Standards for attractiveness, particularly in commercials, also appear to be sexually stereotyped. For example, a content analysis of 4,294 commercials found some form of attractiveness message once every 3.8 commercials and that "attractiveness is more associated with women than with men and that men (via authoritative voice-overs) are forging this attractiveness-women link" (Downs & Harrison, 1985, p. 17).

MTV, Its Audience, and Content

Almost 6 out of 10 television households receive MTV as part of their basic cable service (MTV Research, 1991). As MTV grew in popularity and its audience increased in size, companies who wanted to reach young people found that MTV was an important outlet for their commercial messages. In 1991, 80% of MTV's audience was between the ages of 12 and 34. Moreover, one quarter of the audience was between the ages of 12 and 17, an adolescent audience much larger than that reported for other television networks (MTV Research, 1991). In addition, adolescent viewers spend an average of over two hours a day watching MTV (Sun & Lull, 1986).

Whereas research has not yet examined gender stereotyping in MTV commercials, several studies have analyzed the characters in music videos. For example,

Brown and Campbell (1986), using a sample of music videos from MTV and BET (Black Entertainment Television), found that women and blacks were in the minority on MTV. White men were seen most often and usually were the center of attention, while women and blacks remained in the background. Similarly, Sherman and Dominick (1986) found that women and minorities were underrepresented in samples of music videos on MTV and on network television.

Vincent, Davis, and Boruszkowski (1987), using the consciousness scale developed by Pingree, Hawkins, Butler, and Paisley (1976), found that 56.9% of the portrayals of women in concept music videos (videos that told a story) were condescending. Overall, the depiction of gender roles was traditional, and sexism was high. In a follow-up study using samples of concept videos taken 18 months apart (Vincent, 1989), most of the videos had all male performers and portrayed women condescendingly. There was, however, a significant rise in the number of videos that presented women as "fully equal" to men between the videos taped during the summer of 1985 and those taped during the winter of 1986–1987, from 15.5% to 38.5%. Conversely, there were also small but significant increases in the amount of sexy or alluring clothing (lingerie, bathing suits) and nudity in the later sample as compared to the earlier one. Similarly, Seidman (1992) found that females were more likely than males to wear sexually revealing clothing. Finally, both males and females were portrayed in sex-typed occupations.

These findings to date focus only on the content in music videos themselves, not in the ads inserted into the programs. This study will extend the literature by examining gender portrayals in the ads on MTV. The focus of this study is on the frequency and type of portrayals of females compared to males in the ads.

Two broad research questions guided the study. The first asks how men and women are portrayed in MTV commercials and hypothesizes that both men and women will be portrayed in stereotypical ways. Five specific hypotheses relating to gender images in MTV commercials were tested:

Female characters will appear less frequently than male characters in MTV commercials.

Female characters will be more likely than male characters to be portrayed as having very fit bodies.

Female characters will be rated as more attractive than male characters.

Female characters will be more likely than male characters to wear skimpy or sexy clothing.

Female characters will be more likely than male characters to be the object of another's gaze.

The second research question focuses on whether commercials for different types of products have a male or female gender orientation. In short, are there recognizable differences in terms of the types of products that are associated with men and women?

Method

A sample of MTV commercials was recorded on videotape during five weekdays in mid-November 1991.[1] Six hours of MTV programming were recorded each day, half between the hours of 3:00 and 6:00 p.m. and half between the hours of 9:00 p.m. and midnight, the hours (after school and late evening) when adolescents are most likely to watch MTV.

In total, 550 commercials were recorded. Eliminating repeat commercials, the final sample consisted of 119 individual commercials. These commercials were equally likely to be found in the after-school and late evening hours. The high rate of repetition, both within and across the time parameters, implies that there is a greater likelihood that the images in these commercials will be seen (and perhaps remembered) by viewers. In order to reflect the actual content of the time frame in which the commercials were sampled, the data for each commercial were weighted by the number of times it appeared in the entire sample of 550 commercials.[2]

The recording instrument consisted of two separate units of analysis, the commercial and the major characters. A commercial was operationalized as an advertisement with the intent to sell or promote a product, service, event, etc. This operationalization excluded promotions relating to MTV itself, such as contests, surveys, and MTV programming. PSAs and other informational spots were also excluded.

The type of product (or service) advertised was coded using a 32-product coding scheme that was collapsed into six categories:

Personal products: appearance, hygiene, and health-related products ($n = 31$ unweighted; 136 weighted).

Entertainment: games, toys, musical equipment and accessories, and video game paraphernalia ($n = 26$ unweighted; 121 weighted).

Clothing & Accessories: clothes, shoes, handbags, jewelry, and like products ($n = 16$ unweighted; 97 weighted).

Media Products: books, magazines, movies, television shows, and like products ($n = 16$ unweighted; 84 weighted).

Food & Drink: both nutritious and non-nutritious foods, all restaurants, and alcoholic and non-alcoholic beverages ($n = 18$ unweighted; 68 weighted).

Other: cars, services, household products, and like products ($n = 12$ unweighted; 35 weighted).

Two separate measures of gender orientation were used. The first, visual gender makeup, was operationalized as the physical presence of males and/or females in the commercial. A commercial with a male gender makeup had only males present. A commercial with a female gender makeup had only females present. A neutral gender makeup commercial contained both males and females. Categorizing a commercial as "cannot code" meant that there were no characters. The second measure of gender orientation was the gender of the user of the product. A product user was operationalized as someone who held, demonstrated, touched, or was in any way physically associated with the product. These two measures isolated only male and only female orientations to focus on the most pure cases of gender orientation.[3]

The second unit of analysis was the major character (or char-acters) within a commercial. Major characters were operationalized as humans who were central to the action of the commercial; in short, a commercial's basic nature and selling intent would be changed if this character did not appear. Announcers were not considered characters unless they appeared visually in the commercial. Basic demographic information about the major characters was coded, including gender, race or ethnicity, and social age (stages of the life cycle, ranging from infancy to old age).

Physical attractiveness was assessed by four codings. The first item measured the body type or level of fitness and muscularity of the character. It had three values: (1) out of shape (poor posture, flabby, soft, weak), (2) average fitness (little or no focus on muscularity or the body), or (3) very fit (muscular). Second, the character was rated on a 5-point attractiveness scale, ranging from (1) repulsive/ugly to (5) very attractive (stunning, above average appeal). Attractiveness was defined as the apparent physical attractiveness of the character (as opposed to the actor/actress) as s/he was portrayed within the commercial. Coders relied on the commercial context in making attractiveness judgments focusing on how the producers framed the character in order to eliminate their own subjective assessments of physical attractiveness. Third, coders also judged whether the character wore skimpy or sexy clothing, using a 4-point scale ranging from (1) neutral (non-sexy) clothing to (4) outright nudity. The final attractiveness item assessed whether the character was set up as the object of other characters' attention or admiring gazes.

Fifty commercials (42% of the individual commercials) were selected and independently coded by two separate coders[4] in order to provide data for the reliability analysis. Intercoder agreement was estimated using Krippendorff's (1980) alpha. The following reliability coefficients were calculated: product type (.98); visual gender orientation (.94); gender orientation of the user (.89); gender (.96); race (.88); body type (.75); attractiveness (.91); sexy clothing (.86); and object of gaze (.75). All of these variables were nominal in nature except for two ordinal measures — body type and attractiveness.

Findings

The demographic makeup of the characters in MTV commercials parallels the distribution of characters in music videos (see, for example, Sherman & Dominick, 1986). Almost half of the characters (48.5%) were young adults (about 18 to 25 years), and a little more than a quarter (27.4%) were adults (about 26 to 60 years). Relatively few characters were portrayed as adolescents (11.1%) or as elderly (12.1%). Children (1.0%) were almost invisible in this sample. More than 9 out of 10 characters (95%) were white. The remaining 5% included all other racial/ethnic groups (black, 2.3%; Asian, 2.1%; Hispanic, 0.6%).

There was support for hypothesis 1 (see Table 1).* Males appeared slightly more often (54.4%) than females (45.6%) in the sampled MTV commercials ("goodness of fit" X^2 based on a 50/50 distribution was 4.1, df = 1, $p < .05$). There was also support for hypothesis 2. Women were more likely than men to be portrayed as having very fit or beautiful bodies, X^2 (2, N = 489) = 96.3, $p < .001$. Almost three quarters of the men were rated as

having average bodies, while more than three quarters of female characters (77.4%) were rated as having very fit or beautiful bodies.

There was also support for hypothesis 3. Females were rated as more attractive than males, X^2 (3, N = 517) = 206.6, $p < .001$. More than half of male characters were placed in the middle category of the attractiveness scale, with slightly more than one third rated as attractive. Hardly any male characters (2.2%) were rated as extremely attractive or beautiful. Conversely, more than half of female characters were rated as extremely attractive or beautiful, and almost one quarter were rated as attractive. Few female characters were rated as neutral in attractiveness (15.1%) or unattractive (8.0%).

Hypothesis 4 was also supported. Female characters were more likely than male characters to be portrayed wearing skimpy or sexy clothing, X^2 (2, N = 513) = 148.0, $p < .001$. The clothing worn by almost all (93.5%) male characters was rated as neutral. A small percentage of male characters (6.5%) were coded as wearing clothing that was somewhat sexy. While slightly less than half the women in the sample (46.2%) were coded as wearing neutral clothing, comparatively large percentages of women were coded as wearing somewhat sexy (24.4%) or very sexy (29.4%) clothing.

Finally, there was support for hypothesis 5. Female characters were more likely than male characters to be the object of another character's gaze, X^2 (1, N = 522) = 94.7, $p < .001$. One out of five male characters (19.0%) was the object of another character's admiring gaze. In contrast 6 out of 10 female characters were the ob-

ject of another's gaze. When one character directed his or her gaze upon another character the object of the gaze was a female almost three quarters of the time.

The second focus of the study examined the gender orientation of the commercials. The analysis revealed that a majority of the commercials were oriented toward both men and women in regard to the visual presentation of the sexes and the user of the product. When focusing, however, on those commercials that included only men or only women more commercials were oriented towards men than women. The measure of visual gender makeup indicated that 23.7% of the commercials had only males while 9.6% had only females. The measure of the gender of the user of the product revealed that in 4 out of 10 commercials only men touched, demonstrated, or were physically associated with the product. Women, on the other hand, were primary product users in 2 out of 10 commercials. For both measures purely male orientations were found over twice as many times as purely female orientations.

The relationship between gender roles and the type of product advertised in MTV commercials was examined by looking at the crosstabulations of the type of product advertised with two measures of gender orientation—(1) the visual gender orientation of the commercial and (2) the gender orientation of the user of the product.

The relationship between the type of product advertised and the visual gender orientation of the commercial is given in Table 2.* Most of the commercials had visual representations of both men and women (85.7% of media prod-

*Not included in this publication.

*Not included in this publication.

ucts; 62.5% of personal products; 57.4% of food products; 42.3% of clothing; and 31.4% of entertainment products).

When only one gender was represented, the gender was more likely to be a male than a female, except for commercials for personal products. For example, 38.1% of the commercials for clothing featured only men while only 15.5% of these commercials featured only women. Only males were seen in 32.3% of the commercials for entertainment products while 4.1% of these only featured women.

More than one tenth of the commercials showing only males were for food and drink, 7.0% were for media products, 28.9% for clothing, 30.5% for entertainment, and 17.2% for personal products. On the other hand, there was a somewhat different product distribution for commercials with only females. More than three quarters of these commercials were for personal products (55.8%) and clothing (28.8%) and one tenth were for entertainment products. Only 5% of the commercials showing only women advertised media or food-related products.

Commercials with only male product users were somewhat equally divided among the four categories, but with females almost three quarters of the commercials with only female product users were for personal products (see Table 3).*

Personal products were the only type of commercials more likely to have female rather than male users (55.1% vs. 41.2%). More than half of entertainment commercials had male users and one third (33.1%) had no specific user. Clothing commercials usually had male (39.2%) or both

*Not included in this publication.

male and female users (30.9%). Similarly almost half of the commercials for food or drinks were classified as having both male and female users. Finally, more than 6 out of 10 commercials for media products could not be classified by the specific gender of the user.

Discussion

Commercials on MTV are gender-stereotyped. Even though a large percentage of commercials were geared toward both men and women, the data consistently revealed that when one gender was the target of a commercial, the target was typically male. The visual gender makeup of the commercial and the gender of the user had more than twice as many only male commercials as only female commercials. It is particularly interesting to note that males were far more likely than females to handle or control the object being advertised. This may reveal a bias on the part of advertisers that males are more effectively associated with the strengths of a particular product than females.

The types of products classified as male and female also revealed a gender bias. The product type most often oriented toward males was entertainment-related. In contrast, the product type most often oriented toward females was personal products — products with the primary purpose of improving or enhancing the physical attractiveness of the buyer. While commercials with only male characters included products reflecting fun and action, commercials with only female characters focused on products related to looking good. These gender associations with particular product types reveal that in regard to the specific users of the products and the visual nature of the commercials there were

stereotypical designations of women's and men's roles.

The analyses of character attributes also revealed that commercials on MTV were filled with stereotypical information about gender roles. Female characters in these commercials appeared less frequently, had more beautiful bodies, were more physically attractive, wore more sexy and skimpy clothing, and were more often the object of another's gaze than male characters. All of these findings supported the idea that visual attention was highly emphasized for female characters. The portrayals in these commercials reveal a disturbing message: The primary purpose of women's effort is to "look good" and to be the object of the visual attention of others.

This study revealed that despite MTV's status as a "cutting edge" genre of television, MTV's advertisers continue to utilize stereotyped images and appeals in their commercials. Consequently, the messages about gender roles that adolescents might learn from MTV commercials uphold traditional restrictive views of men and women. On the whole the findings of this study, while examining somewhat different variables, corroborate findings from recent content analyses of commercials in prime-time programs illustrating the persistence of sex-role stereotypes (Bretl & Cantor, 1988; Ferrante et al., 1988; Lovdal, 1989).

This study indicated that MTV commercials preserve and perpetuate stereotypes about women. If adolescents, as is likely, utilize MTV as a source of social learning about gender roles, then they receive warped views of the roles and responsibilities of women in society. While we cannot say there is a causal relationship between commercial content and social problems like rape, eating disorders, and discrimination in the workplace, MTV commercials in no way contribute to a reduction of misconceptions about women and women's roles in society. As a popular maxim states, "If you're not part of the solution, you're part of the problem."

Notes

1. The choice of a week-long sample may be a limitation of the study. This decision, however, was based upon the methodology of previous content analyses of television content, many of which have used week-long samples (see, for example, Bretl & Cantor, 1988; Downs & Harrison, 1985; O'Donnell & O'Donnell, 1978; Signorielli, 1985b).
2. Analyses conducted on the weighted and unweighted data sets yielded similar findings. The weighted data are reported because they represent a more realistic approximation of the imagery seen during a week of viewing.
3. Commercials with mixed genders and those without characters were not included in the product user coding schemes.
4. All of the commercials were coded by the third author; the second coding for the reliability analysis was completed by two other (one male and one female) master's students at the University of Delaware.

References

Bretl, D. J., & Cantor, J. (1988). The portrayal of men and women in U.S. television commercials: A recent content analysis and trends over 15 years. *Sex Roles, 18,* 595–609.

Brown, J. D., & Campbell, K. (1986). Race and gender in music videos: The same beat but a different drummer. *Journal of Communication, 36*(l), 94–106.

Courtney, A. E., & Whipple, T. W. (1983). *Sex stereotyping in advertising.* Lexington, MA: Lexington Books.

Dalton, J. (1985, December). The televisionary. *Esquire,* pp. 380–387.

Dominick, J. R., & Rauch, G. E. (1972). The image of women in network TV commercials. *Journal of Broadcasting, 16,* 259–265.

Doolittle, J., & Pepper, R. (1975). Children's TV ad content: 1974. *Journal of Broadcasting 19,*131–142.

Downs, A. C., & Harrison, S. K. (1985). Embarrassing age spots or just plain ugly? Physical attractiveness stereotyping as an instrument of sexism on American television commercials. *Sex Roles, 13,* 9–19.

Ferrante, C. L., Haynes, A. M., & Kingsley, S. M. (1988). Image of women in television advertising. *Journal of Broadcasting & Electronic Media, 32,* 231–237.

Gershon, P. R., & Gantz, W. (1992, May). Music videos and television commercials: A comparison of production styles. Paper presented to the annual conference of the International Communication Association, Miami, FL.

Krippendorff, K. (1980). *Content analysis: An introduction to its methodology.* Beverly Hills, CA: Sage.

Lovdal, L. T. (1989). Sex role messages in television commercials: An update. *Sex Roles, 21,* 715–724.

MTV Research. (1991). *Marketing report.* New York: Time Warner.

O'Donnell, W. J., & O'Donnell, K. J. (1978). Update: Sex-role messages in TV commercials. *Journal of Communication, 28*(1), 156–158.

Pingree, S., Hawkins, R. P., Butler, M., & Paisley, W. (1976). A scale for sexism. *Journal of Communication, 26*(4), 193-200.

Riffe, D., Goldson, H., Saxton, K., & Yu, Y. C. (1989). Females and minorities in TV ads in 1987 Saturday children's programs. *Journalism Quarterly, 66,* 129–136.

Seidman, S. A. (1 992). An investigation of sex-role stereotyping in music videos. *Journal of Broadcasting & Electronic Media 36,* 209–216.

Sherman, B. L., & Dominick, J. R. (1986). Violence and sex in music videos: TV and rock 'n' roll. *Journal of Communication, 36*(1), 79–93.

Signorielli, N. (1985a). *Role portrayal and stereotyping on television: An annotated bibliography of studies relating to women, minorities, aging, sexual behavior, health, and handicaps.* Westport, CT: Greenwood.

Signorielli, N. (1985b). The measurement of violence in television programming: Violence indices. In J. R. Dominick & J. E. Fletcher (Eds.), *Broadcasting research methods* (pp. 235–251). Boston: Allyn & Bacon.

Sun, S. W., & Lull, J. (1986). The adolescent audience for music videos and why they watch. *Journal of Communication, 36*(1), 115–125.

Vincent, R. C. (1989). Clio's consciousness raised? Portrayal of women in rock videos, re-examined. *Journalism Quarterly, 66,* 155–160.

Vincent, R. C., Davis, D. K., & Boruszkowski, L. A. (1987). Sexism on MTV: The portrayal of women in rock videos. *Journalism Quarterly, 64,* 750–755, 941.

 Article Review Form at end of book.

How do researchers think that stereotype vulnerability interferes with performance? What are two ways that you can reduce the possibility of stereotype threat to someone?

Can Racial Stereotypes Psych Out Students?

Elaine Woo

Two students, one black and the other white, sit next to each other in a college classroom. Both are bright and from middle-class families. They went to decent high schools and did well on college placement exams. But the black student is flunking, and the white one is not.

Why do they perform so differently?

Stanford University social psychologist Claude Steele believes he has an answer. And it isn't genetics, social class, lack of academic skills, family dysfunction or segregation—the usual suspects in the lineup of explanations for the stubborn problem of black underachievement.

Steele says that blacks—or any member of a group freighted with negative stereotypes—constantly labor under the suspicion that the stereotypes about them are true. Thus, women contend with the image of being mathematical klutzes, the elderly with insinuations of forgetfulness, blacks with the specter of intellectual inferiority. This burden alone, he believes, can make an otherwise competent student flounder.

His work is likely to stir up the scientific community, where many researchers believe that a number of factors underlie group differences in academic performance. But Steele's theory, tested in the lab and on campus, turns some common psychological assumptions on their head. In the process, it offers ammunition to both sides of the affirmative action debate.

Steele argues that the possibility of being judged by a stereotype—or inadvertently fulfilling it—can cause an anxiety so disruptive that it impairs intellectual performance. The victim may reject the stereotype, yet can't avoid its glare.

Steele calls this condition "stereotype threat." For black college students, it can deaden the commitment to academics, becoming a barrier as effective, he says, as a lock on the schoolhouse door.

In a paper published last month in the *Journal of Personality and Social Psychology*, Steele and Joshua Aronson of the University of Texas offer proof that pervasive negative stereotypes about blacks' intellectual ability create a "situational pressure" that distracts them and depresses their academic performance.

The trigger can be astonishingly trivial—asking a student to identify his race before taking a test, or suggesting that the test will measure intellectual performance. But defuse the stereotype threat by removing those triggers, their research says, and black students score as well as whites.

Suggesting the phenomenon's universality, Steele and professor Steven J. Spencer of Hope College in Holland, Mich., found the same results in experiments examining women and the image that they are mathematically inept. Steele and Aronson have found even white men may be stereotype-vulnerable: Their scores plummeted in testing situations that implied their math ability would be measured against that of Asians.

"If they can feel stereotype vulnerability," Aronson says, "anybody can."

Yet it is Steele's and Aronson's work involving blacks that has received the most enthusiastic attention, in part because of the promise it holds for solving what has seemed an intractable problem.

Dropout Rate a Problem

Nationally, the college dropout rate for African Americans is 70%, almost twice that of whites, despite three decades of efforts aimed at boosting their academic success.

"It is an extremely encouraging program of research," said Jennifer Crocker, a University of Michigan social psychologist. "It suggests this is a problem we can do something about . . . these group differences in achievement."

The harshest criticism so far has come from a painfully close source: Shelby Steele, the conservative essayist who is Claude's identical twin brother.

In an extraordinary outburst, the San Jose State English professor, an ardent foe of affirmative action, has accused Claude of stealing his ideas and applying them to a more politically correct agenda.

"This has stood between us for some time," Shelby wrote in a scathing letter to the *New York Times* in October, after the newspaper ran an article contrasting their views. What his brother now calls "stereotype threat," Shelby claimed, is really his idea of "racial vulnerability," which Shelby explored in a series of essays published five years ago.

Then Stanford's Steele replied with his own letter, denying the charges and spelling out the differences between his theory and his brother's ideas.

Trying to patch up their relationship, Claude initially declined to be interviewed for this article without assurances that Shelby would not be mentioned. He relented after reaching an agreement with Shelby that neither would comment on the other's work.

Claude began investigating the problem of black underachievement in the late 1980s, while on the faculty at the University of Michigan. Asked to join a committee studying student retention and recruitment, he came upon some astounding statistics: grades and Scholastic Achievement Test scores of blacks and whites who were flunking out.

The conventional wisdom said that when black college students failed it was because they were ill-equipped, felled by substandard schooling since kindergarten.

But Steele found that those with the best preparation—reflected in high SAT scores—were failing more frequently than those with lower scores, and at a rate more than three times that of whites with similar scores.

Among black students, 18% to 33% were bombing out, compared to 2% to 11% of whites. And the dropout rate was the highest among students ranked in the top third by SAT scores.

"That pattern surprised me," Steele said recently. "Something else was going on in that situation beyond just skill preparation."

At Stanford, which hired him in 1991, Steele embarked on a series of experiments with Aronson, then a postdoctoral student, to test the hypothesis that social stigma was hampering blacks' intellectual performance.

In the first two experiments, three groups of undergraduates were recruited to take a test made up of the toughest items from the verbal portion of the Graduate Record Exam, used by graduate programs to assess aptitude.

The first group was told that the test would provide a genuine measure of verbal reasoning ability—a cue that researchers thought could trigger in blacks fear of being judged according to a stereotype about their intelligence.

The second group was given no suggestion that intellectual prowess was being measured. It was told that the test would merely evaluate the factors involved in solving verbal problems.

The third group's students got the same instructions as the second with one addition: The test would challenge them.

The researchers theorized that stereotype vulnerability works, in part, by preying on self-doubt any test-taker may feel when struggling to answer a difficult question.

Giving students an alternative context for evaluating their performance—that their frustration might be caused by the test's difficulty rather than any mental deficiencies—could be another way of shielding them from stereotype anxieties.

Researchers said the results of the study confirmed their hunches. Black students who thought the test would measure verbal ability scored significantly lower than whites in their group, and lower than blacks given other introductions.

"This was the first clear demonstration that we had something," Steele said.

In their next experiment, Steele and Aronson wanted to establish what psychological process was unleashed by the murmur of stereotypes. Did cuing blacks that their intelligence was being measured set off thoughts about the relevant, damning stereotype?

They invited 35 undergraduates to take a difficult test. But just before they began, the students were asked to complete 80 word fragments, some associated with negative black stereotypes (such as race, lazy), and others suggesting self-doubts (such as dumb, shame).

The students also filled out questionnaires asking for personal information, such as musical preferences.

These exercises were meant as a sort of racial Rorschach test, "to find out what is psychologically active in a person's mind" during the exam, Steele said.

He and Aronson found that blacks who were told the test would assess mental abilities completed the most word fragments related to negative stereotypes and self doubt. And they recorded fewer stereotype-related preferences (such as rap music) than other blacks or whites.

Those results, the researchers said, suggested that the mere threat of having their intelligence measured aroused in blacks thoughts of stereotypes about intellectual inferiority. And these students tried to distance themselves from those thoughts by disavowing stereotypical interests.

Fears Can Be Eased

Coming just as their mental powers are being stretched by the exam, self-doubt causes blacks to labor twice as hard, but to ill ef-

fect, Steele theorizes: They reread questions and recheck answers, in the end working less efficiently and making more mistakes.

"When a black kid sits down to take an ability test," Steele concludes, "bang! Racial stereotypes are activated . . . and are probably driving their emotions and behavior in that situation. . . . You're self-conscious, you don't have as much to allocate" to the task at hand.

In the final experiment in this series, all subjects were told they would take a test that would not reflect their ability. The only variable was that half of the subjects were asked to identify their race on the test sheet.

When blacks were asked to state their race, they scored dramatically lower than whites. But when the race question was absent, their scores matched those of whites.

In other words, the barest hint of stigma seemed to dampen blacks' achievement, but lifting it was the key that opened the lock.

"I think that is the major contribution of our work, really," said Steele, "showing that stereotype threat is a situation that can be turned on and off."

Even some proponents of a competing theory—that genetics account for group differences in intelligence—such as UC Berkeley professor emeritus Arthur Jensen, concede that Steele's research may have some merit and is worth further study.

But Jensen—an educational psychologist who caused an uproar in 1969 when he wrote an article suggesting that black children had low IQs that were largely inherited—also said that "stereotype vulnerability" is, at best, a "minor contributor" to racial differences in standardized

tests. He cited a recent study showing that the gap appears as early as age 3, "before any conscious awareness of societal (attitudes) toward blacks have been imbibed."

How well Steele's theory holds up won't be known for years. To answer some of his critics, he is in the midst of replicating his experiments using classic intelligence tests, which Jensen and others consider truer gauges of the ability to think and reason.

What is certain is that the theory already is challenging common views of prejudice and how it affects achievement.

Richard Nisbett, a University of Michigan social psychologist and noted authority on the psychology of stereotypes, observed that Steele's "is really quite a different notion about prejudice than the way people thought in the past."

Black underachievement previously has been tied to prejudice in two ways: Racism shortchanges black children, who wind up with the worst teachers and the most dilapidated campuses. And black students internalize negative stereotypes, which gives rise to crippling self-loathing.

The latter idea informs much of the movement to eliminate affirmative action. Shelby Steele has written powerfully of the danger of such "racial vulnerability" in his 1990 book, *The Content of Our Character: A New Vision of Race in America.*

Affirmative action, he wrote, has perpetuated blacks' "inner realm of racial doubt." That doubt itself, he said, "becomes an unrecognized preoccupation that undermines their ability to perform. . . ."

This debilitating power of stereotypes was part of "an entire framework of ideas lifted without attribution" by his brother, Shelby alleged in his letter to the New York Times. Asked in a recent interview whether he still believed his brother's theories borrow from his, he would only say, "We do not comment on each other's work."

In Nisbett's view, Claude's take on the problem is distinctly different from Shelby's, and suggests a different solution than a wholesale scrapping of affirmative action.

Stereotype threat rejects self-victimization as an explanation for black failures: The problem arises from imperfect situations rather than imperfect psyches.

"The brilliance of it (is) to locate the problem out there," Nisbett said. "There are circumstances that can trigger susceptibility to those stereotypes, and there are things institutions can do to make it more or less likely that people will feel vulnerable to them."

Steele and colleagues at Michigan are five years into a comprehensive effort to demonstrate how that vulnerability can be lessened.

Michigan's 21st Century Program is based in large part on Steele's research. Blacks and whites, randomly recruited, live and study together. They discuss personal and social issues in weekly rap sessions or seminars. Their regular course work is supplemented by evening "mastery workshops" in English, calculus, chemistry and physics, taught by upper-class students and emphasizing collaborative study.

Dramatic Results

By avoiding the self-segregation that is standard at most colleges, the program works against what Steele calls "pluralistic ignorance"—the racial isolation that can lead blacks, for instance, to assume their poor grades are the result of a racist professor. When blacks and whites room and study together, they have the opportunity to see their struggles in a different, nonracial light.

The benefits for blacks have been striking. Last year, the average GPA for 21st Century students was 2.89, almost a point higher than that of other blacks. For the top two-thirds of blacks, it eliminated the grade gap with whites. And in the program's first two years, 90% of blacks went on to graduate.

Whites in the program also earned higher grade averages than other white students, but Steele said the increase was not statistically significant. Some observers say the workshops are responsible for blacks' improved performance. Others credit the unique group culture—the value placed on studying, the collaborative ethic, the socializing that cuts across race.

Steele, who is analyzing the program, believes that black students' strong gains are caused by a combination of these factors.

The effort—which will be doubled to 500 students next fall—embraces what Steele calls "wise schooling": education must have at its heart the belief that every student is "up to the challenge of school."

Stereotypes, he reasons, threaten that principle. So do the remedial program into which so many minorities are funneled.

Instead, Steele says, schools should strive to reinvent themselves in ways that eliminate the stereotype threat. That means ending remedial programs that set minimal goals and rethinking those affirmative-action efforts that, in subtler ways, send minorities the message that they are not up to the competition.

And it means encouraging in students the idea that their ability to learn is not fixed, but expandable—an optimistic counterpoint to *The Bell Curve,* the 1994 book that renewed debate over the genetic basis of intelligence.

The success of these principles, Steele notes, has already been demonstrated by a number of prominent educators, such as former Garfield High teacher Jaime Escalante, who motivated underachieving East Los Angeles math students.

"If there is any single principle involved," Steele said, "it is 'Challenge them, don't remediate them.' Challenge conveys faith in their potential."

 Article Review Form at end of book.

How might people who don't believe that they hold negative stereotypes nevertheless behave in a discriminatory fashion? What are the three ways that affirmative action programs detect the presence of "aversive racism"?

"Aversive" Racism and the Need for Affirmative Action

John Dovidio

John Dovidio is a professor of psychology at Colgate University.

It is clear that court decisions and other moves against affirmative action in Texas and California have discouraged minority-group students from applying and being admitted to college, particularly to professional schools. Certainly we should re-examine preferential-treatment programs critically and carefully to determine their benefits and harms. But we also need to ask whether, as many critics of such programs suggest, the United States now can afford to pursue a colorblind approach to equal opportunity.

Over the past three decades, nationwide surveys have documented significant declines in whites' overt racism toward blacks, including expressions of prejudice, negative stereotyping, and resistance to racial equality. Nevertheless, substantial differences in the social, economic, and physical well-being of blacks and whites persist; the gaps in their income levels and unemployment rates are growing. Blacks continue to report greater distrust of government and other people than do whites. In one survey, for example, only 16 per cent of blacks, but 44 per cent of whites, felt that "most people can be trusted." These data, and similar empirical evidence for other minority groups, challenge the assumption that racial differences no longer are a critical issue for our society.

My own research on whites' prejudice against blacks calls into question whether racism has really declined as much as surveys indicate. Over the past 20 years, I have conducted research with Samuel L. Gaertner, a professor of psychology at the University of Delaware, that explores how overt racism has evolved into more-subtle and perhaps more-insidious forms.

In contrast to traditional forms of prejudice, the emotional reaction of what I call today's "aversive" racists to minorities is not one of overt dislike or hostility, but rather one of anxiety or discomfort. As a consequence, aversive racists attempt to avoid interracial interaction whenever possible. And although they try not to behave in overtly negative ways toward blacks (which would threaten their self-image as unbiased), they frequently express their bias indirectly, by favoring whites rather than discriminating against blacks and members of other minority groups.

For instance, an employer influenced by feelings of aversive racism might subtly re-evaluate the most important qualifications for a job, depending on the race of different applicants. If, say, a

John Dovidio, " 'Aversive' Racism and the Need for Affirmative Action," CHRONICLE OF HIGHER EDUCATION, July 25, 1997. Reprinted by permission of the author.

white applicant had broader experience and a black applicant had more up-to-date training, the employer would decide that experience was more important; if the white applicant had more-recent training and the black more experience, the employer would decide that experience was less important. Thus, the aversive racist would find a way to hire the white applicant without admitting to himself or herself that racial bias played a role in the choice.

Because aversive racists consciously endorse egalitarian values, they do not show prejudice in situations in which discrimination would be obvious to others or to themselves. However, aversive racists do discriminate, usually unintentionally, when they can rationalize their actions in ways that apparently have nothing to do with race. Thus, as in the example I cited above, they will justify favoring one person on the basis of some factor other than race—for example, a particular educational background—or they will say the criteria involved are ambiguous, allowing them to favor a white person with, perhaps, better grades over a black person with better recommendations.

Another way in which aversive racists often unconsciously discriminate is by providing special favors or support—such as mentoring or special opportunities for promotions—to people with backgrounds similar to their own. This allows them to avoid thinking of the actions in racial terms.

White are most likely to manifest aversive racism by failing to help blacks or other members of minority groups, without any overt intention to cause them harm. In one study, for example,

Samuel Gaertner and I found that when whites thought they were witnessing an emergency, they were just as likely to help a black victim as a white victim—if the whites believed that they were the only witnesses and that their personal responsibility was clear. But if whites believed that there were other witnesses to the emergency, and they could justify not helping by believing that someone else would intervene, only half as many of them helped a black victim as helped a white victim. The presence of other witnesses gave aversive racists the chance to justify not helping black victims without invoking race: They could let someone else help the blacks.

The subtlety and unintentionality of aversive racism can contribute to distrust and tension among racial and ethnic groups. Because aversive racists are unaware of their own prejudice and discriminate only when they can justify their behavior on grounds other than race, they tend to underestimate the continuing impact of race. They certainly dismiss racism as a motive for their own behavior, and they think blacks or members of other minority groups see prejudice where it doesn't really exist. Members of minority groups, in contrast, see aversive racists denying their own bias and yet sometimes acting in a biased fashion. As a result, it is not surprising that members of minority groups suspect that prejudice exists everywhere.

Critics of affirmative action frequently argue that "reverse discrimination"—in which members of minority groups are favored over whites who are equally or even more qualified—is now a greater problem than racism.

Empirical research, including some of my own work, demonstrates that reverse discrimination does occur. However, it occurs primarily when the bias carries few personal consequences for the individual favoring minority groups. In more personally significant situations, discrimination against minority groups is still more likely to occur. For instance, we have found that white students favored the admission of qualified black students to colleges as a general principle, but were biased against qualified black applicants who sought admission to their own college or university.

Approaches to dealing with traditional, overt racism—such as passing laws that require desegregation—generally are not effective in combating the aversive racism that we see today. Simply providing colorblind equal opportunity is not enough, because aversive racists are not colorblind. A growing body of research demonstrates that, upon meeting black people, whites immediately think first about the individuals' race rather than about other characteristics, such as sex, age, or socio-economic status. Thus, any negative stereotypes and attitudes that whites have about blacks are automatically activated. My colleagues and I recently have found that when whites see a black person, they experience negative thoughts and feelings even if the whites report—and often truly believe—that they are not racially prejudiced.

Three key elements of affirmative-action programs make them more effective against aversive racism than equal-opportunity policies are. First, affirmative-action programs are designed to assemble, in a self-conscious way that can counteract the effects of subtle bias, a diverse pool of fully qualified candidates for admission to educational programs or for employment or promotion.

Second, affirmative-action programs produce statistics that allow organizations to gauge their progress toward diversity. Systematic monitoring of racial disparities—for instance, in student or faculty attrition, or in the number of employees promoted above a certain level—can reveal the cumulative effects of aversive racism that might go unnoticed, even by the victims, on a case-by-case basis.

Third, affirmative-action programs focus on outcomes, not intentions. Demonstrating intent to discriminate is difficult in cases of aversive racism, where bias typically is not intended.

It is important for us to understand that although aversive racism may be unconscious, unintentional, and subtle, it is neither inevitable nor immutable. Significant changes can occur in individuals and society. Expressed racial attitudes have changed dramatically since Congress enacted civil-rights legislation 30 years ago. The personal, social, and economic well-being of blacks, women, and other traditionally disadvantaged groups has improved since the advent of affirmative action.

We should not delude ourselves, however, into thinking that equality has been achieved, that equity is now guaranteed, or that our society is beyond bias—regardless of court rulings and other actions hostile to affirmative action. Racism is not a problem that will go away on its own if we ignore it, as more than 200 years of history prove. Proponents of affirmative action must work aggressively to find ways to get scholars' research data before the courts, because it is clear that we still need to combat racism actively and self-consciously. Good intentions alone are not sufficient to guarantee equality. Affirmative action is not a perfect solution, but it is still needed.

 Article Review Form at end of book.

What are some of the specific suggestions for reducing prejudice and stereotyping of another person? Which of these do you think would work on a college campus?

Can't We All Get Along?

Overcoming prejudice

Jan Farrington

The football game was half over when Michael Smallwood, a 17-year-old junior at a north Texas high school, saw school officials confiscate a sign from a boy sitting a few rows in front of him. The sign carried five letters, T-A-N-H-O, but no words. Michael, one of a small group of African-American students at his mostly white school, didn't have a clue what the letters meant. A white friend sitting with him said he didn't want to tell him.

But Michael found out soon enough. His school's all-white varsity team was playing its first game against a local rival whose two star players were black. The acronym TANHO stood for "Tear A Nigger's Head Off."

"My own school was doing this!" Michael Smallwood told the local newspaper. "And they know that I go to this school, and that I'm sitting behind them."

It isn't an experience he's likely to forget. And even though school officials say they have "zero tolerance" for racism . . . even though Michael's friends rallied around him . . . the sour taste of racism lingers on.

What's going on here? Aren't we getting anywhere in the fight to push prejudice . . . racism . . . discrimination . . . intolerance out of our life? You hear the stories: bombs in Northern Ireland. Riots and shootings in Israel. The burning of black churches across the United States. Nazi emblems sprayed on the walls of synagogues. College students cruising for a "fag" to beat up. Stories like these grab headlines on the national news and in newspapers almost every week.

But these awful things aren't the only things happening. There's no denying that racial and ethnic tensions run high in this country—and that teens are right in the middle of them. A 1993 study by the Anti-Defamation League found that white teenagers showed a higher level of bias against blacks than older white people do. But at the same time, teens at many schools say they have close friends of other races. "Mixed" groups of teens are working together on community service projects.

Here are a few success stories:

In Brooklyn, New York, the world's first black-Jewish rap group, Dr. Laz & the CURE, are

performing for students from local high schools. A Jewish high school teacher and a black Baptist minister decided that the Hasidic Jewish and African-American teens of the neighborhood needed to get to know each other. They talked about everything—from being afraid of seeing the "other" group on the streets at night, to reasons for wearing dreadlocks and "beanies" (the yarmulkes many Jewish men wear). They've taken their "Increase the Peace" program on national TV, and get teens thinking (and dancing) with raps like "Funky Racists": Funky racists, funky, funky, racists. Funky racists try to keep us all confused. Funky racists funky, funky racists. They go around spreading lies about blacks and Jews.

In San Francisco, California, a creative writing and poetry class at Galileo High School brings white, Asian, Hispanic, and African-American students together to hear the work of writers from different races and cultures—and to write and share their own work, too. "Twice a week," says author Lynn Duvall in *Respecting Our Differences*, "students share and talk about poetry, stories, and essays meant to reveal the human beings behind the skin colors in the classroom."

In Brunswick, Maine, 50 children and teens from New York City's Harlem neighborhood attend a camp to train as "Peacekeepers" for their schools and after-school programs. They learn how to communicate, how to avoid conflicts (or mediate them), and how to set goals for their community and work to make them happen.

Our views on prejudice, racism, intolerance, and discrimination are affected by the good and bad news we hear on TV, radio, and in the print media. But the fact is, what happens to us/our friends/our family affects us more. And that's where the work of getting along needs to start: in the natural settings of our lives—in school, at church, in the community. In *Respecting Our Differences*, Duvall gives good reasons you should want to become more tolerant:

1. The more you learn, the less you fear.

2. Tolerant people are more self-confident and comfortable in all kinds of situations.

3. Tolerance makes life more interesting.

Once you start feeling comfortable with different kinds of people, you can experience American culture in all its richness and diversity. You'll be ready for the "multicultural" world (and workplace) of the next century. And you'll probably be happier. Happier? Because it's usually more fun to meet people on a "you and me" basis . . . instead of dividing your world into "us" and "them."

Need some ideas about how to break the ice with teens of other races? Let's look at how teens in one heartland city are working on the problem.

Bridge Builders

Mario Hendrix is on a 6-foot ladder staring up at the sky. He's about to fall backward into space—and into a different world. Below him, hands forming an interlocking finger "net" to catch him, are other members of Mario's group of "Bridge Builders"—other teens, white and black, who are attending the one-week camp that kicks off this two-year program.

"Ready?" asks a staff member. "Ready!" everybody shouts. "Falling?" And the group below Mario shouts together: "Fall, Mario!" And he does, right into their linked arms.

"That 'trust fall' is a real test of faith and love and trust in your group," says Mario. "You just met these people a few days ago. You were strangers, people of different races. And here you are, falling off a 6-foot ladder and believing they're going to catch you."

Mario came from predominantly black Central High School in Memphis, Tennessee, to the first Bridge Builders camp four years ago. Beth Bilbrey was in high school almost across the street from him, at a private, all-girls school whose students were mostly white.

"Mario was somebody I probably would never have met without Bridge Builders," Beth says. "Now we're both freshmen at the University of Memphis. I saw him at a Coolio [a rap group] concert the other night, and he teased me: 'What are you doing here? You don't listen to black music!' I told him I was just breaking down those racial barriers, you know." Breaking down racial barriers in Memphis was the idea behind Bridge Builders, a program sponsored by the Episcopal churches of Memphis. Founder Becky Wilson thought it

was a shame that the only way most black and white Memphis teens got to know each other was "competitively"—on football fields and basketball courts. She hoped Bridge Builders could give teens who were natural leaders in their schools a chance to get to know each other, and to form bonds that could mean great things for Memphis as these teens grew up.

Mario agrees that he's feeling the "ripple effect" of the program. "Now that Bridge Builders has been going for four years, I meet people I know everywhere—at the mall, at school, at a play I just went to. I hear 'Hi, Mario!' all over town. It's made me feel easier about things, and it's made my life more fun."

Beth Bilbrey agrees that Bridge Builders has had an effect beyond the participants in the program. "It's really made a difference in me," she says. "I have friends of other races, and I'm not intimidated about meeting their friends. We can talk and relate to each other, and every time you get to know a person, that breaks down another barrier and then another."

One of Mario's best memories is of the first night of the program. "I'd been paired up with a white roommate, but he didn't come until pretty late on the first day. We were supposed to have lights out at 11, but we just talked and talked. I think it was about 3 a.m. when we got to sleep." That was the first time in his life, Mario says, that he'd ever sat down and had a long talk with a white person his own age. "It was a wonderful thing," he says.

"We talked through all those stereotypes, you know—about how white people can't rap and black people eat fried chicken every night," he laughs.

Participants in the program meet monthly for two years, sometimes to talk or do role-play or problem-solving exercises—and other times to work together on community service projects. "We've taken homeless kids swimming, painted older people's houses, filled holiday food baskets, and helped build a house for the Habitat for Humanity program," says Beth. "It's a great way to keep up friendship—and lots of us meet for dinner or a movie at other times, too."

Memphis businesses are getting into the act, too. Last summer, a local insurance company paired a white student and a black student as summer interns and let them learn the business together. It's another way the program may be affecting the future of the city—by spinning a network of connections among teens who may be the business owners, politicians, and community leaders of the next century. Mario Hendrix says he still remembers the end of that first camp session. "I had gone from having no trust to trusting these people, and after graduation, I thought, I don't want to lose this feeling. I didn't know if the friendships we had would be there outside the camp, or be there when we met again. But they did last. And now when I walk up to people, I'm not afraid to talk to anybody. I used to be real shy about saying, 'How you doing?' and now I know people can be different—but different is OK."

Breaking the Silence

How are "Things" at your school? Are you all the silent type ("What race problem?") or the jokes-across-the-cafeteria type ("Did you hear the one about the . . . ?")? Are divisions among racial and ethnic groups handled with good humor and frank conversation . . . or only "handled" if there's an incident or crisis at school?

In a recent *USA Weekend Report* survey, almost three-quarters (72 percent) of middle and high school students surveyed said they had a close friend of another race. How about you? In the same survey, almost half the 248,000 students who responded said they had personally experienced some form of racial prejudice in the past year. "The racial tension at my school is pretty bad, but nobody talks about it," a 15-year-old white student in Florida told *USA Weekend Report*. "All the whites feel something against the blacks, and all the blacks feel something against the whites." At her last school in a small Texas town, she adds, "My family had lots of black friends. Here, both sides are afraid of each other, though neither will admit it."

What's more, the conflicts and tension seem to get worse, not better, as middle school students head for high school. Some high school students report peer pressure to stick within the "group"—and trouble from friends when they don't. Others are afraid they'll make the first move toward someone of another race or ethnic group—and be rejected.

Think about your answers to the questions below.

1. How would you describe race/ethnic group relations at your school?

2. Do students at your school segregate themselves by race or ethnic group? If so, how do you feel about that?

3. Have you ever hung out in a group in which you were the only one of "your kind"? Talk about why you haven't—or tell about the experience.

4. Are you close friends with someone of another race or ethnic group? With someone who is gay? With someone who has a physical or mental disability?

5. Would you date a person of a different race? How do you think your parents and friends would react if you did?

6. Have you had a personal experience that affected the way you feel about another group or race?

7. Are students at your school generally treated equally?

8. Do you hear a lot of racist jokes/humor at school? How do you usually react? Is this kind of humor a source of tension/friction/fighting?

9. If a classmate of another race said, "You can ask me anything," what would you ask?

10. Think of just one good idea: What could you and your friends do to improve race relations at your school?

Where You Can Start

Living in a diverse, multicultural, "salad bowl" society can be exciting and life-enhancing—if you are comfortable with the idea that (as our Bridge Builder Mario said) "different is OK."

Of course, you can't wave a magic wand that will take away the awkward moments and racial tensions in your world. But you can start to change the way you act and think—and slowly, the moves you make will affect the world around you.

Consider some of the suggestions and strategies below:

- Admit that you "own" your problems. So much racial and ethnic tension comes from blaming other groups: for the trouble we have finding a job, getting an education, getting ahead. Decide that you can be the source of your success–and, instead of blaming, use all that energy to learn new skills, volunteer to help in the community, etc.

- Look for natural "bridge-building" opportunities. You can't just walk up to somebody and say, "Let's be friends," as you did when you were 6. But if you'd like to expand your world and get to know people of other races, watch for teens who share your interests: somebody who is in the drama club with you, on a sports team, or on the school newspaper staff, for example. Don't be afraid to reach out for new friends.

- Reach out. Offering to help in the community is a great way to be a part of a "mixed" group working together. Teens often feel as if society thinks they're pretty useless; working in a food bank or volunteering to teach kids to read can let you know that you have power, that you can affect your world—and that you aren't anybody's "victim."

- Don't feed off the anger. So many of us seem so angry, so ready to "blow up" at the slightest thing. Too often, we take that anger and throw it at the nearest target: blacks, whites, Hispanics, Asians, gays, old people, foreigners. Stay away from the "culture" of anger: from friends who constantly talk about hating other groups . . . from talk radio shows that try to whip up people's emotions . . . from "hate" groups.

- Be yourself, not a "role" you think people expect. It's too easy to walk around school or the streets being the "role" you think the world expects: tough

black girl . . . I-don't-take-that-from-anybody white guy. It's not easy to break those patterns. How can you begin? Work hard to deal with everybody you meet as a human being, not a "type."

- Stop accepting racist or intolerant talk. You have several options: physically move away from the "scene" (making it clear to the other person why you're leaving) . . . directly confronting the person ("Hey, that isn't true" or "I really feel bad when I hear stuff like that") . . . confronting the person later in private (he or she will be less defensive, maybe more ready to listen) . . . and "playing dumb," a technique in which you just keep asking the other person to explain that joke or that statement—because you just don't get it. It's a good way to make people think twice about what they say—without getting into a confrontation.

- In a tense situation, find ways to "defuse" the bomb. If you were in the wrong, apologize. If you aren't sure why the other person is angry, ask questions—try to find out where he or she is coming from. Give the situation time to cool off—suggest arranging a meeting with a trusted teacher, preacher, or adult friend to act as "facilitator."

- Don't let other people stop you from growing and changing. Bridge Builder Beth says the first year she went back to her private school and told classmates she'd made a good friend who was black, they said, "Oh, come on now, you don't really need to be friends with a black person." Whenever one person shakes up the status quo, other members of the group are likely to pressure them to

"change back" to the way they were. Be friendly—but if you think you're moving in the right direction, don't let other people talk you out of it.

- Ask for adult help. Maybe the thing your school or community needs is a program like Bridge Builders . . . or a teen community service project . . . or a recreation center where teens of all groups can meet. If you have a good idea, bring it to your school principal, your pastor or rabbi, a local community activist, or any adult friend you think might help you.

- Be forgiving. Cut people some slack. Lots of people try to live decent lives. When we fail—when we get angry and insulting—it's often because we're scared, stressed out, broke, overworked, and just plain tired. Be kind.

A Better Place

Letting go of the feelings of racism and intolerance—and letting go of anger at being treated unjustly—is the beginning of opening yourself to the richness of life. Writer Toni Morrison once said that "if you're going to hold someone down, you're going to have to hold onto the other end of the chain." What she meant was that when we try to "hold down" other people, we are keeping ourselves down, too.

Patricia Raybon writes in *My First White Friend* that the important parts of freeing yourself from prejudice and hatred are to begin and continue. Nobody's asking you to become a saint overnight—just to work on making your corner of the world a better place for everybody.

 **Article Review Form at end of book.**

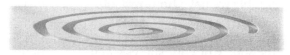

- Race and gender discrimination may be difficult to detect. This may be due to the way in which we learn about discrimination, and due to the new, more subtle forms of racism and sexism. Some researchers believe that racism has evolved to the point where people do not believe themselves to be racist, yet these same people are discriminatory.

- Prejudice and stereotyping are problematic because they may result in people discriminating on the basis of skin color or gender rather than ability. Just knowing that others hold stereotypes about them may prevent some women and minorities from reaching their full potential.

- Although stereotyping may be part of the normal way we think about others, we can control the harmful consequences of negative stereotypes, such as prejudice and discrimination. Simply becoming aware of the potential for discrimination can often reduce its impact. Affirmative action programs have helped to identify and correct subtle discrimination. Intervention programs have helped stereotyped group members to feel challenged in their schoolwork rather than stifled by fear that they will fulfill a stereotype. You can take steps in your daily life to become more sensitive to prejudice and discrimination and to address them when they occur.

R.E.A.L. Sites

This list provides a print preview of typical **coursewise** R.E.A.L. sites. (There are over 100 such sites at the **courselinks™** site.) The danger in printing URLs is that web sites can change overnight. As we went to press, these sites were functional using the URLs provided. If you come across one that isn't, please let us know via email to: webmaster@coursewise.com. Use your Passport to access the most current list of R.E.A.L. sites at the **courselinks™** site.

Site name: Ten Myths about Affirmative Action

URL: http://www.wesleyan.edu/spn/affirm.htm

Why is it R.E.A.L.? This is the web site of a hypertext article called "Ten Myths of Affirmative Action." This piece, which first appeared in the *Journal of Social Issues,* discusses some of the myths that people hold about affirmative action. The author brings relevant statistics and social psychological studies to bear on this timely issue. Can you think of any other myths that he did not cover?

Key topics: discrimination, law, politics, stereotyping

Site name: Atlantic Unbound

URL: http://www.theatlantic.com/atlantic/atlweb/flashbks/blacked/steele.htm

Why is it R.E.A.L.? If you found the discussion of how stereotypes may "psych out" students interesting, you will want to read this article. The article (which originally appeared in the *Atlantic Monthly*) is by Dr. Claude Steele and goes into greater depth than the newspaper article about him that is in this section.

Key topics: attribution, discrimination, self-concept, stereotyping

Site name: The Public Service Commission of Canada: Stereotyping

URL: http://www.psc-cfp.gc.ca/audit/prcb/mono3-e.htm

Why is it R.E.A.L.? This is a review article put forth by the Public Service Commission of Canada on how stereotyping plays a role in our everyday life and how we can change that role. The Public Service Commission states, "Understanding how we create and use our stereotypes improves our capacity to deal effectively with people whose views or behavior is different than our own." See if their discussion of stereotypes corresponds with what you have learned in your class. Would you include any additional information in this public service message?

Key topics: stereotyping, cognitive biases, discrimination, group behavior

section

7

Learning Objectives

- Understand the factors that affect whether or not someone will help another person.

- Understand intervention programs designed to reduce aggression.

- Apply theories of aggression to the phenomenon of "road rage."

- Explain research that demonstrates media influence on violence.

Prosocial Behavior and Aggression

WiseGuide Intro

When we watch the evening news, we often see stories that make us shake our heads in astonishment at the cruelty of which human beings are capable. At other times, however, we can be moved and inspired by stories of extraordinary sacrifice by one person on behalf of others, such as the lifelong devotion of Mother Teresa toward India's poor. In both cases, we are left wondering what can inspire such extremes of viciousness and kindness.

The sad fate of a young woman named Kitty Genovese has become the most famous case study in the social psychology of helping—or the lack thereof. Early one morning in 1965, while perhaps dozens of her neighbors looked on in horror, Ms. Genovese was stabbed to death as she tried to enter her apartment. No one came to her aid, or even phoned the police. Social psychologists wondered if the Genovese case simply exposed the callousness and indifference of the modern world, as many editorial writers claimed, or if instead it told us more about the circumstances that can cause otherwise concerned people to avoid getting involved. Researchers concluded that the "bystander apathy" that probably contributed to Ms. Genovese's death resulted not from the insensitivity of the witnesses but from the unfortunate tendency for individuals in groups to assume that someone else would take care of the problem.

The article by Newcomb and colleagues discusses more contemporary research about helping others. In this case the helping behavior involves no extraordinary personal sacrifice or risk, but is something we have all had the opportunity to do at some point: stopping someone who is drunk from driving. Much like the Kitty Genovese case, situational factors such as the number of other people present influence our willingness to stop someone from driving. This article provides a good overview of altruism research, and it may prove useful in guiding you toward giving the right kind of help the next time you confront this difficult situation.

We move from helping (or not helping) others to the other extreme: an examination of why we harm others. Many people believe we live in an increasingly violent society. Indeed, violent crime rates took a sharp turn upward in the United States about twenty years ago, and have remained at a relatively high level ever since. Still, violence and aggression have been with us from the birth of humankind. The constant presence of violence across cultures and throughout history has led many people to speculate that aggression is an inborn instinct that all humans share, and is therefore something we must simply learn to live with. This bleak perspective is not correct, however. Most psychologists agree that aggression is not inborn and instinctive, but is a controllable, correctable human response. An international conference of scientists from many fields of study issued a statement in 1986 that summarizes diverse areas of research on aggression. The "Seville Statement," as it has come to be known, strongly declared that it is scientifically incorrect to say that aggression is inborn; that aggression is a learned behavior; and that the same creature who can make war also has the capability to make peace. If aggression is a learned behavior, then we have the power to learn new methods of interaction and change the level of violence in our society.

The article by Leonard Eron addresses just how we can unlearn aggression. Dr. Eron has spent the last forty years researching aggression in our lives and in the mass media. He reports on the progress of a longitudinal intervention project designed to reduce violence. He discusses the difficulty of conducting scientifically rigorous research out in the real world, and of effecting change in behavior. He does point to some promising results that show a decrease in aggression, although he expects greater results as the project continues.

Our third article discusses a novel, contemporary, and all-too-familiar kind of aggression: "road rage." Why do otherwise calm and rational people become so hostile and aggressive once they get behind the wheel? Once again, we learn the power of the situation to shape behavior. The article discusses a number of instances of aggression on the roads, and considers some possible explanations.

Our final article, "Violence, Reel to Real," discusses one of the most controversial claims in aggression research: that the high level of actual and dramatized violence portrayed in the mass media contributes to aggressive behavior, especially among children. Although the purveyors of media violence would like to believe otherwise, forty years of research have demonstrated that violent television and film do indeed result in increased actual violence. The article discusses those research studies and talks about the potential for "copycat" violence.

What are the personal characteristics believed to be related to helping? How is this study similar to "diffusion of responsibility" studies? How is it different?

Two Varieties of Helping in Drunk-Driving Intervention

Personal and situational factors

Michael D. Newcomb, Jerome Rabow, Anthony C. R. Hernandez, and Martin Monto

Abstract: *Objective: This study examined personal characteristics and contextual factors among college students who had made an attempt to prevent someone from driving drunk. The study was guided by findings from prior research and the arousal/cost-benefit model of helping. Both passive and assertive interventions and their efficacy were considered. Method: Questionnaire data were obtained from 338 students; 206 (68%) had intervened in a DUI situation (63% women). Self-reports of the person (e.g., moral obligation), the situation (e.g., perceived danger) and the type (passive, assertive) and success of the interventions were gathered. Results: Of all interventions used 73% were successful; the median number of interventions used was three. Of the assertive interventions used in DUI situations 57% were successful compared to 47% of the passive interventions. Path analyses revealed that being older relative to the intervene and greater sobriety of the intervenor predicted more interventions of both types. Personal commitment to intervention, amount of perceived danger and less alcohol consumption increased assertive interventions, whereas talking with someone about the potential DUI person increased the number of passive interventions. The success of both passive and assertive interventions were dependent upon the number of each of these interventions used. However, the more passive interventions were attempted, the less likely the success of an assertive intervention. Conclusions: The current findings extend our understanding of the psychosocial factors associated with informal DUI intervention, particularly concerning the choice and success of passive versus assertive interventions. Several of these significant predictors support laboratory research findings on helping and the arousal/cost-benefit model, while others do not. (J. Stud. Alcohol 58: 191–199, 1997).*

There is a massive body of research on "helping" behavior completed in laboratory or experimental settings (Rabow and Newcomb, 1992). In a summary of this work, Dovidio (1984) argues that the motivational, cognitive and situational factors associated with helping support an arousal/cost-reward model. According to this model, people become aroused as a result of another person's distress. In situations with greater potential harm or danger there is more arousal and hence increased likelihood of intervention or helping behavior. However, the occurrence of this helping intervention depends upon the perceived costs and benefits to acting or not acting.

Despite this large and significant volume of work, little is known about the prevalence, processes or nature of helping behavior in naturally occurring situations (e.g., Dovidio, 1984; Monto et al., 1994; Rabow et al., 1990). one naturally occurring situation, intervening to prevent others from driving drunk, is considered a form of helping behavior (e.g., Newcomb et al., 1991; Rabow and Newcomb, 1992). In this article, we explore the usefulness of an arousal/cost-benefit model to understand informal DUI helping behavior. The decision to intervene and stop another from driving drunk is neither as consequential as the donation of "the gift of life" (Simmons, 1991; Simmons et al., 1987), nor as full of immediacy as the administration of CPR. It does not seem to be the type of helping that is planned helping behavior (Amato, 1985, 1990), nor is it as spontaneous as jumping in a river to save a drowning person. DUI intervention also differs from typical bystander helping or intervention where the victim needs help and knows it, the intervenor is not well acquainted with the victim and the intervenor may be at risk for bodily harm by intervening (e.g., stopping a mugging or assault).

Prevalence of DUI Intervention

Self-reported rates of informal DUI intervention do not seem to vary greatly: 37% for adult Californians (Davis, 1982); 39%, 51% and 56% for California col-

lege students (Rabow et al., 1986, 1990; Wolfinger et al., 1994); 46% for male North Carolina college students (Mills and McCarty, 1983); 40% for youngsters in grades 9 through 12 in give different geographical locations (Vegega and Klitzner, 1989); and from 37% to 43% for five national random telephone samples (Berger and Persinger, 1980). Although one Canadian sample reported a much higher intervention rate (over 90%), these interventions were attempted only with family members and close friends (Adebayo, 1988).

Theories of DUI Intervention

Several key theoretical questions are raised by the prior research on helping behavior. One question involves the variable or ability and action. Are arousal and perceived ability to intervene promoted by assessments of the situation? Further, is this arousal associated with increased costs for not intervening either at a personal (discrepancy with self-perceptions) or situational (likely adverse consequences) level? A second theoretical question relates to the person's self-conception. Feelings of empathy, inequity or moral obligation may be more critical in nonemergency situations. Will these occur and be potent predictors in a DUI situation? We have conceptualized DUI interventions as a quasi-emergency situation (Rabow and Newcomb, 1992). Individuals neither have to make an instantaneous decision akin to an emergency nor do they have days to plan it. The implications of these distinctions are unclear for this class of helping behavior. Since it is not quite an emergency situation, we might be

able to generalize the importance of these self-conception variables to the DUI situation.

Newcomb et al. (1991) surveyed the experimental research on helping and the findings on DUI interventions and selected 28 variables that might relate to intervention in a drunk-driving situation. The 28 variables were categorized as personal (12), relationship (4), situational (5) or individual (7) responses in the situation. Bivariate and multivariate analyses were executed between these 28 predictor variables and intervention among 192 female and 111 male college students. The variables that correlated significantly with intervention were: three personal variables (moral obligation to intervene, number of prior interventions, the belief that intervention reflects self-image), one relationship variable (how well the subject knew the driver), three situational variables (number of persons known, another person intervening, conversation that encourages intervention) and four individual response variables (driver needed help, how badly the driver needed help, thinking about intervening, ability to intervene). Four significant predictors emerged in a logistic regression analysis: knowing the driver well (a relationship variable), having a conversation that encouraged the respondent to intervene (a situational variable), perceiving the driver as needing help and the respondent's feeling able to intervene (individual responses in the situation).

The Newcomb et al. (1991) study raises interesting theoretical issues as to the similarity and difference between laboratory and natural helping behavior. One question has to do with the person: How do personal abilities, morals, self-conceptions and experiences reflect constructs in the arousal/cost-benefit model? Although the bivariate correlations suggested that aspects of the person's prior experiences were related to intervention and personal arousal, the regression analysis established the value of the arousal/cost-benefit model with the exception of having a conversation. We might, however, assume that conversations that encourage you to intervene are likely to increase arousal because of the normative encouragement, to convey a "you should" expectation and to promote guilt for not intervening, and thereby are likely to emphasize the cost of not acting.

In sum, research on DUI interventions, while confirming many of the variables predictive in the laboratory studies and in some ways supporting the arousal/cost-benefit model, has extended variables about the person, the situation and the responses in the situations. One problem is that most research on informal DUI intervention has been conducted without reference to any theory or model. This article sets the stage for careful and thorough post hoc speculation about the value of the arousal/cost-benefit model for understanding informal DUI intervention. To approach this post hoc speculation in an informed manner, we must review relevant aspects of the extant literature on helping in the laboratory and the real world.

Laboratory and Real-World Helping Behavior

Feelings of being similar to or involved with the potential victim increase bystander arousal (Krebs, 1975). Distress, or arousal, of bystanders is affected in a different way by emergency and nonemergency situations. In emergency situations, helpers develop stronger feelings of upset and higher levels of psychophysiological activity (Gaertner and Dovidio, 1977). In nonemergency situations, where arousal is less critical, either empathetic concern (Batson and Coke, 1981), feelings of inequity (Waister et al., 1978) or feelings of moral obligation (Schwartz and Howard, 1981, 1982) generate the helping behavior.

These different explanations reflect the debate about the kind of emotional experiences that promote intervention. Piliavin et al. (1981) argue that "the processes by which another's need promotes helping seem dynamically similar across situations" (p. 236). However, the work by Batson and his colleagues (Batson et al., 1981) suggests that different emotional experiences influence intervention in different ways. Using the arousal/cost-reward framework, they argue that the costs for not helping when one feels warmth and compassion are higher than when one feels upset or alarm.

Other suggestions from the laboratory literature on helping refer to aspects of the person and to the situation. The more the person sees him/herself as the kind of person who helps, the more she/he is likely to intervene (Batson, 1987; Simmons, 1991). In the present study, we consider this personal factor as a latent construct reflecting the moral obligation to stop someone from driving drunk and whether the act of intervention expresses the kind of person the intervenors like to think they are. Another individual difference that has been documented concerns the amount of alcohol consumed. Helping be-havior may be inhibited by alcohol consumption, in that perceived ability to intervene is associated with intervenor's lower levels of intoxication (Rabow et al., 1990). Concerning the situation, the presence of others was an important factor for helping in laboratory experiments (Latane and Nida, 1981), but was not confirmed in research on informal DUI interventions in naturally occurring situations. Rabow et al. (1990) found that the number of persons in the situation and the number of persons known in the situation did not directly predict DUI intervention, although these variables did predict danger, which in turn predicted DUI intervention. Latane and Darley (1976) also noted that discussions among potential helpers were more likely to result in helping behavior. Whether such discussions increase the arousal of others is unknown, but seems likely.

Present Study

We conceptualize the helping process in drunk-driving situations to consist of three sets of variables: (1) personal background characteristics and other general contextual variables, (2) individual subjective and evaluative responses to the immediate DUI situation, and (3) intervention. In our conceptualization, the first set of variables provides a frame and context within which the individual operates. These are the variables that the individual brings to the DUI situation and global aspects of the current event. The second set of variables consists of the individual's subjective and evaluative responses to others and the potential drunk driver. The third set of variables consists of the number and type of interventions used by respondents and their success.

The current research examines helping behavior in naturally occurring DUI situations to determine the variables that are associated with different forms of informal intervention and their success. Few studies have examined the number of attempts at intervention (persistence) and types of interventions used by respondents (Adebayo, 1988; Hernandez and Rabow, 1987; Wilson, 1984). As suggested by Hernandez and Rabow (1987), we categorize intervention into two categories, passive and assertive approaches. In a passive approach the actors approach the driver and the situation in a tentative fashion. They ask the driver if he or she needs help, if he or she would like to sit down and have a cup of coffee. In an assertive approach, the actors more directly take charge of the situation by taking the car keys of the driver or telling him that he or she will not be driving. We conceive of the assertive form of intervention as requiring greater arousal than the passive form and hence as potentially more successful. We are concerned with the factors that influence the selection and type of intervention and whether it is successful in preventing another from driving drunk. We also examine the personal, contextual and situational factors and their influences on the two forms of intervention and the success of these in the prevention of drunk driving.

Hypotheses

This research examines the value of the arousal/cost-benefit model for understanding informal DUI interventions. The three categories of variables (personal, situational and intervention) can be evaluated as contributing to arousal and the perceived costs or benefits of acting or not.

Within the personal domain, knowing others who have been hurt or killed in an alcohol-related situation contributes to greater arousal and greater costs to not intervening and therefore leads to assertive interventions. Frequently being exposed to others too drunk to drive and intervening often should reduce arousal and generate passive interventions (e.g., Newcomb et al., 1986) because of the effect of "mere exposure" desensitization (Zajonc, 1980). "Mere exposure" is a process through which direct experience of a particular stimulus or event reduces the emotional reaction or arousal to the occurrence, thereby increasing the likelihood that a well considered assertive action can be taken. Having a belief that you are morally obligated to stop another from driving drunk and believing that such intervention expresses the kind of person you are may contribute towards having to act in the potential DUI situation and may increase personal costs for not intervening. The challenges (costs) to one's self-conception as a moral person, engendered by the adverse consequences of a potential drunk driver, would seem to require action that is strong and successful.

Concerning the situation factors and consistent with the arousal/cost-benefit model, we also predict that the more danger expected and the greater the arousal and perceived benefits to acting, the more likely that assertive interventions will be attempted. We also hypothesize that discussions with others will increase anxiety (arousal) and hence contribute to the likelihood of more assertive intervention. Using the arousal/cost-benefit model, we also predict that the greater their use of alcohol, the less likely that subjects will use assertive interventions. While we cannot be certain of what occurs with those who drink more in contrast to those who drink less, Turrisi et al.'s (1993) work suggests a plausible rational for a prediction. They found that as drinking increased, the perception of the likelihood of negative consequences decreased and hence this evaluation would lead to judgments of diminished danger. Next, we expect that the greater the number of people in the situation, the less arousal and fewer perceived costs due to the diffusion of responsibility (e.g., Rabow et al., 1990). Finally, for reasons cited earlier, we believe that assertive (more arousal) interventions will be more successful than passive interventions. Path analyses are used to test these hypotheses in a conceptual sequential ordering of variables. Personal and background variables were allowed to predict context and reaction to situation measures, which in turn were allowed to predict the number of passive and assertive interventions. The attempted intervention variables were allowed to predict the success of intervention measures. In addition to this mediated model, paths were also tested from nonadjacent clusters of variables in the model (i.e., from personal characteristics to all types of intervention and success and from context to intervention success measures). This proposed model is based on a theory of how these components might be causally linked and tests our specific arousal/cost-benefit hypotheses, but our analyses cannot prove such a sequence since they are based on retrospective, cross-sectional data. Nevertheless, the selection of variables and proposed ordering is consistent with both prior laboratory and applied research on DUI interventions and other helping behavior as well as the arousal/cost-benefit theory.

Method

Sample

Participants were from three sociology classes at the University of California, Los Angeles, who were asked to complete an anonymous drinking and driving questionnaire as an optional class assignment (the professor left the room and those not wishing to participate were allowed a study break). Fewer than 10 students chose not to complete the survey.

A total of 388 usable questionnaires were obtained. Of the 388 students 303 (78%) reported having been in a DUI situation in the last year. Only those who indicated having been in a DUI situation in the last year and reported attempting to intervene in that situation (N = 206, 68%) were included in this investigation.

Of the 206 students, 63% were women. The average age of our respondents was 20 years old. The academic class standing of the samples was 30% freshmen, 21% sophomores, 21% juniors, and 28% seniors. The ethnic composition was: 48% white, 19% Asian, 17% Latino, 11% black, 3% "other" and 2% Native American.

Measures

A series of questions about the person, context and responses to the DUI situation were used to assess and examine drunk-driving interventions and their success. A DUI situation was described as when the respondent was in a circumstance where she/he considered another person unable to drive due to that person's intoxication. In other words, the definition of a DUI situation was the respondent's subjective perception that another person was too drunk to drive.

Seven questions were used to assess personal or individual factors. The first three questions asked about the respondents' prior experience in DUI situations. They included: whether the respondents knew friends or family who had been hurt or killed in an alcohol-related accident, the number of times in the past year they had been in a situation where they saw someone whom they thought was too drunk to drive; and the number of times they had tried to stop someone from driving drunk before this most recent drunk-driving situation. Two Likert-type questions assessed respondents' beliefs and self-evaluation regarding whether they strongly agreed or disagreed with the statements that they: felt morally obligated to stop someone from driving under the influence; and intervening in a potential drunk-driving situation expresses the kinds of person they like to think they are. Finally, two questions assessed respondents, alcohol consumption in the DUI situation and the number of people present in the situation.

Seven questions were used to assess the context of, and respondents' responses in, the DUI situation. These items included evaluative assessments, feelings and behavioral reactions that occurred in the situation. Questions included in this set were: respondents, self-reported level of sobriety or intoxication (ranging from sober to very drunk); the number of persons known in the situation; whether the respondent had spoken to someone about the poten-tial drunk driver; the amount of perceived danger (ranging from the person was "not at all danger-ous" to "very dangerous"); whether the driver was older, sim-ilar or younger in age; whether they knew the driver (ranging from "barely knew" to "knew very well"); and whether they liked the driver (ranging from "not liked at all" to "liked very much").

Drunk-driving interventions and their success rate were assessed with a series of questions. Previous work by Hernandez and Rabow (1987) suggests that there is a distinction between passive nonconfrontation types of intervention (e.g., asking for the person's car key, asking the person not to drive) and assertive intervention (e.g., taking the person's car key, telling the person not to drive). In the present study, 10 yes/no questions were used to assess intervention (five passive and five assertive). Responses to these questions were dummy coded (1 = yes, 0 = no) and separately summed to create two intervention variables (total passive, total assertive). The success rates of the 10 interventions were also assessed using a yes/no question format. Responses to these questions were dummy coded (1 = yes, 0 = no) and separately summed to create two success variables (success of passive, success of assertive).

A path model depicting the relationships between respondent characteristics, contextual and DUI situation variables and types of intervention, and the success of these interventions, is tested. The model consists of 18 manifest variables and two latent constructs (Newcomb, 1990). The two latent constructs were personal commitment to intervention (as measured by: moral obligation to stop someone from driving under the influence; intervention expresses the kind of person they like to think they are) and affinity toward the potential driver (as measured by: whether they knew the driver; whether they liked the driver).

Results

Of all the interventions by respondents 73% were successful. The median number of interventions used by respondents was three. The use of assertive interventions in a DUI situation had a 57% success rate, in contrast to 47% of the passive interventions. There were no gender differences in the number and type of interventions used, although the majority of potential DUI drivers intervened upon were men. Nevertheless, few interactions were found between gender of the intervenor and intervene in regard to type and success of intervention (Hernandez et al., 1995).

In the initial path model, we fixed one of the indicators for each latent construct at unity to identify the model. We allowed the individual and contextual variables to correlate freely among themselves and permitted each to predict all situation (subjective, evaluative) variables. The residuals of the situational variables were allowed to correlate freely. The individual, contextual and situational variables were allowed to predict the passive and assertive intervention variables as well as the true success of the intervention variables. Passive and assertive intervention variables were permitted to predict the success of both intervention variables. This initial model allowed us to examine all possible paths and to determine empirically those that were significant and could be retained in our final model.

Modifications to the initial model required systematic elimination of all nonsignificant parameters. Using the Wald test (Bentler, 1995; Chou and Bentler, 1990), we removed from the model all nonsignificant correlations and all nonsignificant paths. This process resulted in a final model that fit the data very well ($[X^2]$ = 98.67, 124 df, N = 206, p = .95; normed fit index [NFI; Bentler and Bonett, 1980] = .84, comparative fit index [CFI, Bentler, 1990] = 1.0). Fit in this context is used only in the statistical sense in that the final model accurately reflects the data. It does not necessarily mean that any substantive or theoretical models have been confirmed. The standardized solution for this final model is depicted in Figure 1.* As Figure 1 shows, there were no direct paths from any of the personal or contextual variables to the success of intervention scales. Successful intervention was mediated completely by the two types of intervention scales.

When we examine the personal background factors, we find that neither the number of prior DUI intervention attempts nor the number of others known hurt or killed in a alcohol-related accident had any effect on any of the DUI situation variables, types or numbers of interventions, or the success of intervention. The number of prior DUI experiences of our respondents positively predicted the number of people known in the DUI situation and their affinity toward the potential drunk driver.

Among the situational variables, the more people in the DUI situation decreased the respondent's affinity toward the potential drunk driver. However, in

contrast to prior research affinity had no direct effects on either type of intervention or their success.

As expected, the amount of alcohol consumed in the situation negatively predicted the degree of sobriety. The degree of sobriety, in turn, had a positive effect on the number of passive and the number of assertive interventions attempted. The amount of alcohol consumed also negatively predicted (directly) the total number of assertive interventions used. The respondent's age relative to the potential drunk driver positively predicted the number of passive and assertive interventions: the younger the potential drunk driver relative to the intervenor, the more passive and assertive interventions were likely to be used by the respondent.

The latent construct of personal commitment to intervention had both direct and indirect effects on intervention. Personal commitment to intervention positively predicted the number of assertive interventions used, the amount of perceived danger and the possibility of talking to someone else about the potential drunk driver. The more danger perceived, in turn, positively predicted the number of assertive interventions used. Talking to someone else about the potential drunk driver positively predicted the number of passive interventions used.

The number of passive interventions positively predicted the success of such interventions and the number of assertive interventions positively predicted the success of these interventions. The success of assertive interventions was negatively influenced by the number of passive interventions attempted.

*Does not appear in this publication.

Discussion

Although DUI intervention is less complex than administering CPR (Shotland and Heinold, 1985) and less involved than planned helping, DUI intervention seems to derive mainly from two sets of influences: factors about the person and factors in the situation or context, each of which tends to lead to different types of helping behavior being selected and to different rates of their success.

Implications of Hypotheses

Several hypotheses were generated for these analyses based on the arousal/cost-benefit model of helping behavior offered by Dovidio (1984). As expected, assertive DUI intervention led to greater success than passive DUI intervention. We predicted that assertive DUI intervention would be influenced by greater personal commitment to intervention, greater perceived danger and less alcohol consumption (and therefore greater sobriety). These predictions were supported by the analyses. However, we hypothesized that knowing others who had been hurt or killed in a DUI incident, greater number of prior DUI intervention attempts and fewer people in the situation would lead to greater likelihood of intervention (either of a passive or assertive nature). None of these hypotheses were supported in the path analysis. We also predicted that greater discussion with others about the DUI driver would increase assertive interventions, which was not found. This variable was significantly associated with more passive interventions.

Our available variables did not tap all aspects or critical constructs of the arousal/cost-benefit model. For instance, our assessments can best be construed to reflect various levels of arousal, whereas the cognitive decision regarding the costs and benefits of offering help was not well captured by our measures. Our best approximation of this appraisal is our perceived danger variable, which can capture both a high degree of arousal and serious costs to nonintervention if danger is considered high. Further research on informal DUI intervention needs to assess more precisely the various components of the arousal/cost-benefit model so that a more careful test of this theory in this naturally occurring situation can be made.

The positive associations between sobriety and each type of intervention may reflect a spurious relationship. Although it is possible that becoming more drunk reduces the likelihood of intervention, it is also likely that an underlying personality characteristic may make the respondent drink less (or not at all) and also makes him/her more likely to intervene. In other words, it is not possible to determine whether getting drunk reduces one's propensity to intervene or whether those who get drunk are not the types of people who intervene. Finally, it is interesting to speculate about the negative relationship between number of others present and affinity for driver. On the one hand, the more people present increases the likelihood that the respondent did not know the potential drunk driver. On the other hand, a few people present may indicate that the respondent was on a date with a boyfriend or girlfriend. In other words, one direction of this association may be a surrogate for the nature of the respondent's relationship with the potential DUI, rather than saying anything per se about the actual effect of number of others present.

Integration of Findings

While the total number of passive and assertive interventions predicted the success of passive and assertive intervention (respectively), the sources and inhibitors of these two forms of helping DUI interventions were both similar and different. Consistent with the arousal/cost-benefit model, assertive interventions were inhibited by the amount of alcohol consumed and the degree of drunkenness. A personal commitment to intervention, an assessment of the amount of perceived danger and identification of the driver as younger relative to the intervenor all predicted the number of assertive interventions. These variables seem to increase arousal and hence the assertive form of intervention. The total number of passive interventions was predicted by three variables. Discussions with others about the potential drunk driver and the youth of the driver relative to the intervenor positively predicted the number of passive interventions, which on the other hand were inhibited by the degree of drunkenness. We may tentatively conclude that more firm and direct helping behavior in this naturally occurring situation (assertive intervention) is influenced by a person's sense of self or personal commitment. More passive forms of helping DUI interventions appear to derive less from the person and more from factors in the situation.

Several mediated effects are also evident in the final path model, suggesting the more complex and sequential aspects of the process of DUI intervention (Rabow et al., 1990). For instance, amount of danger mediated the relationship between personal commitment to intervention and the number of assertive interventions (although a direct effect was also apparent between these variables). Talking with someone about the potential DUI driver mediated the relationship between personal commitment to intervention and number of passive interventions. In other words, talking with someone about the situation transformed a personal commitment to intervention, which typically led to assertive interventions, to making more passive interventions. Degree of sobriety mediated the effect from alcohol consumption to numbers of both passive and assertive interventions. Finally, an older age of intervenor compared to intervenee mediated the effect of alcohol consumption to both passive and assertive interventions. These situational or immediate context variables mediate and help shape the effects of personal characteristics and prior experience on the type of DUI interventions selected.

Further, we may see in this act of DUI intervention an enactment of social control. The community of attitudes that says "thou shall not drive drunk and endanger yourself and others" stands in contrast to another community that says "thou shall mind your own business." For at least half of our subjects, the former community's attitudes towards social control have been internalized. Our intervenors bring conformity to selected community expectations through their own self-control. Finally, the total number of passive interventions was also found to negatively predict the success of assertive interven-

tions. The correlation between total number of passive interventions and total number of assertive interventions, however, was positive. These findings suggest that when individuals use more passive interventions they are less likely to be successful if they attempt an assertive intervention. This is an interesting finding, in that it suggests that individuals may have different styles of intervention. Some individuals may rely more on passive nonconfrontational types of intervention, while others may rely on more assertive types of intervention. These different styles may be a reflection of an individual's sense of self. From a practical standpoint, this finding suggests that those who use passive interventions should not attempt an assertive intervention (since it is more likely to fail) and should persist with variations of passive interventions. It also implies that there may be some limits to arousal for some people.

Conclusions

We have been able to identify several variables that predict informal intervention in DUI situations. Certain variables influence particular types of intervention (passive versus assertive), whereas other factors affect both types of intervention and are more general predictors (e.g., sobriety). Several of these conclusions conform to the arousal/cost-benefit model of helping, while others do not. Therefore, the factors that contribute to a personal sense of commitment to intervene and how these are influenced by situational factors in selecting a response to a DUI situation need more careful study. The arousal/cost-benefit model clearly has some impor-

tance, but may be inadequate to describe fully this naturally occurring and unique and complex form of helping. What is clear is that this form of helping behavior, the decision to intervene to prevent another from driving drunk, is a fact of American drinking life. It is complicated, consequential and worthy of deeper study, and the arousal/cost-benefit model seems to be of continuing value in further understanding this process with perhaps more careful operationalizing providing more conclusive results.

There are clearly several limitations of the present study that require further research. First, our results are based on retrospective recall data that may be distorted or altered when reconstructing past events. By focusing on specific and concrete aspects of the situation and context, we hoped to avoid this bias. Further, we did not cue the respondents to the "passive" or "assertive" connotations of a particular intervention and asked them only to describe what they did. Therefore, we do not expect recall to be altered by the passive or assertive quality of the respondents' intervention. In addition, we have limited the recall period to the past year, thereby reducing problems with retrieving very old memories.

Most respondents made more than one attempt to prevent another from driving drunk in a particular situation. Unfortunately, we did not assess the temporal ordering of the various interventions used. For instance, it is plausible that passive interventions may be used first and if these fail more assertive interventions attempted. Determination of these patterns or sequences of helping behavior interventions must await further research.

Our findings are based on a "one-sided story." We have no idea of what processes occur within the potential DUI driver. For instance, certain characteristics of the potential DUI driver (e.g., extreme stubbornness, denial or ego involvement) may elicit more interventions, finally culminating in active ones, simply because the earlier, more subtle ones were not successful. This is a critical area for further research.

Finally, even with the most accurate recall, we must rely on memories of an event that cannot fully capture the intricacies and multiple co-occurring processes that characterize complex human interactions. DUI intervention is far more complex than we have been able to portray in this set of cross-sectional data. It is quite likely that DUI intervention is an evolving reciprocal interaction between intervenor and intervenee and an unfolding process where each participant acts and reacts to the other. For instance, a second attempt after an unsuccessful intervention will lose the element of surprise and allow the potential DUI driver to formulate counterarguments or other evasive strategies.

References

Adebayo, A. Drunk-driving intervention in an urban community: An exploratory analysis. *Brit. J. Addict.* 83: 423–429, 1988.

Amato, P. R. An investigation of planned helping behavior. *J. Res. Pers.* 19: 232–252, 1985.

Amato, P. R. Personality and social network involvement as predictors of helping behavior in everyday life. *Social Psychol.* 53: 31–43, 1990.

Batson, C. D. Prosocial motivation: Is it ever altruistic? In: Berkowitz, L. (Ed.) *Advances in Experimental Social Psychology,* Vol. 20. San Diego, Calif.: Academic Press, Inc., 1981, pp. 167–187.

Batson, C. D. and Coke, J. S. Empathy: A source of altruistic motivation for helping? In: Rushton, J. P. and Sorrentino, R. M. (Eds.) *Altruism and Helping Behavior: Social, Personality, and Developmental Perspective.* Hillsdale, N.J.: Lawrence Erlbaum Assocs., Inc., 1981, pp. 167–187.

Batson, C. D., Duncan, B., Ackerman, P., Buckley, T. and Birch, K. Is empathic emotion a source of altruistic motivation? *J. Pers. Social Psychol.* 40: 290–302, 1981.

Bentler, P. M. Comparative fit indexes in structural models. *Psychol. Bull.* 107: 238–246, 1990.

Bentler, P. M. *EQS Structural Equations Manual.* Encino, Calif.: Multivariate Software, 1995.

Bentler, P. M. and Bonett, D. G. Significance tests and goodness of fit in the analysis of covariance structures. *Psychol. Bull.* 88: 588–606, 1980.

Berger, R. J. and Persinger, G. S. *1980 survey of the public perceptions of Highway Safety.* McLean, Va.: Automated Services, Inc., 1980.

Chou, C. P. and Bentler, P. M. Model modification in covariance structure modeling: A comparison among likelihood ratio, Lagrange Multiplier, and Wald tests. *Multivar. Behav. Res.* 25: 115–136, 1990.

Davis, S. Driving under the influence: California public opinion, 1981. *Abstr. Rev. Alcohol Driv.* 3: 3–8, 1982.

Dovidio, J. F. Helping behavior and altruism: An empirical and conceptual overview. In: Berkowitz, L. (Ed.) *Advances in Experimental Social Psychology,* Vol. 17, San Diego, Calif: Academic Press, Inc., 1984, pp. 361–427.

Gaertner, S. L. and Dovidio, J. F. The subtlety of white racism, arousal, and helping behavior. *J. Pers. Social Psychol.* 35: 691–707, 1977.

Hernandez, A. C. R., Newcomb, M. D. and Rabow, J. Types of drunk-driving intervention: Prevalence, success and gender. *J. Stud. Alcohol* 56: 408–413, 1995.

Hernandez, A. C. R. and Rabow, J. Passive and assertive student interventions in public and private drunken driving situations. *J. Stud. Alcohol* 48: 269–271, 1987.

Krebs, D. L. Altruism: An examination of the concept and a review of the literature. *Psychol. Bull.* 73: 258–302, 1970.

Krebs, D. Empathy and altruism. *J. Person. Social Psychol.* 32: 1134–1146, 1975.

Latane, B. and Darley, J. M. *Help in a Crisis: Bystander Response to an Emergency.* Morristown, N.J.: General Learning Press, 1976.

Latane, B. and Nida, S. Ten years of research on group size and helping. *Psychol. Bull.* 89: 308–324, 1981.

Mills, K. C. and McCarty, D. A data-based alcohol abuse prevention program in a university setting. *J. Alcohol Drug Educ.* 28: 15–27, 1983.

Monto, M. A., Rabow, J., Newcomb, M. D. and Hernandez, A. C. R. Do friends let friends drive drunk: Decreasing drunk driving through informal peer interaction. In: Venturelli, P. J. (Ed.) *Drug Use in America: Social, Cultural and Political Perspectives.* Boston, Mass: Jones and Bartlett Publishers, Inc., 1994, pp. 183–192.

Newcomb, M. D. What structural equation modeling techniques can tell us about social support. In: Sarason, B. R., Sarason, I. G. and Pierce, G. R. (Eds.) *Social Support: An Interactional View.* New York: John Wiley and Sons, Inc., 1990, pp. 26–63.

Newcomb, M. D., Huba, G. J. and Bentler, P. M. Desirability of various life change events among adolescents: Effects of exposure, sex, age, and ethnicity. *J. Res. Pers.* 20: 207–227, 1986.

Newcomb, M. D., Rabow, J., Monto, M. and Hernandez, A. C. R. Informal drunk-driving intervention: Psychosocial correlates among young adult women and men. *J. Appl. Social Psychol.* 21: 1988–2006, 1991.

Piliavin, J. A., Dovidio, J. F., Gaertner, S. L. and Clark, R. D. 3d. *Emergency Intervention.* San Diego, Calif: Academic Press, Inc., 1981.

Rabow, J., Hernandez, A. C. R. and Walts, R. K. College students do intervene in drunk driving situations. *Sociol. Social Res.* 70: 1986.

Rabow, J. and Newcomb, M. D. Informal drunk driving intervention as helping behavior: Theory, research, and practice. *Sociol. Pract. Rev.* 3: 94–101, 1992.

Rabow, J., Newcomb, M. D., Monto, M. A. and Hernandez, A. C. R. Altruism in drunk-driving situations: Personal and situational factors in intervention. *Social Psychol. Q.* 53: 199–213, 1990.

Schwartz, S. H. and Howard, J. A. A normative decision-making model of altruism. In: Rushton, J. P. and Sorrentino, R. M. (Eds.) *Altruism and*

Helping Behavior: Social, Personality, and Developmental Perspective. Hillsdale, N.J.: Lawrence Erlbaum Assocs., Inc., 1981, pp. 189–211.

Schwartz, S. H. and Howard, J. A. Helping and cooperation: A self-based motivational model. In: Derlega, V. J. and Grelak, J. (Eds.) *Cooperation and Helping Behavior: Theories and Research.* San Diego, Calif.: Academic Press, Inc., 1982, pp. 328–353.

Shotland, R. L. and Heinold, W. D. Bystander response to arterial bleeding: Helping skills, the decision-making process, and differentiating the helping response. *J. Pers. Social Psychol.* 49: 347–356, 1985.

Simmons, R. G. Presidential address on altruism and sociology. *Sociol. Q.* 32: 1–22, 1991.

Simmons, R. G., Marine, S. K. and Simmons, R. L. *The Gift of Life: The Effect of Organ Transplantation on Individual Family and Societal Dynamics.* New Brunswick, N.J.: Transaction Books, 1987.

Tuprisi, R., Jaccard, J., Kelly, S. Q. and O'Malley, C. M. Social psychological factors involved in adolescents' efforts to prevent their friends from driving while intoxicated. *J. Yth. Adolesc.* 22: 147–169, 1993.

Vegega, M. E. and Klitzner, M. D. Drinking and driving among youth: A study of situational risk factors. *Hlth. Educ. Q.* 16: 373–388, 1989.

Walster, E., Walster, G. W. and Berscheid, E. *Equity: Theory and Research.* Boston: Allyn & Bacon, 1978.

Wilson, J. R. *A National Household Survey on Drinking and Driving: Knowledge, Attitudes and Behavior of Canadian Drivers.* Ottawa, Canada: Transport Canada, Road Safety and Motor Vehicle Directorate, 1984.

Wolfinger, N. H., Rabow, J. R. and Newcomb, M. D. Reexamining personal and situational factors in drunk driving interventions. *J. Appl. Social Psychol.* 24: 1627–1639, 1994.

Zajonc, R. B. Feeling and thinking: Preferences need no inferences. *Amer. Psychol.* 35: 151–175, 1980.

 Article Review Form at end of book.

What is the difference between the full-range intervention and the two-tier intervention? Which is more successful? What are some of the difficulties of implementing an intervention project like this?

It's Not Easy, But Inner-City Youth Can Unlearn Aggressive Behavior

Leonard D. Eron

If aggression is a learned behavior, as we believe it is, then it should be possible to unlearn it. But it's not that easy in the inner city, despite reports of success in other areas. Effecting behavioral change requires a complex and sustained approach carried out consistently over a number of years and affecting several psychosocial contexts and settings of development. In the ghettos of Chicago, where we are conducting our research, we have not had unqualified success—at least not immediately.

Our Metropolitan Area Child Study (MACS) is a longitudinal research program investigating methods for preventing the development of antisocial and violent behavior in children and for promoting the development of social competencies. We are conducting the study in 16 schools: eight in the inner-city of Chicago and eight in a working-class suburb, Aurora, IL.

Blocks of four schools, two in each community, were randomly assigned to each of three treatment conditions plus a no-treatment control condition. All 12 treatment schools (six in each location) receive general enhancement classroom intervention, which consists of a 15-week teacher training seminar series with consultation, observation and feedback, and a social-cognitive training curriculum (Yes I Can) for all children in grades two through six. This is a series of age-graded workbooks that deal with attitudes, norms, alternative solutions, etc.

In the next condition, four of these 12 schools (two in each location) receive this general enhance-ment classroom component plus a two-year, small-group, peer-based intervention provided to children who have been identified as at risk for the development of aggressive behavior. The children meet with a leader and a co-leader in groups of six peers.

In the most intensive condition, four of the schools (two in each location) receive the general enhancement classroom component, plus the peer-based intervention, plus a one year, 22-session family training intervention. The families of high-risk children from these four schools meet with family trainers on a weekly basis to discuss any practice issues such as behavior management, communication between family members, communication between family and school, problem-solving, and prosocial activities to be carried out in the family context.

Leonard D. Eron, It's Not Easy, But Inner-City Youth Can Unlearn Aggressive Behavior, THE BROWN UNIVERSITY CHILD AND ADOLESCENT BEHAVIOR LETTER, November 1994, Vol. 10, No. 11, p. 1. Reprinted by permission.

Full Intervention Brings Best Results

We have completed the first two years of the six-year program, or one third of the intervention, so the results are intermediate and tentative. What we have found so far is that the largest decrease in the aggressive behavior of high-risk boys has been accomplished in those schools assigned to the full range of intervention conditions: general classroom enhancement, plus peer group training, plus family treatment.

Less of a reduction in aggressive behavior among boys was accomplished in the two-tier conditions: general enhancement and peer group, but no family treatment. Those schools that received only the general enhancement actually saw an increase in aggressive behavior over the two years. The control group that receives no treatment and only pre- and post-assessments appeared to do as well as the group receiving the peer intervention. There were no significant differences among conditions for high-risk girls.

Study Is a Work in Progress

How do we explain these provocative findings? First of all, this is intended to be a six-year intervention. We have criticized earlier prevention studies because of their short duration and use of brief, one-dimensional interventions with no long-term follow-up. What we have shown thus far in our intervention is that it is only with intensive effort over multiple contexts that improvement can be shown to occur in two years.

For primary prevention, in which an entire unselected population is the recipient of a briefer intervention, it may well take a longer time. We will have to wait four more years to see what happens to those schools in which only the general enhancement was applied. It may just take that long to show any effects.

Second, the effects of the intervention in the short run may be quite different for the different ethnic subgroups in our sample. For example, the three major ethnic groups—African American, Hispanic and non-Hispanic white—seem to have responded differentially to the general enhancement, small-group and family treatments. The African American group did better than the other ethnic groups in the general enhancement condition and somewhat better in the small-group condition, while the Hispanic subjects did best and better than the other ethnic groups in the family condition. We are in the process of investigating these inter-ethnic differences, but it is apparent that in designing and evaluating preventive interventions, ethnic groups should be treated differently. What works in one group does not necessarily work in others.

There is another reason for the between condition differences, or lack of them, that we obtained. With only four schools in each condition, and only two in each city, it is likely that real differences among the schools in economics and social characteristics may affect the results even when they are randomly drawn from similar areas. And this was the case, unfortunately, with the schools we randomly selected.

It turns out that the schools in the classroom enhancement condition were probably more disadvantaged than schools in the other conditions. For example, the two Chicago schools in this condition were in areas with the highest percentage of household incomes under $15,000 per year and the highest rule of crimes against persons. Also, one of the schools in this condition changed its principal four times over the course of one year. Can you imagine how much disruption that caused, not only in regular classroom procedures, but also in the implementation of our project's methods?

Daunting Realities

These are the realities that must be accommodated when doing research in Chicago, as well as perhaps in other cities in which the education system is so adversely affected by economic and social disadvantage. We're not going to go in and change ingrained beliefs and behaviors with eight to twelve sessions on "conflict resolution." It will take a much longer, more consistent effort with procedures that have been theoretically derived, are culturally sensitive and have empirical support.

Despite all this, when we look more closely at these results, we have actually done pretty well. A large number of children did reduce their aggressive behavior over two years. At least 22 percent of the high-risk boys reduced their aggressive behavior by 10 percent over two years. Approximately 6 percent. of the high-risk boys reduced their aggressive behavior by 25 percent If this were a public health program in hypertension, for example, and we reduced blood pressure by 10 percent in high-risk subjects, that would probably merit a lead article in the *New England Journal of Medicine* and headlines in the science section of the *New York Times*.

The fact is that inner-city intervention programs aimed at teaching children alternative ways of behaving and solving interpersonal problems are doomed to failure if they do not take into account the extreme and persistent environmental constraints, such as violence, hopelessness and limited social resources, that surround these children 24 hours a day.

This article was excerpted from an invited address given by Leonard Eron at the American Psychological Association's annual convention in August. Leonard D. Eron, Ph.D., has been studying aggression and how children learn it for 40 years. He and his colleagues at the University of Michigan's Institute for Social Research followed the entire third-grade population of a semi-rural county in New York State for 22 years. One of their findings was the predictability of aggressive behavior from age 8 to age 30, including serious antisocial and criminal behavior.

Article Review Form at end of book.

As you read "Road Rage," consider how each of the aggression theories mentioned in your text would explain this behavior. How would both the victim and the perpetrator of "road rage" explain what caused the incident? Have *you* ever committed road rage, or been the target of it?

Road Rage

Tailgating, giving the finger, outright violence

Americans grow more likely to take out their frustrations on other drivers.

Jason Vest, Warren Cohen, and Mike Tharp

Some of the incidents are so ludicrous you can't help but laugh—albeit nervously. There was the case in Salt Lake City, where 75-year-old J. C. King—peeved that 41-year-old Larry Remm Jr. honked at him for blocking traffic—followed Remm when he pulled off the road, hurled his prescription bottle at him, and then, in a display of geriatric resolve, smashed Remm's knees with his '92 Mercury. In tiny Potomac, Md., Robin Ficker—an attorney and ex-state legislator—knocked the glasses off a pregnant woman after she had the temerity to ask him why he bumped her Jeep with his.

Other incidents lack even the element of black humor. In Colorado Springs, 55-year-old Vern Smalley persuaded a 17-year-old boy who had been tail-gating him to pull over; Smalley decided that, rather than merely scold the lad, he would shoot him. (And he did. Fatally—after the youth had threatened him.) And last year, on Virginia's George Washington Parkway, a dispute over a lane change was settled with a high-speed duel that ended when both drivers lost control and crossed the center line, killing two innocent motorists.

Anyone who spent the Memorial Day weekend on the road probably won't be too surprised to learn the results of a major study to be released this week by the American Automobile Association: The rate of "aggressive driving" incidents—defined as events in which an angry or impatient driver tries to kill or injure another driver after a traffic dispute—has risen by 51 percent since 1990. In those cases studied, 37 percent of offenders used firearms against other drivers, an additional 28 percent used other weapons, and 35 percent used their cars.

Fear of (and participation in) aggressive driving has grown so much that in a poll last year residents of Maryland, Washington, D.C., and Virginia listed it as a bigger concern than drunk driving. The Maryland highway department is running a campaign called "The End of the Road for Aggressive Drivers," which, among other things, flashes anti-road-rage messages on electronic billboards on the interstates. Delaware, Pennsylvania, and New Jersey have initiated special highway patrols targeting aggressive drivers. A small but busy community of therapists and scholars has arisen to study the phenomenon and counsel drivers on how to cope. And several members of Congress are now trying to figure out ways to legislate away road rage.

Lest one get unduly alarmed, it helps to put the AAA study's numbers in context: Approximately 250,000 people have been killed in traffic since 1990. While the U.S. Department of Transportation estimates that two-thirds of fatalities are at least partially caused by aggressive driving, the AAA study found only 218 that could be directly attributable to enraged drivers. Of the more than 20 million motorists injured, the survey identified 12,610 injuries attributable to aggressive driving. While the study is the first American attempt to quantify aggressive driving, it is not rigorously scientific. The authors drew on reports from 30 newspapers—supplemented by insurance claims and police reports from 16 cities—involving 10,037 occurrences. Moreover, the overall trendlines for car accidents have continued downward for several decades, thanks in part to increases in the drinking age and improvements in car technology like high-mounted brake lights.

But researchers believe there is a growing trend of simple aggressive behavior—road rage—in which a driver reacts angrily to other drivers. Cutting them off, tailgating, giving the finger, waving a fist—experts believe these forms of nonviolent fury are increasing. "Aggressive driving is now the most common way of driving," says Sandra Ball-Rokeach, who codirects the Media and Injury Prevention Program at the University of Southern California. "It's not just a few crazies—it's a subculture of driving."

In focus groups set up by her organization, two-thirds of drivers said they reacted to frustrating situations aggressively. Almost half admitted to deliberately braking suddenly, pulling close to the other car, or taking some other potentially dangerous step. Another third said they retaliated with a hostile gesture.

Drivers show great creativity in devising hostile responses. Doug Erber of Los Angeles keeps his windshield-wiper-fluid tank full. If someone tailgates, he turns on the wipers, sending fluid over his roof onto the car behind him. "It works better than hitting the brakes," he says, "and you can act totally innocent."

Mad Max

While the AAA authors note there is a profile of the lethally inclined aggressive driver—"relatively young, poorly educated males who have criminal records, histories of violence, and drug or alcohol problems"—road-rage scholars (and regular drivers) believe other groups are equally represented in the less violent forms of aggressive driving. To some, it's tempting to look at this as a psychologically mysterious Jekyll-and-Hyde phenomenon; for others, it's simply attributable to "jerk drivers." In reality, there's a confluence of emotional and demographic factors that changes the average citizen from mere motorist to Mad Max.

First, it isn't just your imagination that traffic is getting worse. Since 1987, the number of miles of roads has increased just 1 percent while the miles driven have shot up by 35 percent. According to a recent Federal Highway Administration study of 50 metropolitan areas, almost 70 percent of urban freeways today—as opposed to 55 percent in 1983—are clogged during rush hour. The study notes that congestion is likely to spread to currently unspoiled locations. Forty percent of the currently gridlock-free Milwaukee County highway system, for example, is predicted to be jammed up more than five

hours a day by the year 2000. A study by the Texas Transportation Institute last year found that commuters in one-third of the largest cities spent well over 40 hours a year in traffic jams.

Part of the problem is that jobs have shifted from cities to suburbs. Communities designed as residential suburbs with narrow roads have grown into "edge cities," with bustling commercial traffic. Suburb-to-suburb commutes now account for 44 percent of all metropolitan traffic versus 20 percent for suburb-to-downtown travel. Demographer and Edge City author Joel Garreau says workers breaking for lunch are essentially causing a third rush hour. He notes that in Tysons Corner, Va., it takes an average of four traffic signal cycles to get through a typical intersection at lunchtime. And because most mass transit systems are of a spoke-and-hub design, centering on cities and branching out to suburbs, they're not really useful in getting from point A to point B in an edge city or from one edge city to another. Not surprisingly, fewer people are relying on mass transit and more on cars. In 1969, 82.7 percent drove to work; in 1990, 91.4 percent did. Despite the fact that the Washington, D.C., area has an exemplary commuter subway system, it accounts for only 2 percent of all trips made.

Demographic changes have helped put more drivers on the road. Until the 1970s, the percentage of women driving was relatively low, and many families had only one car. But women entered the work force and bought cars, something developers and highway planners hadn't foreseen. From 1969 to 1990 the number of women licensed to drive increased 84 percent. Between 1970 and 1987, the number of cars on the road more than doubled. In the past decade, the number of cars grew faster (17 percent) than the number of people (10 percent). Even carpooling is down despite HOV lanes and other preferential devices. The cumulative effect, says University of Hawaii traffic psychology professor Leon James, is a sort of sensory overload. "There are simply more cars—and more behaviors—to deal with," says James.

As if the United States couldn't produce enough home-grown lousy drivers, it seems to be importing them as well. Experts believe that many immigrants come from countries that have bad roads and aggressive styles. It's not just drivers from Third World countries, though. British drivers are considered among the safest in Europe, yet recent surveys show that nearly 90 percent of British motorists have experienced threats or abuse from other drivers. Of Brits who drive for a living, about 21 percent report having been run off the road. In Australia, one study estimates that about half of all traffic accidents there may be due to road rage. "There are different cultures of driving all over the world—quite clearly, if we mix new cultures in the melting pot, what we get is a culture clash on the roadway," says John Palmer, a professor in the Health Education and Safety Department at Minnesota's St. Cloud State University.

The peak moment for aggressive driving comes not during impenetrable gridlock but just before, when traffic density is high but cars are still moving briskly. That's when cutting someone off or forcing someone out of a lane can make the difference (or so it seems) between being on time and being late, according to Palmer.

Unfortunately, roads are getting more congested just as Americans feel even more pressed for time. "People get on a time line for their car trips," says Palmer. "When they perceive that someone is impeding their progress or invading their agenda, they respond with what they consider to be 'instructive' behavior, which might be as simple as flashing their lights to something more combative."

Suburban Assault Vehicles

This, uh, "instruction" has become more common, Palmer and others speculate, in part because of modern automotive design. With hyperadjustable seats, soundproof interiors, CD players, and cellular phones, cars are virtually comfortable enough to live in. Students of traffic can't help but wonder if the popularity of pickup trucks and sport utility vehicles has contributed to the problem. Sales have approximately doubled since 1990. These big metal shells loom over everything else, fueling feelings of power and drawing out a driver's more primal instincts. "A lot of the anecdotal evidence about aggressive driving incidents tends to involve people driving sport utility vehicles," says Julie Rochman of the Insurance Institute for Highway Safety. "When people get these larger, heavier vehicles, they feel more invulnerable." While Chrysler spokesman Chris Preuss discounts the notion of suburban assault vehicles being behind the aggressive-driving phenomenon, he does say women feel more secure in the jumbo-size vehicles.

In much of life, people feel they don't have full control of their destiny. But a car—unlike, say, a career or a spouse—responds reliably to one's wish. In automobiles, we have an increased (but false) sense of invincibility. Other drivers become dehumanized, mere appendages to a competing machine. "You have the illusion you're alone and master, dislocated from other drivers," says Hawaii's James.

Los Angeles psychologist Arnold Nerenberg describes how one of his recent patients got into an angry road confrontation with another motorist. "They pulled off the road and started running toward each other to fight, but then they recognized each other as neighbors," he says. "When it's just somebody else in a car, it's more two-dimensional; the other person's identity boils down to, 'You're someone who did something bad to me.'"

How can aggressive driving be minimized? Some believe that better driver's education might help. Driver's ed was a high school staple by the 1950s, thanks to federal highway dollars given to states. But a 1978 government study in De Kalb County, Ga., found no reduction in crashes or traffic violations by students who took a driver's ed course compared with those who didn't. Rather than use these results to design better driver's ed programs, the feds essentially gave up on them and diverted money to seat belt and anti-drunk-driving programs. Today, only 40 percent of new drivers complete a formal training course, which may be one reason 20 percent to 35 percent of applicants fail their initial driving test.

The Inner Driver

But governments are looking anew at the value of driver's education. In April, Michigan passed sweeping rules that grant levels of privilege depending on one's age and driving record. States with similar systems, like California, Maryland, and Oregon, have seen teen accident rates drop.

Those who lose their licenses often have to return to traffic school. But some states have generous standards for these schools. To wit: California's theme schools. There, errant drivers can attend the "Humor's My Name, Traffic's My Game," school, in which a mock jury led by a stand-up comic decides who the worst drivers are; the "Traffic School for Chocoholics," which plies errant drivers with chocolate and ice cream; and the gay and lesbian "Pink Triangle Traffic School."

But the real key to reducing road rage probably lies deep within each of us. Professor James of the University of Hawaii suggests that instead of emphasizing defensive driving—which implies that the other driver is the enemy—we should focus on "supportive driving" or "driving with the aloha spirit." Of course that's hard to do if (a) someone has just cut you off at 60 mph or (b) you live in Los Angeles instead of Hawaii. Nerenberg, the Los Angeles psychologist, has published an 18-page book-let called "Overcoming Road Rage: The 10-Step Compassion Program." He recommends examining what sets off road rage and to "visualize overcoming it." Other tips: Imagine you might be seeing that person at a party soon. And remember that other drivers "are people with feelings. Let us not humiliate them with our aggression." In the chapter titled, "Peace," he suggests, "Take a deep breath and just let it go." And if that doesn't work, the windshield-wiper trick is pretty clever.

 **Article Review Form at end of book.**

What are some of the factors that affect the degree to which media violence will influence someone? What is the "Mean World Syndrome," and how does it result from television viewing?

Violence, Reel to Real

Does TV and movie violence cause real violence?

John Leland

Abstract: *The fire-bombing of a subway token booth following release of the film 'Money Train,' which depicted a similar crime, has renewed the debate over the influence of TV and film violence on aggression. Existing research is inconclusive. Various research findings are interpreted.*

In the film "Money Train," a man douses a New York subway token-booth clerk with a flammable liquid, lights a match and demands her money. When she pushes a bag of cash toward him, he tosses the match at her anyway, laughing sadistically that he isn't in it for the money. For New York audiences this was a horror revisited: in the 1980s, hoodlums terrorized subway clerks with firebombs and lighter fluid. The movie opened on Wednesday, Nov. 22, and grossed $15 million in its first five days.

But its impact seems to have extended beyond the box office. Late Saturday night, three days after the opening, two men in Brooklyn squirted flammable liquid into the token booth manned by Harry Kaufman and blew his small cubicle to pieces. Kaufman remains in critical condition, with burns over 75 percent of his body.

By midweek two more token booths had been attacked or threatened by firebugs. The makers of "Money Train" ardently defended their film, claiming they were only depicting a real crime method. But the incidents read like the latest case of life imitating art—or perhaps life imitating art imitating life (graphic). Bob Dole, who had reaped political mileage denouncing the entertainment industry in May, again lambasted Hollywood last week, calling for a boycott of the movie: "Those who continue to deny that cultural messages can and do bore deep into the hearts and minds of our young people are deceiving themselves and ignoring reality."

This was an easy shot, especially in the wake of such a reprehensible crime. Who could defend the values of "Money Train," a witless orgy of gratuitous mayhem? But as with most quick attempts to connect entertainments with real-world violence, the story under this was far more complicated. For starters, the hoods responsible haven't been arrested; no one knows whether they even saw the movie. More significant, the incident offers only the most facile look at how violence in the media might affect us. Copycat crimes, even if they hold up under scrutiny, involve only a minuscule fraction of the millions of people who watch the same movie or show. Far more troubling is the question of how our daily immersion in violent media—in aggressive cartoons, brutal sporting events, graphic newscasts, shoot-'em-up movies and TV shows and harsh popular music—affect children and adults in the aggregate.

Beneath the huffy sound bites lie nearly 40 years of extremely murky scientific research on the subject. The evidence holds fascinating clues into how our entertainments act on our minds. But it is also far less certain than many of its adherents claim. Researchers routinely cite thousands of studies. Really, there are closer to 200; the rest are rehashes of data. The press in turn uncritically repeats numbers like annual figures for how many violent acts kids see each year, without noting that the figures include acts of nature, cartoon violence and slapstick along with grisly fare. A closer look at the actual research literature reveals that what we don't know about media's effects is often as dramatic as what we do.

Nobody believes that media by themselves cause aggression. But Leonard Eron and Rowell Huesmann of the University of

Michigan found in a 22-year study following kids from third grade through adulthood that the single best predictor of later aggression—more than poverty, grades, a single-parent home or exposure to real violence—was a heavy childhood diet of TV carnage. "Of course not every youngster is affected," says Eron. "Not everyone who gets lung cancer smoked cigarettes. And not everyone who smokes cigarettes gets lung cancer. But nobody outside the tobacco industry denies that smoking causes lung cancer. The size of the correlation is the same." Epidemiologist Brandon S. Centerwall goes so far as to assert that without TV there would be 10,000 fewer murders per year in the United States, 70,000 fewer rapes and 700,000 fewer assaults.

Much of the most effective research has been done on children, because they are considered most susceptible. As Centerwall puts it, "Later variations in exposure, in adolescence and adulthood, do not exert any additional effect." In the early '60s, Albert Bandura at Stanford was the first to show that kids learned behavior from TV, not just from their parents. Psychologists have used four theories of learning to describe how TV violence may influence kids: they learn to imitate what they see on TV, especially when it is rewarded; they learn from the frequency of violence on TV that it is normal; they become desensitized to real people's suffering, and they become aroused by images on television, triggering violent responses. Early researchers, following Aristotle, thought media violence might by cathartic, purging violent urges, but experiments have not borne this out. In a classic series of lab experiments in the early 1960s, researchers first frustrated a group of preschool kids, then showed them TV footage of a man hitting a "Bobo" or clown doll. Afterward, the kids who saw the violence were more likely to mimic it on a similar doll. Further studies showed that these kids would also spontaneously act out against a man dressed as a clown, indicating that TV violence might spill easily into the real world. In another twist, a group of kids saw a similar footage of a man hitting a doll, but then being spanked for his actions. These children were much less likely to attack the doll themselves.

These last results imply that what matters is the type or treatment of violence: that screen mayhem that's rewarded will encourage aggression, but when it's punished it will inhibit it. By this logic, a heroic John Wayne movie might be more damaging than a senseless slasher movie, especially if the villain is punished. The experiments also argue that simply tallying the number of violent acts is meaningless. In this case, seeing the most acts of violence (both a hit doll and a spanking) made kids the least likely to rumble themselves.

Working with adults, Brad Bushman at Iowa State has shown in lab situations that subjects not prone to aggression were not affected by what they saw, while those previously inclined toward violence were. "Highly aggressive people organize experiences in their memories differently," he says. Violent entertainment "activates their aggressive thoughts, angry feelings." Bushman came to his interest in TV violence the tough way. "My electronics teacher owned an audio store. Just before closing one day, two armed men came in and forced the owner and customers down in the basement, forced them to eat Drano and put duct tape over their mouths, much like in the movie 'Magnum Force.' At trial, one witness testified that these men watched 'Magnum Force' three times the day before."

Other researchers have questioned whether it was the hyperkinetic form of TV, more than the content, that prompted aggression. Two studies published in the early '80s found that programs with heavy action but no violence were just as likely to provoke aggression as those that contained actual mayhem. Dorothy and Jerome Singer at Yale further found that even innocuous programs like the quick-cutting "Sesame Street" or variety and game shows were so stimulating that they prompted aggression. (The producers of "Sesame Street" have since slowed the show down. The problem with lab studies, though, is that their conditions are artificial and limited. They take material entirely out of context, and don't look at cumulative effects of our real viewing patterns. The responses measured—punching a doll or pushing a shock button—are not real violent responses, only approximations. Further, the responses all come with the sanction of the experimenter. They seem like acceptable behaviors, with no threat of retribution.

Two of the most compelling field studies have looked at the way television changed a culture when it was first introduced. In 1973, Tannis MacBeth Williams studied kids in a Canadian town before and after the town got TV. She found that creativity dropped and that within two years after the arrival of the tube, rates of hitting, shoving and biting among first and second graders increased by 160 percent.

In a somewhat related experiment, Centerwall looked at murder rates in the United States, Canada and South Africa after the introduction of TV. In each country, 10 to 15 years after television came in, murder rates doubled. Centerwall explained the lag by reasoning that it took that long for the first young kids exposed to TV to come of age. Even looking at other factors—the baby boom, urbanization, the rise of firearms—he claims that none was as viable an explanation as TV.

Neither of these studies dealt with the content of TV. Both suggest that it may be the fact of TV—the way it changes our social lives, decreases the time kids spend with parents, stimulates material desires—that makes our world aggressive, more than the body count in an episode of "NYPD Blue."

George Gerbner, professor and dean emeritus of The Annenberg School for Communications at the University of Pennsylvania, has been studying television and its effects since the 1950s. He argues that the question of whether violent media causes violence misses the point. "It's a shallow, superficial, law-enforcement approach." The violence on TV, he says, shapes a range of responses beyond aggression. So Gerbner devised what he calls a Mean World Syndrome: a measure of how television cultivates "feelings of insecurity, vulnerability and mistrust, and—despite its supposedly entertaining nature—alienation and gloom." He contends that violence is used to define social relations between characters. "The primary message of violence on TV," he says, "is who can get away with what against whom." In a study covering 1982 to 1992, for example, the researchers found that for every 10 prime-time male characters who commit violence, 11 were victims. But for every 10 female perps, there were 17 female victims. The numbers

are even worse for minorities. For every 10 women of color given power, 22 are victimized. The elderly and the poor are also common victims on television. According to Gerbner, viewers then bend their views of the real world according to these ratios. People who watch a lot of television, he found, believed that women were more likely than men to be victims of violence (in fact, men are about one and one-half times as likely to be victims of violent crimes). "Some kids see themselves as more likely to be victims than other kids, and they develop a greater sense of vulnerability. Or if they see themselves as more likely to perpetrate violence without consequences, they develop a greater sense of being able to prevail through aggression." He also found that heavy viewers were more likely to call for severe punishments for criminals, and to have brought new locks, watchdogs and guns "for protection."

Many researchers, though, question Gerbner's method of counting all acts of violence alike. He answers that no viewer distinguishes between "Henry: Portrait of a Serial Killer" and "Arsenic and Old Lace" and that on TV, even natural phenomena like storms convey a message about power. His work also invites a counterexplanation: people who are predisposed to fear the world are also more likely to stay home and watch TV. Gerbner argues that because we watch TV all our lives, there is no such thing as predisposition, "no before and after. TV cultivates the predisposition."

Even if the evidence is inconclusive, it's hard to dismiss the likelihood of some connection between media and aggression. So what to do? Gerbner rejects the V-chip—a device that would allow parents to block out programs

coded for violent content—as "a technocratic fantasy. It's a mindless mechanism. Who programs it? Do you let the fox guard the chicken coop? If government decides, it's unconstitutional."

Both the Singers and Huesmann have designed programs to try to inoculate children from the harmful effects of television. Huesmann asked a group of second graders to help make a videotape on the effects of TV violence, exploring how TV works: how it is not real life; how copying TV can hurt real people, and so on. Tested later, the kids showed a high skepticism toward media violence; they were also less aggressive in class. Parents can try similar techniques at home, or push schools to educate young kids about the biases and distortions of television. Unfortunately Huesmann does not think the effects of his program will be long-lasting. "I don't believe this kind of curriculum alone can solve the problem. It needs to be coupled with reduction in media violence."

For four decades the entertainment industry has resisted such pleas, no matter how great the pressures on it. The body of research against media violence, though spongy, grows larger each year. We may never understand fully just how our entertainments shape our behavior. For now, all we can say for sure is that the subway clerk Harry Kaufman lies in a hospital room, burned in a crime similar to one in a movie. It's cause for cautious examination, not sound bites. The research has a long way to go, further than its believers claim. But you still might think twice before letting your kids watch Power Rangers.

 **Article Review Form at end of book.**

- Typically, helping behavior is regulated by a number of situational and personal characteristics. In the case of preventing a drunk person from driving, situational characteristics (e.g., perceived dangerousness of the situation) were important, but personal characteristics, such as knowing someone killed by a drunk driver, did not have any effect on one's willingness to help. Assertive interventions (e.g., taking someone's keys) were more successful than passive interventions (e.g., asking someone not to drive).

- Intervention programs to reduce aggression must be long-term. It is also best if they include all domains of a child's life: home, school, and friends. Programs such as these have led to significant decreases in the amount of aggressive behavior.

- Aggression is a part of our everyday lives, yet we can control it. Road rage is an example of a situation where anger and aggression could be reduced.

- The media affect levels of violence in a number of ways. They provide models of violence to follow, they desensitize people to the effects of violence, and they encourage the development of the Mean World Syndrome. These effects may be particularly severe for those who have some previous inclination toward violence.

R.E.A.L. Sites

This list provides a print preview of typical **coursewise** R.E.A.L. sites. (There are over 100 such sites at the **courselinks™** site.) The danger in printing URLs is that web sites can change overnight. As we went to press, these sites were functional using the URLs provided. If you come across one that isn't, please let us know via email to: webmaster@coursewise.com. Use your Passport to access the most current list of R.E.A.L. sites at the **courselinks™** site.

Site name: Access to Justice Network Publications

URL: http://www.acjnet.org/docs/bystajhs.html

Why is it R.E.A.L.? Here you will find an article that summarizes much of the social psychological research on helping behavior and bystander intervention. The article examines personal factors, such as gender and personality characteristics, and situational factors, such as urban stress and number of people present. This should be a good starting point to explore the causes you personally believe are important to predicting helping behavior.

Key topics: culture, gender, helping behavior, motivation

Site name: Center for the Study and Prevention of Violence

URL: http://www.colorado.edu/cspv/

Why is it R.E.A.L.? This is the official web site for the Center for the Study and Prevention of Violence. This site has a number of resources that make it invaluable to someone interested in learning more about violence research, either out of curiosity or for a class project. It has statistical fact sheets on violence, summaries of research studies online, and a list of papers you can request. In addition, you can search "VioLit," the Violence Literature database. Go to this site, and see if you can determine whether levels of youth violence have changed over the last 10 years.

Key topics: aggression, health, law

section

8

Learning Objectives

- Explain the similarities between friendships and romantic relationships.

- Explain the processes by which trust develops.

- Describe the evolutionary psychology model on jealousy, and alternative explanations to the evolutionary model.

- Explain the three types of stable marriages and what differentiates them from unstable marriages.

- Discuss the four problem signs in a relationship and how they can be addressed.

- Explain the three relationship domains that predict individual and joint well-being in dual-career couples.

Interpersonal Relationships

 **WiseGuide Intro**

You probably wish to live a long and happy life, as nearly everybody does. One of the most important determinants of both your happiness *and* longevity will be your interpersonal relationships. Researchers have known for some time that people who are married live longer and healthier lives.

The moment of our birth marks the beginning of our first important interpersonal relationship—with our mother. Soon thereafter, we form relationship bonds with the rest of our family. As we grow, we add to our close relationships—perhaps you can still remember your first best friend. As we reach adolescence, we become more interested in romantic relationships. By the time you are in college, you have a whole series of relationships to manage: family, friends, roommates, and romantic partners. Some of the rewards and challenges of these relationships may include intimacy, trust, jealousy, and conflict. These are some of the topics that social psychologists study.

The scientific study of interpersonal relationships is quite a recent phenomenon. As recently as the 1970s, a U.S. senator criticized research on love and relationships, indicating that this was a matter best kept a mystery and in the bedroom, and many agreed with him. Recognizing the importance of relationships in human life, however, social psychologists persevered and continued to study who was attracted to whom and how people managed their relationships. Because of this research, we now know a good deal more about relationships than we did twenty years ago. The social psychological study of relationships incorporates many areas, including attraction, trust, conflict, intimacy, and social support.

Public opinion about the privacy of relationships has changed, as indicated by the boom in self-help books and talk shows offering relationship advice. In an era where divorce is commonplace, people want to know how to build strong relationships. One goal of this section is to make you a more critical consumer of these popular books and programs. In previous sections we have considered tactics of persuasion and social influence, as well as our occasional shortcomings in social reasoning and inference. Be aware of these phenomena as you read some of these self-help books, and be prepared to check their claims and advice against the relationship research you read about in your textbook. In addition, one of the web sites for this section directs you to a list of more scientifically based self-help books and other psychology resources.

In our first article, Susan Davis talks about a relationship we often pay little attention to—our friendships. She specifically tells of the breakup of her own friendship and then consults with a number of researchers as to how often this occurs and why. You will find some suggestions on how to maintain your friendships over the long haul. The next article, "Trust Me, Please," provides a nice overview of current social psychological research on trust. Trust is the basis for both friendships and romantic relationships, as well as working relationships.

Kotler describes research on the development of trust in childhood and the evolution of trust in adult relationships.

In "Gender, Jealousy, and Reason," we learn about some possible explanations for jealousy, and in particular, gender differences in jealousy. You will first read about a popular model of interpersonal relationships, namely, the evolutionary model. This account posits that gender differences in jealousy are innate, a vestige from our long-ago ancestors. The authors dispute this claim, and argue instead that jealousy is a function of how men and women are socialized to participate in romantic relationships.

In "The Love Lab," the author and her husband take part in a study in John Gottman's marriage laboratory. For the last twenty years, Gottman has been investigating the physiological and psychological symptoms of distressed couples. He has been able to predict, with greater than 90% accuracy, couples that are headed for divorce. In this article you will learn about some of the warning signs of a troubled relationship and how to turn them around.

Our final article discusses dual-career marriages, a phenomenon that has steadily increased over the last thirty years and is surely here to stay. Gilbert reviews the current statistics regarding working men and women in the United States and then talks about how couples balance work and family.

As you read these articles, you will no doubt think of your parents' relationships, your friends' relationships, and perhaps most important, your own relationships. I hope these articles will provide you with some helpful information on what makes a relationship successful, and at the same time familiarize you with the diverse body of psychological research on the topic.

What are the most common precipitating factors in the breakup of a friendship? Is it inevitable that we will grow out of our friendships? Why or why not?

The Enduring Power of Friendship

Adult friendships are more important than many people realize. The emotional burden of experiencing the end of an adult friendship can be very heavy. Unfortunately, there are very few helpful tips on how to nurture friendships.

Susan Davis

Adult friendships—and the loss we feel when they end—are more important than most of us realize.

A few years ago one of my best friends suddenly stopped returning my calls. There had been some tension between us for about a year. We'd all but stopped seeing each other. Given our long history, I figured we would pick up soon again. But for her, it was time to end the friendship.

It was a hard pill for me to swallow. In the 12 years we'd known each other, Kelly and I had gone through a lot together. We shared a house in Boston, traveled cross-country and talked endlessly of our rural roots, our families and our dreams of the future. We wept when I moved to California for graduate school, but we stayed close through letters, phone calls and visits. "We're best friends forever," Kelly used

to say. "We'll grow old together on a porch somewhere."

I always agreed. But when Kelly came to California to start a new life several years after I had, something was out of kilter. I had begun a career and met the man I wanted to marry; she wanted neither a "real" job nor a husband. I wanted to talk about my new feelings. She acted as if I'd betrayed her by even having them.

When Kelly finally stopped speaking to me, I was devastated. We had shared everything. Now my confidante was gone. Worse, she no longer even liked me. I felt unsure and exposed, as if we were schoolgirls on a playground and she were telling stories about me.

Does everyone go through what I went through? As it turns out, many of us do. For years sociologists and psychologists have focused primarily on friendships in childhood and adolescence, because it's during these rich periods that we learn to approach and interact with others. Now they're

realizing that the long decades of adulthood are equally vital. With job demands and "downsizing" increasing your mobility and divorce rates still sky high, family ties are strained to their limits. That means adult friendships are perhaps more important than ever. We learn to make friends in our early years, researchers say, but as adults we learn to depend on these essential links.

It isn't always easy. We like to think friendships are warm, casual, fairly simple affairs. In reality they're more complicated. "Friendships involve a good deal of ambiguity and ambivalence," says Dr. William Rawlins, an interpersonal communications expert at Purdue University at West Lafayette, Ind., and author of Friendship Matters. Every friendship entails subtle, usually silent negotiations over such fundamental questions as whether we're "just" friends, "good" friends, or "best" friends and how generous we'll be with our time. Friction occurs when one friend wants more, gives more or even reveals more than the other.

Unfortunately, guidance on nurturing friendships is sparse. Dr. Diane Prusank, a specialist in interpersonal communications at the University of Hartford (Conn.), looked at scores of articles in eight magazines for women and teenage girls published between 1974 and 1990. She found 125 stories on romantic relationships and families and only nine on friendship. "Our culture is obsessed with romance," says Prusank. "Friendship is secondary; no one thinks it has to be talked about."

It should be. Friendships provide varying degrees of indispensable support, from the agreeable neighbor who lends you his hedge clipper to the former college roommate you can call at any hour of the night for advice or commiseration. But since friendships are voluntary, unbound by obligations of law or kinship, they're especially susceptible to life's ups and downs, particularly when one friend's life changes in a way that the other's does not. Whether it's marriage, divorce or a career switch, these "developmental transitions" make us see ourselves—and our friends—in a new light.

"Sometimes it's something major, like having children," says study author Dr. Donald Pannen, a psychologist at the University of Puget Sound in Tacoma, Wash. "Other times it's just a little thing like a disagreement about a political candidate. But these changes can create barriers and awkward feelings. They can make it more difficult to maintain the friendship." In fact, according to one study of 17- to 64-year-olds who had recently ended friendships,

77% said life changes precipitated the rift.

People have always gone through developmental transitions, but these days two people rarely hit the same transition at the same time. It's quite conceivable, for instance, for a 35-year-old woman to be a stay-at-home mom with two children while her close friend of the same age works 60-hour weeks and goes out on dates.

Certain developmental transitions are more disruptive than others. Career success—and the envy it provokes—can turn even the closest friendship sour. Some friendships may falter simply because two people no longer share the same values, say, about money or politics. Marriage poses one of the biggest threats to friendship, especially for women. Spousal intimacy may weaken a woman's need for a best friend, says Prusank. This seeming abandonment can be hard on the single friends who are left behind.

The hectic pace of modern life also makes keeping up with friends difficult. The new friendships we make on the job are often tenuous, because of the unstable nature of corporate life today. Not only do we leave jobs more often, but we also compete more with our coworkers to hang on to the jobs we have. Add children, hobbies and volunteer or religious activities to the mix, and our social contacts get spread pretty thin. "It used to be that everyone lived and worked and socialized in the same town," says Pannen. "But it takes much more effort to keep friends in today's fragmented society."

It's rare too for an adult to have a single best friend. Most of us have several "very good" friends in different circles. "The bond between adult best friends

isn't the same as in childhood," says Prusank. "The tight connection is diluted by many activities and obligations."

Trouble is, few of us actually acknowledge these pressures, much less discuss them with our friends. "Most people are afraid to burden a friendship with too much talk," says Dr. Julia T. Wood, an expert in communication at the University of North Carolina at Chapel Hill. "If you speak up about what's bothering you, there's a risk that the other person will shy away."

That reticence often continues to the bitter end. Unlike romantic relationships, which tend to break apart with a bang, friendships typically dissolve with barely a whimper. In the Puget Sound study, only 13% of subjects said their friendships ended abruptly, and just 15% managed to have an open discussion of the relationship's problems. "We have no language for describing friendship difficulties," says Prusank. "We don't have 'breakup' conversations, and we don't give back the objects we exchanged. Without these symbolic displays of finality—for example, returning gifts or photographs—it can be difficult to move on."

Both men and women take the loss of a pal hard: Six months after their friendship ended, 70% of the Puget Sound subjects said they felt ambivalent about their conflicts, 50% admitted to still feeling sad and 14% felt angry; only 17% said they were happy to have the friend out of their life.

And once we lose a few friends, whether it's due to work changes, moving, having children or death, it gets harder to approach new people. "Go through a lot of these transitions and you become wary," says Wood. "Older people often withdraw because they have endured so many losses."

Still, most adults tend to make new friends, though often they have to take active measures to do so. "Many people join groups, like local political clubs, or even move to a new neighborhood or city specifically to meet people," says Dr. Rosemary Blieszner, a gerontologist at Virginia Polytechnic Institute and State University in Blacksburg, Va., and coauthor of *Adult Friendships*. If you're shy, try giving yourself "homework assignments," such as approaching two new people a week or reapproaching someone you've met recently and asking them to join you for a cup of coffee.

Of course, low self-esteem or lack of trust in others can make even these minor social interactions difficult. Simply deciding to embark on a friend-making campaign won't make these impediments go away, though a professional counselor can often help.

Much has happened since Kelly and I parted. I've switched jobs, married the man I fell in love with and become closer to my family. I'm sorry that Kelly hasn't been able to share these developments with me. But to endure, adult friendships need to be flexible. And that, says researchers, may be a rare quality.

"Part of what makes a friendship resilient is a mutual ability to weather change and tolerate shifting demands on your friend's life," says Wood. If your best friend suddenly meets the man of her dreams, for instance, the wisest course of action might be to let her go for a while. To maintain a friendship, you need to be willing to come back and rejuvenate it after a period of less contact. "If you always think the silence stems from a lack of affection or care," says Wood, "the bond becomes less stable."

Then again, part of being a good friend is knowing when to let go. One instance, Purdue's Rawlins says, is when an unforgivable betrayal occurs, for example if a friend sleeps with your spouse or damages your reputation. Another is when a friend makes you feel bad about yourself. "There's a value to being able to let go as we take on new roles," says Wood. "This ability to adapt and change is healthy."

I'm not ready to say the breakup of my own friendship was healthy. I still miss Kelly too much. But perhaps my mother, listening to me moan yet again about the loss of my friend, put it best: "You met when you were girls," she said. "You laughed and cried together as girls. Now you're not girls anymore."

 Article Review Form at end of book.

Why do we sometimes trust strangers more than those who are close to us? How do we go about building trust with others?

Trust Me, Please

Who's reliable, who isn't, and when you can know for sure. Here's the latest research on the science of trust.

Steven Kotler

Steven Kotler is a San Francisco-based freelance writer.

We had known each other almost 10 years before I asked her when she had decided to trust me.

"You mean completely, with everything, with all of me?" she said.

"Yes," I replied, expecting a moment from deep in our past.

Instead she said, "Three months ago, when we were lying on the couch in your house, just after I got back from Japan."

"Three months ago? But we've known each other so long."

"I'm not the world's best truster," she said.

Enigmatic and elusive, real trust is the pinnacle of soul-to-soul communication. Trust rests at the core of every meaningful relationship, a part of its very foundation—without trust we have nothing; we are strangers to ourselves and to each other. But while establishing this kind of deep trust is something that we'll attain only a handful of times in our life, we make decisions about whom to trust, when to trust and how much to trust hundreds of times a day. We trust that the restaurant where we eat lunch keeps a clean kitchen, that our doctor can differentiate between strep throat and spinal meningitis, that cars will stop when the light turns red.

And yet, for all this practice, our decisions about trust are often curious. Why, for instance, do we refrain from wearing a seat belt in a taxicab—trusting that the stranger at the wheel will shuttle us safely—while we never fail to buckle up when our most reliable friend is driving? Why do we allow ourselves to lie naked beside a stranger we've only known a few weeks, yet spend our entire lives distrusting our parents?

Because trust is so important to the makeup of our lives and the way we see the world, psychologists have spent years trying to nail down exactly how and why we come to trust others.

The Road to Trust

Our earliest need to trust, said Erik H. Erikson, the renowned psychologist who was a pioneer in the field during the 1940s, comes about because, as infants, we are unable to meet our own needs and must rely on someone (usually Mom) for food and protection. Erikson's research pointed to the fact that infants who are well provided for grow up with a more trusting personality than those whose needs were met only partially. To the latter group, the world is a harder place, inconsistent and threatening.

Trust begins to get tricky when, as children, we start to reach past our families and look for intimacy in the form of friendships. It is this innate, deep-seated desire to be close to other human beings, some psychologists say, that we constantly weigh against our wariness of trusting them. Because trust's nemesis—betrayal—is a wicked charge, a sick feeling more insidious than nausea, most of us are slow to trust, moving forward with caution lights flashing. But our drive for intimacy is so strong that when we embark on a new relationship, our standards for trust often change: Whatever mental "trust checklist" we have prepared for our partner-to-be is usually quickly forgotten.

Stephen Kotler, "Trust Me, Please," SELF, 1995, vol. 17, no. 11, November, pp. 158–159. Reprinted by permission of the author.

"In looking at why people decide to trust one another," says John Rempell, Ph.D., a noted trust researcher and psychologist at the University of St. Jerome's College in Waterloo, Ontario, Canada, "you see that our decisions aren't based on particularly profound information: How someone speaks reminds us of a brother, how they dress reminds us of a good friend—these first choices are based on attraction much more than on logic."

For my friend Susan,* mud was what it took to gain her trust. Certainly Susan was interested in intelligent, attractive men, but for years it was the dirt under their fingernails that initially led her to trust them. It was the dirt that told her they were hardworking, strong and creative. Not until Susan was almost 30, when she felt drawn to Sam,* a carpenter with a history of abusive relationships, did her theory fall apart.

According to Sandra Murray, Ph.D., and John G. Holmes, Ph.D., psychologists who have conducted trust research at the University of Waterloo in Ontario, trust emerges in a two-step process. Imagine a ladder with rungs painted alternately red, then blue. The blue rungs are one process, the red another; trust forms as you climb. Drs. Murray and Holmes have dubbed these processes "detective work" and "the leap of faith."

Says Holmes, "The leap of faith usually occurs when the detective work has just begun, and you are at the point in a relationship where you begin to count on another person beyond the realm of the data available." Susan's decision to trust unmanicured men was a leap of faith based on very limited data. This detail, of course, couldn't actually tell her if

*Name has been changed.

these guys were trustworthy or even decent human beings, but, says Holmes, to one degree or another it's the type of decision we all make. "This happens when people have only superficial information about one another, when they want to believe good things about their partner but don't have the knowledge they need," he explains. Instead, Holmes says, "people create a positive illusion, a fantasy with which to fill in the blanks."

Because our intuitive clarity can only take us so far, it is the very nature of these illusions to fray eventually. When holes start to appear, the detective process takes over and attempts to answer the nagging questions. This process is exactly as it sounds: a careful scrutiny of a partner's words and deeds, a search for safety and security, a further look for proof of trustworthiness.

My friend Vivien* calls it politics. It's what she asks about when her faith in a new friend is challenged. Maybe it's a response to an insensitive comment, maybe he pushes her sexually, maybe it's just a bad feeling. "What are your politics?" she says casually, knowing full well the importance of the question. But she doesn't actually mean politics; she means a set of values. She's not asking her acquaintance whom he voted for; she's asking about the standards he sets for himself and the way he thinks the world should be. In her head she frames these things as political. In her heart she is looking for a deep sense of compassion and justice. "What your friend is really doing is detective work," says Dr. Rempell. "She's looking for a set of core values that prove to her that not only can this new person be relied on, but, more importantly, that he won't hurt her. It's something all of us do."

Sidestepping Mistrust

There is, of course, no standard timeline along which trust develops. Instead, says Lonnie Barbach, Ph.D., a clinical psychologist at the University of California Medical School, it evolves "in direct proportion to your partner's reliability and integrity. There must be an excellent correlation between their words and their deeds." Dr. Barbach, who coauthored *Going the Distance: Finding and Keeping Lifelong Love*, explains that "if your partner is unreliable, breaks promises and makes excuses time after time for being unable to come through for you, you will inevitably discover yourself growing distant and guarded, and the possibility of achieving intimacy will be greatly reduced."

In relationships, especially in the beginning of the ones that matter most, we want to please each other, so we frequently offer to do things we can't possibly do. Barbach suggests that the inability to follow through on these little promises—being on time, picking up a roll of stamps from the post office, remembering the laundry—generates mistrust. If I can't trust her to take care of the small things, the thinking goes, will she be there when I really need her? To avoid this common pitfall, Barbach suggests learning to say no. This response may make your partner unhappy, but in the long run it's much less damaging than creating mistrust.

The Courage Connection

Still, a person can be on time, buy the stamps and remember to do the laundry for five years yet never share his emotional secrets. Reliability makes the process easier, but it will only go so far. In the end, psychologists say, developing trust comes down to courage. "Trust grows through risk; it is an evolutionary process," says Rempell, "but you must take chances for it to flourish."

At the age of 39, Ann,* who worked in a Seattle public-relations firm, took just such a chance. She had returned to graduate school on a scholarship for mid-career minority professionals, quitting her job and relocating. As an undergraduate Ann had struggled academically; now she had to return to the classroom and confront the same fears that had hampered her performance 17 years before.

One of Ann's classmates was a woman named Liz*—young,

*Name has been changed.

friendly, spry and incredibly bright. Ann found Liz's intelligence intimidating. When a professor teamed the two together for a project halfway through the first semester, Ann's old fears returned. She tried calling home to talk with her friends and family, but no one was around.

Ann remembers sitting up late with Liz, working on their project, very upset. She needed to talk to someone, but all she knew about Liz was her differences. Still, there was something in her eyes, something that seemed kind and calm in Liz that let Ann take a chance and trust her with her fears. "Liz believed in me," says Ann. "She believed in my ideas and made sure I got credit for them." What began as a cry for help became a tremendous friendship. Now, two years after gradu-

ation, Ann and Liz have a small business together, a strong friendship and the knowledge that some risks can make all the difference in the world.

Despite all of our detective work and countless leaps of faith, there are no reassurances: Trusts are violated every day, promises are broken, secrets revealed. And once a trust is betrayed, there's often no going back. So how do you know when you really trust someone? "When you stop monitoring your partner, when you stop continuously asking yourself little questions, when you just know *intuitively*," says Holmes. "That's when you know trust exists."

 Article Review Form at end of book.

How does society socialize men and women to behave differently in romantic relationships? How can evolutionary theory explain romance and jealousy?

Gender, Jealousy, and Reason

Christine R. Harris and Nicholas Christenfeld

University of California, San Diego

Buss, Larsen, Westen, and Semmelroth (1992) have suggested that men and women are intrinsically different in the magnitude of their responses to sexual and emotional infidelity, as a result of differing reproductive costs over human evolutionary history. Women, seeking to ensure males' long-term involvement, have evolved to care about their mates falling in love with others, and not to be so concerned about their mates having sex with others. Men, keen not to expend resources on other men's children, should be concerned about their women having sex with others, and not care so much about their falling in love with others. Buss et al. supported their argument with data indicating that when asked to choose whether sexual or emotional infidelity would be more bothersome, more women than men selected emotional infidelity, and more men than women selected sexual infidelity. We argue here that these results can be ex-

plained without suggesting that men and women are innately different in how much they are disturbed by emotional and sexual infidelity.

Although Buss et al. and other investigators before them (Daly & Wilson, 1983; Symons, 1979) proposed an evolutionary account for men caring about sexual infidelity and women about emotional infidelity. Buss et al. argued that "emotional infidelity may signal sexual infidelity and vice versa, and hence both sexes should become distressed at both forms" (p. 255). We suggest instead that men and women may be equally upset by each type of infidelity and that the crucial difference may lie in how much they think that each form of infidelity signals the other.

Imagine a man returning from work one day to discover incontrovertible proof of his wife's sexual infidelity. He might well think that because women have sex only when in love, it is quite certain that she has fallen in love with this other man as well. A women, however, finding the same evidence about her husband, might think that because men often have sex without being

in love, there is no reason to assume he is in love with the other woman. The man, then, is upset by what he takes to be sexual and emotional infidelity, whereas the woman is concerned only about the sexual infidelity. The man will be more bothered by the sexual infidelity than is the woman because he draws a more troubling conclusion from that evidence. The man should have a stronger response to sexual infidelity even if the man and woman care equally about their spouses' actual sexual exploits.

The situation should be reversed with evidence of emotional infidelity. The man, on coming across evidence of this sort, should reason that women can be in love without having sex, and so he need not assume that there is sexual infidelity as well. The woman, however, thinking that men in love are certainly having sex, will assume that both sorts of treachery have occurred, and be doubly bothered.

Thus, emotional infidelity should especially trouble women, and sexual infidelity should especially trouble men. This prediction follows not from any postulated innate difference in responses to

Christine R. Harris, Nicholas Christenfeld, Gender, Jealousy, and Reason. PSYCHOLOGICAL SCIENCE, Vol. 7(6), 364–366, November 1996.

the specific infidelities, but rationally from the hypothesis that men think women have sex only when in love and women think men have sex without love. We tested this hypothesis in a survey, and also sought to replicate the original finding of Buss et al.

Method

Subjects were 137 undergraduate students (55 males and 82 females) who individually and anonymously completed a survey of attitudes about relationships as part of a requirement for experimental participation. Among other questions about sexuality and dating were three questions about sexual and emotional infidelity. The first was taken from Buss et al. and was included to replicate their finding; the other two were designed to measure how much men and women think each form of infidelity implies the other:

1. Please think of a serious romantic relationship you have had in the past, currently have, or would like to have. Imagine that you discover that your romantic partner has become interested in someone else. What would upset you more?

   a. Imagining your partner trying different sexual positions with that other person.

   b. Imagining your partner falling in love with that other person.

2. Please think of a serious romantic relationship you have had in the past, currently have, or would like to have. Imagine that you discover that your mate is engaging in sexual intercourse with someone else.

Table 1 Comparison of Men's and Women's Distress in Response to Imagining Emotional and Sexual Infidelity in a Partner (in Percentages)

Gender	More Bothered by	
	Sex	Love
Females ($n = 81$)	22	78
Males ($n = 55$)	47	53

How likely do you think it is that your mate is in love with this person?

3. Please think of a serious romantic relationship you have had in the past, currently have, or would like to have. Imagine you discover that your mate is in love with someone else. How likely do you think it is that your mate is also engaging in sex with this other person?

The latter two questions were answered on 5-point Likert scales ranging from "not at all likely" to "very likely."

Results

Results for the first question replicated the results of Buss et al. In choosing between the two forms of infidelity, more males than females selected sexual infidelity as more upsetting, whereas more women than men selected emotional infidelity, $X^2(1, N=136) = 9.39, p < .005$. (One female failed to answer this question.) The data are shown in Table 1. Overall, subjects were bothered more by emotional than sexual infidelity, a bias that Buss et al. found also. In fact, in both our data and those reported by Buss et al., the men were close to equally split about which would bother them more, and it is the women's strong aver-

sion to emotional infidelity that produced the effect.

To analyze whether the sexes differ in the extent to which they think one form of infidelity implies the other, we subjected the second and third questions to a mixed factorial analysis of variance, with gender as the between-subjects factor and the two questions as the within-subjects factor. There was no main effect of gender. $F(1, 132) = 1.03$, n.s., and overall subjects thought that emotional infidelity implies sexual infidelity more than sexual infidelity implies emotional infidelity, $F(1, 132) = 12.17, p < .001$. (One female and 2 males failed to answer one of these questions.) The specific prediction, that men think that sex implies love for their partners more than do women, whereas women think that love implies sex more than do men, was tested with the interaction, which was significant, $F(1, 132) = 11.32, p < .001$. An inspection of the means, which are presented in Table 2, indicates that the dominant effect was that women think men can have sex without being in love.

Discussion

The findings provide strong support for the predicted interaction in the extent to which men and women think each form of infidelity implies the other. The pattern suggests that it is reasonable for men to be more concerned than women by evidence of a partner's sexual infidelity and for women to be especially concerned by evidence of a partner's emotional infidelity. Women may report less concern over scenarios of sexual infidelity because they believe that their partners have sex without being in love; men care more about sexual infidelity be-

Table 2 Subjects' Rating of How Much Sexual Infidelity Implies Emotional Infidelity and How Much Emotional Infidelity Implies Sexual Infidelity

Gender	Sex Implies Love	Love Implies Sex
Females (n = 81)	2.70	3.75
Males (n = 53)	3.43	3.32

Note. Cells indicate means on a 5-point Likert scale, from 1 (*not at all*) to 5 (*very*).

cause they think it is unlikely to occur without emotional infidelity as well. It need not be the case that men care more about the sex, but may just be that sexual infidelity accompanied by emotional infidelity is worse than sexual infidelity alone.

Both the approach taken by Buss et al. and our own interpretation can explain why women are more bothered by emotional than sexual infidelity. Buss et al. suggested that this is an innate response based on women's desire that their offspring have involved fathers. We suggest it may be due to women's belief that men may have sex without being in love, but are less likely to be in love without having sex. Emotional infidelity is thus logically a more troubling indicator. The account offered by Buss et al., however, has difficulty explaining men's indifference between sexual and emotional infidelity, a pattern that Buss et al. found in their survey (even after discarding men who have never had a committed sexual relationship), and one replicated here. The evolutionary account predicts that men, not wanting their partners bearing others' children, but not caring so much about their partners loving others, should care far more about sexual than emotional infidelity. Our account, that men care about both kinds of infidelity, and our

finding that they think the two signal each other about equally, is perfectly compatible with men reporting they would be equally concerned to discover evidence of either type of infidelity.

The different inferences about the relationship of love and sex that are documented here could well reflect actual differences in the behavior of men and women in the world. That is, our subjects may be correct in suspecting that women tend to have sex only when in love, and this tendency may reflect an innate dispositional difference (Symons, 1979). However, even if it does, our account would not require one to postulate an innate gender difference in the intensity with which men and women experience sexual or romantic jealousy. Whether or not the difference in sexual behavior is real, and whether or not it is based in innate biological differences, does not matter. As long as women think that men have sex without love but not love without sex, it is rational for them to be bothered more by reports of emotional infidelity than by reports of sexual infidelity.

Ultimately, all differences between men and women have a genetic origin, because the difference between man and woman is one of genes; however, the path from genes to attitudes and behavior may be circuitous and

based on reasoning (Harris & Pashler, 1995). It is not, for example, an innate preference that causes men to micturate standing and women sitting, but a reasonable response to an innate difference. Gender differences in affective responses to jealousy also need not be innate.

One can think of many examples of gender differences in emotions that are based on reasoned interpretations of evidence. Men and women will have very different emotional reactions to lipstick stains on a partner's collar—not because of a difference in their innate responses to lipstick, but rather as a result of their rationally interpreting the evidence differently. What suggests an affair to one sex implies mere sloppiness to the other. Responses to infidelity may likewise not be innate reactions, but instead a result of differences in the way the evidence is interpreted. Men and women need not differ in how much they care about each sort of infidelity, but only in what they think each implies.

References

Buss, D.M., Larsen, R.J., Westen, D., & Semmelroth, J. (1992). Sex differences in jealousy: Evolution, physiology, and psychology. *Psychological Science, 3,* 251–255.

Daly, M., & Wilson, M. (1983). *Sex, evolution, and behavior* (2nd ed.). Belmont, CA: Wadsworth.

Harris, C.R., & Pashler, H.E. (1995). Evolution and human emotions. *Psychological Inquiry, 6,* 44–46.

Symons, D. (1979). *The evolution of human sexuality.* New York: Oxford University Press.

Article Review Form at end of book.

What might be some effective counseling strategies for people considering marriage? How could you extend the suggestions from this article to your nonromantic relationships?

The Love Lab

Linda Fears

Last night we had fight number four hundred and twelve. He was late—again. No phone call, no message. I know he has a long commute to his job as a marketing executive, is on the road a lot and often gets caught in traffic. But somewhere along the way he could give me a ring so I don't worry that he's under a truck. I think he's insensitive; he thinks I'm a nag. But aside from that continuous argument, Chuck, thirty-four, and I, thirty-one, are doing just fine. Aren't we? We've made it past the seven-year-itch without a scratch (anniversary number nine is in September), we've got careers we enjoy, a four-year-old son and two-year-old daughter we're crazy about and a marriage that's rock-solid . . . at least I think it is.

The truth is, no one can be smug about the state of his or her marriage these days. In spite of all the talk about "family values," a recent study of 1985 data from U.S. Census records revealed that one out of every two new marriages (marriages since 1980) will end in separation or divorce.

Since my marriage qualifies as a "new" marriage that could be headed for trouble, I accepted an invitation made to *Ladies' Home Journal* to visit the marriage lab at the University of Washington, in Seattle, where research psychologists are using science-based techniques to uncover the real reasons that marriages succeed or fail. Not only would I be able to see first-hand how all the lab's special equipment works, but Chuck and I would experience a session in the lab as well. I wasn't so sure Chuck would be willing to fly across the country to have research psychologists tell us what's wrong with our relationship, but when I broached the subject, he thought it sounded like fun. (Fun? Maybe we are in trouble—I don't know this guy as well as I thought I did!) The country's first and only marriage lab—formally known as the Family Formation Project— was created by fifty-three-year-old John Gottman, Ph.D., an award-winning research psychologist, professor of psychology at the University of Washington and author, most recently, of the book *Why Marriages Succeed or Fail* (Fireside, 1995). Though the

Seattle lab is just five years old, Gottman has been conducting scientific experiments for twenty years on more than two thousand couples using video cameras, EKG monitors and custom-designed instruments to observe what happens when couples interact (prior to the University of Washington, Gottman taught and conducted his marriage research at Indiana University and at the University of Illinois). "My research teams have compared, microsecond to microsecond, how couples talk to each other," says Gottman. "We've examined their facial expressions, monitored how much they fidget and how they gesture. We wanted to find out what happens to partners' heart rates when they try to work out their conflicts. Do they breathe harder? Do they find it more difficult to listen? Do unstable couples express more sarcasm or contempt in these situations than stable couples do?"

Gottman and his colleagues then take all that data and feed it into a computer. The results, says Gottman, are like a "CAT scan of a living relationship," and they have enabled him to specifically identify the responses and physiological reactions that are essential to a sound marriage—and those that can damage a relationship. The research has also enabled Gottman to predict divorce. "In one study," he says, "we were able to foretell with an astonishing ninety-four-percent accuracy which couples were headed for divorce three years later. It's the highest prediction rate ever achieved by a scientific study on marriage."

What Gottman's methodical and unique approach to marriage research has revealed is that there are three types of stable marriages: validating couples (they listen to and understand each other's point of view and compromise often); volatile couples (they fight passionately and often, but are more affectionate and romantic than most couples); and conflict-avoiding couples (they resolve their problems by minimizing or avoiding them; they accentuate the positive aspects of their marriage, accept the rest). What these three marriage styles have in common is that regardless of how frequently the couples fight or how heated the arguments get, the relationships remain solid because, says Gottman, "the couples are nicer to each other more often than not." And he has the numbers to prove it. "Satisfied couples maintain a five-to-one ratio of positive to negative moments in their relationship," he says. "Positive moments nurture the affection and joy that are crucial to weather the rough spots."

Divorce, on the other hand, tends to be imminent when the relationship becomes more and more negative. If there is a negative interaction for every positive one, the couple is in trouble. Gottman and his team have ob-served a pattern in the divorce-bound marriages they studied. Every couple exhibited the same four disastrous behaviors, behaviors so destructive to a relationship that Gottman calls them, a bit coyly, the "Four Horsemen of the Apocalypse." From least dangerous to most dangerous, they are:

Criticism—attacking a spouse's personality or character.

Contempt—insulting and psychologically abusing a spouse.

Defensiveness—denying responsibility, making excuses, whining.

Stonewalling—removing oneself from a conversation with stony silence.

Of course, every couple exhibits behaviors like these at some point in their marriage. But when such behavior becomes routine, Gottman has found, the couple has very big problems.

So what could he tell Chuck and me after hooking us up to the monitors and observing us for just a few hours? As it turned out, quite a lot. Here's what happened.

Chuck and I walked into the lab on the Seattle campus and were met by Jim Coan, one of Gottman's team of research assistants. Coan placed EKG electrodes on our chests, galvanometer sensors (a fancy name for sweat detectors) and pulse monitors on our fingertips, sat us in hard, wooden armchairs so we faced each other, strapped our arms to the chairs and clipped microphones to our collars. He placed black coils across our chests to register breathing. Video cameras were inches from our faces. It was truth or consequences for real—everything we'd say, every move we'd make (though we couldn't move much) and every expression, no matter how subtle, would be recorded from now on. (Even the chairs were rigged with a jigglometer to record every fidget and squirm.) Coan then handed us questionnaires—a list of ten topics that many couples disagree about: Money, communication, in-laws, sex, religion, recreation, friends, alcohol and drugs, children and jealousy. Chuck and I were to assign a percentage from 0 to 100 to each topic to indicate how much we disagree: 0 percent—we never fight about it; 100 percent—we fight about it all the time. After we completed the questionnaires, Coan chose the three areas that both of us listed fairly high disagreement about: Chuck's long working hours, household chores and money.

We took turns airing our grievances to Coan. Then he asked us to debate the issues on our own and try to resolve them. He said he didn't expect us to solve all our problems, just reach workable solutions that we could take home with us. Coan went into an adjoining room to watch us on TV monitors and analyze our vital signs. The goal: to understand how we were reacting emotionally.

We spent the next fifteen minutes discussing subjects we've had fights about—big and small—for years. And maybe it was because we were strapped down and neither of us could leave the room and change the subject, or maybe it was because we were being analyzed and we wanted to make the most of the experience, but we did manage to reach some important agreements: Chuck promised to call me if he expects to be home later than 8 P.M. He also said he'd select one night out of the week to be home extra early and spend time with the kids (wow—a bonus! We didn't even talk about our son's frequent refusal to go to bed until Daddy gets home). Chuck also agreed to be more conscientious about picking up after himself and promised to have our home office—the messiest room in the house—straightened up and organized in two weeks. I said I'd try not to be so grumpy about his long hours, acknowledged that I wasn't a great money manager and handed the responsibility of bill-paying over to him. I also pledged to be a better saver.

It was exhausting but useful exercise and we did agree to continue to face our problems and work them out. But we wanted Gottman's opinion and feedback. Do we have constructive discussions? Do we handle our differences well? Do we fight right? To find out, the three of us watched the money portion of our video together:

Chuck: "I've been upset for the past five years about how little we've been able to save. I control my spending better than you do. I don't know where the money goes."

Linda: "That's because you don't pay attention to the things that add up. I know where the money goes because I pay the bills. If the kids need new shoes, I buy them. I pay the babysitter, our son's nursery-school tuition, buy presents for our relatives. If you want to know where the money goes, I'll be happy to show you my checkbook."

Gottman: There's a little defensiveness here. Chuck's being defensive, his heart rate is rising, so he's clearly upset, and Linda's whining....

Chuck: "It doesn't bother me all the time—I mean [laughing], I don't lie awake at night worrying

that we won't have enough money for the future. I just get upset when the bills include $1,000 worth of credit-card expenses, considering I haven't used my credit card in months."

Gottman: Here, Chuck uses humor that wasn't reciprocated. So there's tension. Further proof of tension is Linda's pulse, which is speeding up.

Linda: "Have you ever asked me to spend less?"

Chuck: "No."

Linda: "I'd like to save more, too, but you have to remember we've had a lot of expenses lately—a new house, new furniture...."

Chuck: "But it's not just lately."

Linda: "Why are you telling me this now?"

Chuck: "I'm just being honest."

Gottman: Now Linda stops whining and shifts into anger, which is really a healthier reaction. Her heart rate quickens even more. Chuck's EKG is even—he's trying to stay calm and defend himself, but not in a defensive way.

Linda: "Well, what's your solution?"

Chuck: "I'll start paying the bills, and I'll also work out a budget that we can agree on."

Linda: "I don't mind doing that. It's just that all you've been doing is complaining and not coming up with solutions."

Gottman: So the anger built up, but it wasn't destructive to the discussion. Anger is only destructive when the complaining becomes criticism and when it's blended with defensiveness and contempt. Linda is not doing that. She's using anger to open up the

issue. You're talking over each other to some degree—talking simultaneously—but that's not harmful, it's healthy. Your heart rates have dropped, which indicates both of you are becoming more rational.

Chuck: "That's true. I admit it."

Linda: "You've never taken much interest in bill-paying before, or in putting money aside for certain purchases."

Chuck: "That's just part of my procrastinating slob persona."

Linda: "You are a procrastinator. What if you forget to mail the bills on time?"

Chuck: "I'll remember. I'm paranoid about our credit rating. Besides, if you're unhappy with the way I'm handling the bills, we'll go back to having you do them."

Linda: "Okay. That's fair."

Gottman: Again, there's a lot of give and take here, and really a lot of mutual respect. Linda admits Chuck has a point; Chuck sees Linda's perspective. The real strength in your interaction is that neither of you is defensive. You started out a little defensive, Chuck, but you dropped it. And that's a real strength. Defensiveness fuels marital conflict; when people perceive themselves as being attacked, they become more distant from one another. Neither one of you is like that. Both of you are very open. And even when you confront each other, you're considerate. That's essential for good communication. So your marriage is looking good to me!

What a relief! But Gottman's endorsement of our marriage wasn't the best part. What made the marriage-lab experience worthwhile for me was something Chuck said. He admitted to me that until he watched us on the split-screen videotape, he never noticed how upset I looked while we're arguing. He tends not to look me in the face when we fight, but instead looks somewhere off in the distance. I've always accused him of not listening to me enough: Now I had proof. So Gottman suggested that Chuck look me in the eye more often to take in my emotions.

"Paying attention to each other is crucial," he said. "Linda, you may want to develop some sort of signal to italicize for Chuck when something is really important to you—some way of letting him know that 'this is a big one, so don't let it go.' But I think your communication is just fine. There's a big range of what makes a marriage work so that it satisfies both partners. There's a lot more stress in the world today and it affects all of us, especially couples who are raising kids. But getting through the stressful times together without resorting to behavior like being contemptuous or stonewalling each other is crucial for marriage longevity."

It's been two months since we visited the marriage lab, and during that time, we've managed to save more money than we have in quite a while, and Chuck has called or left a message on the answering machine every night that he has anticipated coming home late. But, though he's clearly trying to be neater, our home office is still a wreck, and I still have to occasionally remind Chuck where his keys, wallet and glasses are. But when he thanks me for my help, he looks me straight in the eye.

 **Article Review Form at end of book.**

Is there one best way to conduct a dual-career relationship? What are the three types of dual-career relationships, and what predicts well-being for each?

Current Perspectives on Dual-Career Families

Lucia Albino Gilbert

Lucia Albino Gilbert, Professor of Educational Psychology at the University of Texas at Austin, studies the career development of women and various aspects of dual-career family life. Address correspondence to Lucia A. Gilbert, Department of Educational Psychology, University of Texas, Austin, TX 78712.

In 1969, the Rapoports, working in England, first used the term *dual-career family* to describe what they considered to be an unusual and "revolutionary" type of dual-wage heterosexual family that emerged as the result of complex social changes.[1] Revolutionary from their perspective was the dual-career family's apparent inconsistency with traditional notions of gender. In such a family, the woman and man both pursued lifelong careers, relatively uninterrupted, and also established and developed a family life that often included children. Contrary to tradition, the woman viewed her employment as salient to her self-concept and life goals and pursued occupational work regardless of her family situation. The male partner, in turn, appeared less defined (relative to other married men) by the traditional "good provider" role long associated with male privilege and power.[2]

The notion of a two-career family was met with both excitement and skepticism. It promised to preserve the best of marriage—intimacy and enduring love—but freed partners from the harness of gender roles. True equality between women and men—social, economic, and political equality—seemed highly possible, if not inevitable. Now, some 25 years later, both the excitement and the skepticism appear realistic. Although increasing numbers of couples establish dual-career relationships, the larger promise of true equality has yet to be achieved.

From a theoretical perspective, role sharing in the private lives of heterosexual partners represents the elimination of gender-based role specialization and male power associated with patriarchy. Because dual-career marriages still exist within a larger world of gender inequity, it is not yet possible for the role-sharing dual-career family to emerge as a normative societal marital pattern. Nonetheless, the surprisingly high percentage of employed couples for whom role sharing is an interpersonal relational characteristic attests to this pattern's growing importance.

This article provides an overview of research on dual-career family life. Before summarizing this research, I review current facts on working women and men in the United States. These facts and figures describe the broad social context of dual-career families today.

Facts and Figures on Education and Employment

Currently, women and men ages 25 to 29 are equally likely to have 4 or more years of college. Women also experience fewer barriers to using their education than was the case previously, and a sizable number have entered professional fields formerly closed to them, such as medicine, law, and university teaching. In 1990, women represented 25% of full-time employed physicians, 27% of lawyers, 30% of college and university teachers, and 36% of Ph.D. psychologists; overall, women now constitute about 39% of the professional labor force.[3]

A direct corollary of women's increased educational and occupational opportunities is the dramatic increase in the number of U.S. families in which both partners report full-time employment.[4] Most married women with children under 6 years old are employed; 59.2% are in the labor force, and of these, 69.6% are employed full-time. For married women with children under the age of 18, these percentages increase to 67.0% employed and 72.9% employed full-time.

The average working wife with full-time employment contributes approximately 40% of the family's annual income. Increasing numbers of women view work in professional fields as central to their self-identities, a fact that obviously increases the number of families in which both partners consider themselves to be in careers (as opposed to women moving in and out of the work force depending on their families' needs).

The Kinds of Questions Asked by Researchers

As women's and men's roles have changed, so have the kinds of questions asked by researchers. From a gender perspective,[5] research on dual-career families can be viewed as falling into three somewhat distinct phases. The first phase focused on women's changing roles. Questions centered around how women could "do it all" and continue to meet their traditional responsibilities of caring for husbands and children. Implicit in this approach was the idea that women's roles were changing but men's were not, and that women made any necessary accommodations. Close watch was kept on how women dealt with the stress of their "multiple roles," how their children fared, and how happy their husbands were. Researchers, for example, looked for harm to children and compared children reared in traditional and dual-wage homes; however, results from the many studies conducted showed preschool-aged children to be at no added risk if they received alternate child or day care instead of parental care for some portion of the day.[6]

The second phase is best characterized as gender comparative. A woman's decision to pursue occupational work was viewed as "her right" as well as "her choice." Women began to push for changes within the home and family, and hence for changes in men's behaviors. Assumptions about how to arrange occupational work and family life shifted from women doing all the accommodating to arrangements being worked out between spouses. Both women and men were viewed as having multiple roles. Much of the research in this phase centered on comparisons of women and men. How much were men doing in the home compared with women? Did women and men cope in different ways? Were there gender differences in marital, occupational, or parenting satisfaction?

One major finding was that having multiple roles benefits women and men.[7] Benefits for women include increased self-esteem, better physical and mental health, and enhanced economic independence. For men, benefits include increased emotional involvement and bonding with children, better overall health, and lowered pressure to be financial providers. A related finding was that men increased their participation in parenting.[8] Some studies indicated that when both parents of preschoolers are employed, the combined time fathers and mothers spend in direct interaction with their children is about the same as for parents in families in which only one spouse is employed. The difference is that working parents spend more time with children on weekends and plan more for their time with children overall. Census data on primary child-care arrangements used by dual-wage families indicate that 17.9% of fathers provide primary care for children under 5 years of age. Reports from the Department of Labor indicate that increasing numbers of men use vacation and sick days to tend to newborns and other children, refuse long work hours, and seek flexible schedules or family leave.[8]

This second phase, although providing valuable insights into the day-to-day life of partners, used the behavior of individual women and men as its primary focus of inquiry. Little attention was given to the larger context in which these behaviors occurred. The third, and current, phase, in contrast, broadens investigations of dual-career family life to include the context of societal norms and practices. Thus, this phase recognizes explicitly that how couples combine work and family and carry out their multiple roles depends on much more than partners' personal wishes or preferences. In the case of parenting, research paradigms now include such structural variables as the kinds of care provided, definitions of optimal care, and the type of employer policies available to spouses.[9–11] Maternal employment, which in itself is generally unrelated to child outcomes, is viewed through its effects on the family environment and the child-care arrangements, and these are moderated by parental attitudes, family structure, workplace policies, and other relevant variables.[10] Obviously, the more employers' policies reflect a traditional workplace culture in which women with children leave the workplace and men with children are unencumbered by family responsibilities, the more difficult it becomes for both partners to parent.

Realities of the Dual-Career Family Life-Style

Let us turn to four crucial areas of dual-career family life and briefly consider key findings and key issues. All four areas involve some aspect of spouses' multiple roles. Investigations range from studies of spouses' actual role behaviors to studies of the support spouses need for their roles.

How Partners Combine Family Life and Occupational Work

Although women today have greater economic and legal equality with men than in the past, partners must still act out their private roles as spouses, parents, and homemakers within the larger world of "gendered" occupational and institutional structures and policies. Thus, men still earn much more than women on average and hold most of the positions of power in society. Women can more readily and ex-

plicitly use family-related employee benefits such as parental leave and flextime. Moreover, individuals, female or male, still feel they must accommodate their personal lives to the traditional occupational structures if they expect to be rewarded by employers.

Despite this situation, recent data on the division of domestic labor indicate that the inevitability of a "second shift" for wives is overstated and that although some wives do face a double day, others are in more equitable arrangements. Overall, men's participation in family work has continued to increase from 1970 to the present time, more so in the area of parenting than in the area of household work.[12] There is also important variation among couples. My studies of dual-career families indicate three general marital patterns, which I have labeled conventional, modern, and role sharing. In a conventional dual-career family, both partners are involved in careers, but the responsibility for family work (household work and parenting) is retained by the woman, who adds her career role to her traditionally held family role. Typically, both partners agree to the premise that work within the home is women's work, and men "help out" as long as doing so does not interfere with their career pursuits. Far more professionally ambitious than their spouses, the men in these families typically command much higher salaries and see the choice of whether to combine a career with family life as belonging to women.

In the modern pattern, parenting is shared by the spouses, but the wife takes more responsibility for household work than does the husband. Characteristically, the men in these families are motivated

to be active fathers, a motivation that may or may not be strongly associated with egalitarian views. These men want close relationships with their children but may still see other aspects of family work as more the responsibility of women than of men.

The third pattern—the role-sharing dual-career family—is the most egalitarian and a pattern many couples, and female partners in particular, strive for. In this variation, both partners actively involve themselves in household work and family life as well as occupational pursuits. At least one third of heterosexual two-career families fit this variation, although many spouses who are not role sharing describe their situations as equitable.

Differences among dual-career families involve variables associated with individual partners, employment practices, and social norms. Table 1 summarizes the usual personal, relational, and environmental factors that influence how couples combine occupational and family roles. Satisfaction does not necessarily differ for people with different family patterns; rather, satisfaction with a particular pattern adopted depends on these factors, especially each partner's perceptions of fairness and sources of support.

Perceptions of Fairness: Equity Versus Equality

Spouses' perceptions of what constitutes equity relate directly to marital quality and personal well-being.[13] The issue is not equality of power, but rather perceptions of equity or proportional returns in the exchange of personal and economic resources. Thus, wives who define themselves as co-providers, compared with wives who view

Table I Factors That Influence How Partners Combine Occupational and Family Roles

Factor	Examples
Personal factors:	
Personality	How important is a partner's need to dominate? to be emotionally intimate? to be tops in her or his field?
Attitudes and values	What are a partner's views about rearing a child? about women being as successful as men professionally?
Interests and abilities	How committed is a partner to occupational work? to family relations? Are both partners satisfied with their occupations and career plans?
Stages in careers	Is one partner peaking and the other thinking about retirement?
Relationship factors:	
Equity and power	How are decisions made? What seems fair? How do partners come to agreements about household work? about parenting? about money?
Partner support	Can partners count on each other for support in most areas?
Shared values and expectations	Do partners share the same views of women's and men's roles? Do partners have similar life goals?
Environmental and societal factors:	
Work situation	Are work hours flexible? Is there evidence of sex discrimination or other kinds of gender bias? Are policies prohibiting sexual harassment in place and understood?
Employer's views	Are policies family oriented? What is the general attitude toward employees who involve themselves in family life?
Availability and quality of child care	Is child care available? Does it meet parents' criteria for high-quality care?
Support systems	Do family members live nearby? Are friends and colleagues also in dual-wage families? Is the community responsive to the needs of employed parents?

themselves as persons who generate a second income, feel more entitled to their husbands' participation in family work and feel relatively unsatisfied if they perceive their husbands as not doing their fair share of this work. Similarly, husbands typically involve themselves more in family work when wives make greater financial contributions to the family and when both partners attribute greater meaning and importance to the wife's employment.

Women who perceive themselves as co-providers but who are hesitant to ask their husbands to do more at home may inadvertently act in ways that keep husbands in the dominant position, at the cost of their own marital happiness. Wives who perceive husbands as doing too little, but whose husbands disagree, report lower marital satisfaction and happiness than wives and hus-

bands who agree the wife is doing more or who see themselves as equitably sharing roles. Overall, women and men who achieve desired outcomes through participation in family work are unlikely to be aware of injustice. Desired outcomes typically include family harmony, time for family activities, or care and responsiveness among family members.

Parenting and Role Conflict

Among heterosexual dual-career couples, deciding when to have a child is typically more the question than deciding whether to have a child. The timing of the transition to parenthood has important consequences for parental behaviors, divisions of household labor, and partners' well-being. Once partners decide to parent, decisions about the child's day-to-day care are made in the context of variables such as partners' val-

ues, employers' policies, flexibility of work schedules, and the availability of care.

Generally, role conflict and day-to-day stress associated with parenting and careers are lowest under the following conditions:[14]

- Employers of both partners have benefit policies that are responsive to families' needs.

- Both partners participate actively in parenting.

- Partners feel comfortable sharing the parenting with child-care personnel.

- Partners view each other's involvement in home roles as fair.

- Partners are satisfied with the child care they are using.

- Partners are happy in their occupational work.

- Partners employ cognitive-restructuring strategies in

coping with stress. For example, a parent whose work is never-ending might say, "No sense worrying about what I can't get done. I'll do what I can. Besides, I like what I'm doing."

Sources of Support

Two sources of support are particularly crucial to spouses' and families' well-being. First, significant others have a central and extensive role. The mutuality of spousal support and affirmation is particularly important. Shared values and expectations about love and work and perceptions of fairness enhance the ability of spouses to be supportive.

Second, societal and institutional support is extremely important. Effective coping and satisfaction among partners with children invariably are associated with societal support—equitable salaries for women, flexibility of work schedules, suitable child care, family-supportive employers and benefit policies. Currently, a number of companies offer flexible scheduling in the form of flextime, part-time employment, job sharing, compressed work schedules, or work at home. Companies with supportive work and family policies, good health coverage, and flexible work hours have significantly less employee burnout and turnover than companies without such policies.[11]

Closing Remarks

As recent studies indicate, female and male employees hold increasingly similar attitudes toward relocation, business travel, and child care, and family obligations influence the plans and experiences of women and men.[9] It is now the norm for women and men to combine occupational work and family life across the life cycle, although this pattern is still somewhat out of step with social institutions and with how people define careers and achieve occupational advancement. Although change comes slowly, a new picture of contemporary marriage is nonetheless emerging. For women and men who live in these more egalitarian times, the variations of the dual-career family form stand among the marital patterns available.

Notes

1. The term career, although sometimes used to indicate any kind of employment, is defined in the literature more specifically: A career comprises positions requiring special education and training and undertaken or engaged in as a lifework. Typically, such positions require a high degree of commitment and provide the person with a sense of consecutive, progressive achievement, be it through promotions or other recognition of accomplishments and skills; R. Rapoport and R.N. Rapoport, The dual-career family, *Human Relations*, 22, 3–30 (1969).
2. J. Bernard, The good provider role: Its rise and fall, *American Psychologist*, 36, 1–12 (1981).
3. National Science Foundation, *Selected Data on Science and Engineering Doctorate Awards* (Author, Washington, DC, 1991).
4. S.K. Wisensale, Toward the 21st century: Family change and public policy, *Family Relations*, 41, 417–422 (1992).
5. Gender refers not only to biological sex, but also to the psychological, social, and cultural characteristics that have become strongly associated with the biological categories of female and male.
6. S. Scarr, D. Phillips, and K. McCartney, Facts, fantasies, and the future of child care in the United States, *Psychological Science*, 1, 26–35 (1990).
7. See, e.g., R.C. Barnett, N.L. Marshall, and J.D. Singer, Job experiences over time, multiple roles, and women's mental health: A longitudinal study, *Journal of Personality and Social Psychology*, 62, 634–644 (1992).
8. See, e.g., U.S. Bureau of the Census, *Who's Minding the Kids?* Series P–70, no. 20 (U.S. Government Printing Office, Washington, DC, 1990); U.S. Department of Labor, Women's Bureau, *Employers and Child Care: Benefiting Work and Family* (U.S. Government Printing Office, Washington, DC, 1989); J.H. Pleck, Are "family-supportive" employer policies relevant to men? in *Work, Family, and Masculinities*, J.C. Hood, Ed. (Sage, Beverly Hills, CA, 1994).
9. S. Zedeck and K.L. Mosier, Work in the family and employing organization, *American Psychologist*, 45, 240–251 (1990).
10. L.W. Hoffman, Effects of maternal employment in the two-parent family, *American Psychologist*, 44, 283–292 (1989).
11. J. Aldous, Ed., The impact of workplace family policies, *Journal of Family Issues*, 11(4) (1990).
12. L.A. Gilbert, *Men in Dual-Career Families: Current Realities and Future Prospects* (Erlbaum, Hillsdale, NJ, 985); M.M. Ferree, The gender division of labor in two-earner marriages, *Journal of Family Issues*, 12, 158–180 (1991).
13. J.H. Pleck, *Working Wives/Working Husbands* (Sage, Beverly Hills, CA, 1985); L. Thompson, Family work: Women's sense of fairness, *Journal of Family Issues*, 12, 181–196 (1991).
14. L.A. Gilbert, *Sharing It All: The Rewards and Struggles of Two-Career Families* (Plenum Press, New York, 1988); L. Thompson and A.J. Walker, Women and men in marriage, work, and parenthood, *Journal of Marriage and the Family*, 51, 845–872 (1989).

Recommended Reading

Ferree, M.M. (1990). Beyond separate spheres: Feminism and family research. *Journal of Marriage and the Family*, 52, 866–884.

Gilbert, L.A. (1993). *Two Careers/One Family: The Promise of Gender Equality*. Beverly Hills, CA: Sage.

Pleck, J.H. (1985). *Working Wives/Working Husbands*. Beverly Hills, CA: Sage.

 Article Review Form at end of book.

- Adult friendships require time and attention to flourish, and as in romantic relationships, people may grow apart, leading to friendship "breakups."

- Trust develops in a two-step process that involves learning more about a person and then taking the requisite "leap of faith." This process continues in a cyclical manner.

- Some social psychologists are using an evolutionary model to explain how men and women relate to one another by examining what the relationships of our evolutionary forebears would have looked like. Some sex differences in relationships may be inherited, but many more are a result of socialization.

- Research has found that there are three types of stable marriages; all have in common a five-to-one ratio of positive to negative moments in the relationships. As the amount of criticism, contempt, defensiveness, and stonewalling in a marriage increase, it becomes increasingly likely that divorce will result.

- Dual-career marriages may be more traditional or more egalitarian in nature. The degree of individual and marital well-being seems dependent on perceptions of equity and social support in the relationship.

R.E.A.L. Sites

This list provides a print preview of typical **coursewise** R.E.A.L. sites. (There are over 100 such sites at the **courselinks™** site.) The danger in printing URLs is that web sites can change overnight. As we went to press, these sites were functional using the URLs provided. If you come across one that isn't, please let us know via email to: webmaster@coursewise.com. Use your Passport to access the most current list of R.E.A.L. sites at the **courselinks™** site.

Site name: Social Cognition and Personal Relationships

URL: http://artsci.wustl.edu/~msahrend/SC.html

Why is it R.E.A.L.? At this web site, you will learn more about the mental processes inherent to the formation, evolution, maintenance, and dissolution of close relationships. A short history of close relationship research is provided, as is a discussion of how social cognition research can inform close relationships research. You can read about some current studies in this area and explore related links. Read one of the up-to-the-minute studies on this site. How could you potentially apply the findings of the study?

Key topics: romantic relationships, social cognition, self-help

Site name: Recommended Popular Books on Psychology

URL: http://www-personal.umich.edu/~tmorris/goodbook.html

Why is it R.E.A.L.? As mentioned in the WiseGuide Intro, there is a plethora of bad self-help books on the market. This is a reference list of self-help books suggested by Dr. Charles Morris, author of a best-selling introductory psychology textbook. He indicates that these are well-written, engaging, interesting, and readable books that have something worthwhile to say about one or another aspect of psychology. You might want to print this list out for future reference.

Key topics: self-help, romantic relationships, self-concept, self-esteem

Site name: Human Development and Family Studies at Pennsylvania State University

URL: http://www.personal.psu.edu/faculty/n/x/nxd10/family3.htm

Why is it R.E.A.L.? This is a comprehensive web site that students in Human Development and Family Studies at Pennsylvania State University put together. It includes information on relationships, including dating, marriage, and breaking up; parenting, from pregnancy and dealing with infertility to parenting teenagers; grandparents and brother/sister relationships; family problems, including grieving, alcohol and drug use, and divorce; and intimate violence. See if you can find some helpful information on a family relationship of concern to you.

Key topics: romantic relationships, aggression, biology, culture, friendship, social support

Index

Note:
Entries in boldface type are authors of Readings.

Family roles, combining with occupational roles, 204
Farrington, Jan, 137, 158
Fear, and procrastination, 53
Fears, Linda, 197
Federalist party, decline of, 58
Feminism, influence on U.S. politics, 63
Ferrari, Joseph, 52–53, 54
Fiction writing, decline in magazines, 76
Flexible scheduling, for dual-career families, 202, 205
Flextime, 202, 205
Food advertising, 71, 147, 149
Ford, Charles, 10
Ford, Richard, 102–7
Freedom, challenge of cults to, 99, 100
Free riding, in group settings, 115, 116, 117
Freeways, traffic jam increases on, 179
Friendships
    interracial, 161
    studies of, 186, 188–90
    Web resources on, 206
Furlong, origin of, 112

G

Galileo High School, cross-cultural writing class, 158
Gejdenson, Sam, 129
Gender
    and DUI intervention behavior, 170
    influence on attitudes toward infidelity, 194–96
    and salary discrimination, 138–44
    stereotypes about, 136, 145–50
Gender identity, in African American women, 40, 42, 44–45
Gender roles
    and dual-career families, 201–5
    in MTV commercials, 145–50
Genovese, Kitty, 163
Gerbner, George, 184
Gergen, Kenneth, 35–36, 37, 38
Ghetto
    aggression in, 175–77
    influence on perception of social breakdown, 29
Gilbert, Lucia Albino, 201
Gilovich, Thomas, 1, 3
Gingrich, Newt, 129
Godey's Lady's Book, 74
Goff, Lyn, 15–16
Good Housekeeping, 74
Gottman, John, 187, 197–200
Government
    citizens' attitudes toward, 58–66
    and norms of exclusion, 132–33
    response to perception of social breakdown, 30
Grades (academic), and self-esteem, 49–50
Graduation, increasing rates of, 29
Gridlock, in U.S. government, 61–62
Groups
    bystander apathy in, 163
    conflict between, 128–34

decision making by, 109
identification with, 128–34
membership rewards of, 109–10
motives for joining, 111–13, 128–34
productivity within, 114–18
self-directed work teams, 135
stereotypes about. *See* Stereotypes
Groupthink, 109, 110, 119–27

H

Hair dyes, carcinogenic, 69
Hale, Sarah Josepha, 74
Hale-Bopp comet, 102, 105
Happiness, effect of interpersonal relationships on, 186
Hardin, Russell, 110, 128
Harris, Christine R., 194
Health
    effect of procrastination on, 52
    effect of smoking on, 84
Healy, Elaine, 136, 145
Heaven's Gate cult
    explanations for mass suicide, 98–101
    former member's experience with, 102–7
    rules of conduct for, 106–7
Helping
    arousal/cost-reward model of, 165–66, 167
    and bystander apathy, 163
    and DUI interventions, 165–73
    Web resources on, 185
Hendrix, Mario, 159
Hernandez, Anthony C. R., 165
Higher Source, 105
Hippocampus, role in memory formation, 16
Hispanics, responses to anti-aggression interventions, 176
Holistic dogmas, and attraction to alternative therapies, 22
Holmes, John G., 192
Holocaust, parallels of Milgram's research with, 92–93, 94
Home, perspectives of, 130
Homogeneity, and groupthink, 120, 122–23
Honesty, nonverbal cues to, 18–21
Household income, increases in, 29
Housework, in dual-career households, 203, 204
Huesmann, Rowell, 183, 184
Human Development and Family Studies at Pennsylvania State University, R.E.A.L. site, 206
Hume, David, 133
Hunt, Shawn, 130–31, 133
Husband, Troy H., 14
Hutu, norms of exclusion among, 131–32, 133
Hyman, Ira, 14
Hypocrisy, and cognitive dissonance, 85–87
Hypothesis testing, biases in, 4–5

I

Identification, with groups, 128–34
Identity formation
    among African American women, 39–46
    studies of, 39–41
    and teenage smoking, 79
    theories of, 32–33
    See also Self
Illness, 22
Imagination, effect on false memories, 15–16
Incentives, for group efforts, 114–15, 117
Income inequality, 29, 65
Independence, as reason for teenage smoking, 79
Individualism, influence on concept of self, 36–37
Individual Needs Department, in Heaven's Gate cult, 104
Infancy, false memories from, 16
Infidelity, men's and women's attitudes toward, 194–96
Influence, types of, 89
Informal groups, influence on American society, 64–65
Information, poor searching for, 121, 124, 126
Inner city, aggression in, 175–77
Insertion orders, examples of, 75
Insulation, and groupthink, 120, 122, 126, 127
Intelligence, racial stereotypes about, 151–54
Interest groups, growing role in political campaigns, 62–63
International Carnivorous Plant Society, 113
International Sand Collectors Society, 113
Internet, cult recruiting via, 99
Interpersonal relationships
    developing trust in, 191–93
    evolutionary model of, 186, 187, 194–96
    friendship, 188–90
    relation to happiness and longevity, 186
    as research topic, 186
    romantic, 194–96, 197–200
    Web resources on, 206
Intimacy, and trust, 191, 192
Isolation
    effect on performance, 154
    use by cults, 100

J

Jagger, Mick, 34–35
Janis, Irving, 119, 120–21
Japan
    concept of self in, 36
    cross-cultural studies of group performance in, 116
Jealousy, gender differences in, 187
Joe Camel, 80

Peer pressure
    and racism, 161
    and smoking, 81–82
Pennebaker, James W., 10
Perceived danger, effect on intervening behavior, 168–69, 170, 172
Perez, Danny, 113
Perot, Ross, 59
Personal independence, as reason for teenage smoking, 79
Personality
    multiple aspects of, 34–38
    and obedience, 96
Personal products, MTV commercials for, 147, 149
Phenobarbital, use in Heaven's Gate cult suicide, 102
Philip Morris, *Ms.* advertisements for, 70–71
Physical attractiveness, in MTV commercials, 146, 147
Physicians, women as percentage of, 202
Placebo effect, and alternative therapies, 23–24
Pluralistic ignorance, from racial isolation, 154
Police, efforts to curb teenage smoking by, 83
Political campaigns, changes in, 62, 66
Political parties
    effect of campaign reforms on, 66
    weakening of, 58, 59, 61–62
Politics, 63, 66
Polygraph, 10
Polzer, Jeffrey T., 136, 138
Postmodernism, theoretical expressions of, 37–38
Prejudice (racial)
    indirect, 155–57
    overcoming, 158–61
President, public trust in, 58
Press, role in changing attitudes toward government, 60–61
Primary elections, effect on political parties, 66
Privacy, public opinion about, 186
Procrastination, 33, 51–54, 55
Procrastination Research Group, R.E.A.L. site, 55
Procrastinators Club of America, 53
Procter & Gamble, requirements for ads in women's magazines, 75
Productivity, within groups, 114–18
Professions, women in, 202
Promotional items, for tobacco companies, 79–80
Prophecy, research on effectiveness of, 6
Psychic predictions, research on effectiveness of, 6
Psychological costs, of group participation, 117
Psychological tests, online, 55
Psychology
    influence on disease recovery, 23, 25–26
    recommended books on, 206

The Psychology of Cyberspace, R.E.A.L. site, 135
Psychoneuroimmunology, and spontaneous remission, 23
Psychosomatic disease, and alternative therapies, 24
Public schools, perception of decline in, 30
Public Service Commission of Canada, R.E.A.L. site, 162

R

Rabow, Jerome, 165
Race
    and aversive bias, 155–57
    of characters in advertising, 72, 148
    importance to identity development, 39, 40, 41, 42–43, 44
    stereotypes about, 151–54
Racial isolation, effect on performance, 154
Racial stereotypes, effect on performance, 151–54
Racism
    aversive, 155–57
    and identity formation of African American women, 39–40
    overcoming, 158–61
Rape, mass media influence on, 183
Rawlins, William, 188–89
Reagan, Ronald, 60
Reality
    constructivist view of, 38
    distortions of, 25–26
R.E.A.L. sites
    Access to Justice Network Publications, 185
    American Family Foundation Cult Group Information, 108
    Atlantic Unbound, 162
    Center for the Study and Prevention of Violence, 185
    Counterfactual Research News, 31
    Cyberia Shrink's Tests, Tests, Tests, 55
    Exploring Nonverbal Communication, 31
    Human Development and Family Studies at Pennsylvania State University, 206
    Procrastination Research Group, 55
    Psychology of Cyberspace, 135
    Public Service Commission of Canada, 162
    Recommended Popular Books on Psychology, 206
    Self-Directed Work Teams, 135
    Social Cognition and Personal Relationships, 206
    Social Influence: The Science of Persuasion and Compliance, 88
    Social Psychology Class Paper, 108
    Steve's Primer of Practical Persuasion and Influence, 88
    Ten Myths About Affirmative Action, 162
Reciprocity, influence on perceived effectiveness of therapies, 26

Recommended Popular Books on Psychology, R.E.A.L. site, 206
Recovery from disease, as invalid support for alternative therapies, 22–23
Recruitment, by cults, 99
Relatedness, and self-concept, 37
Relationships, importance to African American women's identity, 43, 45
Relevant comparisons, failure to make, 4
Religion
    importance to African American women's identity, 43–44, 45
    influence on American society, 64
Remission, spontaneous, 23
Rempell, John, 192
Respecting Our Differences, 158, 159
Responsibility
    and theory of multiple selves, 38
    transfer of, 96
Reverse discrimination, and aversive racism, 156
Revlon, reactions to placement of magazine ads, 76
Ricca, Joe Ann, 111
Richard III Society, 111
Risks, failure to consider, 121, 124, 126
Risk-taking, and trust, 193
Rkk, in Heaven's Gate cult, 106
Road rage, explanations for, 178–81
Roediger, Henry L. III, 15–16
Role sharing, in dual-career families, 201–5
Romance
    gender differences in, 194–96
    and lying, 9
Rorty, Richard, 133
Rush hour, traffic jam increases, 179
Rutherford, Beth, 12
Rutte, Christel G., 136, 138
Rwanda, norms of exclusion in, 131–32, 133

S

Safe-sex campaigns, and behavior change, 85–87
Salaries, gender discrimination in, 138–44
Samizdat, coverage in Ms. magazine, 71
Sand, organization for, 113
San Diego Wild Animal Park, Heaven's Gate cult trip to, 105, 107
Sass, Louis, 35, 37
Saxe, Leonard, 8, 9, 10
Schools
    perception of decline in, 30
    racism in, 158–61
Schwarzkopf, Norman, 113
S.C. Johnson & Son, requirements for ads in women's magazines, 75
Searle, John, 37
Sea World, Heaven's Gate cult trip to, 105, 107
Secret Service agents, ability to detect lying, 20
Selective bias, and groupthink, 121, 124
Selective memory, research on, 5–7
Self
    development of, 32–33

Putting it in *Perspectives*
-Review Form-

Your name:_____   Date: _____

Reading title: _____

Summarize: provide a one sentence summary of this reading: _____

_____

_____

_____

Follow the Thinking: how does the author back the main premise of the reading? Are the facts/opinions appropriately supported by research or available data? Is the author's thinking logical?

_____

_____

_____

_____

_____

_____

Develop a Context: answer one or both questions: how does this reading contrast or compliment your professor's lecture treatment of the subject matter? How does this reading compare to your textbook's coverage?

_____

_____

_____

_____

_____

_____

_____

Question Authority: explain why you agree/disagree with the author's main premise?

_____

_____

_____

_____

_____

_____

_____

COPY ME! Copy this form as needed. This form is also available at http://www.coursewise.com Click on: *Perspectives.*